The All You Can Eat Gardening Handbook

Easy Organic Vegetables and
More Money in Your Pocket

Cam Mather

AZTEXT
PRESS

Aztext Press
Tamworth, Ontario Canada K0K 3G0
michelle@aztext.com • www.aztext.com

Library and Archives Canada Cataloguing in Publication

Mather, Cam, 1959-
    The all you can eat gardening handbook : easy organic vegetables and
more money in your pocket / Cam Mather.

Includes index.
ISBN 978-0-9810132-2-0

    1. Organic gardening. I. Title.

SB453.5.M37 2010   635'.0484 C2010-900640-2

Printed and bound in Canada

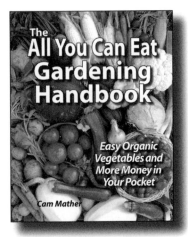

The cover photo taken by my daughter Katie Mather is of vegetables harvested from my garden in the Summer of 2009. The photo was not manipulated in any way. In fact you can see where cabbage worms chewed holes in the cabbage.

This book is dedicated to my father-in-law Lorne Archer who spent his working life in a steel mill that was the manifestation of "Dante's Inferno" and yet managed to plant and nurture a massive organic garden that overflowed with life and energy. Lorne was a positive influence every moment of the 30 years that I knew him and he planted the seed of my passion for growing organically. Lorne was light years ahead of his time on many levels, particularly in his wisdom for working in harmony with nature. I miss him deeply and wish he were here to see some of his knowledge and passion shared with others in these pages.

Acknowledgements

Like everything I do this book was a joint venture with my wife Michelle. She was involved with every component of the book from concept to final editing. She is also my partner in our massive garden and the person who turns most of our garden's bounty into wonderful meals.

I am grateful to my parents Joan and Bruce Mather who allowed me to turn their backyards into vegetable gardens and nurtured my love of gardening and lifelong learning.

My daughters Katie and Nicole took many of the photos you see in this book and have done their share of weeding and watering and manure shoveling. Katie put a great deal of effort into the cover photo which took the better part of a summer day.

I am eternally grateful to all of the farmers who have fed me over the years. Of particular note are:

My friend John Wise, an organic farmer who even manages to grow strawberries organically which is one of the more challenging of crops. John has weathered the ups and downs of growing food for a living with the added challenge of doing it organically and is a model for how we'll all be doing it soon. John has been an endless source of information and encouragement over the years and I aspire to his level of knowledge on all things organic.

My friend and neighbor Agnes Hagerman is without question the most enthusiastic farmer I have ever met. She lives and breathes farming and her enthusiasm for it is utterly contagious. She has been selfless in giving of her time to answer my questions and generous in her gifts of hay that is no longer fit for her cattle but has great potential to enhance my soil.

Joe O'Neill at "O'Neill's Farm Supply" in Tamworth tolerates my never-ending questions with grace and patience. Much of my knowledge on what and when to plant has been gleaned from Joe and at the scale I purchase seed from him it's quite amazing he talks to me at all.

My neighbor Ken Gorter has shared with me many of the techniques his father, a market gardener, used to earn his living and feed his family. I owe Alyce Gorter a huge debt of gratitude for allowing me to haul away a trailer full of the byproducts of her horses each week. This weekly soil amendment has been instrumental in my success at gardening on the scale that I do with the sandy soil that I am surrounded by.

Brian Burt and Ruth Hayward at Burt's Greenhouses in Odessa, Ontario not only provide me with fantastic transplants each spring from their sustainably heated greenhouse but have been a great source of information, particularly as I have experimented with growing sweet potatoes.

John Wilson and Denice Wilkins of Wilson's Organic Blueberries in Tweed, Ontario introduced me to high bush blueberries and were kind enough to read through the blueberry chapter and to provide feedback based on their 20 years of experience growing them.

While these individuals have all provided enormous help to me in the writing of this book, I should point out that any errors or omissions are my own.

Paul Olsen introduced me to Ruth Stout and her mulching techniques and suggested I try the grocery store dried pea experiment.

As always our editor Joan McKibbon put her life on hold to meet our deadlines and for this we are deeply grateful.

And last but not least I'd like to thank Bill and Lorraine Kemp for encouraging me to share my gardening techniques in this book and always providing wonderful feedback about the harvest we share with them.

Table of Contents

PART I

Garden Preparation

1

Introduction

I just came in from the garden. It is magical. It smells wonderful. It's so full of life. It gives off positive energy—health-giving energy.

I brought in some of its bounty. New potatoes. We'll boil them and put just a bit of olive oil and salt and pepper on them. There's no taste like it. I brought in some green beans too. We'll steam them and they'll be amazing, although an awful lot are just being eaten raw as I stand preparing dinner.

I brought in a head of broccoli. Broccoli is a Super Food, an antioxidant-rich powerhouse of cancer-fighting phytochemicals. Sometimes I steam it but tonight I'm just going to stir-fry it in a pan with lots of garlic and olive oil. It will still be crunchy when I serve it, and its wonderful green color will become richer and more vibrant. It tastes sumptuous. None of the healthy enzymes and vitamins and minerals have been lost as it sat in a truck and grocery store for weeks.

I don't measure the garlic I use in "cloves" as so many recipes do; I measure it in whole heads. For our pizza I use at least two heads. For the broccoli stir-fry I'll use one whole head of garlic. Just cutting it I can feel it building up my immune system as garlic does. It doesn't matter how well I wash my hands; I'll have the smell of garlic on them for a while and it'll keep me craving garlic later. Sautéing the garlic in olive oil I just feel my bad cholesterol going down and my good cholesterol going up. I feel some of the plaque that's built up on my arteries getting washed away.

The final item on my plate will be tofu, also stir-fried with the broccoli, olive oil, and garlic. While I've grown everything else on the plate, the tofu was purchased. I did grow soybeans, so I could have made it myself, but there is an art to it and I haven't mastered it yet. Soy protein is exceptionally healthy and a number of major health studies link it to a dramatic reduction in the risk of many cancers. Cooked in garlic like this it's going to absorb some of that rich, wonderful aroma and taste. When it's close to being ready we'll put a bit of tamari on it, which is an Asian fermented soy sauce. We'll also sprinkle it with sesame seeds and it will melt in our mouths.

Once everything is on the plate we'll sprinkle it with chopped parsley picked minutes ago. It makes the meal look absolutely fabulous. Fit for the finest urban restaurant, but much healthier since all the ingredients are freshly picked.

The plate arrives at the table with the potatoes, beans, broccoli, and garlic-infused soy protein steaming and smelling heavenly. Almost everything is from my backyard less than 100 feet away. It's the 100-Foot Diet. There is no cholesterol on my plate. There are healthy and health-giving vegetables full of vitamins and minerals and antioxidants. There is lots of fiber. My gastrointestinal tract is going to love this meal. It's the sort of meal my body was designed to process. My blood pressure is going to love this meal. My heart thanks me for this bounty that is going to reduce its workload, as it doesn't have to push blood through constricted arteries. There is ample protein on my dinner plate, more than enough for any adult. The potatoes contain starches that will break down slowly and give me energy over the

long haul. The broccoli's antioxidants are going to cruise around looking for precancerous cells to remove.

Maybe my journey to the cellular level is a bit simplistic, but the research is overwhelming that this is the sort of meal we should be eating to maintain optimal health. The fact that it came from my backyard is a bonus. The fact that it cost next to nothing is a double bonus. It's funny how sometimes the things that are best for us in one way, like our health, can also be good for us in other ways, like our bank account.

The story of my meal is also a metaphor for how I approach gardening. I absolutely love it. I take infinite joy in it and it provides an unending source of energy for me, year round. Every year I have great success in the garden and every year I have dismal failures. There are other things I would have liked to have on my plate but they were late this year, or with those cool nights in July they just didn't thrive.

I use the end result of the summer's garden as my introduction because the meals that your garden will produce are what it's all about. The very act of growing food is a wonderful, healthy,

spiritual pursuit, but sitting down at the table to the end result is what makes it all worthwhile. I challenge anyone who has grown their own food to honestly tell me that they prefer store-bought produce which could have been picked weeks before and shipped thousands of miles before it got to their plate.

The tofu that I didn't grow for the meal also represents the endless optimism of a gardener. "Next year I'll try…." "My garden next year is going to have way more…." Now that I've mastered growing soybeans I just have to find some time to take the next step and process them once they're harvested.

Hope springs eternal, and that is never truer than with a gardener. Every summer presents unique challenges and un-expected rewards. For many this year was much cooler and wetter than usual, which made for a tough season for many heat-loving vegetables. Other parts of the country were bru-tally hot and dry.

In those locations if you didn't have a strategy for harvesting rainwater and using it efficiently your garden suffered.

In this book I hope to provide as many tools as I can for growing in as many circumstances as readers are likely to find themselves in, whether you have a long or short season, ample rain or water challenges, a small backyard in the city or ample acreage in the country. The principles are all the same; you just have to tweak them a little depending on where you are.

The requirements are going to be the same. You're going to need sun, water, nourishment for the soil, and time. The time is going to be your investment. You're going to have to put in some time. Time to prepare the soil. Time to plant. Time to weed and water and maintain the garden.

The rewards are huge. More independence in your food budget. The increased health benefits of the food you eat. The joy that comes from getting your hands dirty—as Peter Gabriel says, "digging in the dirt." I really believe gardening is a very spiritual endeavor. I think it gets us back in touch with some of the most basic levels of our DNA, when our ancestors realized that you didn't neces-sarily have to hunt and gather, that you could in fact put down roots in one place and let certain plants put down roots to help sustain you. Dig-ging those potatoes out of the ground is some-thing humans have been doing for many thou-

sands of years. Buying potatoes in a grocery store is a relatively recent event in human evolution. I believe it may in fact be a fairly short-lived part of the human experiment, so the more skills you have in the ancient art of growing food, the more resilient to an uncertain future you'll be.

So just take a look at this meal! Doesn't it smell fantastic! The new potatoes! The garlic wafting off the plate! You can feel the health-giving energy radiating from this plate. Get your shovel; we're off to the garden to make this happen at your house!

Bon appétit!

2
The History of My Gardening Habit

Back in 1976 when I was in high school I was into all the usual stuff. My favorite band was Boston, but I liked Kansas and Chicago. There was a geographical theme to band names back then. I loved the freedom that access to my parents' car provided. It helped me to pursue another interest—girls. Part-time jobs were handy for gas money. I tried to do well in school and took all those academic courses to expand my brain. It wasn't until I bought an off-the-electricity-grid house that I realized what a huge mistake I had made by not taking electrical, automotive, and other practical courses that would have actually helped me to learn a few skills.

My interests were girls, music, cars, and school, in about that order. Then I did this weird thing. I looked at my parents' backyard and thought: I'd like to grow a garden. I wasn't into the groovy Woodstock music thing, so this wasn't some hippie back-to-the-land urge. And it wasn't a message I'd received during a chemically induced hallucination either, since I just never could suck that smoke into my lungs. I lived in suburbia. I grew up on cartoons and The Partridge Family. I'd never been to a farm. All my ancestors were city dwellers.

Nope, this was something beyond that. I have yet to figure it out. As I ease on down the yellow brick road of my spiritual life I think perhaps it was motivated by a former life. Perhaps I was a farmer in a previous life and this was part of an unfinished journey. Maybe some force in another dimension was directing me. But it seemed to be something stronger than that. It seemed to be something at a cellular DNA level. This was something rooted deep within me that I needed to deal with. It was completely out of context. My normal activity at the time was seeing how loud I

The kids are alright and they're out in the garden

could play "Stairway To Heaven" by Led Zeppelin on the insanely cool and high-tech cassette deck in my parents' car without blowing up the speakers. What the heck was with the gardening thing?

The gardening thing wasn't to be ignored though, so I took the calling to heart and put in a vegetable garden. I took a shovel and I turned over the sod. The subdivision where I lived had soil that was very high in clay. Clay can be pretty hard stuff to grow in. Back in the 70s when this subdivision was constructed they were still learning, so the developers scraped off all of the topsoil to make it easier to dig foundations and build on a larger scale. They didn't put the topsoil back though. If they had I would have had bad topsoil. Instead what I got was abysmal clay subsoil. The clay content was so high I would have been way better to buy a potter's wheel and start making ceramic bowls.

Luckily at the age of 16 I was too stupid to know this, so I persevered. I added a bag of peat moss hoping it would help break up the clay, which was like throwing a granule of sugar in to sweeten your coffee. Then I planted some seeds and waited. Things did grow, but they did not grow well. After a rain I'd have to go out with the hoe and break up the soil. The rain turned the surface of the garden into a concrete-like substance, like ice on a frozen pond. What this garden needed was a jackhammer to break it up. But a humble hoe and teenage bravado were all I had, so I kept at it.

The results were abysmal. Very few things grew and what did grow did not grow well. An intelligent teenager would have given up there.

But lo and behold the following year we moved to a different city and this time to a home closer to the downtown. The home was a hundred years old and it turns out that a hundred years ago they didn't have fancy earthmoving equipment and limitless fossil fuel energy, so they left the soil that was there alone. Since many cities were actually established near bodies of water, you'll find city soil can be pretty good. The soil at this house was fantastic. It was dark and rich and wonderful. The only problem was that there was a patio right where I wanted to put the garden. My parents were great. No problem, they said. Just move the patio stones closer to the house and that area is yours. Do you have any idea how heavy patio stones were in the 70s? They used concrete and lots of it. And reinforcing rod, so the darn things were basically indestructible.

Once again the strength of my teenage back

My second garden attempt in better soil with better results.

was undaunted and the patio stones began their migration. The soil under the stones was perfect. I turned it over and raked out the weeds and in went my seeds. This time it was a huge success. One of the photos of the garden captured my joy at the prospect of growing in real soil. It also captured my Peter Frampton-like hair. All right, it wasn't that long. I kept my seeds in a North Star shoebox. Back then you wore Adidas or North Star. I believe North Star was the poor cousin and therefore my shoe of choice.

But having a garden where things actually grew was pretty novel. Having my parents rave about how great the tomatoes were was a bonus. Who'd have thought that? You could put in a tomato plant in June and have tomatoes in August. Not that I liked tomatoes. Not that I liked any vegetables for that matter. This was the weird thing about my gardening pursuit. It wasn't as if the outcome of growing vegetables was something that I particularly desired. Now if I could have figured out a way to grow Cap'n Crunch or Cocoa Krispies, then it would have made sense. But I couldn't, and frankly all these healthy green vegetables weren't even on my radar screen for preferred dinner items. Thankfully 35 years later they are indeed the basis of my diet and I enjoy them immensely.

After a year or two away from a garden while in apartments, the bug finally bit me again and this time I discovered a place where I could rent a garden plot in a community garden. The garden required a drive in the car to the other side of town, which was a bummer, but after dinner many nights and on weekends I spent a lot of time there. The garden was actually in Bronte Creek Provincial Park, which was an oasis in a concrete jungle. It was peaceful and quiet and I was surrounded by green. As I worked in the garden I could hear birds. When I'd finished I could walk in the woods. I feel blessed to have had this outlet for my gardening obsession. Some forward-thinking park warden had had the vision to realize just what an asset a publicly owned trust could be and what benefits it could offer its constituents.

While the garden was wonderful it was communal, which did have a few downsides. The biggest was the neighboring plot gardeners' approach to pest control. Some seemed to think the images of Agent Orange spraying in Vietnam were a model to be emulated and felt 2,4-D was a better way to eliminate weeds than a hoe. I still retain the image of a gentleman dusting his potatoes with this thick, white cloud of some unknown toxin that looked like the DDT they covered prisoners with in those grainy black and white movies from World War II. Did he not think that if it could so easily snuff out a potato beetle maybe, just maybe, there might be some long-term effect on him personally? And this was before I had heard about or read Rachel Carson's *Silent Spring* or any of the supporting evidence that was beginning to show a link between these products and negative outcomes in humans from long-term exposure. It just didn't seem right. And it just didn't seem necessary. Oh look, there's a potato bug. How about I squish it? What? No potato bugs? So maybe I won't take precautionary measures and nuke the plants regardless. That was the wisdom of the day: precautionary application of pesticides to avoid potential problems. And we wonder how insects developed broad-spectrum resistance to so many of these chemicals.

I was blessed to finally be in a situation where I could buy my own home, and Michelle and I finally got a place to call our own. As the Dixie Chicks say in "A Home," "Four walls, a roof, a door, some windows, Just a place to run when my working day is through." And it was a small home. I think about 800 square feet on the main floor and a basement that was great for storage. The lot was small, 40 feet wide by 100 feet deep, but it was ours! That first spring I got to put in my first garden on my own property. It was small but it was an older neighborhood so the soil was good. I knew it was going to be a challenge because the wonderful huge tree that shaded our non-air-conditioned house also made a fair amount of shade where the garden was. But I put it in a far back corner and hoped for the best. The best turned out to be pretty dismal and nothing grew well. The soil looked fine. It looked rich and should have had the nutrients the plants needed. I kept it watered and weeded and it got enough sun that there should have been some success, but it was pretty much a disaster.

This is where we learned about research and after some digging realized the culprit was the big tree. And it wasn't even the obvious explanation, which was the shade. The tree was a black walnut and for a vegetable garden that's a death sentence. Black walnut trees, and I mean the whole tree, the leaves, the roots, the nut husks, secrete something called juglone. Juglone is a "respiratory inhibitor," and who'd have thunk it, plants need to respire just as you and I do. So while my tenacious tomato plants were trying to grow and make me proud,

My front yard garden with my peach tree to the left and hard-to-see vegetables encroaching on the far side of the sidewalk.

they were secretly being gassed like some diabolical plan by Dr. Evil in an Austin Powers movie to use nerve gas to extort billions or millions of dollars from world governments.

So it was game over for a while in the vegetable department. This was sort of all right because I had learned a new passion from my father-in-law, Lorne Archer. Anytime a maple tree seed germinated in his garden he always put it in a little pot. Eventually he had a little nursery in his backyard and was happy to give trees away to anyone who admired them. I had planted a maple tree in my front yard and sure enough after a year or two the seedlings were starting fast and furious. I made the rounds on garbage night and picked up lots of the 6- or 8-inch plastic pots that people were throwing out and started my own little nursery. I took those black walnuts that were bombarding my kids on their swing set in the fall and put them in pots. Turns out black walnut wood is highly desirable and I was starting seedlings by the truck-load. Eventually this became the basis for my long-term retirement plans. Since I was never going to make enough money to have a proper retirement, I would find a bit of property, start a black walnut plantation, then 50 or 60 years down the road sell off lumber to pay the taxes.

I didn't stop at these trees though. I grew all kinds of trees. I found an area under a power line where thousands of pine and spruce seedlings were growing. Since the power company was just going to nuke them with an herbicide eventually anyway I grabbed them. Soon my tiny lot was overflowing with seedlings and small trees. One year we had a garage sale and put a few trees out and sold them, which was fantastic. Toward the end of the day a neighbor came over and asked about the pines and spruce. He wanted to know how many I had. "I don't know, maybe a hundred. How many do you want?" "All of them," was his response. It was as if I'd died and gone to heaven! Someone appreciated my trees. Turns out he owns a fishing camp in the north and wanted to grow some natural windbreaks between his cabins. I can't remember what I sold them for. The soil was mostly compost I made for free from leaves that I scrounged from neighbors. The pots were free. The hundreds of hours of my time that I devoted to nurturing them, well you couldn't count that. How about $2 each? He paid me $200 cash and it was one of

Our vegetable garden is coming along well, with radishes and beans up, and we are less worried about revolution than we used to be.

E. B. White

the best days of my life. Oh sure, I was running a successful electronic publishing business. That was good. And the birth of my daughters, oh sure, those were red-letter days. And since Michelle is editing this, my wedding day, now that was the ultimate red-letter day. But selling the fruits of my gardening efforts was off the charts. It's amazing to grow something healthy and beautiful and then share that with someone else. If that person wants to compensate you, it's all the better.

While I was on my tree-growing tear I resorted to growing a few vegetables in the front yard. I would discreetly put a tomato plant or pepper in with our flowers, and you'd hardly notice. The flower gardens were getting bigger and bigger though, so then maybe this year I'd add a few beans plants. Next thing you know, I had a vegetable garden growing in my front lawn. It was great. We ran our business out of the house and our customers who dropped in to pick up artwork thought it so quaint that we had vegetables in our front yard. Quaint and yummy when a handful of tomatoes were included with every corporate annual report layout. I had also planted a peach tree, which thrived, close to the house, and since we were near Lake Ontario, which regulated the temperatures, it was able to stand the winters. One year we picked a hundred wonderful, tasty, juicy, organic peaches.

I used to work like a dog on weekends composting leaves, weeding, watering, and making the garden bigger. I can remember sprawling exhausted on the final plot of grass we had left, late one Saturday afternoon, and a car with two elderly ladies stopped to make sure I hadn't dropped dead of a heart attack. I think it was that and the infamous chiropractor incident that convinced me it was time to move. Each year as the garden expanded so did its selection of crops. One year I could wait no longer and the corn seeds went in. Planting corn in your front yard is a crossing of the Rubicon of sorts. It takes you to that next level, from a hobby gardener to a, well, lunatic. It takes you from the interesting character the neighbors humor to a crazy man the neighbors worry will soon be growing dreadlocks and gardening naked while smoking huge volumes of pot.

But step over the line of social etiquette into the realm of eccentric I did, and put in those corn stalks. And they grew tall and straight and so did my pride in my gardening prowess. In fact everything I've learned since says they shouldn't have produced any corn since you should have three or four rows so that the wind can circulate the pollen properly.

Then one day as my chiropractor was contorting my neck and back into positions that they were never meant to attain, he asked if that was corn he saw growing in my front yard. Now I had a reputation. Now I was the guy with corn in the front yard of his city house. Now it was time I got outta Dodge.

Getting out was something that had been in the works for a number of years. We had been looking for a rural property and trying to figure out how to do it. We looked for about five years using the 15-point guideline we'd developed for what our perfect rural home would include. Along with a solar-powered house and large forested area, it would include lots of room for growing food and ideally would allow the land to be certified organic, meaning that it hadn't been treated with pesticides or herbicides for at least three years. For a number of years we had been running an organic produce coop out of our garage. Ted Thorpe, a local organic farmer, delivered a truckload of vegetables to our garage and told us what he'd have the following week. Sixty families would pick up their vegetables, give us money, and order for the following week. Michelle did all the coordinating, ordering, counting, organizing, paying. It was a huge amount of work, but it was one of the best things we ever did to honor our growing environmental concerns. Ted grew sustainable, healthy, organic vegetables less than fifty miles from our home. The families loved the food, and Ted loved having a ready source of income that he could count on every week.

So when we finally found our place in the country and it had never been sprayed at all that we could determine, we were "over the moon" with excitement. The first spring we put the garden where Jean, the previous owner, had put it, behind the house in a very sandy location. We weren't living there full-time so it was only tended on weekends and suffered for lack of water and attention. That year we had an extremely early frost in the middle of September, and when we went up the next weekend the beans and much of what was left was nipped. Moving to an off-grid house we had lots of other priorities, so we didn't pay too much attend to the dismal failure that was the garden.

When Michelle decided to start putting in flower gardens she asked me if I could find any topsoil. I found a good spot near the old barn foundation and went back to enlarging the garden

Michelle and our friend Ellen try to identify herbs in our original garden left over from the previous owner, Jean.

in the sandy area behind the house. I kept using my shovel to turn over huge areas and then raking the grass out to leave what soil I could behind. It was very time-consuming and tiring, but I loved it. This was the garden I was going to be growing food in until I dropped dead in my potato patch. So I didn't mind the work. The first full summer we were there I planted a large garden in this sand and I think it suffered from the Neonatal Intensive Care Unit term "Failure to Thrive."

I did continue to retrieve wheelbarrows full of

much nicer soil from near the barn foundation for flower gardens and to put around apple trees we planted. I'm not sure when it dawned on me, but eventually a high-efficiency compact-fluorescent light bulb (since we were off the grid) went on over my head: maybe I should actually have my vegetable garden there. I believe the expression that comes to mind regarding my delayed realization is that I'm obviously "not the sharpest tool in the shed." In this matter I do not disagree.

I guess what held me back was the fact that the land around the old barn had four-foot high grass with a tangled, thick network of roots that made removing it a huge hassle. An intelligent person would have looked at that grass and said, "Man, there's gotta be something great nurturing this growth." I looked at it and said, "Man, it's gonna be lot of work turning it into a garden." While my assumption was correct about the work involved, turns out it was worth it.

"Welcome to the Jungle." The beginnings of our current main garden near the barn foundation

I started with a small garden in that area and kept the one out back in the sand. Each year I hacked off more grass and made the new garden bigger. The soil there was much healthier. As much as I enjoy the physical effort of enlarging a garden with a shovel and claw-like cultivator to shake the soil out of the grass clumps, I realized there had to be a better way. Since I didn't own a

tractor to plow it with, and since my rototiller just rolled over and played dead every time I tried to use it, I needed another strategy.

Eventually I realized that many of the farmers around me often ended up with large round hay bales that were not fit for animal feed. So I started purchasing them and using them to kill the grass. I'd roll out a thick layer of hay over the area I wanted to be garden next year, and after about six months the grass underneath would be dead. Then I could rototill the hay into the ground underneath with the added bonus of adding more organic matter to the new area. It worked like a charm, and ever since I discovered this strategy my garden has grown exponentially.

It's now getting close to half an acre, which when you own 150 acres doesn't sound like much, but which when you look at a garden full of weeds that need pulling it is in fact a very large garden. As we got to know the various previous owners of the house, which dates back to 1888, we learned the history of the area where the garden is. We discovered that animals had been kept in the area around the barn and much of the manure removed from the stalls was spread in this area. We also found out from a woman now in her 70s that they had a garden in the same place when she was a child. There's a lot of history in our garden.

The barn was torn down several decades ago, but the concrete foundation still remained. Trees had grown in all around it and it was in full shade. I started cutting the trees back to let more sunlight in. Inside the barn foundation itself was a jungle of sumacs and other small woody trees and plants. I started hacking away at these and discovered that there was actually a concrete floor in the barn. Once I got the overgrowth removed I was able to move all the soil that was left into some raised beds. I made the raised beds with cedar posts I scrounged from the side of the road as the township fixed the wire guardrails. So I now have three raised beds in the foundation. The soil in them is wonderfully dark and rich. I put my heat-loving plants in there, like peppers, eggplants, and tomatoes. This year I tried sweet potatoes there as well as peanuts and okra. We can still have cool evenings well past our last frost date, and the foundation is a great heat sink which absorbs heat from the sun all day and radiates it back at night. I think that even though there is no roof, the walls help cut down on some of the cooler winds that can retard growth early in the season.

My biggest challenge with gardening here is water. The good news about a very sandy soil like mine is that it has great drainage and you don't have to worry about water sitting around and causing problems. The bad news is that it dries out quickly, and we seem to be in a very drought-prone area. Near the barn foundation at one end of the garden is a dug well. This is a concrete-lined well that was built in the 1920s to provide water to the animals. It had an old building that was crumbling around it and a wooden pump that had fallen down into the well itself. Once I pulled down the building and cleaned out the well, I had an excellent source of water near the garden. Eventually I built a solar-powered pump that allows me to move the water to where I need it, either to rain barrels for hand watering or into my irrigation system.

For now I think I have enough garden under cultivation. You can grow a lot of food on half an acre. We have a plant-based diet, which means that we can actually offset a fairly large chunk of our food budget each year with the garden. I continue to try new things. This year I planted several apple trees in a new raised bed I put in the barn foundation. I put in more strawberries and raspberries this year, which I have not had much luck with in the past. I have some things that I don't put as much effort into. We never seem to make much use of the rhubarb, so I haven't been doing anything to keep it thriving. Luckily it's a perennial that comes back every year, even if you completely ignore it.

Having more room to expand my garden into is a dream come true for me after gardening in such restricted areas for so long. The reality now is that until I'm ready to expand my market-gardening business I don't really need it any bigger. I have grown vegetables for several businesses in the area, and while it's incredibly rewarding spiritually, on the scale I was operating on it was next to impossible to make a reasonable return on my investment of time. For now I'll just grow what I need, knowing I can always grow more if I want to.

I just celebrated my 50th birthday, and since my first garden was the year I got my driver's license at 16, that makes 34 years I've been gardening. I do not have a degree in agriculture from a university or college. I have read bookshelves full of works on gardening, I have taken many workshops with gardeners, and like most gardeners I have shared stories with other gardeners for years to find out what's worked and what hasn't worked for them. I hope to bring lots of this experience to you in this book. I don't have all the answers. No one does. You'll have to learn what does well in your garden and in your climate and what doesn't.

Nature is beaten back and the main garden starts to take shape.

Hopefully you'll be able to find a network of other gardeners in your area who like to share their experiences and to learn from yours. Sometimes just seeing someone with a large vegetable garden and stopping in to admire it can create a new friendship where you'll be able to learn all sorts of new tricks and techniques.

I hope you'll be able to take the same joy from growing food that I have. I can think of few activities that are more essential to a human being and that are a better investment of your time.

3
Secrets to Success

There's always a danger in giving away the ending of a story at the start of the book. Someone's going to read it and say, "Hey, that's it. I can put the book down now because I've figured out the ending." That might be true in a novel but not so much in a gardening book.

I'm giving away my secrets now so that you will be motivated to keep reading. I've read dozens of gardening books and discovered a great deal of useful information in them. I've also read many gardening books that intimidate the heck out of me. In fact, after reading one of those intimidating books I feel like an incredible failure, because I seem to be doing everything wrong according to what I've read. Every year I enjoy a huge harvest of wonderful healthy vegetables, but according to some of these books, I do everything wrong!

Often these books have a system, or a strategy, that makes for a great book title, but when you start trying to reduce the basic act of gardening to a system it gets very gimmicky and unnatural. If you throw some seeds in the dirt and get a bit of rain, chances are you'll end up with vegetables you can eat. They might not thrive, but you'll probably get something. In other words, growing vegetables is pretty easy. So the last thing I want to do is scare anyone off.

To grow healthy vegetables you're going to need to enrich the soil to provide the nutrients that the plant needs in order to grow, and you're going to need some water. That's it. That's all there is to having a great garden. That's right, you can put the book down now and head out to the garden.

I share these two basic secrets with you now so that if you reach any point in the book where I make things sound too technical you can just remind yourself that all you really need is some compost and water. Anything else is fluff.

I'm going to provide a few more details because you'll probably have some questions about the best way to do things, and I hope to share what I've learned in the garden and through my reading and my conversations with other gardeners. But ultimately it's just details. As long as you keep providing the soil with some organic matter and water, your plants will be fine.

Your garden will need some of your time. You'll need to take some time to provide the growing conditions to help your plants thrive. The biggest investment of your time will be in keeping the weeds down. If your plants have to compete with weeds for the finite amount of nutrition and moisture in the soil, you will compromise some of their potential. This is especially true early in the season. When your plants are small and their root systems are immature, it's very easy for weeds to crowd them out, and if it's between a delicate, hybrid, crossbred, fancy schmancy vegetable plant and a bunch of gangly, mean-spirited, energy-sucking bully weeds, the weeds will win every time. They're thugs! I observed this time and again in the community gardens where I rented space while living in an apartment. It was obvious that some other gardeners were really enthusiastic about gardening for about one weekend—that first weekend when they planted everything. Then the weeds took over. When I compared the plants in those other gardens to the plants in my garden, where the weeds were eliminated, there was no comparison. The weeds win every time.

You just need to provide some TLC for the garden all season. You need to do your best to eliminate the weeds and make sure the plants get water. The other benefit of your spending a bit of time with your plants is that you'll notice things that are going on with them. Most of the things you'll notice will be wonderful as they grow and flower and start producing the food you'll eat. Other things will require some attention. If they've suddenly become covered with aphids, you may need to get some soapy water to wash the aphids away. If the aphids are really aggressive, you may

want to visit the local garden center and pick up some ladybugs to release on the plants. Ladybugs love aphids and will feast on them.

The amount of time you'll need to spend will be in proportion to how big your garden is, how much you enjoy it, and your expectations. A lot of gardening success is related to the time you invest. Keep the plants weeded, keep them watered, and look for pests. Pretty basic stuff. All that remains are a few details.

4
Eating Energy

I know what you're thinking. This is a gardening book. Why do you need a chapter about energy? Please indulge me for a minute and let me explain.

The incredibly great lifestyle most North Americans enjoy is in large part due to the abundance of inexpensive fossil-fuel energy we've had access to over the last century. Oil and natural gas have made our lives pretty easy and present us with an incredible array of amazing products and food from all over the world. Oil in particular has been important because of its role in transportation, not only giving us great mobility but also allowing food to move long distances to our dinner table. Natural gas has made our homes comfortable but it has also been the major raw material in the production of fertilizer that has allowed farmers to grow more and more food on less land. In the early part of the last century the average farmer grew enough food for 6 people while today he grows food for more than 130 people.

We have been freed from the daily grind of searching for or growing our own food to engage in other activities. Oil has incredible potential energy in it. Three tablespoons of crude oil is the equivalent of eight hours of manual labor. I recognize this myself in my garden. I know how much work it would take me to hoe the garden to keep the weeds down. Instead I can use a small amount of gasoline, which is refined from crude oil, in my rototiller and I will be able to till the garden in a fraction of the time. It is estimated that if you worked your whole life doing manual labor your energy output would be equivalent to only three barrels of crude oil. Man, how depressing is that!

Our diet now is largely dependent on fossil-fuel energy. This dependence starts when the farmer puts diesel fuel into her tractor to plow the soil and plant the seeds, and it continues as fossil fuel fertilizers are added to the soil and insecticides and herbicides are sprayed on the crops. Diesel fuel is used to harvest the crop and to fuel the truck that takes the vegetables to the factory for processing. Natural gas heats the water at the canning plant to process the vegetables, and fossil-fuel energy produces the electricity to refrigerate or freeze the vegetables. There is also the fossil-fuel energy that is used in the manufacture of the plastic bag or glass jar or metal can that the vegetable is packaged in. More diesel is used to get the can, jar, or package to a central warehouse, and more energy is used to keep that warehouse cool. Energy is used to transport food from the warehouse by truck to the store, and then the store uses more fossil-fuel energy for lights and warmth and refrigeration. You probably use fossil fuel in your car to pick up the food from the grocery store or market, and then you use natural gas or electricity to cook the food when you get it home. Essentially we are eating fossil fuels.

The challenge will come if we ever run out of cheap fossil fuels. And it appears that we may be at or getting very close to a point where this happens. There is a geological limit to how much fossil-fuel energy was deposited in the ground millions of years ago through a combination of climate and heat and pressure. "Peak oil" is the point at which we've extracted half of the reserves that are in the ground. We're not going to run out of fossil fuels; they're just going to get harder and harder to get at. A number of geologists who study peak oil feel we've already hit the peak. A number of others say we're very close. The International Energy Agency (IEA) is the organization that developed nations rely on for information about energy. Up until 2008 the IEA suggested that there was nothing to worry about and that the world still had huge reserves left. In 2008 it changed its tune dramatically and announced that the depletion rate for conventional oil was almost 7% as opposed to the 3% stated in its previous report. The IEA also suggested that the world will hit a "production plateau" in 2020. I believe that this is a veiled way of saying "peak oil" and that the IEA has finally seen the light.

So the food you eat is going to get more expensive, especially the food that travels long distances. For many of us that means we're going to have start eating food that's grown closer to home.

At the same time that we're hitting peak oil we've also got a population issue to deal with. People don't like to talk about it but it's the 800-pound gorilla in the room. When I was born in 1960 the

There is huge amount of embedded energy in our North American diets.

population of the planet was 3 billion people. In the year 2000, four decades later, the population was 6 billion. So it doubled in four decades. Now we're at 6.6 billion, on our way to 8 or 9 billion this century. The United Nations believes it may stabilize at that level. It's going to have to stabilize because I don't think the planet can feed 9 billion people. In fact I don't think it can comfortably feed 6 billion. In 2008 when the price of oil hit $147/barrel there were widespread food shortages throughout the planet. While North Americans may spend 10% or 15% of their income on food, many people in other countries spend from 50% to 90% of their income to eat. So when there was a rapid price spike in grains and essential food crops as oil and commodity prices skyrocket, many people across the planet had problems feeding themselves. This is always true for people in many countries when droughts and wars hit, but in 2008 things were different. When these shortages hit many people suffered immensely.

The problem of food shortages isn't going away. Decades ago governments were proactive about commodity prices for farmers. If the price of grain was low governments would step into the market and buy grain, which would drive the price up. They would store it in grain elevators until years with lower harvests to sell it back into the market. In the 1980s the Reagan/Thatcher era swept in a mood of government deregulation and these governments decided it wasn't their place to regulate food prices. So whereas in previous years the world had months of grain in reserve in case of emergencies or famines, today we have days of it. The cupboards are bare. We produce lots of food but we don't store it the way we used to. We use a "just in time" system for our food. This may work fine for an automobile company avoiding warehouse costs by having parts for vehicles arrive just as they are about to be assembled into a car, but I'm not sure it's a great idea for our food. I think there's a little bit more at stake.

This is where this book comes in. You may not be able to convince your government to be more responsible about the food supply, but you can take control of your own. While I talk about lots of different food to produce in your garden I do have a bit of a bias towards the foods that are the easiest to grow and store and that pack a nutritional punch. Potatoes are my favorite example. They grow anywhere, store extremely well with no energy required to store them, and are a nutritional powerhouse. You can live on potatoes, and the starches and complex carbohydrates they are made of are the perfect food to provide the energy your body needs to do everything from cycling to work to hoeing your garden.

I believe that rising energy prices are going to have a dramatic impact on our lives but that they don't have to be negative. In my book *Thriving During Challenging Times: The Energy, Food and Financial Independence Handbook*, I show how taking the steps to reduce your reliance on fossil-fuel energy can have a positive effect on your lifestyle. It also helps to deal with the guilt many of us experience when we drive or use fossil fuels with the knowledge that they have a negative effect on the environment. Having your own garden is the perfect example of how this move to independence will have a positive effect on your life. You'll reduce your reliance on food that has traveled extremely long distances and may be harder to get in the future. You'll dramatically reduce your carbon footprint with every item you harvest from your garden. You'll reduce some of your exposure to rapidly rising energy costs. You'll grow wonderfully healthy and amazing chemical-free foods full of positive energy and the nutrients that your body needs. And finally you'll experi-

ence a huge boost to your spirit with the joy that comes from growing your own food. There is no better single ingredient to deal with challenging times than the right attitude, and that positive approach to life is waiting out in your backyard in the vegetable garden!

Growing and storing your own food is one of the best steps you can take towards making yourself more resilient to energy shocks.

The author spreading the word at a local garden center workshop.

5
Soil Preparation

Here's my fantasy. I buy a new house and in the backyard is this massive vegetable garden all tilled, with a fresh load of composted horse manure just worked in. Yea, that's what I'd like. And a nice row of raspberries all pruned and ready to go. All right, now we're talking. And a row of asparagus. And strawberries. That's what I'd like.

What I'd like and the reality for most of us are two different things. Right now you're probably looking at a backyard with a swing set and lots of grass. That's okay. We can work with that. All we've got to do is get rid of the grass. There are two schools of thought on this. The hard one, the one I always followed, is the "Cancel the health club membership and sharpen your shovel" method where you just start turning over sections of sod, knock off as much topsoil as you can, and get ready to plant. Let's look at this in more detail.

One of the greatest challenges of planting a garden is preparing the place where it's going to be. When you're standing and looking at a patch of lush green grass, it can be pretty discouraging to think about turning over that thick-rooted mass. It's good sign, though, that the area where you're going to put the garden is already green. That means there's some good topsoil waiting. You just need to remove what's growing there now and replace it with your vegetables. In the words of The Terminator, "No problemo."

All you need is an attitude adjustment about the work involved. North Americans have no problem paying for a fitness club membership and burning calories on stairmasters and treadmills, accomplishing absolutely nothing in terms of productive work. Yes, they are maintaining their cardiovascular health, but apart from saving the health care system money and not having to buy larger-waisted jeans, they really have nothing to show for it.

Now turning over a garden, that's an accomplishment. And it's not just cardio you're getting. There's actual muscle work here, and load-bearing exercise that will stave off osteoporosis. Plus you're using your back muscles. When I started my business and worked 12 hours a day at my computer, my back was a mess. I visited a chiropractor regularly to tried to keep my back from seizing up. But I noticed that when I took canoe trips and spent three or four days lugging around huge packs of food or carrying a canoe on my shoulders when I got home my back was great for weeks.

Since moving to the country and having a huge garden and heating with firewood that I cut from my property, my back continues to feel great. I really think there is nothing better for your body than to grab a shovel and get digging. Now you need to be reasonable about it and maybe set some realistic goals if you don't make vigorous physical activity a regular thing. You might want to work at a small section each day until you've got the full garden turned over.

Attire

Rule #1 about turning over soil is to have a good pair of work boots. If you work in crappy sneakers or sandals your feet are going to ache afterwards and you're going to swear off gardening forever, which would be a mistake. Good work boots will have a stiff sole and if you get the safety-certified ones with the green triangle they will have a steel toe and potentially a steel shank. The steel shank will run the length of the sole and will prevent a nail from puncturing your foot if you step on one. Obviously if it'll stop a nail it should be firm enough to protect your foot when you're pounding on the shovel. The steel toe isn't a bad idea either. I'm not saying that I've ever used a shovel recklessly enough to hit the front of my work boot with it, but when I retire my work boots it's usually because the steel toe has worked its way through the leather. Enough said.

A good work boot will also support your ankles, which will help reduce the chance of injury and other leg discomfort. I say this from experience. The first warm day of spring we all get giddy with glee and run around and do things we haven't done in months and then hobble about with shin splints for the next week. Good work boots should last for years, and if you think of the money your garden will save over that time period they're well worth the investment.

When your house was built, the construction crew might have thrown all sorts of wood and nails and other sharp materials around the yard. These might have been covered up by topsoil but may still be lurking in the soil. The action of frost heaves materials up towards the surface, and thin rubber running shoes are not going to offer protection from the sharp objects that lie in wait. I do not mention this to scare you but just as you probably wear a seat belt for safety reasons when you drive, so you should look at a good pair of work boots as a safety precaution that will improve your gardening experience. My garden is located near the foundation of the old barn that was torn down many decades ago. The soil is a veritable smorgasbord of jagged and protruding objects that pose the risk of potential tetanus infection. Since I'm averse to needles and have not

Like a faithful dog, even work boots need to be retired when the duct tape takes over. Look for the Green Triangle designating steel toes.

had a tetanus booster in years, I try to minimize my close encounters of the rusty nail kind.

Stretching

Now that I'm 50 I would even go as far as suggesting that you warm up for your session with the shovel. If you were you going out to play some basketball or hockey you would probably do some stretching. It just makes sense to get your muscles ready for what you're going to ask of them. Turning over a garden is going to use most of your major muscle groups and it's going to be tempting once you start to overdo it. So take a few minutes, find that one piece of carpet you still have with underpad, and do some stretching. You don't have to do this every time you garden, but this first little endeavor may take some effort.

The Shovel

Wow, a whole section on a shovel. How condescending is that, like I don't know what a shovel is. It is not my intention to condescend but if I may I'd like to offer one bit of advice from experience.

Rule #2 of turning over sod is to sharpen your shovel. "Didn't it come sharp?" No, probably not. For shipping purposes a shovel is usually left dull. It's the owner's job to sharpen it. And it will need to be sharpened periodically over its life. The challenge with steel is that the steel that stays the sharpest tends to be pretty brittle. So the steel they use in a shovel will be softer, which will make it less likely to break, but it also means that every

time you hit a stone the shovel will get a little duller. My favorite shovel, pictured, here is getting pretty worn. It used to be pointy! I like it because it's so light. I guess that makes me a 98-pound weakling. Luckily I don't spend any time on the beach any more so bullies can't kick sand in my face in front of my girl.

To sharpen your shovel you'll need a flat file. Put the shovel on the ground; hold it in place with your knee or foot. Move the file away from the handle, repeatedly picking it up after each stroke and moving it back to start again. In other words, you should only go in one direction with a file like this. Don't go back and forth. As you do this you'll notice that the steel on the point of the blade will start to get shiny as you expose new steel. Keep doing this until it looks and feels pretty sharp. Be careful not to run your finger across the blade to test how sharp it is. You should be able to tell how sharp it is by moving your finger in just one direction.

This probably seems like a lot of hype just to go out and turn over some grass. I agree, but from experience I know the sorts of things that can discourage people, and the last thing I want is for you

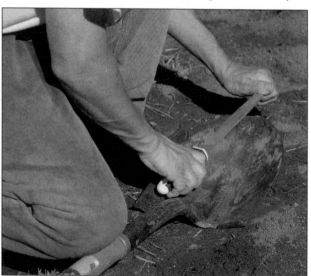

to give up on this project. It'll be worth it, and if you take a few minutes before you start and get prepared properly things will go much better. I'm not proud of how many years it took me to clue into the fact that most shovels don't come pre-sharpened. Sure, if you pound on it hard enough with your boot it will penetrate the sod and soil, but it means more wear and tear on your body than it needs. As I get older, and wiser, I realize that these amazing tools we've created work better when we use them properly.

Sod Busting the Hard Way

When I turn over sod to start or enlarge a garden, I usually make a line with my shovel delineating one of the sides. Then I make another line parallel to it about 8 to 12 inches away, depending on how energetic I feel. Then I make a perpendicular line with the shovel between the other two, again every 8 to 12 inches. Now I can take out these smaller sections that have been cut on four sides. The first row I turn over on the grass beside it. Then the next row I turn over into the spot where I removed the first row. Each subsequent row ends up in the trench beside it until I've got the garden or section as big as I want it. You can take that first row you turned over onto the grass and plunk it down in the last trench or put it in the compost pile. This is something you can do in stages, so don't overdo it. If you're going to make a pretty big garden this year, you don't have to turn it all over on the first day. You can take a few days.

You want to use the shovel and make a grid or checkerboard in the sod, cutting out 10- or 12-inch blocks. The first row you can turn over onto the existing grass and then you can flip the subsequent rows face down in the row beside it. If you're starting this in the fall you can just leave the sod turned over and face down for the winter. If you're in a cold area the frost and cold temperatures will help break up the soil structure. Next spring you can take your cultivator and use it to start breaking up the blocks of sod. What you're after is to remove as much soil from the blocks as possible with as little of the grass and roots as possible.

Now What?

So now you've got a section of your lawn with the sod turned over. What you do next will depend on what time of the year it is and how quickly you want to put in the garden. If you're doing this in the fall you may be able to plant in the spring. Hopefully the frost and colder temperatures will kill most of the grass and its root system. In the spring you may be able to put a thick layer of compost on top and start planting. There is always a risk, though, that you haven't killed the existing grass and that it will just need some sun and warm weather to turn in the opposite direction from the way you left it (face down) and head back towards the sun. This is going to be a huge pain for you and it will be difficult to completely get rid of grass with this deep a root system.

Another option is to supplement your compost with some topsoil, either from another place on your property or from a commercial source. Some beginning gardeners choose to get a load of topsoil delivered. If you can afford this and are up to the work involved in spreading it, great. It's perfect to spread that topsoil on an area where you've turned over the sod. This will ensure that you save the original topsoil but that the grass doesn't have a chance to regrow. You can also purchase some soil in bags from a garden center to cover that turned-over sod.

I do like this system of turning over sod because it means you preserve the topsoil that is such an essential part of the garden's health. It takes decades to create good topsoil and it's a shame to lose it. If you live in a newer subdivision there's a chance that even though you have grass you don't have much "topsoil" under it. Developers learned that it was easiest to scrape the topsoil off areas where houses were being built, using huge earth-moving machines. Then the basements were dug into subsoils, which were then spread around the home. You would hope that the topsoil would have been returned to the yard before sod was put down, but that wasn't always the case. The subsoil, which is often clay, was then much closer to the top and covered only by the narrow band of top-

Cut out a checkerboard in the grass, turn each square into the square beside it, then move the first row you dug to the last row.

Once the sod is turned over, cover it with compost, manure, straw, or leaves to kill any grass that's left.

soil that was returned. The developer didn't have to worry about putting much topsoil back if all he wanted was to get grass to grow to make the place look nice to sell. If you, on the other hand, want to start a vegetable garden with a very thin layer of topsoil and then some horrible subsoil—good luck. This may be a case where some commercial help is initially in order, be it a load of topsoil or bags you bring home in the car.

Another possibility is to turn the grass over in the fall and spread a thick layer of leaves on top. This should help kill most of the grass, and in the spring you can work the leaves into the soil before you plant.

Sod Busting the Slow and Easy Way

The easiest way to get rid of grass is to kill it, and since hiring a small plane to crop-dust with defoliant is frowned on in most areas, you have to be

clever. (And of course I am just joking about this!) The best way to do it is to deny the grass light and moisture, and there are lots of ways to do that. You can spread out layers of newspapers and place rocks or other heavy objects on top to keep the papers in place. Many printers have switched to vegetable-based inks, which should reduce the risk of trace heavy metals and chemicals ending up in the soil. Sheets of cardboard also work well. The tower for my wind turbine came in huge cardboard boxes which I cut open and spread out on an area of grass I wanted to turn into a garden. The following season what was left of the grass was easy to rototill and then rake off. Spreading a large tarp over the grass will also weaken it and make it easier to remove after a few months. One of my favorite ways, though, is to place a thick layer of rotten hay or straw on the grass. (Keep an eye open for bales of rotten hay or straw and then offer to purchase them for a discounted price from the farmer.) The beauty of this is that if it's thick enough it will kill the grass and as it's completing that task it will continue to decay and break down and add organic material to the soil. Finding a pickup-truck load of rotten hay isn't always easy, but if you plan on starting a garden in three to six months or if you want to expand an existing garden it's a wonderful technique.

Shake shake shake…shake shake shake…shake your…grass clump…

Am I showing my age quoting a KC and the Sunshine Band lyric? What can I say? I publicly raved about rock 'n' roll but secretly loved some of those disco tunes.

I use my four-pronged cultivator to spear sod clumps and shake excess soil off if I need to use a new area right away.

If you can find a farmer with some older round bales, they make the perfect garden enlarger.

So that clump of grass you've turned over will be a problem if you don't turn it over perfectly, putting it face (grass) down as you turn it over. Some of that grass may continue to grow back. If you haven't turned it over in the fall or in advance of planting the garden, you'll need to deal with it. But remember, it's not a waste product to be disposed of, as I've seen in the past with some homeowners. It is in fact the very basis for success with your garden because it has so much of that all-important topsoil you want to maintain.

When I've enlarged my gardens by turning over the sod I will often just toss the grass clumps in the area of the garden and then grab them with a cultivator and move them around until most of the soil has fallen off where I want it. Then I place all the sod that's left at the bottom of my compost pile and cover it with a dense layer of leaves. After a season the grass should be dead and I'm left with any topsoil that didn't get knocked off.

Double Digging

For years I've read about a method called "double digging." I didn't get it for a long time, but when I finally did I realized that it's an excellent way to prepare a lawn for a garden very quickly. Like the earlier example where you cut the sod into squares, this time put the first row of sod you remove a foot from where you dug it. Then dig out the soil from where the sod was and place it right beside the row. You're basically digging a shallow trench where that first row of sod was. Now when you remove the second row of sod, turn it over grass side down into the trench you just dug beside it. Once the row is complete dig another trench where the sod was and pile that soil on top of the upside-down sod. By doing this you're making sure that the grass and its roots are buried under a deep enough layer of soil that light will not get down and allow them to live. If you dig the trench deep enough and pile a deep enough layer of soil on top of it you'll be able to grow a garden on top and not have to worry about the sod.

Plus you've saved that topsoil even though it's a little bit lower than it would otherwise be. If you have a healthy soil earthworms will help circulate that topsoil back up higher, as will the action of the frost and other natural processes. I would wait for a year before I used my rototiller or dug deeply with a shovel to turn the soil over. Make sure the grass is really dead before you risk bringing it back into the grow zone by accident.

With this process I'd recommend a very deep layer of compost or compost manure on top because by digging down fairly deep in the trench you haven't brought the best soil to the surface. In time these layers will all get mixed up and you'll

Double Digging

1. First row goes a foot away.
2. Dig a trench and put the soil beside it.

3. Put the next row of sod face down in the trench.

4. Put the soil from the next trench on top of the sod beside it.

5. Continue down each row, first turning the sod face down into the trench beside it

6. Then cover that sod with soil you dig from underneath.

7. Move the sod from the first row and put it in the last row; then put the soil from the first trench on top of the sod in the last row.

have a wonderful, thick, rich upper layer, but for now supplement and make it deep. It wouldn't be a bad idea to mulch with leaves or rotten hay to ensure that no light gets through to that lower layer of grass so you're sure it's dead by next season.

Rototilling

A rototiller is such a huge work saver that I use it in my energy workshops as my example of the energy contained in a barrel of oil, which is the equivalent of more than eight years of human manual labor. So I can spend four or five hours hoeing and weeding by hand once the garden gets going, or I can use a tiny amount of gasoline in a rototiller and accomplish the same work in 15 minutes.

You don't have to purchase a rototiller. Borrowing is always my first choice with a piece of equipment I may not need too often. You can also rent them. I would suggest you rent one a few times and make sure you like it and find it useful before you invest in one of your own.

Rototilling is an excellent way to maintain a garden that has been a garden for a while, but it can be difficult to use a rototiller to start a garden, especially if the area is currently grass. The rotating tines on the back were designed to plunge into relatively soft soil and mix it up, bringing lower soil higher and mixing higher soil down. When they hit a large, matted layer of grass roots they often can't get down through it well, so the rototiller will have a tendency to want to jump or skip over it. This doesn't accomplish the task and can be scary as you try and slow the marauding beast down. I have used a rototiller on a patch of weak and sketchy grass, and it required a number of passes in different directions to accomplish the task. When you're done you still have lots of grass and root that is broken up but still mixed into the soil. These have to be removed or else they're just going to start growing again. I think you're best to stick to using a rototiller to maintain a garden that's already well underway as opposed to starting a garden with one.

Now that I've tried the double dig technique

I think it's excellent. I will admit, though, that I'm getting lazy in my old age and now make sure I've always got lots of rotten hay around so that if I see an area where I'd like to expand the garden soon I can use the hay to kill the grass and add to the organic matter before I even start. After a year under rotten hay, even if it was healthy grass a quick rototill will reveal a rich, healthy grass-free soil to plant in.

If you are going to use a rototiller try and get one with pneumatic (air-filled) tires and with rear tines, which will mean much less vibration for your arms.

My smaller rototiller with solid rubber tires is more maneuverable for weeding, but is not well suited for sod or weed busting.

6
Soil – Digging in the Dirt

It's always a good idea to find out what kind of soil you have in your garden. This can sound complicated and it certainly can be if you use the U.S. Department of Agriculture soil texture classification method which identifies 12 different types of soil.

Gravel	Sand	Silt	Clay
2 mm to 75 mm	0.05 mm to 2 mm	0.002 mm to 0.05 mm	less than 0.002 mm

A simpler classification system is to identify your soil as either clay, sand, or silt. Clay particles are very small, sand particles are much bigger, and silt particles are somewhere in-between. A soil with a heavy clay content is often a reddish color (think of terra cotta clay pots), sand tends to be yellowish brown in color, and the best soil is usually a dark, rich brown or black.

My first garden had very red clay. My current garden, which has excellent soil, is very dark, al-most black, but is also very sandy. You'll discover quite quickly what type of soil you have and how well it holds water. Clay holds water very well, sometimes too well, and it won't drain properly. If you have a big rain and the water puddles on top of the soil, it probably is very high in clay. If the soil stays very soggy in the spring, making it difficult to turn over, it may have a lot of clay. If you take a handful of soil and squeeze it together and it maintains its shape after you open your hand there's probably a lot of clay in it.

If your soil crumbles after you squeeze it in your hand it probably has a lot of sand in it. Sandy soil has excellent drainage, which means that water won't pool on it and it won't become saturated during a big storm. The problem is that the water that's draining away is taking some of the nutrition you want for the plants with it. A clay soil won't drain as easily, and if you get a lot of rain the roots can actually become waterlogged because the water doesn't flow away from them. Clay can also form a very hard surface, which means that if you do get rain a lot of it can run right off the soil and not make it down to where

Dry sand will run through your fingers just the way it runs through an hourglass. Damp sand will stick together a bit, but nothing like clay, and it will brush off your hands easily.

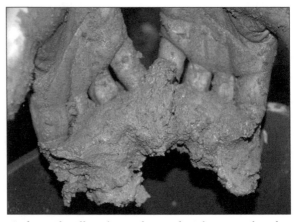

A clay soil will stick together and stick to your hands. This clay subsoil would be great for ceramic pots!

you want it.

So each type of soil has pros and cons but they all require things to make them better, and that's compost and organic matter. Sandy soil needs organic matter to hold onto water and nutrients when it rains so they don't get washed down deeper into the subsoil. Clay soils need organic matter to keep the tiny particles from becoming fused together and hard and clumpy. Organic matter will keep air spaces in the soil that allow the roots to make their way through the clay and also let water drain better. Organic matter will also make the surface of a clay soil easier to break up when you weed and cultivate it.

So regardless of the soil, you have to add organic matter to it. My father-in-law, who was a master gardener, always called this humus, which is the correct scientific name. Now humus is not to be confused with hummus, which is a wonderful Middle Eastern dip made from ground chick peas and often spread on pita bread with falafels. While you could add hummus to your garden, we're talking fairly large quantities here, which would get expensive and would tend to attract a lot of wayward vegetarians wandering around your area.

Humus is really another name for compost. It is degraded or degrading organic material in the soil which helps to make the soil a dark, rich color. If you think of the things you put into compost like leaves and grass and straw, these materials are often only partially broken down when you spread them in your garden. When it rains some of the rain will be absorbed by these materials, which hold the water and release it slowly back to the roots as they need it. This material also keeps the soil particles separated and allows air pockets in the soil. Pretend you're a root just for a minute. Not a big root, like a carrot, but a small, fast-growing tomato plant root. You're trying to make yourself as big as possible so you can absorb as much water and nutrients as possible to send up to the plant. If you're growing in a heavy clay with tiny particles clinging tightly

together, it's a tough slog. If the soil has lots of organic matter or humus in it you can move from air pocket to air pocket, and when you brush up against a nice piece of decaying leaf you absorb some of the moisture it has. As a root, you love organic matter.

Each year you're going to add more and more organic matter to the garden, and over time, regardless of what type of soil you have, you are going to end up with a healthy, rich topsoil. It may take longer than you'd like, but it will be the end result of being very vigilant about adding large amounts of compost and organic material to your garden every year. This is how you end up with the topsoil you see in the fancy brochures at the garden center.

pH

I'm only bringing up soil pH because it seems to be referred to in a lot of places, including seed catalogs. A pH test will tell you whether your

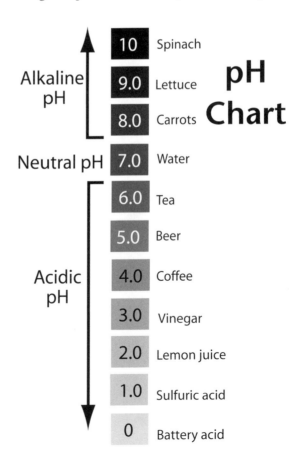

soil is too acidic or too alkaline. On this pH scale you can see that a reading of 7 is considered neutral—not too acidic, not too alkaline. Sort of like the porridge of Goldilocks fame—not too hot, not too cold. Most vegetables will do best with a pH of between 6.5 and 7. But while pH can definitely have an effect on some plants, determining if it is the cause of a particular condition can be pretty difficult. It is also difficult to correct a condition that's affecting one plant without having an effect on other plants.

I have been gardening now for more than 30 years, and I've never done a soil test. There, I said it. It's like saying, "I've never flown on a jet," or "I've never had a Dairy Queen sundae." I know this is something I should do, but I just never get around to it. And for the last 20 years my vegetables have grown very well. If it isn't broken, why fix it?

Sometimes things around your garden may affect the soil's pH. I have a row of very large pine trees near my garden and in a big wind pine needles can be carried quite a distance into my garden. Pine needles tend to make your soil acidic, or move it down the pH scale. A lot of berries like to grow in a very acidic soil, especially blueberries, so putting pine needles around them is a good idea. But if you want to adjust an acidic soil you can buy a bag of lime, which is ground up limestone, and broadcast it on the soil.

Wood ashes

Compost —the ultimate organic boost for the garden

We heat our home with wood and I am able to use wood ashes in the garden instead. I spread them throughout the garden during the winter. Ashes work like lime to move the pH back toward neutral if it's too acidic. I also use horse manure on my garden which tends to raise the pH as well. So my attitude is that even though I have pine needles making my garden more acidic I'm applying ashes and manure, which will restore the soil more towards being neutral, which is a good thing.

Wood ash contains a high percentage of calcium carbonate, which is a form of lime, so ashes are a good substitute to avoid purchasing lime. They also contain some phosphorous, the "P" of the NPK designation on fertilizer, and potassium or potash, which is the "K". There are also some trace elements such as iron and manganese, made popular as a soil enhancer by Bill Murray as the groundskeeper in the movie *Caddyshack*.

Wood ashes have a downside, which is that they can cause scab on potatoes. There are other causes of potato scabs, but neutral or alkaline soils provide the type of environment that the fungi that cause scab like to live in. One way of dealing with this is to avoid lowering the pH of the soil in the area where I plan to plant potatoes by not adding ashes and manure, but I'm not always sure where I'm going to be growing them. I often just keep adding rows of potatoes as the season progresses, especially if I have extras left over in the root cellar. Despite the occasional scab on my potatoes, I've yet to have anyone turn me down when I offer them potatoes in the fall.

So rather than worry about scab and pH, I just take my potatoes as they come. Out of every row I harvest some will be perfect, some will have scab, and some will be a mess, where grubs have chewed them or they've split open or they just don't look that attractive. And while they may not look that good, they'll taste just fine. So I store the best looking potatoes since they're less likely to spoil over the winter, put the ones with scabs next in line to eat, and eat the really ugly ones right away. We have a lot of mashed potatoes in the fall! If you're removing the skins anyway, who cares what they look like? Any time we're having baked potatoes we just make sure to use the ones with the perfect skin.

If you are fanatical about gardening you can spend more time making spot applications. If you know your soil is acidic, you can add lime or wood ash to the area where you're going to plant something that doesn't like an acidic soil.

Compost as a Buffer

The one thing I've learned from the reading I've done and from my experience in my own garden is that compost acts as a huge buffer for your garden in terms of correcting pH. In other words, if you add composted materials regularly, you do not have to worry about the soil's pH. Plants may do best in a specific pH range, but they are really just looking for nutrients that are most likely to be available to them when the soil is in that range. Compost is going to provide these nutrients regardless of the pH, so your plants can access what they need. By adding lots of compost and humus from various sources, you're buffering your plants and giving them what they need. Compost is the great garden relaxer. Just add and relax.

Soil Testing

The way to determine the pH of your soil is to do a soil test. This can take many forms. You can purchase soil test kits, or you can send your soil

Open the capsule and pour contents into vial with soil sample.

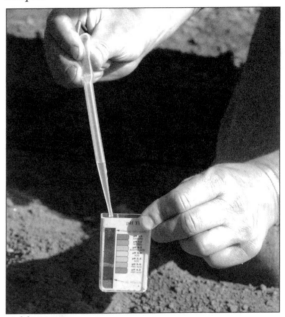

Add water.

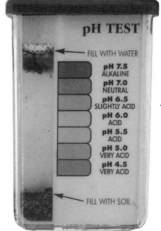

Shake and then let contents settle. After a few minutes compare color against pH key.

off to a lab for testing. You can check with your local department of agriculture to determine if there is a lab in your area. The lab will often suggest that you take samples from a variety of spots in the garden to send off.

The commercial soil testing kits come in many varieties. Some are just pH strips which you dip in a mixture of soil and water with the resulting color indicating the pH. Some soil test kits look like one of those expensive chemistry kits you always wanted to get at Christmas, the kind where you could make a lot of smoke and explosions. Yes, the one your parents never bought for you for exactly those reasons. Not only can you test the soil's pH with these kits, you can also test for nitrogen, phosphorous, and potassium. These will be a little more time consuming but provide more accurate results for more components of your soil.

After admitting earlier that I had never actually tested the pH of my soil, I decided to purchase a kit and test my soil so that I could share the experience with you in this book. The kit I purchased has a small container that you put soil and water into, a capsule of powder, and a colored strip. Once you've mixed the soil and water you add the contents of the small capsule and within a minute the water turns color and you compare it to the strip. I have to tell you, I was pretty nervous taking this test. What if the results were really bad? What if the soil was so acidic it could melt the steel off my shovels? What if plants were dissolving as if they were growing in hydrochloric acid? I felt as though I should have been wearing a lab coat and huge Coke bottle glasses with my hair moussed into crazy spiky points.

Alas, it wasn't so exciting. The pH was close to neutral and the NPK results were good. So apparently you can trust your instincts. Things grow great in the garden, I put in a lot of compost and manure, and the soil maintains itself in a good growing range.

You can also purchase meters that have metal probes that you insert into the soil for readings. You might have seen some that measure the moisture of house plants. I have not tried one of these but a friend of mine is a fellow gardener who grows blueberries commercially. Blueberries love a very acidic soil. He used one of these meters to measure the pH of his soil and it indicated that his soil had a high pH, close to neutral, which blueberries will not thrive in. He applied sulfur to lower the pH to create a more acidic soil. The soil tester continued to tell him he had a neutral soil, so he continued to add sulfur. Meanwhile, despite his activities, his blueberries continued to flourish. Finally he decided to have a professional test done and sent his soil to a lab. The lab results came back saying his soil was below 5, which is extremely acidic. The problem wasn't the soil —it was the tester. So keep in mind that sometimes equipment may not be up to scratch and that trusting your instincts is still the best bet with your garden.

The most important advice of this chapter is once again compost, compost, compost. Add enough compost and you really don't have to worry about all those complicated scientific things you hear about.

7
Compost

If you read only one chapter of this book, this should be it. In fact if you're standing in a bookstore right now because you don't want to spend the money on this book, then go no further than this chapter. The book is a pretty handy reference to have around, so maybe you should buy a copy. If you did buy it I thank you.

Compost is the key to a successful garden. Water and sunshine are equally important, but you have only a limited amount of control over water and the sun. Regardless of your personal feelings of grandeur, the sun and rain are pretty hard to control. Mother Nature bats last, and if she decides that we're going to have an extreme summer of cool and wet weather or one of too much heat and no rain, your expectations for your garden output may have to be adjusted.

Compost is something that you can control and it's as important as anything else you do. Adding lots of rich, nutritious compost to your soil will help you grow wonderful, tasty, healthy vegetables. It will also help you deal with the pests that for many years traditional gardeners have used chemicals to treat. A healthy, thriving plant is the key to dealing with any pest, and the best way to ensure that your plants are healthy is to give them the proper growing environment they need. Compost will build up the soil and provide it with humus or organic material that will help the roots of the plants easily penetrate it and allow water to work its way down into the soil and be available for the plant when it needs it.

If your compost contains a good mix of natural ingredients it will bring the nutrients your plants need into close proximity to the roots so that as they need them they can seek them out and absorb them. Compost is going to add organic material that will help the soil maintain air when it's turned over and cultivated. It will keep

the soil from becoming compacted and forcing that air out. Plants need oxygen just as humans do, and some of a plant's needs are met through its roots. If compost has been added and you've cultivated the soil to keep it light and airy, roots are going to have no problem seeking out the essential elements they need to send up to the plant and ultimately into the end product that you get to enjoy.

Composting is the ultimate form of recycling, where you take other organic materials and break them down and return them to the soil. Much of what I recommend that you add to your compost is readily available in your city and is usually left on the curb on garbage day.

When I lived in the city I started to notice how many bags of garbage people put out and that during the summer and fall it seemed like a lot. I was on the City of Burlington's Sustainable Development Committee in the early 90s and one day we attended a presentation by the city's Chief of Waste Disposal. He shared a chart that showed the weight of the city's garbage as it changed over the 12 months of the year. In the winter it was fair-

An excellent design for a homebuilt compost system. Chicken wire keeps the contents in but allows air to circulate. Front panel can be opened to allow for access to compost. Having two sides allows you to have compost at different rates of decomposition. This was a wet summer so the tarp is preventing it from becoming saturated with rain.

ly low, then started going up dramatically in May, and spiked in June, July, and August. September and October were also pretty high and then the weight dropped off in November and December. So what's with that, I asked? "Grass clippings," was his response. In those days people used massive amounts of nitrogen-based fertilizer to produce lush, green, and vigorously growing lawns. They then cut that grass, vacuumed it up with their lawnmower, and put it in petroleum-based plastic bags. The city then used massive amounts of CO_2-producing diesel fuel to haul it away to the landfill, where it would rot and create methane, a greenhouse gas 20 times worse than CO_2. The city had a landfill that was rapidly filling up. It also had a huge budget crisis because the funding it received from upper levels of government had been dramatically cut. So we asked the city employees to calculate how much money would be saved in diesel and tipping fees at the landfill if grass clippings were banned. It was an enormous amount of money, and once the politicians saw how much money could be saved, regardless of the negative reaction from their constituents they simply couldn't pass up the savings and grass clippings were banned from the garbage.

The public awareness campaign that we sponsored to make the transition was pretty basic. Leave your grass clippings on your lawn. They are a rich source of nitrogen. They will break down quickly and return organic matter to your lawn, which helps it grow well. And guess what? You won't need to buy so much fertilizer every year, if any at all.

During the time that I was growing little trees in pots in my backyard, I needed a lot of organic material and my source for it was local and free. The neighbors took all the leaves that the deciduous trees dropped each fall, put them in green garbage bags, and put them out at the curb. You could always tell which bags held the leaves. The bags were smooth and round and had the imprints of leaves and twigs on them. Garbage, on the other hand, was irregular and had lots of pointed edges from boxes and things. So every night before garbage day I'd set out with my wheelbarrow and grab all the bags of leaves that I could find within about a four-block area. It was great. I got exercise and free compost. The city should really have paid me for all the diesel I was saving.

By the end of the season I'd usually have packed about a hundred bags of leaves into the pile behind the garage. My daughters loved it! They could climb up on to the garage roof and jump into the enormous pile of leaves. In the spring I'd take my pitchfork and start turning the leaves over. I'd move them from one spot to another, each time introducing air into the pile and moving around all the bacteria and natural organisms that were breaking down the leaves. I'd do this every couple of weeks and by the following fall I had a massive pile of dark, rich, wonderful compost.

One of the things that amazed me was the number of earthworms in the soil. They had crawled up into the leaves in the fall and with the volume of the leaves they were kept warm and

There's gold in them thar leaves!

insulated from the cold winter temperatures. As soon as it got warm enough in the spring they got going doing their worm thing, crawling through the pile, chomping on leaves, and leaving behind castings that look just like the best topsoil you can find at the garden center. I made sure that as I was removing the compost/soil to use in pots and in the gardens I held back as many of the worms as I could and left them in the compost area so that they'd be ready to start it all again when I began collecting bags of leaves the following fall.

I hope you will follow my approach to compost and soil building and look around and recognize the huge amounts of organic material that your neighbors are throwing out. They don't see its value, but you should. Those bags of leaves, bags of grass clippings, flower stalks, even the tied bundles of sticks and twigs will break down eventually and return to the soil.

Many municipalities have had to deal with the problem of organic matter in their landfills, which are filling up way too fast. So they have implemented their own source separation programs whereby you have to put out lawn materials like leaves and grass clippings in large paper bags. Initially, many municipalities wanted you to use clear plastic bags so they could see what they were picking up, but it became too difficult to remove and separate that plastic from a large load of compostables. Inevitably some of it ended up in the compost and no one liked that.

As their landfills have become even more taxed, some municipalities have been more aggressive and have gone to a wet and dry system whereby you put all your organic material into a special bin for composting. This is not just grass and leaves but also kitchen waste and the materials most good gardeners would put in their compost bucket on their counter to take out to the compost bin.

These people are throwing out a gold mine of compostable materials. So whether you collect them after dark or you ask your neighbors' permission to grab their large paper bags of leaves, you need to start building up your supply of compost material. This is where an urban dweller has a real advantage over a country dweller. The volume of compostable materials discarded in a city can be astronomical. In the country you won't find such a convenient curbside supply of inputs to your compost. But you will probably be able to find alternatives, and some of them may be fairly reasonably priced. Farmers often have hay that is no longer high enough quality to feed to animals, and they may be happy for you to haul it away. Farmers or your neighbors with horses may also have a spot where they pile the horse manure and will be glad to have you make some use of it.

Wherever you live your task now is to start accumulating materials for your compost pile. Notice I'm not saying "composter," which is what you see in the photo. These are small-scale and a good starting point, but you really want your garden to thrive so you've got to "go big or go home,"

This style of composter won't be big enough for the volume of organic material you'll need.

and you just can't stuff enough organic material into a bin-type composter to produce the volume of vegetables you're going to start growing.

I'm a big fan of the compost pile. It's rather low-tech and not very fancy, but remember that the subtitle of this book promises "easy" vegetables, and having to construct some fancy structure that looks as if it came from an episode of *The New Yankee Workshop* just isn't my style and frankly I don't think offers a huge advantage. To keep the smell down you want aerobic action, or air getting into the process, and if your composter is a solid structure you're more likely to have anaerobic action taking place and that can start to smell. So when you get back with those bags of leaves, it's "Stop, Drop, and Pile."

The design shown in these photos was actually easy and cheap because I had the pallets here.

I also had some wooden stakes to help them stand up. I like the pallets because they allow air to get in and circulate. If I lose some materials through the slats, that's OK. I've got the pile in a spot the garden will eventually expand to, so the compost that makes it out will just get incorporated into the garden eventually.

I also used a small divider, because every two weeks the materials get moved to the other side. This constant turning is going to build my upper body and abs just like on those commercials with the buff people and some strangely shaped work-out device that costs $29.95. It's also going to mix up the materials and speed up the breakdown of the various contents. Buff abs and good, vigorous compost creation—a win-win situation!

Different materials are going to offer different benefits to your compost, whether they be nutrients like nitrogen or phosphorus or perhaps trace minerals that your soil will appreciate. The main guideline I use is that some items will be high in carbon, like leaves, straw and hay, corn stalks, and wood shavings, and some items will be high in nitrogen, such as grass clippings, yard waste, green manures like buckwheat or clover, and your kitchen scraps. There are some commercial supplements you can purchase for your compost, but I'll touch on them later.

The main thing to remember is to try and work on a ratio of about 3:1, three units of carbon for every one unit of nitrogen. I find this gives me a good-quality compost when I'm done and the soil seems to do best with this combination. The microorganisms at work in the composter need carbon for energy and use the nitrogen you supply for protein production. It's a lot of work to break down a big pile of stuff into healthy compost. If I said that I often think of these organisms as a Pac-Man chewing his way around a computer screen, would I be showing my age again?

Here's a look at some of the materials you might want to start tracking down for your composter, but it's by no means a complete list. Wherever you are there's probably some material you should be accumulating that's readily available and ends up being discarded.

Grass Clippings

When we discuss how big your garden should be, I'm going to suggest really big. So if you have a lawn right now, think of it as a "vegetable garden in transition." It's not there yet, but since it's going to be you shouldn't be using its grass clippings for your new garden. You need to let the grass clippings break down and work on building up your topsoil for when you use it for vegetables later. So you should look elsewhere for your clippings. Neighbors are a good start. Try and find someone who has one of those bagger attachments on their lawnmower. Chances are those grass clippings are ending up in the landfill.

Keep your eyes peeled for lawn maintenance companies in your area. Some of their customers probably prefer that they take grass clippings away with them, so they'll be looking for a place to get rid of them, and you could save them a trip to the landfill.

Be careful about how much grass you put in your compost pile. If you use too many grass clippings, you will find that your compost becomes a little too "aromatic." The wheelbarrowful you see in the photograph was 18 hours old when I took the photo. It was amazing to feel how warm the middle of the pile was. In that short length of time the grass clippings were starting to break

My compost piles aren't pretty, but they're cheap and do the job.

down and decompose. Of course anyone who's had a mouse die in their wall knows how quickly things, even tiny things, can smell as they decompose. You've got to be really careful with grass clippings. After just 18 hours, as I was pulling clumps of grass out of the wheelbarrow and mixing them with the other materials, I was amazed by how strong the smell was. It wasn't a really bad smell yet, but it could easily have become a really bad smell. So don't start a war with your neighbors over your compost pile, and be careful with the grass clippings.

Grass is very high in nitrogen and a lot of it is simply water, so it will help offset some of the dryer materials you're using such as leaves or rotten hay.

Leaves

Ahhh… fall. The kids go back to school. The mosquitoes stop ruining outside get-togethers, and a wealth of free organic material rains down from the sky (or at least the trees). Those leaves have spent the summer photosynthesizing and turning energy from the sun and the trees' roots into biomass that will break down readily in your compost and allow you to transfer that stored energy into the plants in your garden. How great is that? It's as if Mother Nature wants you to have a healthy diet full of fresh organic vegetables and provides this wondrous bounty for you every fall. She's quite a gal, that Mother Nature, or so the corporate TV commercials that try and personify her seem to say. I guess I'd agree.

The leaves are going to have a little nitrogen in them, but they are going to be high on the carbon side. Leaves will take a while to break down and nitrogen helps, so it's good to have grass clippings to add. Of course people are cutting their lawns less often late in the fall. My strategy is to grab as many leaves as I can, but I don't add them all to my compost. I hold some of them back. Then once spring starts and I have access to more green things high in nitrogen, like grass clippings, I add those in. Turn the pile over and toss in handfuls of grass every few forkfuls. When you have extra

Grass clippings are an excellent source of nitrogen but must be mixed with materials with carbon, like leaves, to avoid odors.

grass left, you can start adding the surplus leaves into the mix. Since it was getting cold in the fall anyway, you won't have a missed a lot of breakdown of the leaves by leaving them in bags for a while.

Some people suggest shredding leaves to increase how quickly they decompose, but I never have, and I'm not usually a patient guy. I guess the reason I'm hesitant to recommend it is because the subtitle of this book uses the words "easy" and "organic." Buying or renting a shredder, which is a loud and terrifying machine, or running your gas-powered lawnmower through your leaves to chop them up, just seems very noisy and pollution-generating and unnecessary. We're trying to

The convenient paper bags that are now available can be laid over areas where you want to kill grass for future garden expansion.

reduce climate change and our carbon footprint by growing our own vegetables. Firing up another internal combustion engine for this seems counter-productive.

For an urban gardener leaves are going to be the workhorse of your compost pile. They're going to be the basis for great compost and it's going to be worth your while to accumulate a lot of them. If you're in a new neighborhood without mature trees, start scouting out some of the older more established areas that do have big trees. Keep some old blankets and tarps in the trunk of your car, and when you're out take a little detour to one of those tree-lined streets where everyone puts their leaves out in those great big paper bags, and load the trunk up.

Better yet, call City Hall. Talk to someone in Waste Management and ask if they'll drop off a load of leaves at your house. Your house is probably a lot closer than the landfill or the composting facility.

Leaves are wonderful things. They absorb carbon dioxide (CO_2) while they're growing and then they compost down into wonderful organic material to nurture your garden. I'm very grateful for leaves.

Straw/Hay

This source will tend to be in greater supply in the country and will often have a "rotten" moniker preceding it, because if it were good hay some horse or cow would be eating it. This is a good thing because if it is past its "best before date" for eating, then it may already have started some of the breaking down you're after anyway. If it's been exposed to moisture, it could definitely be on its way. Freshly cut and baled green hay can have a fairly high nitrogen component, but the type of hay you'll probably find a farmer willing to part with will be higher in its carbon contribution to your compost heap. Straw, the material left over when grain is harvested, is also going to be a carbon heavy hitter.

Just because you live in the suburbs, don't rule out these materials. Garden centers will often use

them in displays. Once they start looking tattered, offer to take them off their hands at a nominal price. Some of those monster houses with the Martha Stewart inspired fall displays may use them, and they'll be in the trash on November 1st before the switchover to the Christmas extravaganza. Be sure to visit those houses on your "night before garbage day patrol," or just ask the homeowners if they are going to toss them out. Some large churches have those fantastic Christmas pageants with the mangers and live donkeys and sheep on stage. They will be anxious to get rid of those props come December 26th. I've even seen construction crews using straw bales to insulate exposed pipe and concrete in cold climates. I haven't seen them going out of their way to make sure it's properly disposed of. Just another reason to have that tarp in the trunk for when opportunity knocks.

Corn

If you grow corn in your garden, you'll end up with both cobs, after you've eaten the corn off them, and stalks, after the harvest, that will be excellent for a carbon contribution. They are very robust materials, so you may want to take a few minutes and get some wrist exercise cutting them up into more manageable sizes with your pruners or chopping at the corn cobs to break them down into small chunks. Had a bad day at the office? There's always last night's corncob waiting for you out in the compost pile with your boss' face on it. Oh, that seems a little harsh. Corn stalks are often thrown out by people who use them to decorate front porches in the fall, so keep your eyes peeled.

Kitchen Treasures

You know all those potato peels and tea bags and banana peels and carrot tops and orange peels and pineapple tops and…well, they're not waste, they're solid green for the compost. Kitchen scraps are high in nitrogen and a lot of trace minerals

Fresh Grass
Clippings

Woody
material

Garden
Waste
(weeds)

Rotten
Hay or
Straw

Bagged
Leaves

Pea
Pods

Commercial
manure

Soil

Garlic
Stalks

Wood Ashes

Ground
Egg Shells

Dried Grass
Clippings

Peat Moss

Kitchen
Scraps

Coffee
Grounds

Composted
Manure

Wood
Shavings

Water

Everything laid out and ready to mix into my compost. Can you spot the non-organic item here that doesn't belong? Answer on page 120.

that some of those exotic fruits and vegetables from faraway places bring, so get into the habit of collecting your kitchen scraps and make sure you take that nice new stainless steel compost bucket on your counter out to the compost every night, just before you do the dishes, so that it gets washed and doesn't get smelly. You may even want to put in that rice that's been sitting on the fridge shelf too long. Be careful with meat and related animal products, as they will tend to attract rodents and other critters you may not like. When we lived in the city we had a rat we called "Rodney the Fun Rat" that inhabited our compost pile. Our daughters were young at the time and they thought he was quite cute. Here in the country we have a fox that seems to enjoy our compost offerings, even though they don't include meat. We have even had a black bear munching away out there, but of course by the time we got the camera she was gone. Living downtown you won't have to worry about bears.

If your kitchen organic waste volume is low you should take a look at your diet and start buying fruits and vegetables that require peeling and make this sort of waste. Rather than buying frozen curly fries, buy the potatoes instead. Wanting to provide materials for your compost will provide you with a reason to eat fewer processed foods. You also may want to get to know your local greengrocer or fruit and vegetable market. They pay by weight to have trash removed, so whether it's green carrot tops or soft bananas that are unsaleable, they may be happy to give you their organic wastes and this will help you to boost your compost input volume. Just make sure that if you get a load of this stuff you have some bagged leaves to mix it with to make sure it doesn't start to smell. If you're out of

A couple of months' worth of coffee grounds, including the filters, ready to go. Someone's been drinking way to much coffee.

leaves then use this as a great time to turn the pile and add a little of the organic waste in every so often to spread it throughout the pile and get it mixed in where rapid decomposition of the materials around it will help it break down quickly.

Garden Discards

I won't call these just weeds because they can include a lot of things like flowers after the first frost, or the bottoms of your cauliflower plant after you cut off the edible top. These will be fairly high in nitrogen and can add good variety to the pile. You should be a bit careful with weeds if they've gone to seed. In a perfect world your compost pile will get hot enough to kill those weed seeds, but depending on the season and your material mix, your compost pile might not reach a high enough temperature. On the other hand, all my gardens always have weed seeds germinating in them constantly, especially during wet summers. So I don't worry about a few more weed seeds in the compost pile.

Coffee Grounds

Coffee grounds make an excellent addition to your compost pile. You might not produce many grounds at your house, but if you live in the city chances are there are plenty of coffee shops producing lots of coffee grounds. Most businesses pay to have their waste removed, so coffee shop owners are often happy to give you their coffee grounds to cut down on their waste disposal fees. Ask at your local coffee shop and offer to pick up the grounds on a regular basis. Be sure to pick them up consistently so that the coffee shop owner isn't tempted to throw them in the garbage rather than having to store them until you arrive. Starbucks actually has a program called "The Grounds for Your Garden" and are happy to provide its grounds to any takers on a first-come, first-served basis.

Eggshells

Another part of your breakfast meal that will provide materials for your compost is eggs. Once you've cracked that shell and used the part you want, be sure to put the shells in your compost bucket. If you want to keep your doctor happy, you might not want to eat too many eggs, so this is another occasion where you can easily find another source. Local diners break a lot of eggs and end up with a lot of eggshells. Ask the local diner waitress or owner if you can take their shells away for them. Don't tell them they're high in calcium and a rich supplement for your composter. Don't tell them that eggshells make an excellent pest control when they are finely ground and sprinkled around the base of plants. Come to think it, why not tell them? I'm sure they'll be thrilled they're going to good use and not the landfill. La-

bel a bucket "Eggshells and Coffee Grounds" for them to use. Be sure to pick up the bucket after the Sunday morning rush and no doubt you'll have quite a bit of material to add to your compost pile!

Garden Soil

You'll notice in my photos that I add garden soil to the compost pile as I build it up. That soil will already have the microorganisms that soil uses to break down organic material, so by adding it to the pile as you go you're ensuring that they are spread throughout the pile. If you have to wait for them to work their way up from the bottom it will take longer for the compost to break down. Woody plants like straw and corn stalks won't necessarily hold moisture too well, so adding soil will help the pile keep a good moisture balance to speed decay.

Peat Moss

Some environmentalists are very critical of sphagnum peat moss because of the damage done to peat bogs from which it is extracted. However, if you have a really heavy clay soil you may have to resort to using it. I try to use it sparingly and mostly for storing root crops like potatoes and carrots. After we've eaten them, I put the peat moss in the compost pile. I don't reuse it the next year, just in case there are any diseases hiding in there. It is excellent for building soil and helping soil to

maintain moisture, working like a big sponge to soak up water when it rains and release it back over time as roots require it.

Wood Ashes

If you heat with wood or have a fireplace your wood ashes can be used in the garden or added to the compost pile. Ashes contain calcium carbonate, which is like lime, and helps to deacidify soil by increasing its pH. Depending on the wood burned there may be some potash, which you'll find in commercial fertilizers, so the ashes can be a good additive to the pile.

Composted Manure

My neighbor Alyce has horses and she graciously allows me some of the end result of their hay chomping, and it's great for my garden. I put some of it near the compost pile when I first get it to allow it to sit for a while. On a cool day as I unload it the steam just rises out of it, since the concentrated nitrogen helps the breakdown of the manure and straw and wood shavings, producing a lot of heat. After it has sat for a few months I'll start adding it to the compost. You have to be careful with manure because depending on what animal you get it from it can harbor pathogens dangerous to humans, like E.coli. Horse manure seems to be one of the better ones with the least potential for harm, but allowing it to sit and cook for a while to kill those pathogens is an excellent idea.

Composted horse manure is an excellent compost booster.

Wood Shavings or Sawdust

If you know someone with a workshop, chances are they've got a pile of wood shavings from their latest project. I like nice light wood shavings like the ones a planer would make from pine, because they will break down reasonably fast. Some sawdust can be fairly coarse. I've used oak sawdust from my chainsaw and oak takes a long time to break down. It is a natural soil conditioner though, and as it breaks down it can help to hold moisture, so if you have a source for it don't hesitate to use it.

Grass or Sod

Once you get hooked on growing vegetables each year you'll find the garden miraculously expanding. If you're like me, any time the garden expands the lawn shrinks. So I hack off another few feet of sod, grab it with my cultivator, beat it up for a minute to knock as much soil off it as I can, then toss the clump of grass that's left in a pile. Eventually I move that to the compost heap. I make sure I put lots of materials on top of it to ensure that no roots survive. If you don't bury it deep enough in other materials, or if the grass gets close to the outer edge of the pile, it will start growing again, so make sure it's completely covered in a thick layer of other organic matter like leaves.

COMMERCIAL ENHANCERS

Bone Meal

Bone meal is a mixture of crushed and coarsely ground bones and is an excellent source of phosphorus. It is fairly expensive but you don't have

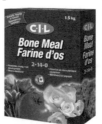

to sprinkle too much into the compost pile to enhance its phosphorus levels. Bone meal's N-P-K ratio is 2-14-0, meaning it's high in phosphorus, and it's also an excellent organic source of calcium.

Brewery Waste

The process of brewing beer uses malted barley and hops and these are discarded afterwards. This makes an excellent compost additive so get to know your local microbrewery or brewpub and ask what they do with their waste. Tell them you'll be happy to make regular visits to pick up their waste, which saves them from paying to have it hauled to a landfill. You also might want to sample the finished product of their process.

Shown here at the Kingston Brewing Co. author Cam Mather gets a bucket for his compost heap from manager Honey-Lee Pratt. Brewer Peter Snell extracts the hops after the brewing process. Later Bruce Mather samples the finished product. Who ever said gardening's not fun!

Blood Meal

Blood meal is dried blood from slaughterhouses and is extremely high in nitrogen, which makes it an excellent addition to the compost heap. It has a high nitrogen level of 12-0-0, so you only have to sprinkle a bit in your compost heap. This addition of nitrogen will promote the growth of the organisms that you want to thrive to break down the organic matter.

Some organic gardeners are hesitant to use blood and bone meal because of the issues with BSE or mad cow disease, which seemed to appear when cows were fed sheep, which they were never meant to eat. While the likelihood of negative outcomes from using these products seems remote, if you're concerned just bulk up on other natural sources in your area.

What Not to Add to the Compost Pile

There are a few things that are best kept out of the compost heap. The first would be diseased or insect-infested plants that you've pulled out of the garden. If the leaves on your tomato turned yellow early and dropped off they might have a blight, so rather than compost them you should remove those plants from the garden and either send them off with your trash or dump them in an area of the yard you don't use.

Some plants like succulents or Bermuda grass, which is a persistent weed in the southern US, will not be killed by the heat generated in the compost pile, so it may be best to keep them out.

Since you may end up spreading some of that compost around with your hands, I'd keep plants like poison ivy out as well. While you can add composted cow, sheep, chicken, or horse manure, don't add dog or cat waste. These can contain pathogens that can be harmful to humans and it's best to keep them out of the composter. While you should be using all your kitchen wastes that come from vegetable or fruit sources, don't add anything related to seafood and meat including bones. These are much more likely to attract rodents.

Turning the Pile

After a few weeks, the microbes and bacteria and earthworms will have begun their job in the compost pile and it's your turn to do a bit of work. This really is one of the many benefits of a vegetable garden. It's not just eating the low fat, low cholesterol, high fiber, and health-inducing vegetables; it's the exercise that it also inspires. It's the "cardio" and it's the "weight-bearing" activity that fights off osteoporosis.

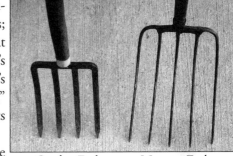

Garden Fork   Manure Fork

There's no use going out to turn over the compost pile, pulling a back muscle on the third forkful, and vowing to never set foot in the infernal garden again. Do some stretching first to make sure your muscles are loose and prepared for a little workout. Remember that yoga DVD you bought a few years back but just never got around to watching? POP it into the DVD player, PLUNK yourself down on that fancy yoga mat, and PLOP your butt down and start stretching.

I like to use my manure fork when the com-

Mixing it up in the compost heap.

Moving the compost every couple of weekends ensures a good mix of compost and faster decomposition.

post pile is still pretty fresh and everything is holding together pretty well. The thin pointy tines plunge into the pile very well, allowing you to grab a good forkful to turn over.

Keep some water handy, from either your rain barrels or a garden hose. If you are finding that the pile seems a bit dry, add some water. Don't drench it, but you do want it moist. Microbes and earthworms like it damp.

After a few turnings the materials will start to get broken up and I switch to my garden fork, which has wider tines and holds the smaller materials better. I figure that with two forks, the first time there's an incident where we local villagers gather to taunt some Frankenstein-like monster

I'll be in the front row and hoisting mine high! You need one too!

The Finished Product

The concept of a finished product is a foreign concept to me because my garden is always a work in progress, as is the compost. After a month or so some of the materials will be broken down enough to use. In fact you could have just dumped those leaves on the garden last fall and worked them in, although it wouldn't be ideal to have them in their full form when you're trying to plant seeds. They will break down, though, with time.

So after six or eight weeks if you think something in your garden needs a top dressing, then by all means take some of the finer compost and spread it on. It's one of the reasons you may want to have several compost piles in various stages of readiness. If one is ready to go in the spring, spread that one on the garden. If you start one in the spring, spread that on the garden in the fall. If you have just one big partially composted pile in July and your corn plants are looking a little tired, grab some of the composted materials and spread it around those corn plants.

There is no hard and fast rule; just be flexible and use your compost as you see fit. The key is to make lots of it and be constantly on the lookout for new organic material to add. There are free compost inputs everywhere, so get creative and lose your shyness. All you have to do is ask.

Compost on the left hand side has had the summer to breakdown. The right hand side has the fresher materials from the fall. By spring the left hand side materials will be ready to start adding to the garden.

8
Soil Amendments

Hopefully I have convinced you of the importance of compost. Composting should always be a part of your home and garden. It is important in your home to reduce the volume of material you're sending to a landfill and important in your garden to make use of that wonderful material which is anything but "junk."

Sometimes, though, you can't produce enough compost for the size of your garden. Perhaps you're shy and don't want to risk grabbing your neighbors' bags of leaves and grass clippings. Maybe you live in the country and drive a Smart Car, without room to carry bags of leaves, or even a bag of leaves for that matter. Good choice of car, but we still need to make up the deficit.

Manure

The next best thing is manure. Animals eat plants and they process this plant material and some of it ends up as great fertilizer for your garden. While you may be squeamish about the idea of using animal waste on your garden, humans have done it for eons and farms which integrate animals and use their waste for manure can be very sustainable.

All manure is not created equal though. The manure you have access to will be the biggest factor in determining what ends up in your garden.

Composted horse manure.

N–P–K

When you purchase many commercial soil amendment products you'll often see a series of three numbers on the package, such as 21-7-7. These refer to the ratio of NPK, or Nitrogen, Phosphorous, and Potassium. **Nitrogen** is an essential building block of amino and nucleic acids, and plants use it to help with green growth. This is why a lawn fertilizer has a high Nitrogen number, to make your lawn green. **Phosphorous** is a component of DNA and helps form cell membranes, so it helps roots and flowers grow and develop. **Potassium** or **Potash** is necessary for all living cells to function, so it helps with the overall health of the plant.

If you have a chicken farm down the road, it'll be chicken manure. If you have a farmer nearby with cattle it'll be cow manure. My neighbor has five (or sometimes more!) horses and I drive over weekly to haul away a trailer full of horse manure. I sure take a lot of sh*t from that woman! Sorry, but it's a pretty common joke between us.

All manure has the potential danger of including pathogens that are harmful to humans, so you have to be careful. People have become sick from drinking unpasteurized apple cider that was pressed from apples that had fallen from the tree and landed near some fresh cow manure.

You have to compost manure and get the manure pile to heat up to kill off the nasty bugs that can make you sick. However, as it sits longer the manure loses nutrients to add to the soil. If you get manure when you can't put it on the garden, for example during the summer and early fall when you're still eating the vegetables, mix some of it with your compost. The high nitrogen content in manure will help speed up the decomposition of the other materials in the compost pile. If the manure contains bedding like wood shavings or straw it will also have a fairly high content of urine, which is very high in nitrogen. This is excellent to get things heating up in a compost pile.

If you aren't going to use the manure right away, you may also want to cover the manure pile with a tarp or layer of hay to keep the rain off it. Too much rain will wash away some of the nutrients you want.

The best strategy with manure is to apply it in the fall, after you've finished eating from the garden. This allows you to put a very generous amount of manure on the garden and then work it in. I put about an inch of horse manure on the soil throughout my garden. Then I work it in with my rototiller. I'm not concerned about working it in too deeply, because I want it to stay in the upper layer of the soil so that it will be readily available for the plant roots next spring. The earth worms will get into it and start breaking it down further to make it even more available to the plants. By next spring that upper layer of soil will be ready to quickly pass nutrients to the roots of the new plants once they start growing.

Manure not only is an excellent fertilizer but also adds organic matter to the soil, which will help improve the soil's ability to hold moisture, provide aeration, and improve the basic soil structure. This chart shows the approximate nitrogen, phosphorous, and potassium levels of different types of manure. These will vary depending on what the animals were fed, how long the manure sat around before you got it, and whether it was rained on.

Manure Content

This chart shows the NPK content of manure as well as some other components of manure that are helpful for the garden. The actual content of the manure you use may differ from this depending on a number of variables, but this gives you an approximate guide for deciding which manure may have the best value for your garden.

Commercial Products

There are many commercial products available to help you condition your soil, and which product you purchase will depend on what's closest. If you have a garden center or hardware store with

Composted cow manure. All the soil value without the smell!

Manure Type	N %	P %	K %	Ca %	Mg %	Zn ppm	Cu ppm	Mn ppm
DAIRY solid	0.61	0.17	0.50	1.54	0.36	95	29	107
SWINE solid	0.90	0.47	0.56	--	---	172	103	--
POULTRY solid	2.37	1.11	1.17	4.6	0.28	238	33	204
BEEF solid	0.73	0.23	0.57	1.5	0.41	129	36	112
SHEEP solid	0.76	0.27	0.70	1.5	0.38	170	20	140
HORSE solid	0.42	0.13	0.36	1.7	0.56	73	23	113

N = Nitrogen, P = Phosphorus, K = Potassium, Ca = Calcium, Mg = Magnesium, Zn = Zinc, Cu = Copper, Mn = Manganese　　　*Source: www.omafra.gov.on.ca/english/crops/field/news/croptalk/2005/ct_1105a6.htm*

bagged gardening products, this is probably going to be what ends up in your garden, and that's great. This may seem counter-intuitive to you, but you should always keep your eyes open for bargains in the fall. Ideally this is a good time to be spreading this type of product on your garden. Most people are more enthusiastic about gardening in the spring and this is when most of these bagged products are sold. By fall many people have lost their interest and many garden centers will still have pallets full of these soil amendments.

Commercial topsoil can be helpful when you're getting started with poor soil.

While some garden centers will tarp them to sell the following year, the plastic will deteriorate and it will be harder to sell them for full retail, so they may want to move them out in the fall. Some garden centers are set up just for the season in grocery store parking lots. These make excellent targets for bargains on commercial products.

So borrow your neighbor's pickup truck and take some cash. When you find a center with bags of composted manure or topsoil, make them a ridiculously low offer to take them off their hands… today… for cash. I think you'll find some great savings doing this: inexpensive soil supplements that are ready to spread on the garden in the fall. If some of the bags are open or taped up, all the better, because the retailers will have difficulty selling these to most people.

Now, if it's spring and you're ready to get going with the garden, by all means, if you don't have access to local manure, use these materials. Since they are pre-composted they are ready to spread and you don't have the worry about their being too high in nitrogen content that might burn vegetables.

As manure dries it becomes lighter and is easier to move and transport. It also concentrates the nutrients on a weight basis, meaning that you don't have to apply as much as you do with fresh manure. So if you can afford commercial bagged manure, by all means go for it. This is an excellent way to give your vegetables a boost, especially if this is a new garden you're working.

Garden centers tend to have more traditional amendments like composted manure and topsoil. More rural co-op stores have a broader range of materials you can use for your garden. They usually have vegetable meals that offer another alternative supplement for your soil. A trip to the local farm co-op will reveal an array of cool-sounding products like alfalfa meal, soybean meal, and cottonseed meal. These can be fed to livestock, but you can also use them on your garden or in your compost. They will be rated as to their Nitrogen, Phosphorous, and Potassium levels and you'll have to decide which offers the most cost-effective way to supplement.

This "sea compost" comes from ground-up sea and crustacean shells.

There's also fishmeal and seaweed meal. This photo shows a bag of dehydrated seaweed meal. It has a number of properties that make it helpful for animals and my local feed mill sells it as a feed supplement. I like it because it contains a variety of trace minerals, which you should try and replenish in your garden. I also like the fact that it's solar dried, which helps reduce its carbon footprint and maintain its mineral content. Farmers near the seashore have fertilized their fields with seaweed for generations. I love it because when you smell it it's just like being at the seashore. So think of how much money your garden

This seaweed meal is a great soil supplement and smells like a walk on the beach by the ocean!

will save you this year when you use dehydrated seaweed meal. It fertilizes the garden and saves you all that money on gas and hotels driving to the seashore. Put a small bowl of this beside your bed, dump some sand on the carpet in your bedroom, and it'll be just like going to sleep by the ocean.

There are also a number of organic fertilizers on the market now that give you one more tool if you feel you have a nutritionally challenged soil to grow in. These are based on the more traditional fertilizers using the NPK ratio. While a lawn fertilizer is high in nitrogen, for example, 21-7-7, a fertilizer for growing vegetables is more balanced, or 7-7-7. The "organic" designation can be confusing from a chemical perspective since "organic" means containing one or more atoms of carbon. The organic fertilizer you find at the garden center will use the "organic" designation more as a description of where the material originated and whether it is suitable for a farm that sells vegetables organically, meaning without the addition of any commercial fertilizers or pesticides.

If you are growing in a severely challenged soil then by all means give one of these products a try, but long-term they are not the solution you need. Realize that the NPK designation, say 7-7-7, does not add up to 100%, so there are other materials in that commercial fertilizer to bulk it up so that someone using it won't overfertilize and "burn" plants. Do some research on the product and find out whether you're comfortable with the other elements that make up the fertilizer. Even with a commercial product you still need to continue to add compost and organic matter from plants to build up the nutrients and trace elements that plants need and to add the decaying material that the soil needs in order to be healthy.

Green Manures

Another option is to try a green manure or a cover crop. This simply refers to a crop you grow in the garden and then turn under to add nutrients and organic matter back to the soil. Not only does a green manure crop keep the soil from eroding and cut down on weeds, it will produce some of the nutrients crucial to a healthy garden. Many green manures are "nitrogen fixers," which means that they take nitrogen from the air and fix or transfer it to the plant and to its roots. Plants have symbiotic bacteria called rhizobia in nodules in their root systems which

Clover with its large and deep tap root and nitrogen nodules.

allow them to complete this amazing process. Nitrogen constitutes almost 80% of the earth's atmosphere, and as you know from the NPK designation nitrogen is helpful for growing healthy plants. So plants like clover and alfalfa are actually able to put nitrogen into your soil naturally. All it costs you is the seed. In the photo you can actually see the small nodules that have formed on the roots of clover I planted as green manure. When I turn the clover under that nitrogen in the plant and roots gets worked into the soil. As the plant material breaks down it adds organic matter to the soil. A green manure is a really sustainable way to enhance your soil.

There are other crops you can use as green manures, such as oats, ryegrass, and buckwheat. I like buckwheat because it germinates easily and grows vigorously, so that once it gets going it really crowds out weeds. Then when you cut it down it adds a tremendous volume of material to the soil. I use what I call a golf

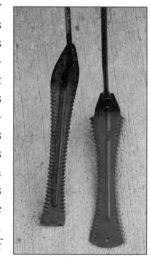

club cutter. It has the handle of a golf club but a flat, sharp blade. Then you just "T" up the buckwheat as you would a golf ball on a driving range and let 'er rip. If you have a big enough crop you can swing in both directions to cut faster. Once the buckwheat is cut you should leave it lying on the soil for a day or two before you turn it under with a shovel or the rototiller.

A green manure is a bit of luxury if you have a fairly small garden plot. It really means you have to take a section out of active production for a year and devote it to a green manure. If you don't have the space then you might want to use a commercial amendment to enhance the soil. Or you might want to get creative with interspersing some green manures with your regular crops. Oats are a very easy-to-grow grass-like green manure that can grow quite tall. You could plant several rows of it on either side of your lettuce plants. Once lettuce starts growing, shade helps slow it down so it doesn't go to seed, or "bolt." So the shade from the oats help the lettuce, and then you can turn those oats back into the soil as an enhancement. This is a gradual way of replacing organic matter and nutrition which other plants are removing from the soil as they grow.

If you do have a large area to plant with a cover crop, you'll probably just want to use the broadcast method of throwing handfuls of seed on the soil. Then you can rake the seed lightly to get some worked into the topsoil. If it's dry when you sow you'll need to water the seed to get it to germinate and keep it well watered until it seems to be thriving. It will require some weeding in the early stages, but once it gets going it should be able to crowd out most weeds.

Some seed catalogs now have green manure sections which are really helpful if you're thinking about using a green manure to enhance your soil. Johnny's Seeds has a Fall Green Manure Mix which includes winter rye, field peas, ryegrass, crimson clover, and hairy vetch. It's a handy mix because once you get this planted the peas, clover, and ryegrass will be killed by cold temperatures in the winter and will provide organic matter to

Buckwheat makes a beautiful green manure.

Cutting it down before it goes to seed with my golf chopper... remember to follow through on your swing.

The cut buckwheat: after a day or two you can rototill or use a shovel to turn it into the soil.

the soil. The hairy vetch and winter rye will re-grow in spring to add more nutrients to the soil. When you finally mix them into the soil they will have added a tremendous volume of the essential materials your soil needs to be a healthy place for vegetables to grow.

Mulch

The use of mulch on a garden is the addition of a natural material to keep down weeds and maintain moisture in the soil. You can use a variety of materials, including many of the same things that you put in your compost pile. I like to use rotten hay because there is lots of it available from farmers in my area. You might like leaves if you're in a city. Some people use pine needles and wood chips. Probably the best material you can get is straw, but around here straw is hard to come by because so many farmers like to use it for bedding for their animals.

Spreading mulch around the plants in your garden helps suppress weeds. This can be a real time saver, as it helps to cut down on the time spent weeding. The mulch will also keep the soil surface from drying out on hot sunny days and help maintain moisture in the soil. I have mulched over the years with mixed results. If you don't put the mulch on thickly enough you'll still get weeds

This garlic was mulched with straw to keep the weeds down and preserve moisture in the soil.

growing through. And if you use a material like rotten hay, there will be weed seeds in the actual mulch ready to germinate and start growing. During a dry season mulch can be great for keeping moisture in the soil, but in a wet summer this is actually a disadvantage. Also, many crops like warm soil, and with a mulch you're actually limiting how warm the soil will get. For heat-loving plants mulching is probably not recommended unless it's plastic mulch.

Ruth Stout has written many books about the benefits of mulching, and in the upcoming potato section I'll actually discuss growing potatoes in a thick layer of mulch. There is no question that mulch can be a huge benefit to poor soil, especially since as it breaks down it's providing the soil with essential organic material.

I personally am not a huge mulching fan. My neighbor Ken claims that "Cam likes to do everything the hard way." Well yes, I prefer to keep the weeds down the old-fashioned way, with a hoe.

The Difference between Hay and Straw

Sometimes you'll be able to recognize a city person by his lack of knowledge concerning straw and hay. There is a difference between the two but someone who hasn't grown up on a farm might be tempted to just lump them together as one thing. As a former "citiot" (city idiot) I know I kept my new country neighbors amused with my indiscriminant and interchangeable use of the two terms.

Straw is the material left over from growing grain. Grain forms a long, tall stalk with a head that contains the grain seeds. Grain is cut by a combine harvester, which processes the plant by separating out the grain and storing it until it can empty it into a grain wagon pulled by a truck in the field. The combine shoots the unused material, including the stalks of the plants, out the back. This leaves rows of straw which a farmer can then gather and put into round or square bales.

Hay, on the other hand, is grown from a variety of grass-like plants and is used as feed for livestock. The grass is sown in a field and often remains there for years. In the summer when the grass has grown tall and often has seed heads, the hay is cut and left to dry. After several days the hay is baled into either round or square bales. Hay is what you feed to horses and cows. Smaller square bales are piled high in haylofts and there are also large round bales that can be moved only with a tractor. These round bales often sit outside unprotected until fed to livestock. After several years the quality of the hay deteriorates and the farmer may be happy to sell old bales fairly cheaply because it doesn't offer the animals much nutritional value.

Straw makes a much nicer mulch if you can get it. It doesn't have the weed seeds and breaks down nicely as a soil enhancer. It also keeps fruit like strawberries off the ground and during a heavy rain or watering it keeps water from splattering on fruit and vegetables that you want to keep cosmetically attractive.

Now you can sound like an expert when discussing the ways of the country!

Legumes like these peas not only produce a great crop but also add nitrogen back into the soil.

Symbiotic bacteria called rhizobia help the legume convert nitrogen in the air into nodules of nitrogen that improve the soil and are free fertilizer for the next crop to grow where they were grown.

9 How Plants Grow (Roots, Shoots & Leaves)

Roots, Shoots & Leaves is of course a play on the title of the book *Eats, Shoots & Leaves*, which is about proper punctuation and has nothing to do with plants. But I thought a little basic plant biology might be important. It never hurts to revisit our grade 8 biology class to see what makes a plant tick on the off chance that we can find a way to make it work better, or grow faster!

A plant consists of a root, a stem, leaves, and, if you're lucky, a flower that will turn into what you eventually eat. There are of course variations on this, like carrots, where you actually eat the large taproot.

Water and minerals are absorbed by tiny root hairs and move through vascular bundles to the upper parts of the plants. The root has a cap that gets pushed into the soil by cells behind it that divide and lengthen to push the tip further into the soil. Obviously the more air pockets and fewer obstacles there are in the soil the easier it will be for the root to grow and therefore absorb more of what the upper plant needs. The roots also act like an anchor, holding the plant in place.

The stem has a vascular system which carries the water and minerals throughout the plant. It also has buds that develop into leaves, newer smaller stems, or a flower.

Leaves also have vascular tissue to accept the water and minerals from the roots. The underside

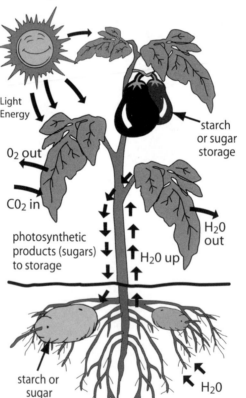

Light Energy

O₂ out

CO₂ in

photosynthetic products (sugars) to storage

starch or sugar storage

starch or sugar storage

H₂0 out

H₂0 up

H₂0

of the leaves have "stomata," which are tiny holes that allow transpiration, where water leaves as water vapor. They also contain palisade cells, which contain chlorophyll that absorbs the sun's energy. I grew up thinking chlorophyll was something that chewing gum had in it to keep bad breath away. Am I showing my age again?

Carbon dioxide from the air combines with water in the leaves using the sun's energy to produce carbohydrates, which is the plant's food. The process also produces oxygen. This is why plants and trees are so great for the planet. They take in the climate-changing CO_2 and store it, while releasing oxygen into the air. Food that's not needed right away for growth is stored as starch.

We are aware that some plants, such as potatoes, store lots of this starch in their roots, which we eat. Others, like rice, store the starch in the grains that are left after they flower. Humans can use these starches for food energy as well.

So those are the basics of Plant Biology 101. There are a lot more things happening in a plant, but this gives a little background on what's happening in that wonderful green thing in the garden. Everything you do, from nourishing the soil with compost and providing water to the roots, helps the plant to optimize this process. Some diseases and pests try and interfere with this process, and we'll discuss ways to deal with them in future chapters.

10
Winter Preparation

There is nothing nicer on a cold winter day than remembering a warm summer day in the garden. It makes the winter seem just so much more manageable. We heat with a wood stove and from time to time in the winter we like to take a bag of our frozen garden tomatoes and put them in a pot on the wood stove. We throw in some minced garlic (also from the garden) and some basil that we puréed with olive oil and froze in sheets just before the frost hit. As it all cooks and bubbles away, the aroma is fantastic. Not only does the inviting aroma remind us of summer, but the taste does too. It really makes all that summer work in the garden worth it.

One of the best ways for you to get excited about gardening is to order your seeds, and winter is the time to do that. Seed catalogs are wonderful sources of information, and the colorful photos and descriptions of the vegetables are very therapeutic for a winter-weary North American. This may be less of an issue in the south, but in the north seed catalogs are definitely a way of dreaming of sunny gardening weather.

I've listed a number of seed catalog companies in the appendix at the back of the book. There are others that I may have missed and my listing is provided only for reference; it's not a recommendation. I have ordered from some of them but not all of them. Like many consumers, once I find a company I like and its products perform well I stick with it. Over the last few years I've ordered from a few new companies and have yet to be disappointed by any seed company I've dealt with. I suppose if a large percentage of my seeds weren't germinating I'd get concerned and might want to switch, but that's never been the case. The seeds I save myself have much lower germination rates than the ones I buy from seed companies. I realize that if I do have low germination rates, it's usually my own fault or the fault of Mother Nature. Sometimes the weather just doesn't cooperate and the conditions aren't right for some seeds, and often I've gone off half-cocked and planted things much earlier than I should, always rushing the season.

I am not making a recommendation about specific vegetable varieties in this book because I think it's very personal and because there are so many available. There are actually gardening books that list all the varieties for different vegetables. I have a confession, and it's that I'm not that fussy about this approach. I know I should be adamant about how Lincoln peas are far superior to Little Marvels, but there are just so many variables when you grow a plant that I can't always chalk everything up to the variety. This isn't always the case. With corn, for instance, we found a variety called "Precious Gem" which we really like, but I also like "Peaches and Cream," which some people can't stand.

So that's the fun part about a seed catalog. It offers a whole gardenful of potential without the reality of having to get out on a hot day and weed.

One of the keys to finding what works best for you and what the family likes to eat is to use some sort of record keeping. Ideally you should have a notebook that you use to keep track of

Everything that slows us down and forces patience, everything that sets us back into the slow circles of nature, is a help. Gardening is an instrument of grace.
May Sarton

what you've grown each year. I use a large piece of heavy cardboard that I tape a piece of paper to, and I attach two pencils to it. I use pencils because pens always run out at the crucial time, and I attach two because if I just use one it'll come off and get lost in the garden. As I'm planting each row I write down the variety that I planted in that row. That way I can refer to it throughout the season and make a note of how well it does. If you have the time, a notebook is an even better idea so that you can record more details that will provide you with a synopsis of how the plants did that year. For example: "Planted 4th week of May, germinated well, grew slowly in June because of lack of heat, were ready to eat second week of July, and went to seed very quickly." Then when you sit down to order for the next season, you might want to see if they have a variety that matures earlier.

As much as we all like to think we have a memory like the Rain Man, the reality is there's a good chance that by the following January you'll have forgotten how your peas did last June. I like my garden map because it also helps me remember where I planted things the year before so I don't put them in the same spot the next year.

You may notice the word "cultivar" in seed catalogs. It is basically a fancy word for variety. It comes from a combination of "cultivated" and "variety," and each vegetable will have a variety of different cultivars, such as "Peaches and Cream" corn or "Sugar Baby" Watermelon. Don't be

scared of the word; just use it a lot when you talk gardening with your neighbors. They'll think you're a genius.

Here's a sample seed catalog entry so we can discuss how to read it.

> ## TOMATOES
>
> **BIG BEEF (F1):** 70 Days (ASC, ST, N, TMV) Puts the beefy in beefsteak! Better flavor, garden performance and all around higher quality. Fruit oval 350g, meaty sweet flesh, easily twice as much fruit as a regular beefsteak
> PKT $3.95; 250 Seeds $8.95; 500 Seeds $16.00; 1,000 Seeds $26.95; 5m @$23.20

Days to Maturity

After the cultivar name you'll usually see a number of days, for example 54 days. This is days to maturity, or how long it should take from the time the seed germinates to the time you have something you can harvest and eat. There's often a big range from one variety to another, and you can use it to your advantage. The last thing you want is for everything in your garden to mature at the same time. When this happens you end up eating peas every night for a week and people can lose their enthusiasm pretty fast.

So you can use the seed catalog to choose several varieties, some early and some late. Since you can never be sure exactly when your vegetables will be ready to eat, you have some wiggle room to spread the season out a bit. Some vegetables may have a fairly short harvest, so starting an early and a late one should spread it out. Using two varieties also hedges your bets with the weather, insects, and some of the other variables that may cause a bad year for something in the garden.

Some vegetable varieties have two timelines, like "28 days baby, 46 days full-size." With things like lettuce you'll be able to start eating baby lettuce within 28 days and it will continue to grow and by 46 days will reach full size. You can see that by starting lettuce every two weeks during

My garden clipboard with tied on pencils I can't lose. And if one pencil is good, two are better.

planting season you should be able to have some to harvest throughout the season.

General Description

The seed catalog will then give a detailed description of the variety and what you can expect from it. The descriptions always make the variety sound great, and when confronted with 10 different varieties you'll want to plant one of each. Unfortunately you'll have to make a choice, and you'll develop a sense of what you like. You'll find that there are some characteristics you simply don't like. For instance you may like the bicolor corn of the peaches and cream type and dislike pure yellow or white corn kernels. This will help you eliminate some varieties from your potential list, and then it's just a matter of what you think you'll like the most. I often pick an early variety and one that matures later in the season to try and spread out the harvest as much as I can.

Disease Resistance

Some vegetables are susceptible to certain diseases, and a seed catalog will usually list them after the description. These are often the confusing abbreviations that don't seem to make any sense. When you see what tomatoes are susceptible to you'll want to cross them off your list and slam the catalog shut. There's no need to freak out. The good thing is that seed breeders have been finding varieties that already have a resistance to these diseases and breeding this resistance into hybrid varieties to make your life easier.

It's probably a good idea to try a non-hybrid variety each year and see if it seems to have any problems that the hybrids don't. If the leaves of the non-hybrid yellow and the leaf stem weakens, causing the plant to look wilted, it might be verticillium wilt. This is assuming of course that both varieties have had a comparable amount of water and sunlight. Now if you watered the hybrid and let the non-hybrid dry out, well then it's not a disease, it's just bad plant care. A fungus causes Verticillium wilt and there is very little you can do about it from what's called a "cultural" standpoint, such as rotating crops, because many spe-

cies are susceptible to it. You can, however, plant cultivars or varieties of plants that have been bred to be resistant to it. So if your tomatoes often seem to end up with yellow leaves that turn brown and fall off early, and if your tomato plants die much earlier than your neighbors', try a hybrid variety with some resistance already built in.

Tomatoes are particularly prone to various diseases. Tomato cultivars will often have these letters after them which indicates it is resistant to that disease.

V –	Verticillium Wilt
N –	Nematodes
LS –	Leaf Spot
ST –	Stemphylium
F –	Fusarium
TMV –	Tobacco Mosaic Virus
ASC –	Alternaria Stem Canker

Selling Details

The final part of the cultivar description will be the price. Seeds are sold in many ways: by the package, by the seed, and by weight. I would suggest that you just order a packet of seeds to start. Most seed companies will put enough seeds in a package for the average home garden. Once you get gardening, if you find something you really like then you might want to start looking at ordering larger quantities. A pound of seeds is a lot, and you may be hard pressed to use them up in a reasonable time period. If you have extra seeds

It's easy to get a little carried away with your seed order. We have a big garden and we'll have enough of some of these seeds for next year too.

left over you'll be fine planting them in the next year or two. After a while, though, your germination rate with older seeds will go down, which is why you'll probably want to place a seed order each year.

There will be a tendency when you're getting started to use a lot more seeds than you should. The seed package will tell you how to plant them, but invariably you'll think more is better, because you can always thin them later. This is true, but it doesn't give you the best return on the money you invest in your seeds.  If you're buying fresh seeds from a reputable seed catalog and you plant them within the optimal time frame (not too early and not too late), you'll get a very high germination rate. So you really shouldn't have to overseed. Follow the directions on the seed package until you get comfortable with planting; then you can start playing fast and loose with the instructions.

Hybrids

One of the first things you'll notice in a seed catalog is that many of the varieties will have (F1) after them, for example, Big Beef Tomato (F1). This means they are a hybrid or a plant that comes from two different pure parent lines. Seed companies will take plants that have different characteristics and cross them to achieve a new plant that incorporates the best traits from each of the parents. This may mean that the plants produce a heavy yield of fruit, that they produce fruit early, that they have certain disease resistance, or that they handle drought conditions better. I think the concept of hybrids is great and I think they often provide a much better yield in your garden.

Some people are not fans of hybrids and they prefer to go with heirloom seeds. These are seeds that are true to the variety the way it was grown decades and even generations ago. It all comes down to personal taste. I've had some heritage varieties I liked and some I didn't. The nice thing about heirloom seeds is that it's often easier to save the seed if you want to use your own seed in the future. With hybrids you can't save the seeds, or at least if you plant the hybrid seeds you saved you can't be sure of the results. I talk more about this in the seed saving chapter. Some people don't like the idea that the person who developed the hybrid has control over the seed, but the reality is that it took them many years to create the hybrid and they want some compensation for that time. I would suggest that as you're starting out you should experiment with lots of different varieties or cultivars.

As you learn more about seed saving you may want to start moving towards non-hybrid cultivars. Some seed catalogs designate each variety as hybrid after the name (F1) and some will list all their hybrids together at the beginning of a section and then list non-hybrids later. If you get the seed-saving bug, keep your eye on this.

Seed Types

I've already talked about hybrid seeds, but there are other factors to consider. Some people prefer non-hybrids and use seed varieties that have been planted for many years. Others want to go even further back and plant homestead or heirloom or heritage seeds. This simply means that the seeds are from cultivars that have been grown for a long time and have not been hybridized, or bred with other varieties. With some vegetables that are open pollinated, or pollinated by bees with the pollen from other similar plants, it can be hard to ensure that an older variety is true to its origins. But many people like these older seed varieties and some seed catalogs are responding by offering them.

I have been gardening organically since I started, which means that I have never used a commercial fertilizer or pesticide. Some hard-core organic gardeners may feel I should also be using heirlooms seeds, and I see their point. Unfortunately I've had too much luck with hybrid seeds and I often purchase transplants from a local greenhouse, and when I do that I have little control over what's been planted. So my garden isn't completely pure to what a gardener was growing a hundred years ago.

One thing I do avoid is treated seed. These are becoming less common, but there are still some seed companies that treat seeds with chemicals such as fungicides to help preserve them over the winter and increase their germination rate. If you've ever stood in a garden center or farm co-op and looked at the bins of bulk seeds, you've probably noticed some pink seeds. These are usually corn or peas or other large seeds and the pink color suggests that they have probably been treated.

I fully understand the rationale behind treating seeds and I certainly support farmers who choose this seed. Their income depends on a seed germinating and thriving, and treated seed is one way to lessen their risk. I always choose not to have treated seeds for my garden because there isn't that same urgency and I would prefer to keep the chemicals out of the garden. Yes, there will be a very trace amount, and yes, it's just on the seed and probably won't be incorporated into the vegetable I eat, but I prefer to steer clear nonetheless.

Many companies now offer organic seeds, which ensures that seed hasn't been treated. It also ensures that the plant that the seed was harvested from was grown to organic standards. Organic seeds are more expensive, but you are sending a message to seed growers when you purchase them that you want the food you eat to be as free from chemical inputs as possible.

Trust the Grower

You may labor over which cultivars of each vegetable to order, but you should be pretty mellow about the end result. The varieties listed in a seed catalog have been tested and refined over the years, so your results should be excellent. Seed companies often have a section for new cultivars early on or flag them throughout their catalog. I know that when I purchase transplants like tomatoes and peppers at my local greenhouse the

owner, Brian Burt, has done a lot of the agonizing for me and has chosen cultivars that will do well in my gardening zone.

It's in the best interest of seed companies to offer seeds that will thrive, because they want me as a regular customer. About the only time I haven't had good luck with seeds is when I've been tempted by a ridiculously low price and bought some at the dollar store. I've often seen those oh-so-cheap seeds and thought "what a bargain." That's until I planted them and saw how few seeds actually germinated. There really is a link between price and quality in the seed department. Sure, if you can buy seeds really cheaply and get some to grow it seems great, but when there are big gaps in some rows or rows that don't come up when you think they should, you'll find it frustrating and you'll often lose an opportunity to get things growing at their optimal time.

The Accessories

Most seed catalogs have at least one page of accessories with tons of the coolest-looking garden add-ons and geegaws that you can imagine. You might want to hold off until you've been growing for a few seasons before you load up on these. It's usually after you've had a problem with something, like having carrot seeds come out of the package all at once, that you'll find a handy tool to help.

Starting Seeds Indoors

Most seed catalogues offer seed starter kits, and these can be very helpful for starting plants indoors ahead of time. You will also find these at a variety of places like hardware stores and building and garden centers. There are lots of wonderful and creative ways to make your own pots, too. You can compress newspaper, use the bottoms of waxed milk cartons or yogurt containers…the sky's the limit. I'm not focusing on these in this book since I decided to use the term "easy" in the subtitle and don't want it to seem like too much work. Now, if it's winter and you're desperate to spend as much time as possible working on garden projects, then go for it. You'll find lots of great ideas if you do an Internet search on "make your own seed starters."

I have experimented with these over the years, but for the cost of the containers that I have been able to reuse for many years, I prefer the commercial brands. I also reuse some of the plastic containers and trays I get when I buy transplants at the garden center. The one thing you have to be aware of when reusing containers is the possibility they may have organisms that may not be helpful for your seedlings. It's a good idea to wash these containers out when you've finished with them each year and let them dry well in the sun. You should also use new potting mix each year. The soil is the most likely place for wilts and blights and other diseases, so by using new potting soil each year you'll significantly reduce the odds that plants won't thrive.

Which seeds you start indoors and when you start them is subject to many variables. First, there are some seeds that are best started right in the garden. They are beans, beets, carrots, corn, peas, radishes, pumpkins, and spinach. These seeds will send out a large initial taproot and stem and will just not transplant well. With most of these you'll also be planting them in such large numbers that it would be too much work to start them early.

I have some vegetables that I start inside but also plant directly in the garden, like broccoli, cauliflower, cucumbers, lettuce, melons, and squash. Then there are some that you'll definitely want to start indoors or purchase as transplants at the garden center, namely eggplants, peppers and tomatoes.

My perspective on starting plants indoors is unique compared to that of other North Americans in that I live off the electricity grid and produce all my own electricity from the sun and wind. As I improve my electrical system I am getting close to being able to use grow lights to start plants indoors, but so far I have been hesitant to. While the late winter can have lots of cool but brilliantly bright days which my solar panels love, we can also hit those spells where "April showers bring May flowers," and if we have a prolonged cloudy spell having grow lights going continuously can deplete the electricity reserve in my batteries.

So I do two things to get around this, and if you live in a state or province that uses a lot of coal to produce electricity, which contributes to climate change, I would suggest that this is not a bad idea to try if you want to help reduce your use of electricity. We start several flats of seeds late in the winter and use the type of seed flats with a plastic greenhouse top. We put them in front of a south-facing window, and as the day progresses and the sun moves we move them several times to keep them in the sun. This may seem like a lot of work to some people, and if you work outside the house it may not be feasible. But for us it works quite well.

The other thing we do is purchase some of our transplants from the local greenhouse. When I say "transplants" I'm just referring to vegetables that have been started as seed and are now partially grown. I use them to get a head start and I

will transplant them from the plastic cell they're in to the garden. What I'm doing is shifting the task of starting seeds to the greenhouse grower. In my case I feel pretty good about that. Burt's Greenhouses, where we buy our transplants, has a very responsible environmental approach. They use IPM or Integrated Pest Management to reduce or eliminate the use of insecticides and pesticides and will often use alternative techniques, such as introducing beneficial insects that prey on the pests.

Gardening in the north as we do also presents the dilemma of heating, and if the greenhouse is being heated with natural gas or other fossil fuel you are contributing CO_2 to the atmosphere. Burt's Greenhouses have installed a biomass burner for heat. They actually burn salvaged lumber, which is basically ground up wooden pallets and construction waste, to produce their heat. Heating with wood is carbon neutral because the carbon dioxide the wood releases when it's burned was taken from the atmosphere and stored when the tree was growing, so burning it only releases carbon the tree sequestered while growing. Burt's is also looking at other sources of biomass material such as switchgrass. Switchgrass is a perennial prairie grass that, once established, grows vigorously each year and can be cut and dried and burned for heat. This is another carbon neutral way to heat, and I'm pleased that the place where I get my transplants takes a positive approach to the environment. They also grow amazingly healthy, vigorous, beautiful plants that thrive in my garden. I hope to one day have my own greenhouse, but right now with writing books and other projects I have on the go, I leave some of the startup work to someone else for my heat-loving plants, namely peppers, eggplants, and tomatoes.

If you're going to grow plants inside you may want to use a grow light. Building your own grow light system is a great winter project and you can find lots of plans for one on the Internet. A search on "build your own grow light stand" brings up lots of designs. If you're handy enough to take on a project like this, all you'll probably need to do

is take a look at a commercial model like the one shown in the picture and you'll come up with a design that works for you. You'll need a shelving system and some large fluorescent light fixtures, which you can purchase from a hardware store or building center. It's helpful if the system is adjustable to allow the lights to start out quite close to the soil and then move upwards as the plants emerge and get taller. They will need about 12

My homemade growlight stand isn't fancy but it works. I used scrap lumber and a fluorescent light fixture from the hardware store.

This high quality commercial unit rolls around easily on casters and the light fixture can be adjusted up and down with a window-blind-like pull cord.
Photo: Veseys Seeds Ltd, www.veseys. com.

Pour your potting mix into the cells, spread it around and press it down a bit, put in your seeds, add some more potting mix on top, and water.

hours with the lights on or 6 hours of good strong sunlight. One of the biggest challenges most people have with starting seeds indoors is that they become too tall and gangly, and this is simply caused by lack of light. You can purchase special "grow" lights, but regular fluorescent tubes will work fine.

Seedlings grow best in a temperature of approximately 65°F (18°C), so keep this in mind when you locate your grow light. If it's too cool the plants will not thrive and you may have a problem called "damping off," where the seedling starts but falls over and dies fairly soon after starting. The virus that causes damping off thrives if it's too cool. Some commercial grow systems actually have a heated pad that the seedling tray sits on to keep it at the optimal temperature. Seedlings prefer a slightly warmer place to germinate so if you can, put them on top of your refrigerator or over a furnace vent. They don't need light to germinate, just heat and water.

Plant the seeds in the trays and cover with a thin layer of potting mixture, then press them down lightly, put a bit more soil over them, and water. Keep the soil moist but never let it get soggy because this will also encourage damping off.

The challenge with starting seeds indoors is calculating when to get them going. Some vegetables such as broccoli and cauliflower can handle a bit of cool weather, so I start them three to four weeks before the last frost date in my area, and if they get out a little early they should still do fine. Other vegetables such as eggplants and peppers will not handle cool weather well, so I wait almost three weeks until after the danger of frost is past before I plant them in the garden. I may still start them six to eight weeks before the last frost date, but they'll get an extra two or three weeks indoors before they end up in the garden.

Hardening Off

After your seedlings have been growing under grow lights or in a sunny window, you'll need to get them prepared to be moved into the garden. This is called "hardening off." On a warm day

I take the flats outside and leave them out for a couple of hours. As long as it's warm enough I do this each day, gradually extending the time they remain outside. The days can be warm enough that you'll be tempted to just put them in the garden, but the nights will still be cold and this will either retard their growth or kill them if it's cold enough. By introducing them to full sun and outside conditions slowly you are conditioning them for their eventual move to the garden. Hopefully you have a cat or dog that you need to bring in at night, which should help you remember to bring in the flats of seedlings.

Cold Frame

A cold frame is a helpful device for hardening off plants and getting some green on your plate in the spring. I found four windows at the local dump that I screwed together and put against a south-facing concrete wall. It gets lots of sun, which helps warm up the concrete, which then radiates the heat back at night. As soon as the soil is workable I put in some lettuce and spinach seeds, which start growing soon after. They don't mind the cool nights. I also keep a section of my cold frame empty for some of the more hardy plants that I've started inside in flats, like my brassicas (broccoli, cabbage, cauliflower). I can leave them outside for a week or two before I put them in the garden. If there is late frost the cold frame is enough to protect them.

Late in the summer I plant a new crop of lettuce and spinach in the cold frame and I can enjoy these right until the ground freezes. Even covered in an early November snow there can be nice green lettuce growing inside that we are still able to eat. Cold frames are easy and cheap to build and allow you to start growing earlier and harvesting later than with a regular exposed garden, so these mini-greenhouses are a good investment of your time.

Experimenting and Covering Your Bets

Each year you'll get better at knowing what cultivars to order and what works best for starting indoors. When you are just beginning, be sure to avoid relying on any one system, and use as many inputs into the garden as you can. Start some seeds yourself, try some transplants from a reputable garden center, and even see how transplants from your local grocery store do. Make sure you have a notebook to record what goes where, because using those plastic row markers that come with the transplants will never work. They'll have disappeared, like socks in the dryer, by fall, only to turn up again when you're turning over the garden next year, and there's nothing less natural than a big hunk of plastic in that beautiful garden soil.

Take your notebook out into the garden with you once a week as soon as you start harvesting things. How did the peas do? Did you get a good crop of beans? Did the "Early Tomatoes" in fact have ripe fruit before the cultivars that said they had a greater number of days to maturity? Did the "Black Beauty" eggplants have more fruit than the fancy, long, slim Japanese hybrids? Did they taste any better when you grilled them in olive oil and garlic and added black bean sauce? Taking notes will require a bit of discipline but will pay real dividends as you discover what works best and what your favorite varieties are.

A cold frame is an inexpensive and excellent way to get things going earlier and keep them growing later.

11
Planning the Garden

One of the greatest things about gardening is visualizing how the garden will look in the late summer and fall as you stroll up and down the rows, nibbling on beans, pulling up bright orange carrots, and digging a few potatoes for dinner. Of course, there's that intermediate step of actually planting and nurturing to get to the harvest stage. But that's the beauty of growing food—there's always the anticipation.

How you lay your garden out will be determined by how much room you have. As you know from Chapter 4 on "Eating Energy," I'm a firm believer in growing as much food as you can. So the bigger you can make your garden the better, and if that means stepping outside your comfort zone and hiding a few tomato plants in the front flower gardens, so be it. When you see the beautiful purple flowers of eggplants and the lush purple "aubergine" richness of the eggplants that grow from those flowers, I see no reason why a front yard bed of eggplants, peppers, and tomatoes can't be just as beautiful as a flower garden. Okra forms a lovely flower before the fruit sets, so it actually should be part of your flower gardens. In Chapter 61 I'll discuss companion planting and explain why you should be interspersing marigolds and nasturtiums and other beneficial flowers with these vegetables anyway, so a front yard garden like this is a fabulous idea!

There are a number of books that promote confined area gardening. One is *How to Grow More Vegetables Than You Ever Thought Possible On Less Land Than You Can Imagine* by John Jeavons. This book has been wildly successful since it was first published in the 1970s. It promotes "bio-intensive growing," which is a holistic approach to maximizing the yield of a limited amount of land.

Another popular book is *Square Foot Gardening* by Mel Bartholomew. It follows the same approach, which is to build up very rich soil and plant your crops very close together. Bartholomew actually suggests dividing the garden into sections with narrow walkways in-between. Each section is further divided into smaller sections that you plant strategically. You pack in as many plants as you can and then harvest as soon as possible to allow others to fill in the spaces. By planting everything closely together you reduce how much weeding is required, because once the plants get big enough they crowd out the weeds. You also reduce moisture loss because less soil is exposed to the drying sun.

These and related books are excellent resources for growing a lot of food in a confined space. The key to being able to do this is to have very rich and healthy soil, and from the amount of space I've devoted to soil enhancement and composting you can see that this is very much my philosophy. My only observation about these books is that they were written at a time when there wasn't the same urgency about food security that I believe there is today. So while it's an excellent idea to grow lots of green leafy vegetables intensively, this is not going to offset a significant portion of your yearly food budget. No question it will help during the summer months, but as a vegetarian of 25 years I can tell you that you can't live on salad. You need to have some starches and carbohydrates and grains, and that means growing a lot of food that stores well. To do that, you're going to need more space. Potatoes are big bulky plants and yes, you can grow them intensively and in containers and in all sorts of exotic ways, but if you want to put 15 or 20 buckets of them in your root cellar this fall you need to have a fairly large area to grow them in. This may mean sacrificing some of that beautiful lawn or finally putting your dream of a backyard pool to rest once and for all. Think of the expense of a pool, the energy to keep it warm, the chemicals to keep it from going green, and the ongoing maintenance costs. Now think about a backyard full of potatoes that keeps money in your pocket year after year.

To me the basis of square foot gardening is a salad garden that keeps you supplied with some vegetables all summer. That's great, but I think you should ultimately be taking your garden to the next step and having a big garden that allows you to not only offset much of your summertime food budget but also provide some food into the fall and winter.

But you have to start somewhere and if a 10 foot by 20 foot plot is what you've got to work with then jump in and get going. If it's your first garden consider what you like to eat and what you think would be fun to try. Perhaps this first year you should try a little of everything and see what does well and what you enjoy. The seeds that you purchase do have a limited lifetime, but they will probably last more than one season. In fact some can last many years. In subsequent years you'll probably find that not as many seeds germinate, but with the price of seeds still fairly reasonable this is an acceptable compromise.

Seed packets are going to have a recommended planting strategy. They will tell you how deep to plant the seeds, i.e. 1/2 inch, how far apart to plant the seeds, i.e. 4 inches, and how far apart the rows should be, i.e. 36 inches. This is where it's easy to be intimidated in the early years if you have a smaller garden. You might look at three seed packets and think that if you follow the instructions they're all you'll have room for, and you were expecting the variety of an all-you-can-eat salad bar. Don't despair. Sometimes not playing

by the rules and not doing what you're told is an OK thing. With a smaller garden you should follow the intensive planting strategy and simply grow things closer together than recommended. If the rows should be four feet apart and you plant them two feet apart you'll probably be all right. For the early part of their growth the plants will be manageable and your garden will look great. As the summer progresses and the plants start getting

In their square foot garden our friends Ellen and Jerry have divided the raised bed into 16 one square foot sections. Each section is planted intensively with vegetables.

bigger you'll end up losing some of the walkway in-between the rows. While it may not look immaculate and organized you'll still get lots of food. It just means you'll have to be a bit careful as you walk in your garden.

This might inspire you to make more permanent walkways in-between the rows with some non-pressure-treated wood. These will help to keep the weeds down. You should keep your vegetable plants off of these pathways and train them to grow more vertically.

Every year my garden has some rows that end up being just the right distance apart, some that are way too close together, and some that are ridiculously far apart. I'm not a fanatic, and after growing for 30 years I try and visualize how big the plants will get and therefore how much room they'll take up. When potato plants start, if you've planted the rows four feet apart it can look as if you're just wasting space in the garden. By August, though, it makes complete sense. The shoots will get very tall and then start falling over. And if a big wind blows through, one of those summer storms with heavy rain and wind and hail, those shoots that can be two feet long will now all be lying between the rows. They'll be fine and still

Our friends Janet and Ed like raised beds and have grass around them. These peppers will be aided by the extra heat that the exposed sides will generate for the soil. The twigs are not meant to be artistic but are in fact to discourage cats from digging in the dirt.

be able to convert all that sunshine into energy for the potatoes that are growing under the soil, but they'll be pretty straggly looking. Ultimately those tops are going to start dying anyway, telling you that the potatoes are ready to harvest, so if they end up looking rough midway through the summer don't despair; they're going to die back soon anyway.

I like having rows between my vegetable rows that are just soil. No planks. No walkways. No mulch. Just soil. Yes, weeds are going to grow there. But I don't mind weeding. And each fall I rototill and make the entire garden one big mass of dark rich soil again and get to start fresh next spring. If I had permanent walkways in-between I wouldn't get this opportunity to wipe the slate clean every season. It also allows me to change the orientation of my rows each year.

One technique some gardeners like to use, especially if they are going to grow intensively, is raised beds. As long as you don't make them too big, raised beds can be great for vegetables, making it easy to reach in and weed. You can decide what you want between the raised beds, whether it's grass you have to cut, or bark, or even gravel. The nice thing about raised beds is that they make it easier to keep track of what was where in terms of rotating your crops. To avoid the pests and diseases that strike one type of vegetable from getting too established, if you keep moving where things get planted many pests will have trouble keeping up.

You have to be really careful with the material you use for raised beds. Use rock or concrete block if you can. Cedar or other untreated woods are nice but may be expensive unless you can reclaim some. Do not use railroad ties or pressure-treated wood. Railroad ties are treated with creosote, a very nasty coal-tar-based polycyclic aromatic hydrocarbon, which you don't want near your food. Likewise, some pressure-treated wood can contain copper arsenic, a nasty chemical that you don't want near anything you eat. With the concern about the safety of this chemical in residential applications, many companies are no longer treating their lumber with it, and I would recommend that you steer clear of it. Try and make the edges as natural a material as possible.

Raised-bed gardens offer some advantages but also have some drawbacks. As I've mentioned, they can be convenient for reaching in and weeding with less bending. If you have some good kneepads or a foam gardening pad to kneel on, you can plunk yourself down in the middle of the row and weed away. Raised beds are also helpful if you live in a colder growing area, because they warm up faster than a regular garden plot. The raised sides of the bed allow the sun to really warm those areas up. On a cool night, though, those sides are more exposed to the cooler air, which can offset some of the positive effects of the heating. And a downside of the increased heat in a raised bed is the increased evaporation. You'll have to pay attention to make sure that the soil does not dry out. If you spend extended periods away from home, a raised bed garden may not be the best option.

I often see photos of raised-bed gardens that have been planted very intensively. This is great as long as you've done your homework and made sure that you've added lots of compost and there's enough organic matter and nutrients to go around. If it seems as though your harvest isn't what it should be, perhaps there's too much competition for the material available. It's all part of the "compost, compost, compost" philosophy. You've really got to pile the compost on.

Part of your decision about how to set your garden up will be based on your general philosophy of the universe. Wow, that sounds profound! If you're one of those people who believe in things being neat and organized then you'll want to make sure you leave lots of space between the rows. If you're someone who subscribes to the chaos theory and doesn't mind things being jumbled and disorganized, then it doesn't matter how close things are together. The reality is that by late summer the garden is not going to look as pristine as it did earlier in the summer when things were just starting. It's the trade-off with a garden. It looks best when you're getting the least amount of benefit from it, and once the vegetables are being harvested a lot of the plants will start getting unruly. I should qualify the statement "getting the least amount of benefit from it." I mean not getting as large a harvest. When your garden is just starting to grow and the rows are all neat and organized you'll get a huge benefit from it, but the benefits you'll get will be less obvious. You'll be filled with great anticipation about what's to come. That vegetable garden will be an endless source of joy and contentment. It represents the potential for food independence, and every head of broccoli you grow yourself and every bucket of potatoes you put in the root cellar leave more money in your bank account.

The other main consideration when planning your garden is to think about crop rotation. This

Raking up soil to form a raised bed can help accelerate heat-loving crops and increase yields early in the season.

simply means that you don't want to grow the same things in the same place every year. Pests and diseases would prefer this, as it saves their having to look around to find their favorite hosts every season, but you want to avoid it. Some potential problems are obvious, like bugs that hide in the soil waiting for the next opportunity to reproduce. Other problems include nematodes that are microscopic or blights that can reside in the soil and wait to attack plants that are vulnerable. Most plants are resistant to some pests and susceptible to others, so by moving your vegetables around you reduce the potential for problems.

Different vegetables also make different demands on the nutrients in the soil. Some are heavy feeders and remove a lot of nitrogen from the soil. Others, like the legume family, which includes beans and peas, actually take nitrogen from the air and store it in nodules in their roots that are then left for next season's crop. So moving your vegetables around each year ensures that you don't have poor results because the area where they are growing is depleted of potential food supplies. Soil also has trace minerals and micronutrients that are important to plants. Moving the plants around ensures that they can find what they're looking for as they create their massive root systems.

Some people like to be organized and have a very set rotation system. So if the garden were square or rectangular in shape, they would divide it into four equal parts and move each of their main vegetable types one section over each year.

Below is a sample rotation schedule.

I'm afraid I'm not this organized. While I strongly believe in the concept of rotating things, I don't usually have a strategy until the season begins. The one thing I do is change the orientation of the garden every year. So if the rows ran north and south last year I change them to run east and west. This at least ensures that things will move a bit each year. I also make sure I move my heavy feeders to a new place each year, although I seem to be a bit against the grain in terms of what makes for a heavy feeder. I like to use my intuition to figure out how heavy a feeder a plant is. To me corn is a heavy feeder. It sends up this massive plant which can be five or six feet high with lots of leaves, a huge tassel on top, and, of course, one or two ears of corn which seem to be a be a pretty concentrated source of protein. When I look at

Crop Rotation

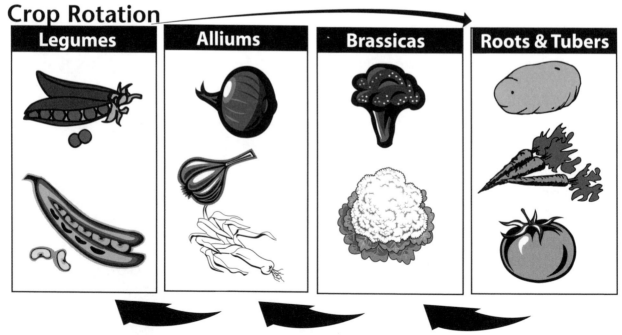

A sample of how you might rotate vegetable families through your garden each year.

a corncob I marvel at the work of the corn plant in producing such a work of art. I think about how this little tiny seed grew into this massive corn stalk and how it contained all the coding and information it needed in order to know when to send out a leaf and when to send out a seed pod and how every kernel in that corn cob has a tiny filament that leads to the top and when we look at the silk we're seeing all those tiny hair-like receptors waiting to be pollinated. A corn plant is a thing of wonder, and I think it requires a lot of the soil and the sun and the rain to bring it to maturity.

A bean plant, on the other hand, is pretty small, and while it does produce these amazing seed pods that we eat—beans—it seems pretty compact and easy on the soil. Of course beans are legumes and they actually get a lot of their nitrogen from the air, so I don't have to worry about growing them in a particularly fertile part of the garden.

I always like talking to other gardeners to find out what they consider to be heavy feeders. I once spoke to a local market gardener, Rick Dawson, from Desert Lake Gardens, and he told me that he liked to keep his peppers in a weak part of the garden because if he put them in too prime a location they didn't produce as well. Up until that time I had thought of peppers as something that probably needed a pretty prime spot. After that I worried about it a lot less and became more concerned with putting the peppers in as sheltered a place as possible because they are very sensitive to cold weather.

Each year my garden is this free-flowing work in progress that changes as the season goes on. I start out with certain constraints because some part of the garden is taken up with the garlic that I planted the previous fall, and this fall I also planted winter wheat, which will reduce my growing areas a little bit more next year. I often start at one end of the garden, putting in my early stuff like radishes and peas. Then as the season progresses I plant based on the temperature and what I think will grow best at that time. Since I stagger plants

Here's a good combination for an early raised bed. The fast-germinating and quick-to-mature radishes mark the row. The tiny seedlings you see emerging are the slow-to-germinate carrots. As you thin the radishes the carrots will have more room to grow, and by the time all the radishes are harvested the carrots will be well on their way.

and grow some things from seed and some from transplants, every garden is a whole new work of art. I'm happy with this system. I may get things too close to where they were in previous years sometimes, but it doesn't happen too often and I've never been able to attribute poor performance by a vegetable to not moving its location.

When you think of commercial agriculture you think of regions that are known for growing something well. Potatoes in Idaho, corn in Nebraska, wheat on the prairies. These areas have a climate and soil well suited to growing these crops, but when you "monocrop," or grow the same thing year after year, pests can be problematic. You can also put extra stress on the soil if you're not replenishing it with nutrients and organic matter. Make sure that your garden doesn't fall prey to this and that things get moved around.

If your garden is relatively flat, its moisture level should be fairly consistent. My garden has a bit of slope to it, and the lower part of the garden has more moisture than the upper portion. This means that I have to pay attention to where I water, and if we experience a drought I concentrate on the upper areas that I know will dry out faster.

Pay attention to what happens with water in your garden and see if there is a natural drainage pattern to it.

Gardening has limitless possibilities and you have lots of options for setting your garden up. Try different things. If growing everything in a confined area doesn't work then open up more area next year and spread things out. If your raised beds dry out too quickly, next year try to plant in more traditional rows. This may be one of the best reasons to not invest in any one system. Be-

fore you go out and spend a lot of money on cedar to make raised beds, why not try one bed this year and have some more traditional beds as well. See what you like. See what works with your soil and your climate and your lifestyle. Maybe you can only really weed on Saturdays and you like having a more restricted area to weed with your raised beds. The possibilities are endless. Now have fun with them!

My most basic strategy for crop rotation: horizontal or east-west one year and vertical or north-south the next. The odds are good things will not end up in the same place, and pests will not have an opportunity to become established in one area.

12
Planting

Put the seeds in the ground. Cover with soil. Water. Wow, that was a short chapter. Well it's pretty easy. There is lots of debate about various elements of the process, but these are the basics. When you are out in the garden with your seed packages you should read the package and follow the directions. The package will give you the "optimal" spacing for the distance between rows and between plants. I say optimal because if you're using a raised-bed garden you may want to plant closer than recommended. And if you're going with rows but have a limited amount of space you similarly may want to cut back on the distance between rows. This just means things will get a little crowded and unruly early on in the growing season. As long as you've provided a good base of compost the plants can handle it, and as long as you're not too obsessive about organization and can stand a little chaos, then go for it.

In the following chapters on each of the main crops I'll provide planting details. I'll also offer some tips on ways I've found to make planting easier and increase your success. One thing I talk about is succession planting. This is key to extending your season. The first time you plant a vegetable garden, you'll be tempted to throw all of your seeds in that first weekend and fill up the garden completely. Then six to eight weeks later you'll have way too many vegetables to eat and what you can't freeze you'll end up giving to your neighbors. And then even though it's still good growing weather, all of your beans and lettuce and broccoli will be gone.

With succession planting you'll just plant a half of the row, or even a third or quarter of the row. Then every couple of weeks you'll plant another few feet of that crop so that the harvest is staggered and you extend the time frame when that vegetable is available to you. You may still have periods when you have too much, and this is when you should go into freezing mode and save some for the winter.

One of the challenges you'll face is actually planting to the depth recommended on the seed package. If you have a soil with lots of clay that clumps and the lettuce package says "Sow ¼" (6 mm) deep" or the corn package says "Sow ½" (1cm) deep," what happens if a big 1" clump of clay falls on some seeds? The best way to deal with this is to make sure you've really worked the area you'll be planting and turned it up well. Once it's been turned over and mixed up, use a rake and remove as much of the large material as you can so that you're left with as fine a soil as possible. Then when you dig a ½" trench for the corn seeds you'll have small enough clumps so that seeds will germinate and grow up through them when you fill the soil back in.

Planting seeds - something humans have been doing for millennium.

Some people recommend using the seed size as a guide for how deep to plant it. For instance, plant the seed three times as deep as the seed size. Depending on the shape of the seed this can get confusing. I like to just follow the directions on the seed package. Even though I have fairly sandy soil it can still be pretty chunky when I go to plant seeds. So I often dig a trench as deep as recommended but don't fill it right to the top. I like to leave a little space so that I can backfill around the seedlings once they get up. Especially early on when it's a bit cooler I want the sun's warmth to be able to get to the seeds as much as possible.

When you water the newly planted seeds, some of the excess soil will wash down into the row, so if you don't overfill when you sow the seeds, the water will usually finish the job.

Transplants can really help speed up the season, so whether you start them indoors yourself or purchase them from a garden center they are a useful part of your planting strategy. Starting plants from seeds yourself will generally be cheaper than purchasing them, but it can be hard to have them as vigorous and bushy as commercial transplants.

What follows is a detailed guideline for growing vegetables and some fruits common to North American gardens. There are always new plants that are introduced from other climates and cultures which you may want to experiment with, but the ones outlined here are tried and true and have a history of producing well. Mix and mingle, experiment, try new things every year, and get ready for the Top 40 Countdown of All Time Garden Favorites!

Here's a watermelon plant I started inside 6 weeks before I planted it outside. I waited several weeks after my final frost date before planting it to ensure it gets the warm weather it likes.

Sometimes when planting long rows I use a rope as a guide so my rows don't wander too much

PART II

"The Top 40 Countdown" of All Time Garden Favorites

13 Asparagus

The greatest vegetables to grow are the ones that come back every year without your having to do anything. These are called perennials. Most of the vegetables you plant will be annuals, meaning that they'll survive only one year in your garden and you'll have to replant them the following garden season. With asparagus, once it's planted it's the gift that keeps on giving. Like most things in life though, it doesn't come without a price, which is a little more work and expense up front. If you love asparagus as much as Michelle does though, it's well worth it. Nothing says "spring" like some asparagus spears steaming on your dinner plate.

The thing to remember about asparagus and rhubarb and berries is that they'll come back year after year, so you need to select a place with that in mind. Often people choose to put them at the side of the garden. If you put them smack dab in the middle, it can be a challenge to rototill around them. So using them as a border is a nice idea.

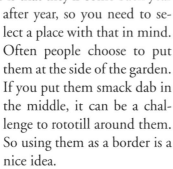

All vegetables are good for you, but asparagus is particularly nutritious. It has vitamins A, C, and K and also lots of the B complex vitamins such as B1, B2 (riboflavin), B3, and B6. Asparagus contains tryptophan (an essential amino acid) and minerals like manganese, copper, phosphorous, potassium, iron, zinc, magnesium, and calcium.

Asparagus also contains folate, which is essential for a healthy cardiovascular system.

Folate, which comes from the Greek word "leafy green", is readily available in green leafy vegetables, but lots of people don't get enough of it. It's critical for fetal development, which is why the government has had bread makers add it to ensure that pregnant women get enough of it. Asparagus contains potassium, which combines with an amino acid called "asparagines" to produce a noticeable diuretic effect. If you like asparagus I'm sure you've discovered this. So don't be eating too much of this if you're about to go on a long car ride without rest stops.

You plant asparagus as a root which you can order from a seed catalog or purchase at your garden center. The root needs to be planted about 8 to 10 inches from the surface, so if you like digging ditches asparagus is your crop! Once you've dug the trench you should carefully place the roots on a small hill of soil and spread them out from the central "crown" which sends the spears up to the surface. Make sure the crowns face up, or you'll be very disappointed.

Asparagus likes a sandy, well-drained soil because the roots are going to sit fairly deep. If you have clay soil or if you dig your trench and hit a layer of clay that will prevent water from easily draining through it, then you'll have to take corrective action to drain it. Dig the trench really deep and then backfill it with larger rocks, then gravel, then sand before you add back some soil for the roots. If you don't there's a good chance the roots will just sit in water and rot.

The key to growing great asparagus is to locate it in really rich soil. When you backfill over the roots you've just planted you want to use the richest soil you can. Mixing soil half and half with compost is a good strategy. Asparagus has traditionally been grown in manure, so if you have access to some good-quality horse manure or composted manure of any kind, this is the place to put it. You can see by the size of the root system that this is quite a plant you are nurturing and it needs you to provide lots of nutrition. Eating asparagus is like taking a multivitamin, but for the plant to provide all those wonderful vitamins and minerals it's going to need lots of good stuff in the soil to draw from. Since I have access to manure from my neighbor I put a thick layer of manure on my asparagus every fall.

You may want to just backfill about half the trench until the spears start emerging. Keep it weeded and then fill with more composted manure or compost later in the summer.

You can also grow asparagus from seeds that you order through a seed catalog. Soak them for several days before planting. They take four to five weeks to germinate, so you might want to plant a few radishes in the row just to mark where it is, because radishes will sprout quickly. After the first year, you should dig up the asparagus roots and then plant them permanently in a deeper trench. After growing a garden, every time you sit down to a meal you'll appreciate how much work farmers put into their produce.

Harvesting

The first year that the asparagus grows in the trench (which would be the second year if started from seed) you shouldn't harvest any. I know how hard this will be. You invested in the plants, you dug the trench, you purchased some wonderful composted manure to fill the trench, and now you've got to watch your asparagus grow without eating any of it. Think of it as a fine wine; it needs time to age. In fact you should only cut spears lightly in the second year. By the third year you'll be able to harvest normally. We usually harvest about half of the spears that eventually sprout up. You have to leave some of the spears to form the beautiful ferny tops that use the sunshine to send energy down to the roots for subsequent years. You might want to put heavy stakes at each end of the row and wrap a big rope around the plants because they will tend to blow down in high winds and you really want them to stay healthy all sum-

mer to produce a good harvest next year.

It is recommended that you cut asparagus spears a couple of inches below the surface of the ground to deter walking and crawling insects that would see a stock opening as an opportunity. However, we usually cut our asparagus spears just above the ground and have had healthy plants. Asparagus is susceptible to a fungus called fusarium, which can be spread from plant to plant on a knife, so some people actually snap the spears when they harvest them. When you purchase your seed or roots you should try and get a variety that is already resistant to fusarium.

In the fall the ferny tops will eventually brown and you can cut them back. I usually cover the row with some old hay or leaves to help protect it from the cold. In the spring you'll pull this back and add more compost or manure before the asparagus starts growing. It really needs a good cold climate so that it will go dormant for the winter months. In some warmer southern states the plant doesn't go completely dormant and can be killed or injured by frost. It's not very often that northern gardeners have reason to celebrate, but we do have a better climate for growing asparagus!

Asparagus plants can last for 15 to 20 years, but to fulfill your side of the bargain make sure they get liberal mounts of compost, mulch, and/or manure every year.

An asparagus root should be planted in a deep trench and backfilled with rich soil, manure, and compost.

14
Artichokes (Globe)

An artichoke flower, which you technically shouldn't see if you harvest the buds to eat.

Globe artichokes are a pretty exotic vegetable to grow and I wouldn't suggest you grow them if you're just starting to garden. After a few years you may want to give them a try. Traditional artichokes are perennials that typically don't produce the edible flower until the second year. For someone growing in a warmer climate, Zone 7 or warmer, this is fine. For northern gardeners this is a challenge because the cold winter will kill the plant, so you have to transplant it into a pot and keep it alive all winter. From my experience this is difficult, so it's great that there is now an annual artichoke for northern growers called "Imperial Star."

Artichokes are an excellent source of the B vitamins, including Thiamine (B1), Riboflavin (B2), Niacin (B3), B5, B6, and Folate (B9), as well as vitamin C, calcium, magnesium, and phosphorus. So they're well worth the effort when you're up for it.

The seeds with take two to three weeks to germinate, so you should sow them about eight weeks before the last frost. As soon as the seedlings emerge put them in two- inch or four- inch pots so they can mature in a larger container before you set them out. You don't want them to be hit by a frost, but it's optimal if you can transplant them so they get a week to ten days' worth of 50°F (10°C) temperatures. This will induce them to form a bud earlier, which is the whole purpose of growing them. If you're trying to get artichokes in a colder climate, you have to use strategies like this.

If you're a flower gardener who likes exotic plants, this is the one for you. If you put the vegetable garden in the backyard and have flower beds in the front, put some artichokes in with the flowers. The plants have beautiful spiky leaves and can grow up to three or four feet in height. The flower buds are unique looking and if you don't harvest them in time they produce a brilliant purple flower that's an explosion of color. I took this photo of a flower the first year I grew artichokes, before I realized that I should have harvested the bud before it flowered. Whoops! Oh well, everyone who toured the vegetable garden enjoyed seeing it.

Some of the flower stalks have multiple stems on them, so when you harvest the earliest and largest stems the smaller ones will receive more energy to mature. If you live in a warmer climate where the plants will survive through the winter, when the season is over let the leaves die back on

Artichokes are an exotic addition to your flower garden.

top of the plant and add some straw or leaves to protect the roots. You'll need to remove this the following spring. In the second and third year you should have some excellent buds to harvest. Next spring the artichoke will send out offsets or suckers, as many bulb plants do. Take a large knife or spade and carefully remove these and plant them separately. Get as much root as possible. These suckers will provide a good harvest the following season.

Artichokes produce multiple heads.

Artichokes (Jerusalem)

Just to confuse the artichoke issue, there is also the Jerusalem Artichoke, which isn't really an artichoke at all but is actually a member of the sunflower family and is grown for its tuber roots, like a potato. It is a perennial so if left in the ground it will spread, but most people dig them up each year like potatoes and replant them in the spring to help maintain a good quality tuber.

The tubers or roots are pretty gnarly and knobby, look like ginger root, and have the consistency of potatoes but are crunchier and sweeter and have a nutty taste. Plant and harvest them as you would potatoes. In good soil the stalks can get very tall and have a beautiful yellow flower. These may be a candidate for a section of the flower garden!

Dirt is the New Prozac

Discover Magazine recently reported that by injecting the soil bacterium Mycobacterium vaccae into mice, a set of serotonin-releasing neurons in the brain are activated. Serotonin is a neurotransmitter than controls mood and drugs that control serotonin in the body are the most commonly prescribed antidepressants. This suggests that simply inhaling M. vaccae while working in the garden can elicit a joyful state of mind. According to the study leader Christopher Lowry, "You can also ingest mycobacteria either through water sources or through eating plants—lettuce that you pick from the garden, or carrots." I always experience an overwhelming sense of wellbeing in the garden, but I just thought it was the fresh air and time away from my computer. Apparently there is a scientific explanation for my elation!

http://discovermagazine.com/2007/jul/raw-data-is-dirt-the-new-prozac

Jerusalem Artichokes are actually perennial sunflowers that are grown for their tuber root, which is similar to a potato. (Courtesy of Johnny's Selected Seeds, www.johnnyseeds.com)

15   Beans

There is an amazing variety of beans and they are used in many ways. They are easy to grow, lots of work to pick, very good for you, and an excellent source of protein you can grow and store for the winter months.

Why Eat Beans?

Beans are a great source of vitamins A, C, and K, as well as manganese and dietary fiber. They contain folate, tryptophan, omega-3 fatty acids, and lots of the B vitamins such as B1, B2, and B3. Beans are also an excellent source of minerals such as calcium, iron, magnesium, copper, phosphorus, and potassium. They are good for your heart, have Vitamin C to lower your risk of colon cancer, are anti-inflammatory. and also contain iron.

Most North Americans are obsessed with getting enough protein, and they really shouldn't be. Most of the protein we get is from animal sources, so it comes with the saturated fat and cholesterol and other things that give us heart disease and diabetes and cause a variety of illnesses. We don't usually pay attention when dieticians say that the protein food group includes beans, but they are a high quality protein and with all the fiber they contain they result in a healthy digestive system, from the stomach to the colon.

There are lots of different types of beans—bush beans, wax beans, lima beans, and kidney beans, among others—and they fill a number of pages in the seed catalogs. Try a few different kinds. If you have limited space, pole beans are a good way to maximize yield in a small area.

Bean flowers.

Planting

Beans are a good vegetable to plant because they are a legume, which means that they can manufacture their own nitrogen and don't need to be planted in a particularly healthy soil. This is a plus if you're getting your garden going and you haven't had much time to improve the quality of your soil. As a bonus, beans can "fix" nitrogen from the air into the soil. How great is that! Free fertilizer. "So you mean I get to eat these insanely healthy beans AND they leave nitrogen in the soil for next year's crop?" That's right. They're almost too good to be true! That's not to say that you shouldn't still be providing some compost to the area they'll be growing in; you just don't need to be quite so obsessed about it.

Bean seeds like warmth to germinate and grow, and I've often jumped the gun and planted them too early and they haven't germinated. The soil temperature should be 60°F (15°C). Bean seeds have a tendency to "damp off," so make sure you move them around to avoid the fungus that causes this, which you should be doing anyway since they are so good for the soil. I usually plant more bean seeds than recommended because I lose some to cutworms, but once they're established I thin them to four to six inches apart. When you see how big a bush bean plant will grow, you'll understand why you shouldn't crowd them too close together.

Once beans get going they pretty much do their own thing. When watering, try to water the soil under the plants and not get the water on the leaves. Beans can be prone to mildew, and by

Green "bush" beans ready for picking

keeping the leaves dry you minimize the risk. A soaker hose or drip irrigation system helps a lot when it comes to watering beans. This year was brutally wet here, so some of my beans did end up with some mildew. If you're having wet weather or are in the garden early in the morning when there's been a dew, try and stay away from the bean plants because you may inadvertently spread a virus, fungus, or rust to the plants.

I love beans because once they get growing they have such lush leaves that they keep the weeds down underneath them. A good hoeing or rototilling between rows will keep the growing area free of weeds that will compete with the beans for water and nutrition.

You have to keep your eye on bean plants because one day the beans will seem too small to harvest and a few days later you'll have some that look too big. You should start picking when they are big enough to make it worthwhile in terms of the volume you end up with to eat, and you should start picking when they are a bit on the small side, because picking the larger ones encourages the growth of smaller ones. You'll see a number of flowers on each stalk and each will turn into a bean, so be careful as you pick to just take the bean and not the whole stalk; otherwise you waste a whole lot of time and effort.

Yellow wax beans

Bean Varieties

Most of the beans I grow are green bush beans and yellow wax beans. Some people call these "snap" beans because before you cook them you usually snap the tip and stalk off. Lima beans are an exceptionally nutritious option, so you should try some of these. With lima beans wait until the thin flat pods get fat and plump, indicating that the beans inside are ready.

Some people grow dry beans to save for later. If you leave any bean pod and don't pick it, it will eventually turn brown and leave a number of seeds inside which are dry and ready to be stored and cooked later. If you want a lot of dry beans, though, you should select a cultivar with this in mind, meaning that when it's smaller and green it won't be as attractive to pick and eat young, it's better to leave it to mature and you'll end up with lots of seeds to dry for the winter.

Many years I've had a variety of beans that don't get picked and when I finally clean out the garden in the fall I dry and harvest the seeds. I put these in glass jars and I think they're absolutely beautiful. I can admire them all winter and marvel at my skills as a gardener. You will too. Some of these we eventually add to soups for added nutritional value and some I use to grow new bean plants the following year.

Pole Beans

If you have limited space in your garden I think pole beans are an excellent option. Rather than forming a bush they send out a main runner which searches out something to climb on and then winds its way around it and climbs up, working its way towards the sun. This would have been the type of bean grown in the story *Jack and the Beanstalk* that got Jack into trouble. I usually make a teepee of sticks before I plant the seeds. I use scrap lumber but you can certainly use any sticks you pull out of the neighbor's trash on yard waste day. Push them into the soil and then tie them together at the top. Make sure the structure is fairly secure, because once the upper part gets covered in foliage it will become a big sail for the first big wind that comes along, and it can be very upsetting to see your pole beans blow over. (Not that this has ever happened to me…more than once.) You can also use strings or a trellis for pole beans to climb.

Once the teepee is secure I plant bean seeds all around the base. As they are growing I give them a hand finding the stakes if they aren't doing it on their own. I gently move them towards a string or stake and partially drape the tendril over or around it. It doesn't take long before the plant clues into the fact that it has hit pay dirt, and "woo hoo," off it goes, winding its way up the pole. If you're vigilant about keeping the beans trained you'll actually have space under the beans to grow another crop like lettuce. Lettuce doesn't always handle the brutal hot sun at the peak of summer, so planting lettuce under your pole beans will provide them with the shade they need to keep from bolting or going to seed and remain as tasty as possible.

Pole beans are an excellent alternative to bush beans if you have a limited amount of space in your garden. They will produce a great harvest that is easier on the knees.

We usually grow a cultivar called "Scarlet Runner" because it produces a brilliant red flower. Your pole beans will become the prettiest plants in the garden. When you see how great a trellis with Scarlet Runners looks, you'll realize there's no reason not to have it in the front yard. Who declared that it was acceptable to have clematis in the front yard but not pole beans? Join the Pole Bean Growers of America and rage against the flower bigotry that keeps vegetables out of people's front yards.

If you have knee or back problems, pole beans are a great option because you don't have to bend so low to pick them. You might have to bend down to get them started—or you could convince your spouse to sow the pole beans for you.

Soybeans

Soybeans are getting lots of press these days. It's partially because soy products have so many amazing health benefits, the main one being their ability to fight cancer. There is also lots of negative publicity about so much of the soybean harvest being from genetically modified seed owned by multinational corporations. You can fight this by growing your own.

Soybeans are cool because they tend to ripen all at once, so you if you want to harvest them to dry they'll all be ready to go after the leaves turn brown and fall off. You can then pull out the whole plant and hang it to dry. Once you notice the pods starting to dry and open you can "thresh" them by putting them in a bag and beating it up either by stepping on it lightly or hitting it with a stick. Save this until the day your boss tells you that the report you just wrote "sucked." For northern gardeners soybeans are superior to lima beans because they are better suited to a cold climate and have more protein and better yields.

Soybeans are not common to most North American gardens, although soy is becoming much more prevalent in our diets, which is a good thing. Researchers believe that one of the reasons Asians have lower rates of cancer and heart disease is because of the large amounts of soy they consume, along with fresh vegetables, while eating less

Soybeans are an easy-to- grow source of high quality protein and nutrition.

night of the first frost to protect them. I always find it frustrating to have an early frost and then go another month before the next one, and I find bean leaves will get nipped with that first frost which leads to a rapid demise of the plant.

Inoculants for Legumes

If you're reading a seed catalog and you see a product like "Garden Inoculant" in the bean or pea section, it refers to bacteria or fungi that are added to soil and form a symbiotic relationship with the plant's root systems. The most common is rhizobacteria, which live within specialized nodules and process atmospheric nitrogen into a form the plants use. The plants do this regardless and there is some rhizobacteria in the soil naturally, but adding it improves the process. I've never used an inoculant, but it is recommended to increase the amount of nitrogen that the legume adds to the soil. If your soil isn't great or you don't have access to lots of compost or manure, investing a few dollars in an inoculant for your beans and peas is a good idea.

animal protein. Using soy as your protein source is an excellent idea, so growing some yourself isn't a bad idea either. Soybeans have more than 100% of the recommended daily intake of iron, and lots of vitamin B6, calcium, magnesium, phosphorous, potassium, and zinc.

You can also eat soybeans when they're young and green. If you boil them for five minutes and put some salt on them you've created the Japanese appetizer called "edaname beans."

Fava Beans

Fava beans are a favorite in the British Isles because unlike most beans they like cold soil and must be planted early, so they mature when the nights are still cool. So if you like lima beans and are in a colder climate, these are a great idea.

Planting fava beans also allows you to extend the season. Get them going early, and then your bush or snap beans will mature later in the summer. With beans I usually plant half a row first, and once they're up and well established I plant the second half of the row to extend the time when I'll have beans at their peak. I also start a second planting well after the first. This second planting will often be at their peak around the time of my first frost. I'll throw a tarp over my beans on the

Peas and beans can be a fair amount of work to pick so it's good to have a crew willing to work for their dinner.

16   Beets

When it comes to novelty vegetables, nothing can "beat beets". I mean, what other vegetable can make your pee turn red, which of course can be scary if you've forgotten that you just ate beets. Betanin is a food dye that is made from beets and it's used in a variety of foods to make them redder, like tomato paste and candies. I can remember buying some veggie dogs and being surprised that they were colored with beef juice. Then I read it again and realized it was actually beet juice.

Beets, like so many root vegetables, are a nutritional powerhouse with folate, manganese, potassium, vitamin C, iron and phosphorous. Beets contain betacyanin, which is a powerful antioxidant cancer-fighting agent, especially against colon and stomach cancer. So it's time to start eating some beets! Not only can you just cook them and eat them, lots of people like to make borscht soup, or you can peel and dice them, toss them with some oil and roast them. Pickled beets are popular as well.

Beets tops make a great addition to a salad or cooked on their own, and they sit on top of a nutritional powerhouse waiting underground.

Planting

Beets like a sandy soil that allows the root to develop and it helps to add lots of compost in to keep the soil light. Beets like phosphorous in the soil so if bone meal or ashes have been worked into the soil recently it should help. Beet seeds are sort of crazy looking, and actually contain 2 to 8 seeds in a cluster, like a small Willy Wonka Gob Stopper, but healthier. I find if I plant them too early they often don't germinate well, so if you want them to germinate well you may want to wait until the soil gets a little warmer. Since people like to plant beets early some seed companies treat beets with a fungicide, so if you're fanatical about avoiding these sorts of products be sure to purchase untreated or organic seeds. For instance, almost all of Johnny's Seeds are sold as untreated. They also sell organic, and add a "T" suffix following the product number to indicate treated seeds. Stokes Seeds on the other hand indicates in their seed catalog that most of their beet seeds are treated, and that to avoid them you should order seeds with a product number that starts with a "UT".

With the multiple seeds on each seed head you may want to thin them to 3 or 4 inches apart once they get going. Beets can get pretty big, so thinning gives them room to grow. They need to be kept well watered and if you have a summer with extremes of wet and dry you may find that the quality of your beets suffers. You may notice white rings in your beets if moisture is not consistent. Beets will have a tendency to "bolt" or send up a seed stalk when you have sudden weather changes.

Beets work well with succession planting, so plant some early and then keep planting more every couple of weeks. You can thin some to eat as the summer progresses and then save others to harvest in the fall. For winter storage cut the tops off, wash and dry them well, then store them in the root cellar. Make sure you only store the ones that look the best. If they have a lot of scab or blemishes that look prone to rot, eat those ones first. The fall is a great time for borscht!

When you go through your seed catalog you'll see lots of cool novelty beets. It used to be that you could get beets in any colour, as long as it was red. Now you can get white beets, and orange beets, and beets with white and red rings that look like bulls' eyes when you cut them. I'm still a fan of plain old red beets. Round beets are considered best to harvest and eat during the summer. The longer or more cylindrically shaped beets are considered better for storage or pickling.

Don't forget the tops! Some of the people that I supply with beets actually prefer the tops to the roots. Them make an excellent addition to a salad, adding some wonderful vibrant colour and lots of healthy nutrition at the same time. As you're thinning them early in the season make sure you add the thinned tops to your salads. Remember when preparing beets to not wear your Sunday whites, because that red juice they produce can stain.

17 Broccoli

Broccoli seems to be one of those vegetables you either love or hate. I know people who absolutely loathe it and I know people who eat it all the time. The broccoli lovers are probably going to outlive the haters because broccoli is a super food, especially when it comes to fighting cancer. Numerous studies have shown that broccoli contains several compounds which protect against breast, colon, and prostate cancer. The whole brassica or cruciferous (as it used to be called) family, which includes kale and cauliflower as well, can lower your incidence of lung, bladder, and ovarian cancer. Broccoli can even repair sun-damaged skin, lower your risk of heart disease, prevent birth defects, promote stronger bones, boost your immune system, walk the dog, and take your garbage to the curb. Okay…I made up the last two.

One cup of steamed broccoli has more than 200% of the recommended daily value of vitamins C and K. There don't seem to be many vitamins and minerals it doesn't have.

I grew up eating broccoli covered in cheese sauce. I think it was to hide the taste. The more I ate it, the more I started to appreciate the taste. The more I grew it myself, the more I realized that there is quite a difference between broccoli that you have cut from your garden just before dinner and broccoli that was cut in California 10 days earlier. As I've come to appreciate the taste I've also learned to cook it less, which is a good thing, since the more you cook it the more of the beneficial effects you lose. That's not to say you shouldn't cook it thoroughly if you prefer to. Eventually, though, with the tons of garlic we grow, I started steaming it for five minutes and then tossing it in a pan of olive oil and minced garlic, and it really tastes great. This summer I stopped steaming it. I just threw it in the pan raw and tossed it with the garlic and olive oil for five minutes, and it is fantastic. I

Broccoli will seem to be spaced very far apart at the beginning of the growing season, but it grows into large plants.

guess that if you take this its logical conclusion, next summer you'll find me on all fours grazing on raw broccoli right off the plant!

The people who have eaten our broccoli have noticed a big difference between our fresh, organically grown broccoli and the stuff that's traveled 2,500 miles. I've actually had some people tell me that they prefer the grocery-store broccoli. When I ask why they claim that fresh, organically grown broccoli tastes too strong…or actually tastes like broccoli! One of the things that I love about this

Lettuce prefers it cool and shady while broccoli can handle the sun. In the upper left you'll notice a lettuce "companion" plant enjoying the cool and shady microclimate created by the broccoli.

new technique of just tossing it with some garlic and olive oil is how the color changes. Broccoli is a beautiful green at the best of times, but after you cook it like this for 5 minutes the color becomes really intense. I can't even describe how it changes, it just gets better. It is truly one of nature's small miracles.

So have I convinced you yet to plant some broccoli? I hope so. If you want to do it organically it will require a bit of attention on your part. Cabbage loopers love broccoli too, and they'll track your plants down one way or another.

Planting

Broccoli likes cool weather, so you should try and get some going early and also plant some later to mature in the fall. I now start all of my broccoli plants indoors and then transplant them to the garden a few weeks before the last frost date, because they're pretty hardy. I've tried starting some broccoli as seeds in the soil over the years, but because the seeds are so small it helps to plant them in the plastic trays where you can put two or three seeds in each cell. If they all take you can separate them into individual cells. I like the transplant system because I'll put in half a row of broccoli every two weeks until the end of June.

Broccoli really does prefer cooler weather, so we find the best-tasting broccoli is the stuff we harvest in either the early summer or later in the fall. We do eat it all summer, but it's not a big fan of hot weather. I have tried putting a few transplants into the spot where I've removed my garlic in the third week of July, but many years the plants don't have enough time to form a large enough head to bother eating.

When the seed catalog says to plant broccoli 18" apart in rows 3' apart you'll probably wonder why, because a head of broccoli isn't that big. What gives? Well the plant itself will be very large, so you should try and follow the directions here.

Harvesting

Broccoli is the sort of vegetable that just keeps giving and giving. Not only is it a super vegetable for your health, but just one plant can be quite prodigious. When the first main head in the center is ready, cut it about four to six inches down. Don't wait too long. You'll be tempted to wait just a few more days so the head will get even bigger! Unfortunately what will happen is that the little green buds will actually start blossoming into little yellow flowers, at which point it will be too late because they'll be past their prime. So cut the main head early. You'll notice side shoots that take over when the first head is removed. They generally won't grow as large, but there will be enough of them for another meal or two. Again, don't wait too long to harvest them or those buds will blossom and you'll miss the window for optimal eating.

You can now buy broccoli cultivars that are more heat tolerant, but our favorite broccoli is always planted late and eaten in the late summer and fall. Even after the first few frosts the broccoli plants will be fine and will taste sweeter and better than ever!

Pests

Cabbage loopers love broccoli. There are several ways to keep them away. You can use row covers that prevent the flitty little white butterflies from landing on the plant and laying eggs on it. I find row covers to be a bit of hassle in terms of weeding and watering around them, so I don't use them. I use "Plan B" or "Bt" for Bacillus thuringiensis, which is considered safe for organic growers. Bt is a bacterium that pests ingest; it prevents them from eating and they die within the day. It is non-toxic to humans, although some of us when confronted with the reality of the bathroom scale probably wish there were a safe way for us to lose our appetites. Remember, though, that if it's fresh vegetables from the garden it's "All You Can Eat" without any guilt!

I don't spray very often and prefer to try and stay on top of cabbage loopers by whacking the little white butterflies with my trusty badminton racket and looking for eggs or young loopers on the plants. In a busy summer when I haven't taken the time to spray, sometimes the little green caterpillars make it through my inspection. I warn

In the center you can see where the main head of broccoli has been harvested. Around it are new smaller heads that will now grow larger and continue to keep you supplied from the same plant.

If you don't harvest the broccoli heads they will eventually flower. The bees and pollinators in the garden love these flowers, and eventually you'll be able to save the seed from the seed pods.

people when I give them broccoli to be on the lookout. We usually spot them when we cut the broccoli up, and if you soak them in some salt water you'll see the odd one abandon ship and float to the surface. Don't freak out. Caterpillars are part of nature. If you still eat meat, it was once a living thing too, don't forget. Caterpillars won't hurt you, but they also won't add much protein to your diet, so do keep an eye out for them on your broccoli.

18   Brussels Sprouts

When I think of being punished as a kid, I think of having to eat Brussels sprouts. I don't think it ever happened, but I guess that would have seemed like a pretty horrible price to pay for setting fire to the plastic paratrooper's parachute as I tossed it off the roof. Not that I ever did that…more than once.

It's funny how things change, because I've pretty much lost my taste for Cap'n Crunch cereal, but I really like Brussels sprouts. Even my daughters like them. They have all the heath benefits of broccoli, such as vitamins C and K, folate, vitamins A, B1, B2, B6, and E, omega 3 fatty acids, iron, and calcium. You name it, Brussels sprouts have it. They have the phytonutrients that enhance your body's natural defense again cancer. They even make your skin healthy so you can save money on fancy moisturizers. The vitamin C also helps guard against rheumatoid arthritis. A "super vegetable" by any other name!

Planting

Brussels (with an "s" because they're from Brussels I guess) sprouts can be a bit tricky to grow. You really want them to mature when it's getting colder, which can make the timing a little tricky for planting. I find that if I plant them a week or two after the last frost date they are usually timed well to be ready for fall. If you have a long, hot growing season you may not have too much luck with them. The plants can be quite large and produce a lot of Brussels sprouts,

Brussels sprouts are a big healthy plant that you'll need to leave lots of room around in the garden.

so you'll want them to be growing in a rich, well composted area in the garden. Like all crops it's best to make sure you rotate them and don't grow them where they've been grown for the last three years in order to minimize pests that are attracted to them.

If your first frost is September 30, you should count back about four months to determine when to put transplants in the garden. I usually put them in two or three weeks after the last spring frost, about the same time I'm putting in my heat-loving peppers and eggplants. With Brussels sprouts I'm not putting them in because they're heat loving but because they're a cold-harvested plant. I want them to be mature just about the time I'm getting frost, which will really enhance their flavor.

Each plant produces a good harvest, so you don't have to put in too many. I usually purchase just one cell pack of four Brussels sprouts transplants from the garden center. Now that we have a freezer I'll start putting in more. In the past we haven't eaten all of the Brussels sprouts from just four plants, so the deer in the area have developed a taste for them. The plants are really big, so you should leave about two feet of space between them. I know this will seem crazy when you put them in, but when you see how big they become you'll understand. You'll also want to make sure you have almost three feet between a row of Brussels sprouts rows and anything else.

Maintenance

Brussels sprouts might be a good plant to mulch to help maintain moisture and provide a good supply of nutrients to the roots. If you're not a mulcher you may want to top-dress with compost or put some around the base as the summer progresses. Once the sprouts start to form you should start removing the leaves near them, starting at the bottom and working your way up as the summer progresses. The sprouts are really just mini-cabbages and it's very interesting to watch them develop. Once you get 10 or so rows of sprouts started you'll want to remove the crown or central growing point, a rosette of small leaves at the top of the plant. Rather than having the plant continue to try and get bigger, later in the summer and early fall you'll want it to put all its energy into the sprouts that are already growing, so removing that leader will get it to refocus on what it has already produced. Leave three or four rows of leaves at the top so the plant has some mini-solar panels to absorb sunlight and photosynthesize. It's like a mini-space station with solar panels, only rather than a crew you have Brussels sprouts.

Harvesting

If you're living in a southern state I feel a little sorry for you when it comes to Brussels sprouts, because they really are at their best in cold weather. They're very hardy and will tolerate light frosts, and heavy frosts, and even blizzards. We have often eaten them after an early snow if the deer have left them for us. You can cut as many Brussels sprouts off as you need as the fall progresses, starting at the bottom where they are the biggest. I usually remove the outermost leaves, which are often loose and marked with some insect holes and yellow around the edges. I have also pulled whole plants out by the roots and hung them in our woodshed to protect them from the marauding bands of deer who enjoy them. This is a convenient way to harvest just a few when we want them. You can also hang them in your root cellar, which should be close to zero degrees by the time you put them in, and they should last another four to six weeks. Keep your eye on them, though, because any member of the cabbage family that "goes" can create a bad smell pretty fast. It's a sulphur-like smell and the compound that causes it is sulforaphane, which is actually one of the healthy cancer-fighting agents at work in a brassicas.

You can boil Brussels sprouts or steam them, and we like to add some butter and salt to bring out the flavor. They really seem to go nicely with a warm dinner on a cool fall night.

Pests

Since Brussels sprouts are basically mini-cabbages, cabbage loopers will like them, but I've found that the butterflies that lay the cabbage looper eggs tend to be more interested in actual cabbage plants, so Brussels sprouts aren't affected by this pest as often as cabbages are.

For the most part I've found them to be fairly pest free. Some growers get root maggots, which I discuss in Chapter 60, as well as aphids, but if you plant Brussels sprouts late enough you should be able to avoid aphids. If you do get cabbage loopers on them you'll probably have them on all your brassicas, so you'll want to spray periodically with Bt. If you're completely adverse to spraying, even with a natural bacterium like Bt, you'll have to use floating row covers to keep the butterflies off your plants.

Brussels sprouts are basically "mini-cabbages" all stacked up and at their prime after a frost.

19 Cabbage

What's weird is that it wasn't until I was writing this section of the book that I realized that all the brassicas start with B or C. I have puzzled over the difference between the brassicas and the cruciferae family, but apparently they are one and the same, with brassica being the current official name for the family and cruciferae the old name. And both families start with "B" or "C," as do broccoli, Brussels sprouts, cabbage, and cauliflower. How cool is this bit of trivia!

Cabbage has all the same health benefits that I mentioned for the previous brassicas, including lots of vitamins C, K, and B and minerals. It also has those phytonutrients that are antioxidants, taking on free radicals that can damage DNA. Red cabbage has been found to have more phytonutrients and also contains polyphenols, which may be protective against Alzheimer's. I prefer red cabbage because it makes it easier to spot cabbage loopers and cabbageworms, which are bright green and show up more easily against the red cabbage.

Sulforaphane

I have a memory of riding my bike to my future wife Michelle's house, 25 miles away in the country. It was in the fall and next to her house there was a huge field of cabbages that had been harvested but the stalks and outside leaves had been left behind. There was a very strong smell of rotten eggs because of the sulfur in brassicas. Well, it turns out that smell was a good thing. It comes from an organosulfur compound called sulforaphane, which has anticancer, antidiabetic, and antimicrobial properties. Young sprouts of broccoli and cauliflower are very rich in it (so don't wait too long to eat them) and Brussels sprouts have the highest concentration of it. These brassicas all have it, and it is important to eat lots of it in this world where our bodies are bombarded daily with a smorgasbord of cancer-causing agents.

Planting

Like all brassicas, cabbage really is a cold-weather plant, but there are cultivars you can buy that are designed to mature early. I usually put in a few of the early variety and hold back and put most of my efforts into the crop I'll plant later. When you cut a cabbage head in half you'll see how thick and dense all the inside leaves are, so even though the head may not be huge a fair amount of organic matter and nutrients have been required to get it to that stage. So plant them in a spot with lots of compost and consider top dressing as the season goes on.

I start some seeds in a tray about four or five weeks before the last frost date and I harden them off in the cold frame closer to the frost date, when I'm going to put them out. I also start my late cultivars in trays early in July. Then I wait four or five weeks until the seedlings have four or more leaves before I plant them in the garden, usually the first week or two of August. This way I have some cabbages that mature early for coleslaw in the summer and more that mature later for fall eating and storage right into the winter.

You can direct seed cabbage in the garden if you want, but with the tiny seeds you'll probably end up putting in too many, which is fine as long as you thin them once the seeds emerge. The plants should be 18" apart, which means it can be tough to get them to direct seed well, so I like to start them in cell packs and then transplant them.

A seed packet has a lot of seeds and the tendency is to just toss them all in, but this gets wasteful. I know that with all the other vegetables we're eating in the summer I probably only need 3 or 4 cabbages for the summer then 8 or 10 for the fall and winter. So starting them in cell packs where I can control how many I sow and how many end up in the garden makes a lot of sense.

Pests

The real challenge with cabbage is the pests, and there's an advantage to planting the bulk of the crop in the summer. The ones you plant in the spring will tend to be deluged with cabbage-worms and cabbage loopers and serve as sacrificial plants. As long as you stay on top of them in the early crop, your second crop won't have so many. I am not hung up on how vegetables look, so I don't mind if my cabbages end up looking a little "ragged," but I'm also not a huge fan of green worms. So some summers I do resort to Bt. In Chapter 60 I'll be demonstrating my awesome badminton racket pest control technique. I prefer the cabbages I will be storing to be pest free, and good-looking heads are a little more important because once they get into the dark, humid conditions of the root cellars any of those holes and blemishes have a tendency to be the place where mold starts or rot sets in. So there's some incentive to try and keep the bugs off them.

Harvesting

You probably thought a machete was just for hacking your way through tropical jungles. It turns out it can come in pretty handy for harvesting your brassicas. The stems of cauliflowers and cabbages can be really thick and strong, and it can be hard to cut them. I often use pruners to cut my way through, but we ran an organic co-op in the city once and I remember the farmer arriving with a machete strapped to his waist. I thought he had a flair for the dramatic until I started growing my own brassicas, and he was right. So if you don't have a machete, keep a good sharp knife or pruning shears around to harvest these.

Purple cabbage makes it easier to spot the bright green caterpillars that are one of its main pests.

Chinese Cabbage

Seed catalogs now often feature a variety of Chinese cabbage because of its popularity in salad bars and as an ingredient in Asian cooking. It could be compared to a large head of romaine lettuce with a tangy, sweet flavour.

Chinese cabbage is fairly hearty and easy to grow, and you can grow it all summer, starting some early and planting more later for fall harvest. Often the biggest challenge is bolting, where it sends up a seed shoot before you can get the cabbage harvested. This is a problem with many vegetables and is why you should use succession plantings where you don't plant too much of a variety all at once. By spreading out your plantings you can hopefully keep on top of harvesting and eating the cabbages so they don't have a chance to bolt and waste all your effort. If they do get ahead of you, be sure to read Chapter 64 on saving the seeds.

20 Cantaloupe - Muskmelon

Muskmelon which I call cantaloupes, get their name from their "musky" sweet taste. It's taken me some time, but I've finally developed a taste for them. I think it's because they are so ubiquitous as a garnish in restaurants that I just got tired of wasting them and started eating them. They are an acquired taste I think, but I like sweet things so it was inevitable that I'd start to enjoy them. They are a nice summer and early fall addition to my breakfast.

Cantaloupes have almost 100% of the recommended daily allowance of vitamin C and vitamin A, as well as some B6 and B3, plus folate. The orange color of cantaloupe is a giveaway that this is a healthy food because that orange comes from its betacarotene, which really bumps cantaloupe up a notch on the health scale. This is an excellent fruit to add to breakfast or even to have as a no-fat sweet dessert after any meal.

Planting

Melons need a long growing season and they like heat. I usually start seeds indoors about four weeks before the last frost. They like warm soil to germinate. Once they're established, I start moving them outside during the day to harden them off. Melons are best started in peat pots so that you don't disturb their roots too much when you transplant them into the garden. I generally take the smaller cell-pack root and put it into a three-inch plastic pot to give the roots more room to spread, and they have been able to handle this.

I also start some seeds in the soil when I set the transplants out because I have had bad luck some years with my transplants. I guess I'm covering my bets. If there are cutworms in the area that lop off all of the transplants, at least I know I have seeds germinating to take their place. Since I notice the transplants being knocked off, I can eliminate the cutworms before the next round of melons start growing. I've also had bad luck with cooler weather. There have been years when I put in melon transplants a good two weeks after the last frost date just to make sure they didn't get nipped, but the transplants just sat there in sus-

This young cantaloupe is hanging from one of the trellises I used for vines this year. Trellises can really help increase yields when you're growing in a confined space.

As a spreading vine, melons need a fair amount of room, but you can actually train them to grow up a trellis. This year I raised some cantaloupes on a trellis and they did just fine without any help. Ideally I should have used some form of netting to hold them up as they got heavier, but the vines managed to hang on until the fruit was ripe. So even if your space is limited there's no reason not to grow melons.

pended animation. I think they were shocked by some cool nights that stunted their growth. Inevitably the direct seeded plants that came later did better. My attitude is to always have a "Plan B" when it comes to the garden.

I plant my melons in hills with three melon plants each. I use my cultivator to rake up soil in the surrounding area and then make a hollowed-out interior for the plants. This leaves a wall around them, like a small swimming pool, which traps water. The hills are at least five to six feet apart because all cucurbits, like pumpkins and melons, spread like crazy. You can see the benefits of training them on a trellis if you have space challenges.

Many seed catalogs recommend using mulch on melons, and it's a good idea. A black plastic mulch helps warm the soil and keeps it from cooling off so much at night, and this is what these heat-loving plants prefer. You can also use a floating row cover, which has the added advantage of helping keep some of the insects off . The downside is that you have to remove it to water and also make sure it's off when the flowers set so bees will pollinate them. Be careful using the black plastic mulch in southern areas because it will actually warm the soil too much. And while you can use natural mulch like straw, which keeps the weeds down, it also provides a good hiding place for pests like the squash bug.

I don't use any of these techniques. I wait until I know there is no chance of frost, plant the melons in hills, keep them watered, and watch for insect damage. You tend to get into a groove with your garden and go with things that work for you. But don't ever hesitate to try new things, because often they can really help.

Care

Melons will need lots of water, especially until they start setting fruit. Once they are well established and on their way I just water every two or three days if we're having a dry spell. Melons have fairly shallow roots, so I don't let them dry out for too long. I'm also careful when I weed. I use

This cantaloupe is off the ground on a high-tech solar heater (a juice can) which keeps it off the cooler ground at night and makes it less prone to disease.

my cultivator in the large open area around the hills before it starts getting filled up with vines. Around the plants themselves, though, I weed by hand, because using a cultivator can harm shallow roots.

When I water I do it early in the morning, and I try to keep as much water off the foliage as I can. I usually have rain barrels with taps in them nearby, so I put the hose from the rain barrel into one of the hilltop pools I have the melons growing in, let it fill up, and after five or so minutes move to the next hill. This gives me five minutes to be doing something else while the hill is getting watered.

If you grow melons on the ground and don't use a trellis you might want to consider putting the ripening fruit up on something like tin cans, plastic pots, or pieces of wood. The first benefit is that the melon is less likely to come into direct contact with a disease or a land-loving bug like a slug. The added bonus is that the fruit is kept off the ground, which can really cool down at night. Even on a hot day the ground around the fruit is cooler than the air. You are essentially putting the melons up on a little solar heater that will help speed up the ripening as well as keep them off the cold ground. It just takes a minute, but the melons will reward you by ripening sooner and being less prone to problems.

Pests

Squash bugs and cucumber beetles are my biggest challenge with cucurbits, whether they be squash, pumpkins, or melons. If you notice leaves that

The leaves on the cantaloupe vines have died at just about the same time that the fruit is ready to harvest.

have been eaten or if some of the leaves wilt and then turn black and die, this is probably a sign of squash bugs. Squash bugs tend to hang out near the base of the plant. They make their way out to the leaves to eat and to lay their eggs on the underside of the leaves. You'll see the eggs in organized little clusters on the leaves near the leaf stem. I just scrape them off when I find them and

hunt around and kill the squash bugs when I see them. They are slow and easy to grab. Or you can use a technique that also works for slugs: place an old board near the base of the plant; the squash bugs will take shelter under it at night; lift it up each morning and eliminate any that you find.

Cucumber bugs will fly onto the plants and tend to do more damage when the plants are small. They can also spread bacterial wilt and viruses, so you can use a commercial organic spray that includes pyrethrin to control them. I like to just stay on top of them and keep squashing them. Sorry, but in this case they're the enemy and need to be eliminated by whatever means I have. I like to use the military term "terminate with extreme prejudice."

If you ever examine the leaves up close and notice tiny, soft-bodied insects they may be aphids or mites, which are sucking insects that will damage the plant. Spray them with an insecticidal soap or blast them off with water from the hose.

You may find your leaves wilting on really hot days. There are a number of diseases that can cause this, but as with other plants, try and buy cultivars that have resistance to these common problems. If the leaves wilt during the day when it's hot but then return to normal in the morning it may just be heat stress. Keep them well watered and don't worry about this. As long as the leaves aren't wilting and dropping they are doing their job and you should still end up with melons to harvest. You should also make sure you rotate where you plant things in the garden to keep any diseases from getting established.

Harvesting

Knowing when to pick your melons is one of those decisions that everyone has a strategy for, but it's difficult to know exactly when it's time. Usually with cantaloupes it's when the greenish parts begin to change to a more yellow color, but every cultivar is different so you can't rely on this. If a cantaloupe looks ready and you tug on it lightly and it separates from the vine, then it's ready, and since you've picked it there's no turning back anyway. Hopefully you have enough on the vines that if you pick one a little early you can afford to waste it. I find cantaloupe don't ripen much after you pick them, so you can't really pick them and hope that they'll ripen eventually. The longer you can wait the sweeter they'll be.

If a bunch of melons ripen at the same time you can store them in the fridge for a few weeks, but they aren't the sort of thing you can put in the root cellar. You'll need to gorge on them during the time they're ripening, get sick of them, and then be craving them by the time the next season rolls around. This is the way we used to eat when grocery stores didn't stock the same fruits and vegetables 52 weeks a year. It was simpler then, and I think it makes more sense.

The Well-Dressed Gardener

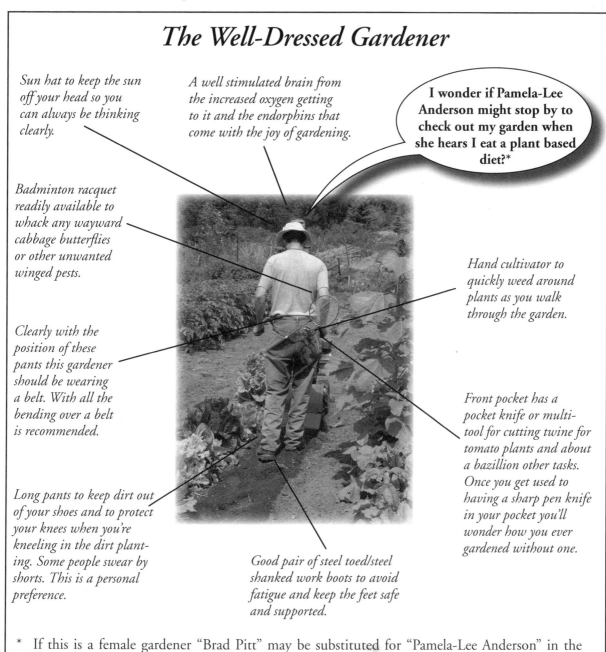

Sun hat to keep the sun off your head so you can always be thinking clearly.

A well stimulated brain from the increased oxygen getting to it and the endorphins that come with the joy of gardening.

I wonder if Pamela-Lee Anderson might stop by to check out my garden when she hears I eat a plant based diet?*

Badminton racquet readily available to whack any wayward cabbage butterflies or other unwanted winged pests.

Hand cultivator to quickly weed around plants as you walk through the garden.

Clearly with the position of these pants this gardener should be wearing a belt. With all the bending over a belt is recommended.

Long pants to keep dirt out of your shoes and to protect your knees when you're kneeling in the dirt planting. Some people swear by shorts. This is a personal preference.

Front pocket has a pocket knife or multi-tool for cutting twine for tomato plants and about a bazillion other tasks. Once you get used to having a sharp pen knife in your pocket you'll wonder how you ever gardened without one.

Good pair of steel toed/steel shanked work boots to avoid fatigue and keep the feet safe and supported.

* If this is a female gardener "Brad Pitt" may be substituted for "Pamela-Lee Anderson" in the thought bubble.

21 Carrots

I believe if I'd been fed a diet of carrots comparable to my diet of watching the cartoon character Bugs Bunny eating carrots, I wouldn't be wearing glasses today and would be able to enjoy a carefree walk in the woods on a moonless night without the benefit of night vision goggles.

Carrots are the richest vegetable source of vitamin A. They get their color from beta-carotene, which our bodies metabolize into vitamin A. They also provide us with lots of K, C, and B vitamins as well as minerals. Their antioxidant properties provide those cancer-fighting characteristics we like.

The RAF developed the urban legend that carrots can help you see in the dark to cover up the fact they were actually using radar to shoot down German planes during the Battle of Britain. A lack of vitamin A can cause poor vision, including night vision, which can be restored by adding lots of vitamin-A-rich foods like carrots to your diet. If you eat bushels of them you will not be able to see in the pitch black, but you may develop carotenosis, which won't hurt you but will turn your skin orange. Keep that in mind for Halloween next year.

Carrots are a fantastic crop to grow because you can eat them all summer and leave them in the garden until it freezes or all winter if you mulch them well. They store exceptionally well in your root cellar, so along with potatoes they should be one of the crops you focus on to get maximum financial and health benefits from your garden.

Planting

Carrots need a well-tilled and loosened soil to thrive. You'll probably have to do more than just hoeing or rototilling the area. This is the time to put on your work boots and get out your shovel and plunge it deep into the soil and turn it over. You can visualize what a nice, long 8" or 12" carrot looks like, and for it to send its tap root that deep into the soil it needs to be as unimpeded as possible. If you have a really heavy clay soil you may actually want to first remove the top five or six inches of topsoil and then go down deeper with your shovel to loosen the soil. Once that lower area is loosened, toss in lots of compost and peat moss to keep it broken up and give the carrots a path down. Then you need to rake the topsoil back into the trench that you dug out and add more compost to it. It needs to be "loosey-goosey" for juicy carrots.

Stones and rocks are not a carrot's friends. As that main taproot grows, it can split if it encounters a rock, and you'll end up with a carrot that's straight on top with two skinny "legs". While these are always great novelty vegetables, fun to dress up in Barbie and GI Joe outfits (because they have legs), this won't be the most productive use of your space. So if you can remove as many of the stones from the carrot patch as possible, it will be worth the time.

Carrots seeds are very small and a plastic seed sower like this can make sure you don't waste seeds by controlling how quickly seeds come out.

Carrots are tiny little seeds and they're hard to handle. Before I started saving seeds I bought this handy little plastic device that lets you set how quickly you want seeds to come out, so you can just go down the row tapping it and having a good steady stream of seeds fall out. Once I started saving seeds I ended up with so many that now I just sprinkle them very heavily into place. I also don't plant them in a narrow row but scatter the seeds across a six-inch- or eight-inch-wide row. I like harvesting a good mass of carrots, and this ensures that you get a good dense row to dig carrots from. Planting like this means you'll probably have to thin more later, but I don't mind thinning.

I often have trouble getting carrots to germinate. There have been many years when I've planted rows of carrots and had very few of them come up. While carrot seeds should be able to handle a late frost, I have the best luck when I wait a bit. I plant two or three rows, two to three weeks apart. If there is something that prevents them from germinating or stresses them during the summer, like a drought, having carrots that are at different stages of maturation means that some will handle it better. When they emerge from the soil, carrots are very delicate and fine, so you'll want to try and avoid having the soil form a crust over them while you're waiting for them to germinate. If you have a lot of clay in your soil, or if you plant them right after a rain, you may find that the top of the soil forms a hard crust that the tiny carrot shoots have trouble breaking through. So make sure that the soil has some compost in it to keep it loose, and keep the soil moist to make their emergence easy.

This year I read a tip about covering your seeds with a wooden plank or burlap for seven days after you plant to improve germination. I decided to give this idea a try and sure enough, five days after sowing the seeds I took the board off the row and some of the seedlings were already an inch high. I'm now a real believer in this system.

You may not want to overdo it with fertilizer for carrots, and back off on the manure in the area where you're going to grow carrots. Too much manure can make the carrots hairy, and

who wants hairy carrots! The hairs are just fine roots that grow out of the carrot, and while they can be easily brushed off they're not optimal for storage.

After the carrots are about two inches tall I usually thin them. If they seem to have a fairly good distance between them I may let them go, but you don't want them running into their buddies and having their growth restricted. About one carrot every two inches is optimal. I also like to make sure that the soil is moist when I thin so that I don't pull out the neighboring plants while I'm at it. Of course in my garden the thinning is part of the weeding process that happens at the same time. Since it's two or three weeks or more before I finally get to thin, the carrot patch will have lots of weeds emerging at the time I'm thinning.

Carrot Varieties

There are two main types of carrots: Nantes and Chantenays. Nantes are the more traditional cylindrical carrots, like the kind the rabbit puppet tricked Captain Kangaroo into giving up during every show. Can you believe how gullible that Captain Kangaroo was! Can you believe that I remember this stuff! Chantenays are shorter and look a bit like spinning tops. You'll recognize the difference when you go through the seed catalog. If you have a nice light soil

The fine, fernlike carrot tops are not only beautiful but form a great mass to keep the weeds around them suppressed.

and you can easily till down 10 or 12 inches, go for the more traditional Nantes. But if you have heavy clay or a soil with a lot of stones and gravel then go with Chantenays.

Pests

I've been very lucky with my carrots over the years and haven't had many pests. Sometimes grubs chew on a few of them, but with the number of carrots I grow that's not a big deal. I also have wireworms that leave little tunnels on the carrots. I give these carrots to my neighbor who provides us with horse manure, because horses love carrots and don't seem to be bothered by some cosmetic marks. You are more likely to get these pests if you're growing in a part of your garden that had grass or sod on it recently.

Carrots bolting to seed is caused by high/low temperature stress at the 5-6 leaf stage. To protect yourself, plant successive crops.

The carrots you plant later in the spring will be more likely to miss the carrot rust fly, but if you want to be sure to avoid this pest you can use floating row covers. I offer this is as a possible solution, but it's one I won't use. Carrots are very easily disturbed when they're small, and laying fabric over them is likely to damage them. You'd almost have to build a little wire greenhouse to keep the fabric off the carrots. Then you'd have to remove it every time you wanted to water or weed the area. My attitude is to plant lots of carrots and give away the ones that have some marks on them.

Harvesting – Winter

During the summer I keep thinning the carrots, but I'm actually just grabbing a couple for dinner or a snack and I take these from an area where they are still pretty dense. As the summer rolls into fall I start digging up bunches to have in the fridge. Then when we get into the frost zone I will start digging some for winter storage.

You don't have to rush digging carrots, though, because they're below ground and you can leave them in the ground until the ground freezes. If you want to get really creative you can even mulch some for winter eating. In warmer growing zones this is even easier. I have put a really heavy mulch of straw or hay on carrots in November before the ground gets frozen. It has to be really deep to avoid freezing. Then for the next few months I've been able to go out and scrape the snow away and dig carrots. Even though they're buried under 8 to 12 inches of straw, it always amazes me that the deer roaming through the garden in the winter know the carrots are there and will actually dig away the straw and chew off the green tops and then start to chomp down two or three inches into the soil to eat the carrots. No wonder we have such healthy deer around here!

Storage

I store potatoes in dry peat moss, but I store carrots in wet peat moss. I'll fill up a bucket with peat moss and start adding water and mixing until the peat moss is moist throughout. Usually I'd be concerned about moisture causing mould and premature spoilage in a vegetable, but my carrots seem to really like this. It always amazes me in March when I take a carrot out of the root cellar and snap it in half and it's crunchy when I eat it.

Carrots are slow to germinate, which means that when it's time to thin the delicate seedlings it will also be time to weed them.

22   Cauliflower

This will be a short section because we've been through all of this before. Cauliflower is part of the brassica family, full of great nutrition and cancer-preventing properties.

I plant cauliflower the same way I plant broccoli, starting it in seed flats beginning in the late winter and then planting four or eight more cell packs every couple of weeks all spring so that I have lots maturing all summer and into the fall. I find cauliflower doesn't do as well in the summer as it does in the fall, so I aim to have the bulk of my plants maturing when the weather is cool. Cauliflower plants have fairly shallow roots, so try not to hoe and cultivate too deeply around the base. It would be better to hand weed since their broad leaves prevent most weeds from germinating near them and once the plants get to be a reasonable size they pretty much crowd out any weeds.

We often find that the cauliflower that matures in the heat of the summer doesn't always form the nicest heads, which is why we try and focus on getting most of our crop to mature in the cooler weather in the fall. If you have problems with heads, such as leaves growing through the head, or buttoning, where the small heads form before the leaves get large enough, it's probably because of extremes, either of temperature, with fluctuations between heat and cold, or of moisture, too wet then too dry or vice versa. The challenge is to try and keep the plants uniformly watered, and if nature plays fast and loose with the temperature, make sure you have succession plantings so that the ones that mature later will be of better quality.

Blanching is the key to good cauliflower. This refers to keeping the sun off the cauliflower itself. The cauliflower head is called a "curd." While you could design fancy little sun umbrellas, a better option is just to take the large leaves and tie them together over top of the head with some binder twine. This prevents the sun from hitting the head itself, which will keep it nice and white. I usually do this once the head is a couple of inches in diameter. It's amazing how quickly a head will be ready to harvest, so keep your eye on it. Sometimes heads are ready to cut within a week of blanching. And don't leave them too long, because they'll quickly become too big and gangly, with the florettes starting to shoot out.

Cauliflower is something you'll need a good, big, sharp knife to harvest. It will keep for a week

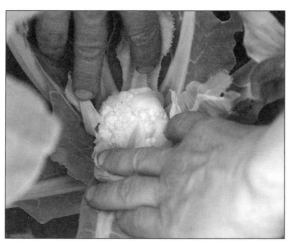

When you see cauliflower heads starting to form, it's time to blanch them.

or two in the fridge, but we find that freezing is the best way to save it for the winter.

To blanch you just pull the large lower leaves up over the head and tie them together with a rubber band or binder twine. This will keep the sun off the head and keep it white, and it will also keep out dirt that may splash up from the soil during heavy rains.

23   Celery (Celeriac)

Celery is one of those interesting foods that has inspired urban legends. People think that celery is the ultimate diet food and that you actually burn more calories chewing and digesting it than it provides, making it the perfect food to prevent weight gain. Well, sure, if you ate only celery maybe, but most people would start to get a little peaked if this was all they ate.

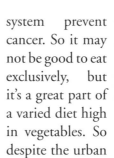

Celery is a good source of vitamins K, C, A, B1, B2, and B6. It also contains folate, potassium, molybdenum, manganese, calcium, magnesium, tryptophan, phosphorus, and iron. Because it's rich in vitamin C and compounds that prevent free radicals from damaging cells, celery helps the immune system prevent cancer. So it may not be good to eat exclusively, but it's a great part of a varied diet high in vegetables. So despite the urban legend, it is a healthy vegetable and is in fact a pretty heavy feeder, meaning that it grows best in a rich, well-composted soil.

I like to plant celery that I've started indoors or purchased as transplants from a local garden center.

Planting

I usually purchase celery transplants from the greenhouse, but you can certainly start them indoors well in advance of the last frost. It will probably be 10 or 12 weeks before you transplant them to the garden. The seeds will take 10 to 20 days to germinate, so don't get too excited when they seem to be taking a lot of time. Be patient. This is why you're starting so far in advance of transplanting. When you're ready to transplant to the garden, wait for a week or two after the last frost, because they prefer to be warm and tend to bolt if you get an extended cool spell after they're transplanted. Celery is a plant that likes boron, and if your soil is deficient (i.e. if you had a professional test done and this was noted) you might want to mix one-eighth of a teaspoon of borax with a gallon of water and use the mixture to water the soil around the plants.

Make sure the soil is well watered when you transplant. I usually dig a trench and put the transplants six to eight inches below the regular soil level. You can put in a celery transplant every six inches since they are relatively compact plants.

After a few weeks I start filling the trench back in with a mix of compost and soil. This will keep the lower part "blanched" or white, like commercial celery. I think this also helps keep the celery less bitter tasting and acts as a good moisture retainer. You can use leaves or straw or compost as well. These will all help keep the roots cool and moist, which is what celery really needs. If the celery gets dried out during the summer it's likely to get bitter.

Pests

Celery loopers, which are green caterpillars with white stripes like to munch on celery. Bt spray will help to handle this. You may get "black heart," which can be caused by a lack of water or calcium deficiency. Aphids can cause problems such as mottled leaves and twisted stems. Look closely for these small insects and blast them off with water or spray them with insecticidal soap. Since celery is part of the carrot family, you may get carrot rust flies that damage roots. The best way to avoid many celery problems to is to ensure that you grow it in a different part of the garden each year so the bugs and bacteria that cause problems won't be in the area.

Harvesting

I like to dig celery up by the roots with a shovel and then prune the roots back with pruners. It will store for a few weeks in the fridge. With the plants that mature later you can actually dig them up by the roots and put them in the root cellar, where they should last for a few months. There is nothing nicer than the taste of crispy celery with a meal.

I plant celery in a shallow trench and then backfill gradually to blanch it and keep the lower part white and tender.

Courtesy of Johnny's Selected Seeds
www.johnnyseeds.com

Celeriac

Celeriac is becoming quite popular and it's something you may want to try. Celeriac is like celery except that it's eaten for the root, which looks like a tropical forest plant, something like a kohlrabi. To eat it you remove the outer skin and eat the insides. I really like it. To me it tastes like celery, but it's stronger and nuttier. The nice thing about it is that it will store well since it's a root. So grow it the same way you would celery and make sure you dig up the whole root. The upper leaves will seem wimpy in comparison to those of regular celery because more effort is being put into the root. Celeriac is a great addition to soups and stews in the fall and will give whatever you add it to a rich celery taste.

24 Corn

There is a lot of talk about how much of the North American diet consists of corn and its many forms. Many of these aren't necessarily a good thing, like the high-fructose corn syrup that makes my Friday night Dr. Pepper so yummy! Drinking two liters of high-fructose corn-syrup-sweetened beverages a day does not make for a healthy diet, even if corn is a vegetable.

Eating corn grown from your garden, on the other hand, is a delicious and nutritious part of a healthy diet. Corn is a good source of the "B" vitamins, containing a quarter of the recommended daily intake of B1 or thiamin as well as B5 or pantothenic acid, which is essential for protein, lipid, and carbohydrate metabolism. It also helps your adrenal glands work properly and has the phytonutrients that are so important as an antioxidant.

I've always felt that I became a real vegetable gardener when I first started growing corn. Sort of a rite of passage into "gardener-hood," as it were. There's something about it. It's a big plant. It looks like what you see in a farmer's field. Many urban dwellers like to buy corn stalks to adorn their homes in the fall, but I've always preferred to have them in the garden. I love how noisy corn can be in the wind, especially in the fall as it starts to dry out and brown. This can be a bad thing if you were scared by the movie *Signs* or *Children of the Corn*, but I find it a wonderful and peaceful sound.

Corn is one of those classic sorts of vegetables that country folk have a lot of sayings about. "Plant corn when oak leaves are the size of a squirrel's ear." I realize you've probably been groaning more than laughing at my vegetable jokes since they are so "corny," but I'll take my lumps. I've read way too many dry gardening books. I love gardening and I think it's a blast, so the last thing I wanted to write was a gardening textbook. You should enjoy yourself in the garden, and you should enjoy reading a book about gardening.

Planting

Corn is a heavy-feeding and large plant, so you may want to wait until your garden has expanded before you give it a try. The biggest challenge with corn is pollination. When you look at the silky tassel of an ear of corn, you need to realize that each one of those strands of silk needs to be pollinated to form a corn kernel. So if pollen doesn't hit a strand, you'll end up with a gap in the row and you can end up with misshapen ears with irregular kernels. The key is to make sure the wind blows pollen onto all of those tassels. If you plant one long row of corn there's a good chance you'll have pollination problems. If, instead, you plant four shorter rows in more of a block formation, it's more likely the wind will blow the pollen around to each of the plants.

One of the biggest challenges of planting corn is deciding what variety to order from the seed catalog. There are usually pages of corn varieties,

This may be a bigger crop than you want to plant, but remember to plant corn in a box shape to ensure proper pollination.

and they all look fabulous. Ordering in winter will really make you long for those warm August days with a big plate of corn. With my admitted sweet tooth for Dr. Pepper (but only on Friday nights) I'm a big fan of sweet corn. My mother, on the other hand, always preferred the heavier, darker yellow types. I'm not a big fan of this type and I always felt as though I needed a hairbrush to dig the corn out of my teeth after eating it. That's the beauty of having so much choice. Each year I generally go with one cultivar that we know we like and then try a couple of others. I also make sure they have different maturity times so that I get some early and then have as extended a corn-eating season as possible. Keep in mind that when I suggest planting four rows in a square block you should do this all with the same seed. If you start mixing different varieties in each block you may get some unintended results. Or, as in the movie *Signs*, aliens will begin frequenting your corn patch, and no one wants to be bumping into aliens at night in the corn patch. Always be careful not to tell secrets in the cornfield, because there are way too many ears.

Some seeds catalogs will offer four kinds of sweet corn. Johnny's Seeds describes them this way:

Normal Sugary "su" will have moderate degrees of sugar.

Sugary Enhanced "se" will be sweeter and the kernels will be more tender.

Shrunken "sh2" is really sweet and is sometimes called "Super Sweet"

Synergistic has 75% "se" kernels and 25% "sh2." It should be picked when fully mature as the sugars develop later.

Make sure you plant corn in an area where you've added lots of compost or composted manure. When those plants are five or six feet high you'll get a sense of just how much energy they sucked out of the ground and converted from the sun, so make sure they have a good base to start. In the fall when you pull the stocks out you'll also get a sense of how far down the roots went to get

the nitrogen they need. Another advantage of that huge root system is to anchor the corn stalk during high winds.

You should direct seed corn into the ground once the soil is fairly warm 60°F (16°C). You can try and plant it earlier, but I have found that in cooler, wet soil the seeds have a tendency to rot and the germination rate is poor. It's worth waiting for an extra week or two so that you have good, consistent germination. I have experimented many times with getting some plants started earlier than I should and then planting some closer to the optimal specified date. Vegetables need sun and heat

to really grow quickly, and what inevitably happens is that regardless of when I start the early stuff, the plants mature at roughly the same time. At a certain point I just accept Mother Nature's wisdom rather than arguing. Michelle wishes I'd follow the same philosophy with her.

I plant my seeds between half an inch and one inch deep and actually tamp the soil down with my hoe so that the seed makes contact with the moist soil. Then I water the row well. I plant the seeds two to three inches apart, and once the plants are five or six inches high I thin them to about six inches apart. Once I started saving my own seed and planting more densely than this I created a huge problem for myself, because it's so hard to thin. You look at those lovely little plants and it breaks your heart to thin them. If you don't, though, you'll end up with lots of mediocre stalks rather than tall, healthy ones.

Since I have access to manure and compost it, I like to use it to top-dress corn. Halfway through the growing season I weed the corn and then put several inches of composted horse manure all around the plants. I really think this helps give the plants a nitrogen boost, and since it's usually starting to get drier in the summer heat the composted manure, which has some wood shavings in it, also serves as a good mulch to retain moisture.

If you are growing in a sandy soil, as I do, and

Corn is a heavy feeder and is a good candidate for drip irrigation, especially in this dry, sandy section of my garden.

are in a wind-prone area, you actually might want to hill up around the base of your corn stalks. Take your hoe or cultivator and drag some of the soil from the walkway between rows over around the base of the plants. This will help anchor top-heavy plants in a light soil. Watering the soil before a windstorm can help to add some weight to the soil holding the roots.

Some hybrid corn stalks send out extra shoots from the base. I consider these suckers and prune them off. They won't amount to much and take energy away from the main stalk. I always grew up thinking that you got multiple ears of corn on a single plant. There must have been a picture of one on the wall in my Grade Two class that I never got out of my mind. Most of my corn stalks only produce one ear. This year some of my Peaches and Cream had two. I tried to pick the biggest one fairly early, but most of the second ears didn't amount to much, so while it looks great to have more than one ear, one seems to be optimal in my growing zone.

Little Pests

The main problems with corn are corn borers and corn earworms. I have had good luck and get very few of these, which I think is because I rotate my

plantings and remove the corn stalks from the garden in the fall. Corn borers will overwinter in the stalks, so if you leave the stalks in the garden it's easier for the borers to jump to the new crop each year. Better to decorate the porch with the stalks in the fall and then compost them away from the garden. For the corn earworms you can spray with Bt or put a few drops of mineral oil on the silk after it wilts to discourage them from laying eggs.

Your corn might also get yellow, wilted leaves, which can be caused by nitrogen deficiency (time to top-dress), lack of water, which is easy to remedy, or one of the many blights out there. When you select corn, look for varieties that have resistance to these. Johnny's Seed Catalog, for instance, lists five blights, wilts, rust and smut and indicates which cultivars are resistant. And yes, you noticed the word "smut." Amazing how that jumps off the page at you! Smut is a fungal disease that causes galls to form on the ears. These galls start out white and then get spongy and filled with a black powder that looks like some prosthetic special effect from a horror movie. As soon as you see one of these be sure to remove the whole plant and throw it out. Don't compost it. That black powder is filled with spores from the fungus and these will blow all over your garden if you leave it too long. Get rid of it early. And yes, as your Sunday school teacher taught you, smut is a bad thing.

If you know someone who has grown corn in your area you may want to ask if they've noted any specific blights and diseases so that as you go through the seed catalog you can look for hybrids that are resistant.

Big Pests

When I grew corn in the city the squirrels loved it and generally got more corn than I did. I could have used a live trap to move them to another area of the city where people weren't growing corn. In the country my enemy is raccoons. They are smart, crafty little monsters and have ripe corn radar. I may never see or hear a raccoon anywhere near my garden the rest of the year, but somehow they know when there is mature corn in my garden and at some point I'll arrive in my garden first thing in the morning to find they've had an orgy of corn gorging. They really annoy me because they don't just take an ear and eat it. They open about 50 ears and take one bite out of each. You can use electric wire fences and live traps for raccoons, but I have a secret weapon. He's called "Morgan the Wonder Dog." I feed him and shelter him 50 weeks of the year, and he pays me back by sleeping in the garden for 2 weeks of the year. Morgan is a sheltie with thick fur who loves sleeping in dirt during the hot summer months. So at the height of corn season he sleeps in the garden to protect it from the marauding bandits. I explain the important nature of his task, and I praise him and thank him each morning when I let him out of the fenced garden, rewarding him with a treat fit for his nickname, a piece of Wonder bread. What is it with dogs and people food? He relishes the responsibility and acknowledgement. Michelle may love her cats, but they've never kept a raccoon out of the corn patch. Morgan the Wonder Dog, on the other hand, is the Tony Soprano of Cam's Corn Patch. "Woke up this morning, got myself a dog…."

Harvesting

I have grown corn for years and sold it to Desert Lake Gardens, which supplies organic produce to families in the city of Kingston near where I live. I've sold dozens and dozens of ears and yet I'm still not that confident about knowing when it's ready. I usually use the silk as my guide and wait until it has turned brown. In *Dick Raymond's Gardening Year* he suggests that you should pinch the top of the ear. If it comes to a point it still needs to grow, but if it's flat then the topmost kernels have fleshed out and it's ready.

I inevitably pull the husk back on an ear to see if it looks mature. If it's not and I leave the husk loosened it is more susceptible to pests, but since I grow a lot of corn I don't mind taking that risk. Once we get into harvesting mode sometimes I pick some a little early, but it just means that those smaller kernels will be even more tender.

Corn won't store too long, so we pick it and eat it right away. If you do have to keep it for a few days, leave it in its husk in a bucket with the  lower part of the ear in several inches of water. Some people can corn but we've become big fans of freezing it. Anytime we're having a feed of corn I always cook way too much. We generally cook it for five minutes in boiling water. Since we've already used the energy to heat that water up, it makes sense to cook extra to freeze. After the cobs cool off we cut off the kernels and put them in freezer bags. There is nothing like warming up frozen corn in the winter. It's like eating summer sunshine. Reminds me of the can of Florida Sunshine I bought as a kid and then opened years later only to discover that I'd been ripped off, because it was empty. You won't be disappointed with corn that you grew yourself.

Fresh, sweet, crisp, organic corn just picked off the stalk and ready for a corn roast.

25   Cucumbers

As an adolescent-like 50-year-old, I still like the idea of growing a vegetable that can make you burp. Have you heard of people who can burp the whole alphabet? It takes growing cucumbers to a whole new level of comic genius! Maturity has never been one of my strong points. There doesn't seem to be a definitive answer as to why some people burp when they eat cucumbers, and the "burpless cucumbers" in catalogs are often Asian varieties.

Sliced cucumbers are an essential element in those ubiquitous images of people at spas with their hair wrapped in a towel and mud on their face. Cucumbers contain silica, which is good for muscle and bone, and because of their high water content they are very hydrating, so putting them on sunburns and swollen eyes makes sense. You don't need to go to an expensive spa to do this, though. Cucumbers belong to the cucurbit family, sometimes called melons or gourds, that includes squashes, pumpkins, melons, and watermelons. When I forget their fancy name I just call them my "vine" plants.

Cucumbers are great in salads, and I love them with tomatoes and thinly sliced onions and let-tuce in a sandwich. It's like a salad bar on a bun.

Cucurbits are all bothered by the same insect pests and a number of wilts, mildews, and scabs, so you should make sure you don't plant cucumbers where other cucur-bits have grown in the last three or four years. The soil needs that time to rid itself of these problems. Cucumbers can climb really well because they send out curly tendrils that hold on as they climb, so they work well in a confined area and can even be grown in pots on your deck.

Planting

I usually start some seeds inside and plant some directly in the garden a week or two after the last frost, because cucumbers really like warmth to germinate. I plant them in hills with lots of com-posted manure. I hill up all the soil for a foot or two around the plant, and once I've got it about a foot wide I hollow out an eight- or ten- inch spot in the middle for the cucumbers. I like doing this because I can fill the hollow with water and have it stay put. It's like a mini swimming pool. By starting some seeds as transplants four or five weeks before the last frost and direct seeding, I usually end up with three or four good plants per hill, which is my goal. Sometimes cutworms lop them off, and sometimes they'll succumb to some unknown microscopic invader. By having four to six transplants per hill plus eight or ten seeds, I should end up with a couple that will survive to fruit.

I usually have two or three hills of cucumbers: a traditional slicing cultivar, a long English-style edible-skin type, and a pickling variety. And yes,

Cucumber plants in a hill with lettuce "sacrificial" plants to attract the cutworms first.

pickles are just small cucumbers! Who figured that out?

While some people suggest mulching cucurbits, mine always seem to have more than their share of cucumber beetles and squash bugs, and the mulch just gives them a good place to hide. I want to be able to see the little bugs to hunt them down and take them out before they do their damage.

Last year was the first year I tried growing cucumbers on a trellis, and I really liked it. It got the fruit off the ground, which made it easier to check for pests, and since they're heat loving I think getting them off the cool ground at night helped produce better cucumbers. I used string on a frame I built, but just putting some chicken wire on some wooden stakes would work fine. Put the trellis about six inches away from the plants, and once the plants get big enough and are starting to put out the curly tendrils, move them so that they can find the chicken wire and start climbing. Try and put the trellis east to west, so that the cucumber will be spread across this exposed to the southern sun.

Cucumbers send out both male and female flowers. You can tell the female flowers because they have a little cucumber between the stalk and the flower. The male flowers appear first and eventually fall off, so don't freak out if you start seeing flowers dropping off. If you see bees crawling in and out of the flowers you'll end up with the female shoots setting their fruit. Gardeners who use floating row covers to keep insects off their plants will find that the bees won't be able to do their pollination thing. If you're going to do this you'll have to hand pollinate, which involves getting a small paint brush and dusting it around the male flowers and then using the same brush to dust the female flowers. This will make you feel very powerful and Mother Nature-like. It's the way hybrid plants are created, as we'll discuss in Chapter 64 on seed saving.

Harvesting

With pickling cucumbers, start harvesting them when they're pickle size. With slicing cucumbers

you can let them get bigger. Be careful to hold the stem as you remove the cucumber so you don't take the whole plant with you. Most cucurbits have small thorns on the stems that can find their way into your hands, so either wear gloves or lightly scrape the stems off before you grab them. Plants will keep producing for an extended period of time, and I do try to have a later succession planting to keep them going as long as I can. While the leaves may succumb to the first frosts, the cucumbers will be fine for a little longer.

Growing cucumbers on a trellis makes for easy picking.

Pests

In some years my cucumber leaves will yellow and sometimes curl up and fall off. This can be caused by a number of things, but it's probably blight or a mosaic caused by aphids or cucumber beetles. The best defense is to try and grow cultivars that are resistant, and it makes sense to grow a few different varieties to increase the likelihood that one will have a good year. If the vines wilt suddenly, it's probably squash vine borers burrowing into the stems of the cucumbers. You'll recognize them by the pile of sawdust they dump out of the hole. Use a sharp knife to remove them and then put that section of the stem back into soil so it will regrow roots.

Cucumber beetles look like yellow ladybugs but a bit smaller, with either black spots or black stripes. They attack young leaves and leave them yellow and holey, but the biggest problem with them is that they often spread wilt, so you want to try and eliminate them as early as you can. I try and pick them off, but if you are having a real problem you can use a pyrethrin spray.

Squash bugs are prehistoric looking, up to

half an inch long and brownish black. You'll know you've found one when you squish it, because it

I usually have all my cucurbits or vines growing in the same area. Here are cucumbers, cantaloupe, watermelon, and squash.

lets out this really strong smell that's a mixture of vinegar and Irish Spring soap. It's crazy! You'll see their eggs on the underside of leaves, just like potato bugs. I squish both the adults and the eggs on the leaves and try and peer all around the base of the plant looking for any that are hiding. You can also put a board near the plants and check it regularly, because they'll like hiding there.

Cucumbers won't store that long, perhaps three to four weeks in the fridge or root cellar. This is why most people pick them when they're small and pickle them. There really is nothing nicer on a cold winter day than a bowl of rich homemade soup made from vegetables from the garden, with some fresh bread and pickles to garnish the plate and add a crispy bite to the meal.

26 Eggplant

When I was a kid I had a job cutting the lawn and weeding the garden for our neighbors the Cohanims. They were from the Middle East and they had this great vegetable garden. In the garden was the most bizarre plant I'd ever seen. It had green finger-like tendrils gripping this crazy purple fruit. The movie *Invasion of the Body Snatchers* with Donald Sutherland was out, and I was quite concerned that these plants would one day grab me from behind while I was weeding and create a zombie-like duplicate of me while I shriveled up into a dust ball. Now years later I chuckle, as eggplants have become a fairly big part of our diet.

We often roast eggplant and add garlic to make the wonderful, smoky *baba ghanouj* dip that we spread on pita bread or eat with nachos. It's also a great alternative to using veal (something that many consider an inhumane food) in a delicious dish of eggplant parmesan.

Heating-loving and blemish-free organic vegetables from the garden.

Eggplants have lots of the B vitamins (B1, B3, B6) and potassium and are an excellent source of fiber, especially when you leave that beautiful skin on. Some people actually call eggplant "aubergine" and I'm not sure what came first, the color or the eggplant. Eggplants are a very cool-looking vegetable and make an excellent addition to a front-yard flower garden. They produce wonderful purple flowers that become one of the most beautiful vegetables you can imagine. So get some in the garden this year—vegetable garden or flower garden!

Seed catalogs have some crazy eggplant varieties, and since it's a weird and wonderful plant to begin with these just add to the fun. They come in crazy colours, like white, and all sorts of crazy shapes. I usually like to stick with the standard egg-shaped, aubergine-coloured variety, but this year we did try an Asian-style that is long and slender. We were hoping to duplicate a dish that we have enjoyed often at one of our favorite restaurants in Ottawa, Ontario called "So Good". They make this incredible black bean eggplant dish that melts in your mouth and triggers the pleasure receptors on your taste buds helping you achieve nirvana. We haven't been able to reverse engineer it yet despite our constant pestering of the owner of the restaurant, Peter. The man is a genius, and he knows that as soon as I figure out how he makes this amazing dish he will have lost his best customer.

Planting

Eggplants are heat-loving plants that originated in the tropics, so they can be challenging to grow in colder, more northern growing zones. It took me years to get a reasonable harvest because I always put in my transplants on the weekend after the final frost. My attitude was, "Well, there's not going to be another frost, so I'm safe." Eggplants are like peppers, though, and if you put them out too early, those cool nights will cause problems later on. Now I wait until the middle of June, two or three weeks after the final frost date. Yes, it might seem awfully late, but it really is better to wait. Since you're busy enough on those early weekends anyway, it's good to have some planting to hold back.

Since I'm in a colder growing area and eggplants do best in warm conditions, I put my eggplant in the old barn foundation. They are in a raised bed which actually sits on a concrete floor, so they enjoy the added bonus of the sun warming up the concrete and radiating it back at night. We can still get cool nights once I've planted my eggplants, so the concrete walls help to both radiate heat and protect them from the cold. You might want to try a small greenhouse or similar structure to help the eggplants stay warm at night and on cloudy, cool days early in the season. Even a hoop-supported floating row cover will help.

This past summer was very wet and cool and the harvest was marginal. During previous summers that were hot and dry we enjoyed a bumper crop of eggplants. You can always tell a tropical vegetable because they love the heat!

Harvesting

We start picking eggplants when they get three or four inches long. You don't have to wait too long. You should use pruners or a sharp knife to harvest them rather than pulling them off, because they won't be released easily and you'll damage the branch and plant if you try to yank them off.

Pests

Eggplants are part of the solanum family, which includes potatoes, and Colorado potato beetles actually prefer eggplants, I guess because they have expensive, fancy tastes. Keep your eye on the underside of leaves. Look for the orange egg clusters and scrape them off if you see them. I find that since I put my eggplant plants out a bit later than my early potatoes I can usually eliminate most of these pests on my potato plants and they rarely affect my eggplants.

Eggplants can stand on their own, but a tomato cage ensures that the fruit stays off the ground.

27 Garlic

Finally, garlic! My favorite chapter! And favorite thing to grow! Oh, and potatoes. And onions. Anyway, I love garlic. I love to grow it. I love to eat it. I love to sell it. While it won't be a huge percentage of your diet by weight or volume, I think it's one of the coolest things to grow in the garden. If you have people coming for dinner, just sauté two or three heads in olive oil before they arrive and your house or apartment will smell like a five-star restaurant. As we walk around downtown Kingston and smell all the trendy restaurants pumping those wonderful aromas out on to the street to entice customers in, we realize "It's the Garlic!" It's that simple.

I think one of the reasons I'm so enamored with my garlic is that it took so long before I figured out how to grow it. It took years, in fact. I always planted it in the spring. You need to plant it in the fall. I planted some tiny little reject cloves from a neighbor and surprisingly they turned into crappy, useless little garlic heads. Then Michelle found me a great little book and we haven't looked back since.

This year we grew about 3,000 heads and sold some of it at a variety of local outlets. Garlic is extremely labor-intensive and time-consuming, and for what I sold it for I would have been much further ahead financially to flip burgers at a fast food restaurant or panhandle on Main Street. It doesn't matter. I enjoy every step in the process and there is nothing more satisfying that packaging up one-pound bags of garlic

Garlic cloves placed in trenches in October, ready to be covered over. Black buckets are always available to collect stones.

to sell.

One of the greatest things about garlic is that, like potatoes, after an initial investment in a few heads you should never have to buy them again. It's like Free Food for Life! Each year you'll eat some and hold some back to plant for the next year, and you'll just keep expanding your base. The 3,000 heads we grew this year started from a $10 investment in organic garlic that we made about 10 years ago at an environmental fair. At that time we bought about 20 heads with six to eight cloves in each. We planted those that fall and the following summer we harvested about 150 heads, 75 of which we ate and 75 of which we planted that fall. The 75 we planted amounted to 500 cloves, so the next year we had 100 heads to eat and 400 to plant, times seven cloves per head, so that's 2,800 heads the following year, and so on. We have gone to a few garlic festivals and added some new cultivars to the gene pool, but the bulk of what we grow today came from the original $10 investment. Try and get that kind of return on the stock market!

Hardneck / Softneck

There are two major types of garlic; softneck and hardneck. Softneck is nice if you want to braid it. Since I'm not patient enough to braid my garlic (heck, I'm challenged tying a knot in a tie once a decade for a wedding) I prefer hardneck. My heads are big and strong and I like the results. You should experiment with both and see what works for you. Hardneck is considered more winter hardy, and we have pretty cold winters here. Softneck will not send up scapes the way hardneck does. There is a third type of garlic called "elephant garlic," and as its name suggests, it's huge. It has a milder taste and is not as winter hardy as hardneck, so I don't grow it, but if you want a big harvest from a small space and don't mind milder-tasting garlic then give elephant a try.

Health Benefits

Garlic belongs to the Allium family of vegetables, which includes leeks and onions. Not only does garlic add a great deal of flavor, it also provides a number of important nutrients to your diet. It is a good source of manganese, vitamins B1, B6 and C, tryptophan, selenium, calcium, phosphorus, copper, and protein. The strong aroma of garlic, like that of onions, is caused by sulfur-containing compounds that are considered to be health promoting.

It is believed that garlic has a positive effect on your cholesterol levels. Garlic is also promoted as providing some prevention against many types of cancer, including breast, ovarian, and prostate. Garlic has been touted as an aide in the prevention of heart disease as well as common colds, flu, and stomach viruses.

Planting

I plant my garlic anytime from late September to November, depending on how busy I am. You can plant before or after a frost, but I like to wait for a frost so that I don't get too much growth before winter. A garlic head is made up of 6 to 10 cloves. I break apart a head and plant the cloves about three to six inches apart, about two inches deep. This is deeper than I'd plant seeds, but I do want the cloves to have a bit of protection from the really cold weather. I have mulched the garlic some years to protect it from the cold weather, but it does just fine even with our consistently below zero (Celsius) weather during the winter.

With the volume of garlic I grow, I now plant three rows about six to eight inches apart, and then leave two feet between the next three-row planting. This way I can get a cultivator between the three tightly spaced rows for weeding and get the rototiller between the garlic row groupings.

When you're planting garlic, make sure you plant it so that the bottom of the clove is pointing down. If you look at the cloves closely as you break them up you'll probably see small root buds already starting. Push these down into the soil and then cover them back over with lots of well-composted soil. In the fall the clove will send out roots and start getting established. Some years when I have planted early the garlic actually sends up its first green shoot before the snow flies. It's pretty cool to go out after a light snow and see the lovely green shoots sticking up through the snow. Garlic is obviously a pretty hardy plant. Most of us have planted tulips and other flower bulbs in the fall before; this time you're just planting something that when chopped and heated in olive oil sends your olfactory receptors "to the moon!"

In the spring, garlic will be the first thing up in the garden. It will eventually send out six or seven leaves, and then it will send up a seed shoot that will form a cluster of bulbils or miniature cloves. This seed stem is called a "scape," and if you leave it alone it will become a curly, pigtail-like growth with a seedpod on the end. You could let this go and harvest the seeds, but if you leave it the bulb will put all its energy into the seeds and forget about the clove. So you want to cut this off. We go down the rows with pruners lopping them off. You can use these scapes in a variety of ways. You can cut them up and fry them to add to pasta or a nice omelet or add them to a stir-fry.

This is probably more garlic than you'll grow in your garden.

It's always difficult to remove these scapes because they are a beautiful addition to the garden, but you want all the plant's energy to go towards forming a nice big head, so they have to go. Most softneck garlic won't send up a scape, so you won't be faced with the agonizing decision to lop it off.

Garlic scapes on hardneck garlic should be removed so that all the energy is diverted into the developing head.

Stop watering your garlic a week or two before you harvest it. The dryer it is when harvested the better.

Harvest

I generally harvest garlic about the third week in July. This may seem early, but by then it has done most of its growing. Remember that it has been in the ground and growing since you planted it in the fall. Once the bottom two leaves turn brown, I start harvesting it. Hopefully you haven't had too much rain prior to harvesting, because you want it as dry as possible. You can use a shovel to loosen your garlic or if you have good big strong heads like mine you can just pull them up by the stalks.

I shake off the loose dirt and try not to bump the heads together too much because they will bruise. The long roots tend to hold the dirt, so you need

Here a garlic scape has been left to develop. It's better to use actual heads for seed for next year rather than these bulbils.

to dry the garlic before you start preparing it for storage. We dry it by hanging it all in our horse barn where it's protected from the sun and the rain with a breeze blowing through to help with the drying process. We prepare it for hanging by gathering up 10- 12 garlic plants. Holding them in one hand, we begin gathering up their leaves in the other hand as we wrap them around the bunch. Once we've gathered and wound them up enough that they are bundled together, we tuck the loose ends in and hang the bunch up on a nail. We use racks that I made with long, thin pieces of wood. I hammered a nail every six to eight inches or so, just enough so that the nail is held firmly in the wood but enough of the nail sticks out so that we can hang garlic on it.

Garlic needs to be out of direct sunlight while it's drying, so a shed or garage is a good place to hang it. If some breeze will circulate around it that's good too. You want to leave it for three or four weeks so that the outside layers of skin and dirt dry well.

This year we had a very wet July, which meant that the heads were wet when we harvested them. We knew from our experience the previous year, also quite wet, that the garlic did not store as well because of the moisture, so the better you dry it the better it will last the winter.

Preparing to Store

After the garlic has spent three or four weeks in the barn and is well dried, we take the bundles down from the racks. We cut the heads off the stalks and gather up the stalks to add to the compost pile. To clean the garlic, I sit with a bucket between my legs and pick up each head, cut off the roots, trim the stalk leaving half an inch or so, and then take an old toothbrush and carefully flake off two or three layers of skin. Each of those six or seven large leaves of the plant corresponds to a layer of skin around the cloves inside the garlic head. So if you take two or three layers off, you should still have three or four more layers underneath for protection. And remember that when you remove these, each clove is individually wrapped as well.

Garlic is ready to be harvested fairly early in the season. Watch for the bottom two leaves to start turning brown. Don't leave it too long or you'll lose some of that protective skin when it dries. Wire mesh wagons like this allow dirt to fall through and are great for drying.

If this were man-made packaging, you'd probably think of garlic as being over-packaged. It's all organic and natural packaging, though, and shows that nature intended it to store well. I always marvel at the miracle of it all.

Once you've flaked off those outer layers, which are probably banged up and dirty, you're left with beautiful, clean, white skin and an amazing head of garlic that will lower your cholesterol and reduce your risk of heart disease. If you grow enough garlic it will elevate not only your good cholesterol but also your oneness with the universe as you sit mindfully cleaning the heads and solving the great mysteries of the cosmos. You can't get that from whacking a little white ball around prime agricultural land trying to get it to land in a hole!

Storing

Garlic should be kept in a cool, dark place but not in the root cellar or fridge. We actually store it in our bedroom because it's farthest from the woodstove and is on the north side of our house, so the garlic stays quite cool. I have to admit that the garlic has been working amazingly well, because we have never, and I mean ever, had a vampire in our room. And if you see what the kids these days are reading and watching, there are vampires everywhere! Yay garlic!

I know very few people who don't love garlic, and homegrown is so much better than what you can buy in the grocery store. I would never be critical of other people's customs, but much of the garlic we get in North America comes from China. When you start growing it you'll realize just how time-consuming it can be and how on a large scale having access to cheap labor is the only way to keep the costs down. The garlic grown in China is often fertilized with "humanure" (human waste). Even though I'm sure it's relatively safe to fertilize with humanure, I would much prefer to know that my garlic came from my garden and was fertilized with the healthy compost I created and watered with rainwater from my rain barrels. Sometimes a low price doesn't represent what's best for you.

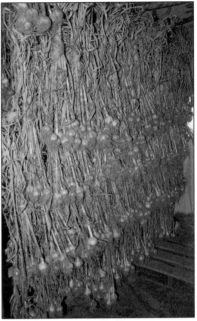

One of our four drying racks where the garlic spends three to four weeks. Air circulation helps speed the drying process.

After the garlic has dried, take a toothbrush and peel back and remove the dirty outer layers to expose the clean, white skin underneath. Don't take too much; leave some to protect the cloves inside.

28   Herbs

Fresh herbs are an amazing way to enhance the fantastic taste of those fabulous vegetables you've worked so hard to grow. They add nuance to the meal and can really enhance the visual appeal of the food on your plate. You can also use them to improve the name of otherwise fairly plain dishes. I always impress breakfast guests with my "basil-infused scrambled eggs" and I like to serve dinner guests our "rosemary and thyme roasted new potatoes." You've heard dishes described this way at fancy restaurants and it's really just an effort to get you to part with more of your hard-earned money. I think it makes more sense to make these delicious treats at home with herbs and vegetables from your own garden.

Many people are looking for alternative methods to get and stay healthy. Many people have discovered the magic of herbs. Many herbs can be fairly obscure and hard to find, so I've kept my herb section fairly mainstream. Most of us think about herbs in their traditional sense as a way of seasoning and enhancing other foods, but many of the common herbs have beneficial effects beyond adding some taste and additional fiber. You've probably heard that a can of ginger ale can help settle an upset stomach, so you're already aware of the health benefits of herbs. They provide lots of other benefits with their antioxidant and anti-inflammatory effects and are also a good source of vitamins and trace minerals. Sure, they're pretty to look at and smell great and make things taste better, but they can help in a variety of other ways as well.

There are dozens of herbs you can grow, but I'm just going to describe the ones I grow on a regular basis. As you expand your garden repertoire each year you'll probably start adding more herbs, and you may also start growing them in amongst your flower garden to keep more room available for vegetables in the garden.

I never seem to have problems with herbs and I think you'll probably find them pretty pest- and problem-free as well. Lots of sun, consistent water, and rotating them to new places each year are what you need to keep them thriving.

Basil

Luckily the first herb in my alphabetical list is also the one I grow the most of: basil. There is simply nothing like the smell of basil. It's one of the secrets we use to impress friends when we deliver a box of vegetables to them during the summer months. We always make sure to tuck a few big stalks of basil into each box of veggies and it makes the box smell heavenly. It suggests the essence of someone with a green thumb even if you're still a rookie gardener.

Basil is a good source of vitamin K as well as iron, calcium, vitamins A and C, manganese, magnesium, and potassium. Basil contains flavonoids, which have been shown to protect cell structures from radiation from the sun or other sources. Basil contains lots of (E)-beta-caryophyllene (BCP) that some studies have shown has an anti-inflammatory effect that helps fight arthritis or inflammatory bowel disease. It's just like my wife's description of me: how can someone who looks so good be so talented? Or in the case of basil, how can something that looks, smells, and tastes so great be so damn good for you? Okay, I'll come clean here; Michelle has never said that about me that I know of. She should though.

You can grow basil from seed in the garden but we like to start it inside in cell packs. We also keep starting some seeds in cell packs well into the summer to set out later. Basil seeds are very small and hard to handle in the garden. You can be a little more careful when you plant them first in cell packs. If you end up with three or four plants in each cell pack, once they've got about four leaves you can take them out and separate them into their own cell. Then when you're ready to transplant them they'll have had a good head start. We put the first plants out after the danger of frost has passed. Then I keep setting them out every couple of weeks until August. With succession plantings I have fresh, tender plants ready to harvest for a good part of the summer.

As the basil plants get larger you'll find that they flower and then go to seed. You should cut off these flowers to encourage more growth elsewhere in the plant. With full sun and consistent moisture my basil always thrives.

The Johnny's Select Seeds catalog has almost two and a half pages of different basil cultivars. If you love basil as I do I suggest you splurge and try lots of them. They have some specially designed for pesto, Thai basil, sweet basil, purple basil, lemon basil—the variety is fantastic! Reading pages like this in January and February makes you ache to be out in the garden harvesting herbs and vegetables.

Borage

Several years ago I grew borage and enjoyed seeing its beautiful, edible blue flowers. The seed oil is a rich source of gamma-linolenic acid (GLA), which is a fatty acid used to treat problems with inflammation and autoimmune diseases. While the effectiveness of GLA in this regard may be open to debate, using borage flowers in salads or as a garnish on your plate or in a glass of iced tea is simply beautiful. Be careful, though, because I planted a few plants and they were monstrous and took up a huge area. The bees absolutely love borage, so if you want to encourage bees to visit your garden and help with pollination, plant some.

Chamomile

Most of us have heard of chamomile tea, and many of us find it a very soothing herbal tea to aid diges-

tion and help us fall asleep. After a day of weeding and watering the garden you'll be less likely to need help to sleep, but nevertheless it's a wonderful herb to grow. The plants are large and produce small, daisy-like flowers. If you are space restricted you may want to  limit how much chamomile you plant because, like borage, the plants can get very big.

Chives

I love chives because they are a rugged perennial that comes up year after year and spreads with each successive growth. They're also one of the earliest green things in the garden and are a constant garnish on my plate and in just about anything we prepare for a few weeks in the spring. Later chives send out a beautiful purple flower that bees love. Chives are an excellent addition to any perennial garden. They're like green onions that spring up through the snow and are ready to green up with the early spring sun.

Cilantro/Coriander

Remember the Certs TV commercials—"It's two, two, two mints in one!" Well cilantro is just that. The foliage is a wonderful herb and a key ingredient in salsa and Indian dishes, and the seeds, which are edible, are called coriander. Chopping fresh cilantro into your fresh salsa made with tomatoes just harvested from your garden  is pretty fantastic. Coriander seed oil is said to have fungicidal and antibacterial properties and is thought to chelate or remove heavy metals from the body. This herb smells great, tastes great, and is good for your health. The plants can be very tall. You can keep taking leaves off as you need them. As they mature the flowers will turn brown, and this is when you'll want to harvest the seeds. I always miss some of the seeds and I end up with cilantro volunteers starting all over my garden every year. I rarely have to start any new plants; I just transplant the volunteers into the herb section each year.

Cumin

As we've evolved our diet into a plant-based one we've grown to love Indian food. We have begun to crave curry if we don't eat it often enough. Cumin is a common ingredient in Indian cooking. We tried growing it this year, which can be a challenge in northern growing areas like mine. It didn't thrive and I think it was because we had such a cool, wet summer. Cumin prefers hot, dry climates. If we'd started it indoors earlier and had a typical hot, dry summer we might have had better success. Cumin seeds are the second most popular spice worldwide after pepper, so next year we'll pamper our cumin and hope to grow some ourselves.

Dill

Pickles are the quintessential canned vegetable and dill is the quintessential pickling spice. The plants are tall and fantastic looking. Like so many spices

dill is best fresh and loses some of its flavor when dried, which is why it's so good to use for pickling and for flavoring summer dishes and fall soups. It likes a long, hot season, so start it indoors and give it a fair amount of room, because the plants can be big.

Fennel

You've got to love a plant that smells like licorice, and that's fennel. It looks surprisingly like dill and the leaves are a nice addition to salad and cole slaw. The seeds can be used for flavoring as well. We have some Tom's of Maine toothpaste with fennel right now, and it's very pleasant tasting. Fennel is a perennial, so plant it where you don't mind it coming back on a yearly basis.

Mint

Have you seen the horror movie *Mint Took Over my Garden!* Well it could be a title of a scary film! Mint is a very vigorous perennial which can get highly invasive, so make sure you plant it where you don't mind it spreading. It may be a good candidate to grow in a container where you can control it. It smells amazing and the bees love the flowers. Mint is considered a good companion plant

for discouraging insects such as white flies and aphids, so you could put a small plant near a vegetable that you've had aphid problems with, but be careful that it doesn't take over the area. Most of us are familiar with mint being recommended for stomachaches, and mint tea is a very popular herbal tea. You can get spearmint and peppermint seeds in many catalogs.

Oregano

It's amazing how I can be weeding around the herbs and suddenly find myself craving pizza. I don't need an excuse to crave pizza, but the smell of fresh oregano makes me crave anything with tomato sauce. Oregano is a great antioxidant with its phenolic acids and flavonoids and it has antibacterial properties that fight food-borne pathogens. According to *Medical News Today*, researchers from a UK university and members of local businesses and an NGO in India have discovered that the essential oil of Himalayan oregano has strong antibacterial properties and even kills the hospital superbug MRSA. Methicillin-resistant staphylococcus aureus or MRSA is one of those super bugs that we have almost no effective means of treatment for and it spreads around hospitals easily. The researchers hope these findings will lead to the development of hand soaps and surface disinfectants containing oregano in hospitals and other health care settings. I'll bet the cafeterias in hospitals with oregano-flavored hand soaps will have people lined up all the way out the door for pizza and pasta with tomato sauce every lunch hour.

Oregano is a perennial that loves the sun.

Parsley

If you grow only one herb, make it parsley. Once it gets growing it is very hardy and should come back each year. It is as versatile a garnish as you'll ever get. It's a great source of vitamin K and also contains vitamins A and C as well as iron and calcium. It has a number of medicinal uses as a diuretic and digestive supplement, and if you've just had a meal with lots of garlic, chewing some parsley will help your breath.

Parsley seeds have a coating that can make them difficult to germinate. Sometimes planting them in the garden in the fall helps them get going. You can also try putting them in the spring garden while it's still cool. If you have trouble getting them going consider buying a plant at the garden center. Parsley is a perennial. You can prolong the season by transplanting some into pots in the summer to bring inside in the fall or can grow it in a pot or container right from the start. We grow both the traditional curly-leafed parsley as well as a flat Italian parsley.

Parsley is considered a great companion plant because it attracts predatory wasps, which in turn kill some garden pests. Its strong smell is said to help repel pests around tomatoes.

Rosemary

If you really want to impress your guests, along with your "basil-infused frittata" serve some "rosemary-roasted new potatoes." Have your butler serve it and they'll think you've won the lottery. Rosemary is a beautiful, compact plant that looks like a pine shrub because of its needles. It should come back each year as a perennial. It contains nutrients that help aid digestion and stimulate the immune system. It adds a wonderful flavor to meals and you can also use it to make your home smell great.

Sage

No Simon and Garfunkel set is complete without the "Parsley, Sage, Rosemary and Thyme" for sale at Scarborough Fair. Sage has been used throughout history to flavor food and for its medical properties. It has some of the same antioxidant and anti-inflammatory characteristics of rosemary and may also boost brain function, which we can all use. Sage is a beautiful plant, and the variety we have keeps coming back each year and has a dusty grey-green hue to it. Once you get a plant going it will attract bees to your herb garden, and it has a wonderful aroma.

Thyme

Anchoring the Scarborough Fair foursome, thyme is a real medicinal powerhouse and is an excellent source of vitamin K and iron. It has the essential oil thymol, which is the main antiseptic ingredient in mouthwash. Prior to antibiotics it was used to medicate bandages because of its antiseptic properties. Herbal tea made from thyme can be used to treat coughs and bronchitis, and it's helpful for respiratory infections. It almost seems like a waste to flavor food with it.

Thyme is a compact perennial and bees love its flowers, so having it in the garden will help all those tomatoes and melons and apple trees by providing bees for pollination. It has delicate needle-shaped leaves and is easy to grow in full sun.

29 Kale

We like to joke about kale at our house. Whenever we try and pretend we're healthy vegetarians, we brag to other people about how much kale we eat. Kale is just one of those insanely healthy green, leafy vegetables. If you got cancer and wanted to do everything possible to knock it out of your body, going on an all-kale diet would probably do the trick. The cancer cells would get a load of it and just give up.

The problem is that it tastes like something a horse or giraffe would like to chew on. Sorry if I've offended the Kale Growers Association, but I just haven't been able to develop a taste for kale yet. I know lots of people who love it, and I'm working on it. I grow kale, and eat some kale, but that doesn't mean I have to like it.

Kale is a brassica (that doesn't start with "B" or "C") and contains just about every vitamin known to man. It's got phytonutrients to prevent just about every cancer out there, and studies show that when you chew cruciferous vegetables like kale it tells the liver to produce enzymes that detoxify cancer-causing chemicals, basically convincing them it's better to just do themselves in rather than hang around Kaletown. Kale has vitamin A and beta-carotene to help your eyes, lots of vitamin C to protect against arthritis, manganese for a healthy nervous system, calcium for healthy bones…just let me know when you want me to stop. Have I convinced you yet? You need to grow kale, and you need to eat that kale. Leaving it for the deer to eat in the winter will not help your body fight off cancer. I must remind myself of this each time I harvest kale and walk glumly to the kitchen as if I'm about to have a root canal. Michelle has to tell me to "stop your whining and eat your kale, Cam!"

Growing

Kale is really easy to grow and lasts really well into the fall, so you can enjoy it right up until the snow starts flying! Isn't that great? I usually start a few plants in the late winter to plant in the garden early, and then I start a few more in the spring to plant in the late spring and early summer. Because it will do so well in cold weather I like to start lots to mature later, after the lettuce and most other green, leafy vegetables have been zapped by the frost. Frost seems to enhance the taste of kale.

Kale plants can get quite large, so leave a good foot of space between them. Once they're in all I do is make sure they get water and are weeded and they do just great. Since they're a brassica I would expect them to get cabbage loopers and cabbage worms, but I rarely see these pests on kale. I think these insects are in fact brassica snobs and prefer the snootier, high-class broccoli, cabbage, and cauliflower instead, not that I blame them. Whoops. Sorry. My lack of enthusiasm for the kale wonder plant reared its ugly head again.

You are best to pick leaves before they get to their maximize size. In fact, the smaller the better. If you harvest the ones closer to the top, don't get too close to the central growing stock, which will continue to produce new leaves.

Still thriving after several hard frosts, kale is a nutritional cold-weather powerhouse.

COLLARDS

Many seed catalogs list collards or collard greens" along with kale since they are from the same family. Collards are very popular in warmer climates like the southern US but can be grown like kale in the north. While they can be eaten fresh or in salads, with their slightly bitter taste they are often sautéed in butter or oil with garlic and onions and salt.

Like kale, collards are a nutritional powerhouse full of sulforaphane with its anticancer properties. A substance called dindolylmethane in brassicas such as collard greens triggers the body's immune response, which includes antiviral, antibacterial, and anticancer activity. All right then, I'm sold. As I write this in October my kale has had some frost, so it's at its tasty best. I will be cooking it up with a whack of garlic and salt and lovin' it! Now if I could just order it at McDonald's!

30   Kohlrabi

In terms of sheer bizarreness, nothing looks cooler in your garden than kohlrabi. It's as though little alien spaceships have landed right next to your lettuce. Kohlrabi look like the original Russian Sputnik satellite. They are in fact another healthy brassica and one to consider, since they will mature quickly in the spring before you have broccoli and cauliflower to eat.

Kohlrabi have a crisp, apple-like white flesh that has a nutty flavor if you eat them raw and tastes more like cabbage if you cook them.

Planting

You can plant kohlrabi before the last frost so as to enjoy them early and again in late July or early August to harvest in the cooler weather. I start a few plants indoors in the late winter to put out in late April for my spring harvest. Then I start some in seed packs in May and June to put out later in July. I could start the seeds directly in the garden for that later planting, but I find that by then I'm pretty distracted with weeding and watering. If kohlrabi are started in cell packs it's much easier to pop the small plants into a spot where I've already harvested something. I grow a lot of garlic, so when I harvest it in the third week of July kohl-

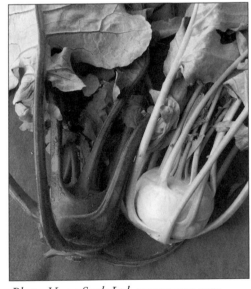

Photo: Veseys Seeds Ltd, www.veseys.com.

rabi are one of the succession vegetables I plant in its place.

Kohlrabi should have the same pests as the other brassicas, but I've never had any pest problems with them. They grow quickly and don't need a particularly fertile soil. The trick is to not let them get too big because they'll start to get tough. You should harvest them when they are about the size of a tennis ball. And believe me, if you let them go they will get much bigger than that.

I have stored kohlrabi for about a month in the root cellar. They should last longer than cabbage since they're more like turnips or beets but won't last the whole winter, so try and eat them early.

31   Leeks

My daughter Nicole loves leeks, so I grow leeks for her every year. I like them too, but you'll find that you start taking great joy in growing food for other people when you discover what they like. It's similar to a theme I share in my book *Thriving During Challenging Times.* So often accomplishing the most basic tasks, like cutting firewood or growing food, can bring you the greatest joy. Whenever my 98-year-old grandmother raves about how fabulous my potatoes are, I take great joy in such a simple accomplishment. So once you find your "vegetable groove," exploit it and relish it. Being identified by your prowess at growing exceptional-tasting and healthy vegetables is really a pretty fine thing.

Leeks are a mild member of the onion family and we often make potato leek soup as the foundation of a winter evening meal. They can handle frost well so I like to have lots in the garden in the fall.

Planting

Leeks take a long time to germinate and grow in preparation for planting into the garden, so they should be one of the first seeds you sow indoors in the winter, 10 to 12 weeks before the last frost date. When you look at the lovely photos of leeks in seed catalogs you'll notice that the white area above the root extends three to five inches up to the first green leaves. Leeks won't develop this way on their own. If you want to achieve this you'll have to hill the soil up around them to blanch them and keep the lower section white. If you don't it's not a problem; you'll just have more green in the lower region.

I usually plant mine in a trench about six inches below the soil line. Then once they're established I start backfilling the trench, which blanches them. I have a tendency to plant onions quite close together and then thin them as the season progresses, but I don't plant as many leeks. They grow very slowly, and I plant them six inches apart right from the start to avoid having to thin them. I also find that I don't usually eat them much in the summer and prefer them as a fall thing, sort of like football.

I also buy some leeks from the local greenhouse. These are well established, but their roots have become densely intertwined while they've been growing. If you try and just pull them apart you'll lose a lot of the roots, so I place them in a water bucket and swirl them around to remove the soil and loosen the root mass. I carefully remove the leeks one at a time preserving as much of the root as I can. Then I place the transplants in the trench and backfill. I then go down the row and press down on both sides of the plant and get it to stand up straight. It will probably right itself and begin growing towards the sun, but I like straight leeks so I do everything I can to get them growing straight. Then as the season progresses I pull more soil up around the base of the plants to blanch them.

I do think that leeks taste best in the fall, which is the other reason to wait a bit. You can keep harvesting leeks right through the winter if you mulch them. Cover them with a really thick twelve-inch layer of straw or hay. The first year I tried mulching them I think I put about six inches on, and when I went to dig them up they were pretty much frozen. Even so, when we fried them in butter and put them in soup they were especially tasty. The extreme cold had caused wild things to happen with the sugars in the plant, converting them to more complex carbohydrates or some crazy natural process which just enhanced the flavor. I wouldn't recommend doing this, though, because later we had a thaw and the ones that had frozen started to rot.

You can also dig some leeks with their roots and put them into sand and keep them in the root cellar. I have never had any pest problems with leeks, which is another reason to grow them.

The matted roots from greenhouse leeks can be hard to separate. Swirling them in water and gently working them apart will keep as much root as possible.

After placing them in the trench and backfilling, straighten each leek by packing the soil down around the plant.

32   Lettuce

Remember that great 1970s movie *That's Entertainment*, with the theme song that included the line "Lettuce, entertain you." What lettuce had to do with that movie I never understood. But for sheer entertainment value nothing can compete with the lettuce sections of seed catalogs. The lettuce sections are fantastic. They are huge. They are colorful. And the variety and shapes and colors of lettuce today are mind-boggling. I grew up eating iceberg lettuce. It was like eating crunchy water. I believe it could be the only vegetable that actually does not contain any dietary fiber. All right, I'm being a bit hard on it. I think it's the kind of lettuce they still use on fast-food burgers.

Most of us have made the leap to lettuce with a little higher roughage value. I still love iceberg on a veggie burger with fries at Harvey's, but I'm not there for my gastro intestinal health. It's just a treat once in awhile. If you haven't done so already, it's time to start expanding your lettuce world.

Lettuce is a good source of vitamin A and folic acid and is a low-calorie, fat-free vegetable. The challenge is to eat it in a "fat-free" or as low-fat a way as possible. Smothered in Caesar salad dressing and topped with grated parmesan cheese does not fit this bill. You should try experimenting with more oil-and-vinegar-based salad dressings or start making your own. Lettuce is a great source of fiber and roughage for your diet, so the less fat you add to it the better. Caution: Do not eat a big salad before long drives or working with heavy equipment. Lettuce contains lactucarium, which is a mild opiate. The Romans and Egyptians ate it at the end of a meal to induce sleep. So put down those sleeping pills and chow down on a big salad to cure your insomnia.

Varieties

There are hundreds of different cultivars of lettuce, but here are the main varieties you're likely to find in seed catalogs.

Leaf – There are hundreds of different types of leaf lettuce in every shape, size, and color.

Butterhead – This lettuce comes from Europe and is considered to have a buttery taste. It has ruffled leaves around a bunched head. Buttercrunch is my very favorite lettuce to grow and eat.

Romaine or Cos – This is my second-favorite and is the backbone of a good Caesar salad. There's nothing more gratifying than growing a head of romaine lettuce that looks just as good as the ones in the grocery store or farmer's market. You feel like a real farmer when you can grow a nice head of romaine.

Iceberg or Crisphead – The lettuce we grew up on, with the tight heads and crunchiness, high on crunch but low on flavor.

Summer Crisp or Batavian – Crisp like romaine or iceberg but sweet and not bitter. Probably a good transition lettuce if you still like iceberg but think that perhaps it's time to embrace all those exotic leaf lettuces.

Asian Greens – You can't be sure what part of a seed catalog you'll find these in, but many Asian greens are leafy or lettuce-like, even though they may appear in other sections of the catalog.

Mesclun and Lettuce Mixes

If you really want to impress your friends sometime, tell them about your mesclun addiction. They'll assume you mean mescaline or 3,4,5-trimethoxyphenethylamine, a psychedelic alkaloid drug made famous in movies, but you'll actually mean the amazing salad mixes so many seed catalogs offer today. They have a wide assortment of colors and tastes and interestingly shaped leaves. They make a salad a work of art, and when you find a nice balsamic vinegar and oil dressing they taste fantastic, add great fiber to your diet, and make you want to eat something that's good for you without a whack of fat.

Planting

Lettuce is really easy to grow, so it's one of the best vegetables to start with as a new gardener. It has fairly shallow roots and needs a compost-rich spot to grow in. I always start some in seed trays four or five weeks before the last frost date. I sprinkle a few seeds into each cell and then separate them into individual cells once they germinate. They like warmth to germinate. Once established, lettuce can handle some cold, so I start putting the plants out in the cold frame as we get closer to the final frost date to harden them off. Once I can get the garden rototilled I plant some lettuce. If we get a warm spell it will germinate and grow. If we don't get a warm spell, I just plant it again later. Lettuce is also one of those crops that will self-seed, so each spring there will be lots of volunteers sprouting up where you had lettuce the previous year. I usually transplant these to one of my new rows. I call these plants that start on their own "volunteers."

Around my final frost date I start planting half rows of lettuce. I plant the remainder two or three weeks later so the lettuce is staggered as it matures. With a combination of volunteers, transplants, and direct-sown seed, I'll have a good supply of lettuce all season. I keep planting some every couple of weeks. Lettuce does not like really hot weather, which is why it's nice to start some in trays that you can keep out of the worst heat of the day. When I dig my garlic up near the end of July I plant more lettuce after rototilling this area. I keep planting it every couple of weeks in August as well, because it will handle the cold. In August

When my lettuce goes to seed I save the seed pods so that next year I can plant lots of it and thin it regularly for salads.

I also plant some in the cold frame and I'll be able to harvest it until December.

Lettuce likes to grow quickly and unencumbered by weather extremes, so try to keep it well watered. While some plants prefer not to have water on their leaves, lettuce doesn't mind it, so it's a fine plant to water with a watering can or a spray mister on your hose. If you see the lettuce bolting, or going to seed, this usually means it's been too dry or you've had too much heat for it. This is why it's a good idea to keep planting it so that you have it maturing at different times. When lettuce bolts it sends up a main shoot where small flowers bloom. Each one of these flowers has seeds in it. If

your lettuce has bolted, just let it go, and once the flowers have formed their seeds pods, grab these to plant next year. If you let the seeds fall on their own that area of the garden will be full of volunteers next spring!

Since lettuce doesn't like the brutal heat and would actually prefer some shade during hot summer afternoons, it's a good crop to plant interspersed with other larger plants. You could plant some under your broccoli or cauliflower plants, which provide excellent big leaves to shade the lettuce. You could even start some with your corn.

I like to harvest my own lettuce seeds, so I always have lots of them and I tend to plant them fairly densely, especially leaf lettuce. I know I'm going to be thinning all summer and fall as we make salads, so I don't mind having lettuce pretty thick to start with, which gives lots of room to expand I as pull mature leaves out of the spots where the lettuce is most dense.

Lettuce seeds are very small, so if you want to be organized and plant them in rows you may want to purchase one of the inexpensive mini hand seeders that you see in seed catalogs and at garden centers. You put some seeds into the seeder and then set the dial according to how quickly you want them to come out. Then you can go down the row tapping it, and the seeds will fall out. In my case I have so many seeds that I've saved each year that I just sprinkle them in fairly densely and then thin them once they get going. Lettuce thinning is just harvesting those first spring salads, so it works out great.

Since lettuce won't store too long it's a crop you use in succession plantings. And if you build yourself a cold frame you can keep going as long as possible.

Pests

I have this fantastic organic pest control book and it has three pages of potential problems with lettuce: yellow leaves, mottle leaves, and just about everything else you can imagine. I have had very few problems with lettuce. I make sure my garden has lots of compost and composted manure. I keep my lettuce watered. I move it each year to a new spot. I plant a wide variety of types. That's about it. The last two summers have been wet so I've had more slugs than usual, which I've been trapping with my beer traps. Yes, that's beer and not "bear" traps. I'll describe these more fully in Chapter 60.

33 Okra

One of the neatest things about my garden is the old barn foundation where I grow my heat-loving plants. This past summer I had eggplants, peppers, some tomatoes and sweet potatoes growing there. For the first time I also tried growing Okra. I had been interviewed on a southern radio station about the gardening DVD I produced, and the interviewer raved about okra, so I figured I'd better get growing it. I placed it in the garden near where I have some of the to-matoes we use for pasta sauce, a cultivar called "Roma". So whenever I had someone tour the garden and I pointed out the okra, I also pointed out the tomatoes and explained that I called this area of the garden "okra-roma".... Where the wind comes sweeping down the plain… and yes, I burst into my best musical rendition of the classic song. Some people laughed as I'd hoped, most of them groaned, and several ran screaming never to be seen again. What can I say, like Rodney Dangerfield "I get no respect for my vegetable comic genius."

Our favorite food to eat at restaurants is In-dian food, and while I had eaten okra many times this was the first year I grew it. I assumed it really was a southern heat loving plant explaining why it's so popular in places like India and in southern US cooking where it ends up in "gumbo". While it wasn't a huge harvest I did get some fruit from the plants and they are simply beautiful to watch grow. With the amazing flower they produce this is another vegetable worthy of your front yard flower garden. Okra is part of the Hibiscus family and when you see the flower you'll see the resem-blance. The plants can reach 7 feet (2 metres) in height if you are in a warm enough climate with a long enough warm season to help it get that big. I'm hoping I never have one that big in my gar-den because it will mean that global warming has extended my season way too long.

Planting

Okra requires about 60 days of heat to really mature and in most places you can get this. It should be a plant you start as seed a good month before you can plant it outdoors after the last frost. In warmer growing zones you can direct seed it in the garden if you like. It is not a big fan of having its roots dis-

Okra's Hibiscus flower makes it worthy of the front yard flower garden.

turbed when transplanted into the garden so you may want to start your okra in peat pots that you can plant directly into the garden, without hav-ing to remove the roots from a cell pack or pot. If you're planting seeds plant them every 3 to 4 inches, then thin to 12" apart. Or if you're plant-ing transplants put them a foot apart because the plants can become quite large.

I was able to keep my plants well watered during the growing sea-son, but a plant like okra would probably like to be mulched. In an area with cool nights this would help to keep the soil a bit warmer around the roots. Growing with a black or clear plastic mulch would also help keep that heat in which is so important with plants that originated in the tropics like this.

Those flowers turn into "lady fingers" as some people call okra.

I had some problems with my plants this year. Some of the leaves yellowed and wilted which could be blight or nematodes in the soil. We had a very wet, cool summer so I'm assuming it was a blight, which a compost tea might have treated. If it was nematodes you can add parasitic nematodes to the soil to go after them, but I did have a lot of marigold plants in the area, which help control nematodes naturally, so hopefully they will help if

there is a problem next year. I did remove the plants from the garden and will not compost them, and I will grow okra in a different part of the garden next year.

I also found some stink-bugs on the plants. You can tell they're stink bugs because they are shaped like a shield and they smell bad when you squish them. You could try spraying them with pyrethrum if you're squeamish, but I think it's better to keep your eye on the plants and squash the bugs when you hunt them down.

I do believe our cool wet summer was not optimal for okra, so I'm hoping next year we'll have one of our more typical hot and dry summers, where the challenge is just to keep things watered.

Harvesting

With this being my first summer I was so enamored with the hibiscus like flower and then the crazy 5 sided, pentagonal fruit that resulted that I forgot to harvest the okra early enough. So the okra got too tough and didn't taste quite as good as it does at our favourite Indian restaurant Curry Original. Optimally you should harvest the pods when they are small and tender. When you pick okra cut the stem and leave it attached to the pod. You can remove it when you prepare it, but leaving the stem on during storage helps it to keep better. Use a sharp knife or pruners to cut the pods. Okra is like the squash family and has small spines that get stuck in your hands, so I usually brush them off the area where I'll be cutting. You could also wear gloves to avoid them.

The pods won't store too well so you should cook them up right away, or put them in the fridge. You can also pop them into bags and put them in the freezer without blanching. When you cook okra the pods can become slightly gooey, so it's common to stir-fry them so you can cook that moisture away.

Compost Page "Popcan" Quiz

If you look carefully in the compost photo on page 37 under the bagged leaves, what doesn't belong in the photo is a can of Dr. Pepper. Sure, it's got high fructose corn syrup in it, but aluminum cans belong in your recycling box not your compost heap.

34 Onions

I have a sacred triumvirate of storage vegetables that I base my garden on—potatoes, carrots, and onions. I'm convinced that you could live comfortably with just these vegetables stored in your root cellar. Some oil and salt would be great, but if worst came to worst these three powerhouse veggies could get you through anything. In many cultures and at many times in history these have been the backbone of people's diets and they've done okay.

I love onions. I love growing them. I love cooking them. I love eating them. I love onion soup. I love to cut up a big onion and sauté it in oil and butter and then add last night's leftover mashed potatoes and enjoy a big plate of hash browns with my eggs for breakfast. And what a treat that I grew them myself.

Years ago, in my job as a desktop publisher, I did the artwork on a catalog for a company that sold parts for large industrial sprayers, the kinds farmers use to spray pesticides. The cover image was a tractor with a spray boom on it that must have been a hundred feet wide. The tractor was spraying onions. I completely understand why farmers spray their crops. They have a huge investment and this is their life. This is how they make money. I also know that I don't wish to eat food that has been grown this way. My onions are not uniform, like the ones you see in the stores, and sometimes they have blemishes. But as Joni Mitchell sang in *Big Yellow Taxi* (*They Paved Paradise Put Up a Parking Lot*) way back in 1970, "Give me the spots on my apples, but leave me the birds and the bees."

Many of us can remember using onions in science class when we were studying cells. Onions are used because when you look at a sliver of onion under a microscope it has very large cells that are easy to identify. These cells are a problem when we cut them because they release enzymes called allinases that irritate our eyes. Michelle wears contact lenses, so cutting onions doesn't bother her, but I do the whole "SNAG" (Sensitive New Age Guy) thing and cry a lot when I cut onions.

Onions have lots of B vitamins and trace minerals, so they are really good for you. Like all members of the allium family, which includes garlic, they promote good cardiovascular health and offer anti-inflammatory and antibacterial benefits. I think it's great that we tend to increase our consumption of them in the fall and winter just as the cold and flu seasons arrive, and I rarely suffer from either illness anymore. Hiding from humanity in my off-grid house in the woods probably helps too.

Planting

Onions come in lots of varieties, like Spanish, red, mild, yellow, and mini. You can plant them in a variety of ways: direct seeded in the garden, as

transplants, and as bulbs. Onions are slow growing, so I've had limited success direct seeding them in the garden. I generally focus on transplants and bulbs. I start seeds two to three months before the last frost date. That requires lots of planning, but remember that it's winter when you start them, so those green shoots will be a tonic to your well-being during the cold winter months. I transplant them into the garden close to the final frost date. They'll handle the cold, but they'll get growing more vigorously as the soil warms.

Garden center onions have matted roots like leeks, so use the bucket technique to loosen and separate the roots before planting.

I also buy transplants from my local greenhouse. They do a marvelous job. The cell packs have a bunch of onions crowded in together and the biggest challenge is getting them apart. I've learned to just dunk the whole bunch into a bucket of water, which helps remove the potting soil, and then it's easy to gradually loosen up and release each of the individual onion plants and its mass of roots. Once I have an onion separated I lay it against one side of a trench and then refill the trench with the onions a couple of inches apart. I keep them fairly close at this time because I plan on thinning them as the season progresses. Once I've backfilled the trench and covered the roots, I press down around each onion and get it standing upright, ready to absorb the sun.

The easiest way to grow onions is from bulbs or onion sets, and

Onion bulbs are an easy, cost-effective way to have a great onion harvest.

I generally have much better luck with bulbs than with seed or transplants. Someone has done a lot of the hard work to get bulbs to this stage, so when you plant them they're ready to send up a green shoot and get growing quickly. I've read that they do not store as well, but I've had trouble confirming this since by the fall I've generally mixed mine all together and don't know which onions I grew from seed and which from sets. I like sets because they're easy to plant and they grow vigorously. One of the biggest challenges with onions is keeping them weeded, and I find it especially difficult with the ones that I direct seed because they're so fine and delicate when they emerge, like a blade of grass, that it's difficult to weed around them.

I plant onion bulbs like garlic, in groups of two or three rows one cultivator length (about six inches) apart. Then I can run the cultivator between the rows to conveniently remove the weeds. I also like this system because now that I use drip irrigation for watering, I can run the hose between two close rows and water two rows of onions at one time. I don't plant the bulbs too deep, just dig a trench one to two inches deep and place the bulbs in. Then I cover with the soil I pulled back to make the trench. I want the top of the bulb fairly close to the surface so it can feel that sunshine and get growing quickly.

Onions grow very close to the surface so you need to apply lots of compost just before you plant them. The roots won't go very far, so they need lots of nutrition readily available. With their roots fairly close to the surface they're also going to be more susceptible to drought, since the roots haven't gone down deep to find moisture. So make sure they're well watered.

Pests

Weeds will be your number-one challenge with onions. They're one crop that you'll need to hoe and cultivate regularly, and you'll have to get down on your hands and knees and hand weed around the onions themselves. If you let the weeds get ahead of you they'll compete for the nutrients and moisture that the onions need, and if the weeds get too big they'll disturb the surrounding onions when you finally do pull them out. So stay on top of them. Onions may be one crop you want to mulch to keep the weeds down.

When you're planting the onions be on the lookout for wireworms and cutworms. You'll know you've got cutworms if your green onion gets to be about three or four inches tall and then suddenly topples over. If you examine the remaining plant closely, you'll often see that a cutworm has chewed it off. The best solution is to dig around in the soil until you find the cutworm and "off" it. Trust me, it doesn't matter how much of an animal-loving, PETA-supporting pacifist you are, after you discover that your beautiful little onion plants have been lopped off you won't hesitate to kill the offending cutworms.

Some gardeners have problems with onion maggots. A small, gray fly lays these early in the spring. One way to deal with this is to plant some early decoy plants from the onions you had left over in the root cellar. Hopefully the flies will lay their eggs on these and you can pull them up and get rid of the onions and the eggs. Don't compost them because onion maggots will thrive in a compost heap. The other way to control onion maggots is to use floating row covers as soon as the onions send out green shoots. Beneficial nematodes may also work by infect-ing the maggots in the ground. Onion maggots tunnel into your onions and the plant wilts and yellows. If you find a lot of this, pull up some of the problem onions and see what's happening. If there are no maggots it could be blight or wilt. If the problem persists you'll want to start ordering onions that are resistant to these problems.

I like planting two rows of onions close together, which makes it easy to put the drip irrigation line down the center and water both rows.

Pull up and dry your onions on the soil in the sun for several days before moving them onto drying racks.

I've been lucky, and other than cutworms early in the season I haven't experienced any problems with my onions. I think having healthy soil helps, and I also think it helps to keep moving things around so that problems don't remain in the soil.

Harvest

When the green tops of the onions start to go brown the onions are close to being ready. By now you'll see the top of the onion bulbs showing through the soil and they'll have a brown skin on them. As the bulbs get larger, if the tops fall over I don't worry about it. In fact my neighbor told me that his father, who was a market gardener, would walk down his onion rows close to harvest time and knock all the tops over so that the plant would put all of its remaining energy into the bulb.

I'm always tempted to leave onions in the ground a little longer thinking that they just might get a little bigger. The problem is that they probably won't and I'm just increasing the chances that some will start to rot. If the tops are totally brown they should come out. I pull them out of the ground and just leave them lying on the soil. If it's sunny I leave them there for a few days. Then I collect them, knock off as much soil as possible, and dry them on racks in the horse barn. (I found the racks that I use at the dump. I think they're large industrial freezer shelves.) I'm careful to leave them in the sun for just a few days, but it's important to let them dry in the shade for three or four weeks before I put them in the root cellar. I like the racks because the air can circulate around them, but the onions could sit on a shelf in your garage. Wire wastebaskets from the dollar store are an excellent place to store onions, as they help to keep the onions dry.

After the onions have been drying on the shelves for a week or two I cut all the tops off with pruners. Onions have a tendency to rot or get moldy where the bulb meets the stalk, so I cut off the stalk to promote drying and hopefully prevent these problems.

Storage

After the onions are really dry I put them in the wire wastebaskets and hang them from nails in the ceiling of the root cellar. As you're taking them off the drying rack and preparing to store them,

These discarded refrigerator shelves allow air to circulate around the onions for a few weeks before you store them in the root cellar.

give each one a light squeeze. If it's soft, use it right away; if it's really soft, compost it. You don't want to risk one going bad over the winter and infecting the others around it in the root cellar.

I bring onions up from the root cellar all winter and keep them in a bin in the kitchen. I inevitably end up with some left over in the spring. My root cellar is completely dark, and because it was the old cistern with one-foot-thick concrete walls it maintains a steady temperature of close to zero. But somehow the onions know when it's time to sprout. In late winter/early spring I begin to notice that my stored onions have begun sprouting green shoots. I take the sprouted onions and plant them in various places in the garden. I use them to attract cutworms in the potato rows, because they already have a green sprout that the cutworms can't resist. And since this will be their second year of growing, these onions will send up a seed stalk which you can harvest seeds from later in the summer if the cutworms don't get them.

Scallions

For years the expression "scallions" puzzled me. I would see them listed as an ingredient in recipes but the authors never explained what they were. It was a real epiphany when I learned that they're just green onions. What a comedown. "Scallions" sound so exotic, but they're actually quite mundane. Seed catalogs sometimes list scallions as "bunching onions." These are just onions that you plant fairly close together and harvest when they're immature, before they've formed real bulbs.

I don't plant "scallions" per se. I plant various onions in large quantities fairly close together and then I just thin them all summer to give me "scallions" or small green onions. Either way it's nice to have green onions available for omelets, to top baked potatoes, to throw in salads, or to use in a variety of other ways.

35 Parsnips

I can still hear my Grandma Micklethwaite telling me to eat my parsnips. As I child my preference was always Fruit Loops over winter crops, but since she lived to be almost a hundred, she must have known what she was talking about. Now that I'm fifty, I've finally decided to pay attention!

Before potatoes arrived in the New World, parsnips were used for many of the dishes that we now use potatoes for. They look like carrots but are paler and have a stronger flavor. For many people roasted parsnips with their sweet nutlike flavor are an essential part of Christmas dinner. Parsnips are actually richer in vitamins and minerals than carrots and contain lots of potassium.

Planting

Parsnips are just like carrots, so make sure you really work the area where you're going to plant them. They are a big root and the easier it is for that main taproot to punch down through nice, fluffy, soft soil, the better. If you've got clay be sure to use peat moss, compost, mulch, rotten hay, and everything else you have to loosen it up.

Like carrots, parsnips need to be direct seeded into the soil when it's cool. They'll take up to three weeks to germinate, so don't panic if they don't show up right away. Plant them very shallow and just put a small amount of sandy soil or peat moss on top of the seeds. They may have trouble breaking through if you plant them too deeply. They'll come up as very fine shoots and they'll be competing with all of the weed seeds that got left in the garden the previous fall. So keep the area well weeded before the parsnip plants emerge and keep it weeded once you're able to differentiate the weeds from the shoots. Once they get going you should thin them to two to three inches apart.

If you let carrots or parsnips dry out during the summer they'll be tough and tasteless and have a tendency to split so they will need plenty of water all summer to keep them juicy.

Harvesting

Parsnips really are a cold-weather plant so you should plan on leaving them in the ground as long as you can. Not only will they survive a frost but it will enhance their taste. It makes them much sweeter. So plan on leaving them in the ground for as long as you can, and harvest them as needed. When I dig carrots or parsnips I use a shovel and loosen the soil around the plants before I pull them out. You can get lazy and just try and pull them by the tops, but if you've done your job they should be big and deep and you're likely to end up with just the tops.

You can store parsnips in the fridge if you're going to use them fairly soon, or in the root cellar in a bucket of moist peat moss or sand. I leave them as late as I can in the garden, and then I mulch some of them with a thick layer of straw to keep them in the garden for even longer. If you mulch them well enough you can even try harvesting them in the spring.

36   Peanuts

If this were an audio book I'd be tempted to play the theme from the Charlie Brown Christmas cartoon because I grew up on *Peanuts* and love those shows. I also love things with peanuts in them, like peanut butter—and Oh Henry! bars, but I guess Just Peanuts ground peanut butter with organic peanuts and no added oil, salt, or sugar is way better for me than a chocolate bar. Peanuts are an excellent source of protein and are easy to grow, so they should be something you want to try at some point as you expand your gardening repertoire.

This may drive you a bit nuts, but peanuts are not true nuts. They are actually a legume like beans, lentils, and peas. Not only do they provide protein but they're also a great source of monounsaturated fats, which can actually contribute to a healthy heart. They have antioxidants with their cardiovascular benefits as well as niacin, which may protect against Alzheimer's disease. Roasting peanuts actually increases many of their health benefits. Dan Buettner's book The Blue Zones: Lessons for Living Longer from the People Who've Lived the Longest suggests that the people with the greatest longevity eat a lot of nuts. So don't shy away from them.

Peanuts require a fairly long growing season and are grown commercially in the Southern U.S.

We all know of the humble peanut farmer who became president. But you can grow them further north if you work at it. The good thing is that they like a light, sandy soil that doesn't have to be overly fertile, which means they'll grow well if you have marginal soil.

Planting

Peanuts are a legume, which means they get their nitrogen from the air, so you don't have to go crazy preparing the soil with compost. Since they'll be growing under the ground, like potatoes, if you have a lot of clay in your soil try and break it up with peat moss or other organic matter to keep the soil soft and airy.

If you live in a more northern growing zone you'll want to start peanuts indoors. Since they don't like having their roots disturbed we grew them in peat pots, and you can see from the photo that the roots were happy to grow out of the pot once they were planted. Once the soil has warmed to 60°F (15°C) you can transplant the peas to the garden. If you live in a warmer area you can plant the seeds directly in the soil. They are going to require 100 to 120 days to mature, so time them accordingly if you choose to plant them as seed. Make a small hill to plant the peanuts in. This ensures that you've pulled loosened soil into the hill, which will help the peanuts form, and it also ensures that the plants will capture the solar heat they need.

Since I grow in a northern region I decided to experiment with peanuts this year. I tried growing one row in uncovered soil, and I put black plastic mulch on one row. The mulch is actually a biodegradable material made from cornstarch, so it breaks down quickly. I'm not usually a fan

In a colder growing zone consider starting peanuts in peat pots so you don't disturb the roots when you transplant them.

This biodegradable black mulch is made of corn starch and was just about gone by the winter.

of using plastic mulch, but it really worked with my peanuts. The peanuts in the row without the mulch did not mature and I didn't get any peanuts. The mulched ones did produce peanuts. It wasn't a bumper crop, but we had a very cool and wet summer, and peanuts do better with some heat. Most years we've had very hot and dry summers, so I think they'll do very well here.

Peanuts are actually fairly drought resistant, which means that they can do well even in areas with little rainfall. The main problem you may encounter with peanuts is a mold fungus, which produces aflatoxin. This is more common in the south where peanuts are typically grown, but you still want to be careful to dry the peanuts properly.

The way peanuts reproduce is quite interesting. They are self-pollinating, which means that the plant has both male and female flowers. After the small, yellow female flowers are pollinated they turn downwards and penetrate the soil for several inches until they reach the area where the nuts will form. The pods absorb nutrients and the peanuts form inside, usually two but up to four per shell.

Harvesting

Late in the growing season you can dig around the base of a plant and pull out a peanut or two to see how they're doing. If they are white and spongy leave them for a while. The longer they're in the

ground the darker the shells will become. If you're in a frost-prone area and you still need some time you can always mulch them with straw to try and extend the season a bit. Since they're growing below ground they should be able to handle a light

The plants I grew without mulch did not produce any peanuts, while the plants grown under the mulch had a reasonable crop considering the cold, wet season we had this year.

frost. If you're growing in a warmer zone you'll have lots of time to grow mature peanuts.

When they're ready, dig up the whole plants with a shovel. Shake off the loose soil and leave the peanuts on the plants until the foliage on the top of the plants has dried completely. You can leave them upside down on the soil if you have a sunny week coming up, or you can hang them in a warm, dry place. Once the tops are dead you can remove the peanut shells and store them in a dry place. Roast them in the oven before you eat them to enhance the flavor and some of their antioxidant effects.

Growing peanuts was one of the most interesting experiments I've ever conducted in the garden. Even though I love peanuts, I always as-

The small, yellow flowers grow to the ground after being pollinated to produce the peanuts.

sumed that I wouldn't be able to grow them. Most of the seed catalogs that I purchase from don't even offer peanut seeds, but we finally found one that did. By the time we paid for shipping the seeds were expensive, but if we had included them with our whole seed order it wouldn't have been noticeable. Our harvest wasn't great this year because of the cool, wet summer, but I still ended up with a few peanuts. The plants were frequently a topic of conversation when I showed people around the garden and I ended up feeling great about taking on a new challenge and succeeding. Growing food is awesome!

37   Peas

As someone who grew up eating only canned or frozen peas, I remember the "ah-ha" moment I had eating peas in one of my first gardens. I picked a pod, opened it, and ate the peas raw. It was like the Hallelujah chorus from Handel's *Messiah*. I had no idea that peas could taste this good. Next thing I knew, half the harvest was gone. This is really the best way to eat peas, standing in your peaceful and lush green garden, getting all of the nutritional benefits of eating a raw vegetable and then tossing the pods anywhere you want since this is organic waste and good for the earth. All of that lovely sweetness in a pea will be converted to starch a few hours after picking, which is one of the reasons they taste so much better raw. When you buy fresh peas in a grocery store they'll have been picked many days before. Frozen peas are processed quickly after picking to help maximize this sweetness.

Advocates of raw food talk about the nutritional value that is lost when you cook vegetables, and I can certainly understand their point when I think about eating raw peas. I prefer many of the vegetables that I eat to be cooked, but peas are definitely an exception. Peas are a rich source of vitamins K, C, A, B1, B2, B3, and B6 and also contain manganese, folate, copper, iron, zinc, potassium, and protein. Vitamin K is good to help keep calcium in your bones. It also helps your blood to clot. And as a vegetarian I'm happy to know that I'm getting lots of iron when I'm chowing down on peas.

Planting

Peas are a cool-weather vegetable and they grow better during cool periods, so they're one of the first seeds that I plant and I always plant them directly into the soil. As soon as I've run the rototiller through the garden in the spring I plant my peas. Since they're a legume I don't worry about putting much compost in the area, but I sprinkle it with wood ashes to bring the pH up a bit. I plant them half an inch to an inch deep. I use a trellis with my peas, so I actually plant two rows about six inches apart and I place a trellis in-between the two rows. A trellis sounds so fancy. In reality, to make my trellis I take a length of chicken wire and tie it to a stake at each end of the row and one in the middle.

Be careful if you have a clay soil or if you're planting peas in a low area in your garden, because the seeds tend to rot if you plant them in a really wet area that doesn't have good drainage. Add some organic matter like compost to ensure that the seeds won't sit in water. I plant the seeds one to two inches apart since I assume I'm going to lose some to cutworms. If they all survive then I let them go. They seem to handle being grown densely.

Many gardeners and seed catalogs recommend that you use an inoculant with peas. This is a special bacteria that helps the roots of the peas "fix" nitrogen, taking it from the air. An inoculant should help the soil around the roots and cause the plants to grow bigger and increase their yield. It will come as a powder that you put the moistened pea seeds into before planting. Some seed catalogs sell inoculant and it's not too expensive, so it may be worth investing in. I have to confess that I have never used inoculant. It's just

Peas getting started on my chicken-wire trellis.

one of those items on the list of things I know I should do…drink more glasses of water…walk more…the list is endless. I know I should use an inoculant but have just never done it. I have always been happy with my legume output, but I also have a good source of horse manure to help in the nitrogen department. I even checked at my local farm co-op store this past spring, as I was prepared to purchase an inoculant and try it, but they don't stock it anymore. So now you have the

The "All You Can Eat" Pea Salad Bar awaits! Meet you in the pea patch.

information. If you have soil you want to nurture and don't have abundant sources of materials to compost, inoculating your pea and bean seeds is an excellent way to help improve your soil.

I generally plant two or three varieties of peas with different maturity dates, which helps spread out the harvest. I always have an early one and a late one, and I grow one with an edible pod. The edible pod variety is usually referred to as "snow peas," and while they eventually form pea seeds inside, it takes a while and gives you lots of time to harvest them and use them in stir-fries and pasta sauces. Once the pea plants get big enough they start sending out curly tendrils to cling onto something, so if they don't find it on their own I coax them on to my chicken-wire trellis. I decided to experiment this past summer and tried growing a row of peas without the chicken wire trellis. Some of these plants stayed close to the ground but there was one dense section where a number of plants supported each other as they grew up. The yield from these untrellised plants wasn't quite as good and it was less convenient to pick the peas that didn't have a trellis to climb up.

Since peas are planted early you need to make a decision about whether to use untreated seeds or seeds treated with a fungicide to prevent problems early on. Wet, cool soil tends to cause more seeds to rot, so if you use treated seeds you'll probably have a higher germination rate. If you go with untreated seeds you might want to plant a slightly higher number to compensate for losses.

You can also plant some peas in the summer with the hope of harvesting them in the cooler weather of the fall. I have not tried this, and you have to remember that they like a cool soil to germinate. So you may want to provide some form of shade to get them germinated and started. If you start them late enough hopefully they'll make it through the worst of the summer heat and be ready to harvest late. The plants should survive a light frost, and I'm sure that would make the peas even sweeter.

Care

The only problem I have ever experienced with peas is cutworms. I plant lots of extras and eliminate the cutworms as they start cutting off the seedlings. There are lots of diseases like wilts, blights, and mosaic that can affect peas, but I've never had difficulty with them. I think it's because many of the cultivars I buy are already resistant to the more common problems you might encounter. Your seed catalog will list the various diseases and will state whether the cultivar is resistant to them. Remember to keep moving peas around. This helps avoid some problems that remain in the soil and also allows other plants to benefit from the nitrogen that the peas have added to the ground where they were growing.

Harvesting

As soon as the pods are large enough, start harvesting them. Don't let them go too long or they'll get too big and the peas will taste bitter. By keeping them picked you'll encourage the plant to send out more seed pods. Pea flowers are beautiful and I can't think of a more attractive plant than the pea plant. If you put in enough of them you'll eventually get to the point where you can't eat all of the peas standing in the garden. That's when you start adding them to salads and pasta sauces or cooking them with a meal. At the peak of the pea season we pick them and freeze them. We don't do anything special, just put them in freezer bags. When you eat them a few months later they taste just like summer. They're also handy to have in the freezer to pop into stir-fries and rice and various other dishes you make in the colder months. Instant summer goodness!

> *The most common disease is pea root rot (Fusarium) which causes foliage to brown from the ground up. The best control is to plant peas in well-drained soil and to rotate crops.*

The peas that don't get eaten in the garden or with dinner can be placed in freezer bags and frozen, ready to keep your garden giving year round.

In the roots of these recently harvested pea plants you can see the nitrogen nodules that this "legume" has produced from nitrogen in the air. These will provide a great fertilizer for the next crop grown in this section of the garden. If you use garden inoculant you should get even more vigorous production than this.

Lifelong Learning - The Great Dried-Pea Experiment

I love how much I get to experiment with my vegetable garden. This year we purchased dried peas and commercial pea seeds from a grocery store. We placed the dried peas on a damp cloth in an aluminum pan and waited until they germinated. We then planted them in the pea patch. While we did get peas from them they produced fewer pea pods. The plants sent out an inordinate number of tendrils that peas use for climbing. It's as if these peas had some touchy issues and were desperate to cling onto something, but I'm not a pea psychologist. While they were cheaper than seeds from a catalog I think I'll be sticking with traditional seeds.

38 Peppers

I'm a "pizza-tarian," so peppers play a big part in my diet. Since I could in fact live on pizza, and since peppers are an integral component of a delicious and healthy pizza, being able to grow them has been one of the stellar achievements of my life. After years of buying these amazing, smooth, sweet, crisp works of art in a grocery store, it's an amazing feeling of accomplishment to be able to just head to my very own garden on a Friday night and harvest most of the pizza toppings I need, peppers included. I emphasize Friday night because it has become the habit in my part of the world—Friday night is "Pizza Night." It's a wonderful meal to celebrate the end of the workweek and the beginning of the weekend. During the growing season, Tuesday night is often "rice and stir-fried veggie night," which means another trip to the pepper patch, and Thursday's dinner might be a pasta primavera, requiring more peppers.

It's good to grow and eat peppers so prodigiously because they are indeed very good for you. They pack a real vitamin C wallop. Along with vitamin A, peppers have a high concentration of carotenoids such as beta-carotene which are antioxidants that help prevent heart disease, macular degeneration, cataracts, and some forms of cancer. Peppers also

have some B vitamins, folate, and other trace minerals, so they're not only pretty and delicious, they're healthy.

Peppers are a tropical plant so they love heat. If you are growing them in a northern zone and have considered purchasing a small greenhouse, peppers would be a good candidate for planting in it.

Planting

Peppers have a long growing season so you'll need to put transplants in the garden. If you start them yourself you should start them 8 to 10 weeks before the last frost date.

They are slow to germinate and prefer warm soil to get going. I have found it difficult to get good, bushy plants myself without using grow lights. For peppers I head to Burt's Greenhouse where they use a wonderful biomass heating system in their greenhouses and the peppers get lots of heat and light, which is what they really need. Their pepper plants are much healthier and larger than any I've been able to start myself. Pepper plants are one plant you should probably leave to the professionals with the greenhouses.

I usually buy my pepper plants at the same time I buy my tomato and other bedding plants—on the May 24th weekend, which is considered the last frost date for my region. I don't plant them that weekend though, and it took me a number of years to learn to hold my pepper plants back.

The evenings here during the end of May and beginning of June are usually still too cool for peppers. I actually wait until almost the middle of June before I plant them in the garden. Nighttime temperatures should be above 50°F (10°C) before you put out pepper plants. If they experience temperatures cooler than this it will delay their growth and hinder fruit from setting later on. It's hard to imagine how cool nights early in June would harm the plant's ability to set fruit, but it seems to be what happens. We have experienced hot summers when my peppers should have produced prodigiously but didn't. I realized afterwards that I had been impatient and planted them at the end of May with all of my other transplants. Sure, the days were getting warm, but the nights were cool and this was the problem.

Here I've just used a wooden stake to support pepper plants.

Peppers are also a plant that benefits from compost, but you shouldn't overdo it with nitrogen. When I first planted peppers in some new, raised-bed gardens with extremely rich, black soil, I had massive pepper plants and very few peppers. Too much nitrogen will do this. When I get my plants from the greenhouse they are often getting root bound, and since I know I may wait another two to three weeks before planting them out, sometimes I transplant them into larger pots. While it's always best to minimize the stress roots experience, in this case I think it's the lesser of two evils, and I'd rather cause a little stress from transplanting than have them root bound.

I grow my peppers in raised beds in the old barn foundation. The concrete floor keeps them warm and the walls absorb the sun's heat during the day and radiate it back at night. Peppers will also benefit from black plastic mulch, which helps maintain the heat around the roots. Many seed catalogs advertise mini-hooped row covers. These consist of evenly spaced semicircles of wire covered with plastic. The wire keeps the plastic off the plants and the plastic protects the plants from the cooler night air. If you want a lot of peppers and live in a cooler zone, it may be worth investing in something like this. You could also make your own quite easily.

By the time I plant my transplants they often have flowers on them. Keep your eye on these and see how they do. I usually lose some, but if the conditions are right, the blossom will turn into a pepper. I also plant my peppers fairly close together, sometimes just a foot apart. I stake some of them or put them in tomato cages, but some I leave on their own without support. If they are grown fairly densely they can support each other. The downside of growing them too close is the danger of pests or disease being able to cross from one plant to another. If you have a good year and your plants produce lots of peppers, you'll be glad you used cages to support the extra weight.

Pests

One of the common problems I've experienced growing peppers is called blossom end rot. The tip of the pepper goes black and soft. Irregular wa-

In anticipation of each one of these blossoms turning into a pepper I've got this plant supported by a tomato cage.

*Need to put out the fire when eating a **hot pepper**? Try eating pasta, potatoes or bananas, but not water. Since capsaicins (the ingredients that make peppers hot) are oils, they don't mix with water, but any oil absorbing food will help reduce the burning.*

tering can cause this, so it's important to keep your peppers well watered. Drip irrigation is the best method because peppers are one plant where it's best to try and keep the water off the leaves when you water. If you're going to use a watering can, try and water just the soil around the base of the plant. Blossom end rot can also be caused by a lack of calcium in the soil. If you find that your peppers are suffering from blossom end rot on a regular basis, purchase some dolomite limestone and put it in the soil around where you plant the peppers.

If your plants aren't doing well or have inconsistent color it may be a virus such as tobacco mosaic virus. Many of the common cultivars of peppers you get today are resistant to this, but it's possible you purchased seed that didn't have this resistance. Some viruses can be spread by aphids, so watch out for them. If you do spot them wash them off with insecticidal soap.

Harvesting

We start harvesting peppers as soon as they look big enough. Obviously the bigger the better,

but if we have some that are almost ready, I'd rather harvest them too small than have to take another trip to the grocery store. I cut them with a sharp knife or pruners and leave about half an inch of the stalk on them. I was always confused by the difference between red and green peppers. Turns out red peppers are just green bell peppers that have had longer to ripen. I think I was always too impatient and picked them too early. If you have a good harvest you may end up with a whole peck of peppers so that you, like Peter Piper, can pick a peck of pickled peppers. Obviously yours won't be pickled. I believe that with our shorter, cooler growing season it can be more difficult to get many red peppers. It helps to select cultivars with the earliest maturity dates and keep them as warm as you can to get those blossoms turning into fruit as soon as possible to maximize the possibility of red peppers. The redder they get the sweeter they are and the higher in vitamin C, so it's worth the effort.

These hot peppers make me sweat just looking at them.

I do not like hot spicy food, but I always grow some hot peppers for friends and neighbors who appreciate them. I remember the first time that I decided to use a hot pepper in my cooking. After cutting a hot pepper I rubbed my eye. I have never repeated that mistake.

Peppers will keep for a few weeks in the crisper. When we are at the peak of the season we start freezing them as well. We just cut them into "pizza-size" chunks and put them in freezer bags in the chest freezer. We place the smaller bags into larger ones because even after freezing the smell of peppers can permeate the entire freezer. It's not a bad smell but it can be strong. All winter we can grab some to throw onto pizzas and toss into homemade pasta sauces.

39   Potatoes

The Most Important Thing to Grow in Your Garden

This chapter is about plain old potatoes or "solanum" potatoes as opposed to sweet potatoes. The potato is native to South America but it has taken the world by storm and is a big part of people's diets throughout the world. And for good reason too.

Potatoes are rich in carbohydrates, which makes them an excellent source of energy. They have more protein than human breast milk, and since our protein needs are greatest when we're newborns and are doubling our weight every six months, it's obvious that we can get all the protein we need from a potato. The amino-acid pattern of the protein in a potato is well matched to what humans need. Potatoes are very rich in many minerals and vitamins, providing one-fifth of our daily potassium requirement, and are particularly high in vitamin C. A single medium-sized potato contains about half the recommended daily intake of vitamin C, so if you're having a crisis of conscience about that morning glass of orange juice that's trucked from the south to your breakfast table, don't worry; the potato has you covered.

A medium-sized potato with the skin on gives you 45% of the recommended daily allowance of vitamin C, 18% of your potassium, 10% of your vitamin B6, and trace amounts of iron, zinc, nia-

cin, thiamin, riboflavin, folate, magnesium, and phosphorous. A potato with the skin on has the same amount of fibre as many whole-grain cereals and breads.

The carbohydrates in potatoes are a starch, which is a good basis to form your diet around. Some of the starch in potatoes is resistant to digestion by enzymes in your digestive system, so by the time it gets to your large intestine some of this starch is still intact. This is good from a fiber standpoint and provides protection against colon cancer. It also improves glucose tolerance and insulin sensitivity, so it helps you avoid those crazy sugar spikes in your blood and leaves you feeling full longer. This is what you want to eat, a carbohydrate that is going to make you feel full and release its energy to you over a long period. If you're going to spend the day hoeing the garden, start your day with a big plate of home-fried potatoes and eggs or tofu. A breakfast like this will give you the energy you need for the whole day. This is how the people who live the longest eat: a huge breakfast and progressively smaller meals as the day wears on. I know that if I'm going to be spending the day in the garden or cutting firewood, if I start the day with a big plate of fried potatoes I'm going to last much longer than if I

just have tea and toast.

The United Nations declared 2008 the International Year of the Potato because: "The potato produces more nutritious food more quickly, on less land, and in harsher climates than any other major crop—up to 85 percent of the plant is edible human food, compared to around 50 percent in cereals." This is a really important statement and you might want to take a second to reread it. What I take from this is that even if you don't have great soil, potatoes allow to you to maximize the nutrition you get out of the soil by producing a healthy, long- lasting source of food energy. Their ability to store well with almost no energy inputs make them the perfect food for the future.

In my book *Thriving During Challenging Times: The Energy, Food, and Financial Independence Handbook*, I suggest that the converging challenges of peak energy, climate change, and the economic crisis are going to result in a future that will look different from the present, and it will probably include scarcity. Shortages in fuel and food are going to be very foreign to most of us, but with the events that are unfolding in the world today I believe they will be a likely occurrence. So part of the strategy I recommend in the book is to make yourself more independent in terms of your food supply. This can be achieved through

After a winter in the root cellar these potatoes have sprouted and are ready for planting.

a combination of storing inexpensive, nonperishable food in a pantry and canning, freezing, and root cellaring your garden's bounty.

Your root cellar is the key to the whole process, because it doesn't require any energy inputs, which are going to become increasingly expensive. And the potato is the big-name, superstar headliner of your root cellar. So getting up to speed on growing potatoes is a priority. The fact that they are cheap and easy to grow is an added bonus. One of the reasons potatoes are so inexpensive to grow is that some of the potatoes you harvest each fall will end up being your seed stock for the following year. So once you've invested in seed potatoes you shouldn't ever have to spend another dime on them. I would suggest that you'll probably want to keep adding some new seed stock to your mix to keep it diverse and healthy, but theoretically you can use the offspring of those original potatoes forever.

There are thousands of varieties of potatoes worldwide, so you'll want to try some new ones each year just to take advantage of this cornucopia of wonderful new cultivars.

Planting

Potatoes like a sandy, well-drained soil. Since they're going to be growing below ground you don't want them sitting in water. If you have clay you'll need to get in there and break it up. Add lots of peat moss and compost, and even some sand from the local building- supply store. Be careful not to load up with too much rich compost or composted manure. If the soil ends up with too much nitrogen the result will be too much green growth up top

Make sure you have a least one vigorous sprout on section you cut to plant.

and not enough energy going into the potatoes down below.

I plant one row of potatoes early, several weeks before the final frost date, because I want these up as early as I can get them going. I call these my "sacrificial potatoes." These will be the potatoes that the Colorado potato beetles will find when they come out of hiding to feed and lay eggs. Since there's just one row at first, I'll be able to inspect it diligently and eliminate the egg-laying parents in large numbers. Then as I start planting more rows two to six weeks later there will be fewer potato bugs out looking for their lunch.

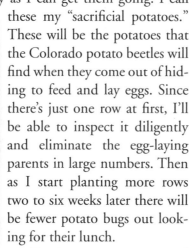

Since I have lots of potatoes left over each spring I don't bother to cut them.

To plant a potato you need a seed potato. You can purchase these from some seed catalogs and some seed potato specialty growers or from your local co-op or greenhouse, or you can just use some potatoes that have sprouted in that bag in your pantry. I would suggest you start with some good quality-stock from a reputable source. There are blights and diseases and you don't want to introduce them to your garden with bad seed. These problems can find you easily enough without your helping them.

I start with potatoes from my root cellar that I stored the previous fall but didn't get around to eating. I

I cover the newly planted potatoes in a shallow trench and hill them as soon as they start growing.

always overdo it and end up with way more potatoes than we can eat over the course of the winter. With so many potatoes to spare I plant a whole potato. I used to cut my seed potatoes into sections, making sure that I had at least two eyes in each piece, or more if I could. Since the sprouts are going to need to take energy from the potato when they start growing, you don't want to make the pieces too small. If you're going to use this technique then you should let the potatoes you've cut harden up in the sun for a few days. Leave them in a sunny place so a skin will form where you've cut through the flesh. This will minimize the chance of their rotting in the soil. At least this is the way most books tell you to plant your potatoes. Whenever I've cut my potatoes I have always just plunked them right down into the soil without drying them and I've never had a potato plant fail to grow. I'm just passing along the "harden-off method" to enhance your odds of success. Since you're going to cut them eventually anyway why not do it three or four days before you actually plant them. I like using whole potatoes because I can plop them in the ground without worrying about their rotting, and I figure that since the potato is the starch reserve the sprouts are going to use until they get their own roots established, why not give each plant as big a head start as you can.

Potatoes like to grow in hills. I used to make the hill before I started and then make a trench through the hill for the potatoes. Now I plant them in well-tilled and loosened soil close to the soil line. Once the potatoes start growing and sending up shoots I hill them up. Every couple of weeks I go down the rows pulling the soil from between the rows up onto the potato hills that I'm forming. This offers the added bonus of weeding the area between the rows as you go. New potatoes will form around or above the seed potato that you plant, so you want to make sure they have a loose soil to grow into. The more soil you move onto that hill the more room you're making for the potatoes.

I plant the potatoes about a foot apart and make sure the rows are about three feet apart. Potato plants are very bushy and if you don't give them enough space you'll just end up with a big mass of potato tops you can't walk through. If you have limited space then by all means grow them closer together. Growing them densely will help crowd and shade out weeds as well, so this is the upside of more compressed planting.

Potatoes should be kept watered and while they're growing you should attempt to keep them from drying out. If they experience extremes of wet and dry you're more likely to end up with potatoes that have cracks or are knobby. They'll taste fine but they won't look quite so nice. With my drip irrigation lines I can keep the rows well watered. It's also important not to overdo the water, since this will cause scabbing and other problems. I have a very sandy soil and during droughts it's difficult to keep everything properly watered. There were years before my irrigation system when I know the potatoes were too dry, and yet every year I have a great potato harvest. It's one of the amazing things about them, that they are so resilient.

Pests

As I've already mentioned, the Colorado potato beetle will be your mortal enemy when you grow potatoes. When I moved to my current location, which is three miles from the nearest neighbor through solid bush, no potatoes had been grown here for decades. The very first year I put in potatoes I had potato bugs. I don't know whether they were dropped in by helicopter, had been hiding in the woods for years, or blew in on some wayward windstorm, but they appeared. The good thing

about them is that they are slow and not that smart. They are easy to spot with their orange and black stripes on a 1/3" inch round body. They'll either be hanging around on the

The adult Colorado potato beetle.

Larvae at work making a meal of your potato plants.

Orange egg clusters on the underside of leaves.

The "badminton racquet" technique and resulting dead larvae.

leaves or in the soil under the plants. If they're on the leaves they'll be either eating or laying eggs. You'll see their damage, as they start at the outside of leaves and work their way in. Their egg clusters are fluorescent orange and are easy to spot on the underside of the leaves. The contrast with the green leaves makes them almost impossible to miss.

As I mentioned, I plant my sacrificial potatoes two to three weeks before the rest. Then once the growth emerges, which can take a few weeks, I start checking them daily. First I go down the row looking for the bugs, and then I straddle the plants and gently pull back the green growth exposing the 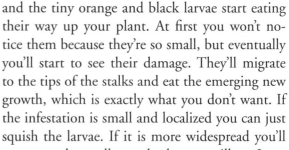 underside of the leaves. The orange egg clusters will jump out at you and you can just squish them against the leaf with your fingers. I used to drown the adults but now I squish them as well, leaving a big orange mess on the leaves or dead bugs on the ground underneath. I do this as a warning to their brothers and sisters to stay away, although there is no scientific basis to this and it really just makes me feel better. I strongly recommend that you start a few plants early if you can and follow this same system. I think you'll find that the bulk of the potato bugs will appear early and you'll be more successful at eliminating them.

As the season progresses and I plant my other rows of potatoes I tend to be less vigilant about looking for potato bugs. There have been many years when I've just had too many distractions with work and other demands on my time and I haven't been able to stay on top of monitoring the potato plants. When the eggs are allowed to remain on the plants, they hatch,

When the tops die it's time to harvest.

and the tiny orange and black larvae start eating their way up your plant. At first you won't notice them because they're so small, but eventually you'll start to see their damage. They'll migrate to the tips of the stalks and eat the emerging new growth, which is exactly what you don't want. If the infestation is small and localized you can just squish the larvae. If it is more widespread you'll need to call out the heavy artillery. I use a badminton racquet and a bucket with an inch of water in it. I go down the rows knocking each branch with the badminton racquet, which brushes the larvae into the buckets. If they miss going into the bucket I stomp on them. A few years ago we produced a gardening DVD and I used the line "Drowning, Stomping, and Squishing" to describe how I deal with potato bugs. This is my variation on the 1980s Journey song with the title "Lovin', Touchin' and Squeezin'."

One way or another, I stay on top of the bugs. If you don't deal with them they will happily chew off all of the green growth and the potato plant will have nothing left with which to photosynthesize the sun's energy and store it in the tubers that you eat. The plants can handle some damage, but if it becomes too significant your harvest will be compromised.

You should be careful where you plant your potatoes each year. Make sure you don't plant them where potatoes or other members of the nightshade family have been grown recently, which includes tomatoes, eggplants, and peppers. The soil might harbor some of the problems that will affect potatoes, such as nematodes. If you plant them where there was grass in previous years watch out for wireworms or grubs. The grubs are large and white and easy to spot when you're preparing the soil, but wireworms look like one-inch-long yellow- or white-colored roots. If you grab a wireworm it will wiggle, so get to know what these look like and squish or drown them.

Many of the other problems you might experience with potatoes will be in the soil, which is why you should rotate them each growing season. Harvest them when the time is right, because if you leave them in the ground too long they're much more likely to get late blight that can cause blemishes and prevents them from storing well. I also find that if I've had a season with too much rain, if the season has had too many extremes of hot and cold, or if it's been too wet late in the summer and early fall before I harvest them, the potato skins will tend to be scabby. There's nothing wrong with a scabby potato; they just don't look great and the skins aren't as attractive for baked potatoes.

Lately I've also found that some of the potatoes I harvest are huge but have a black spot or hollow black spot in the middle. This seems to be caused by too much rain, so I'm finding that it's better to harvest them earlier rather than later. Previously I thought that I might as well just leave them in the ground as it meant less time in the root cellar, but in order to avoid some of the problems that I've mentioned it makes more sense to harvest them early.

Remember as well that you have to keep hilling up the soil over the potatoes. The tubers should not be exposed to the sun. If they are, you'll get green spots on the potatoes and these contain a poison called solanine, which you shouldn't eat. If you do harvest potatoes that have green areas

it's recommended you throw the whole potato away. The poison develops in the exposed area as a defense against being eaten by animals, but the solanine will be spread throughout the potato, so get rid of it. And yes, if you find a potato chip with green on it, don't eat it, even if it's the last chip in the bag.

Harvesting

As the summer wears on you'll find that the green tops of the potato plants will start to become brown and dry. This is perfectly normal. It's the signal that the tubers are ready. You don't have to wait for this to harvest some of your potatoes, though. During the growing season you can stick your hand into one of the hills and root around until you find some potatoes. You can just pull out a few potatoes for your dinner or dig up the whole plant. This is a great way to have "new" potatoes as a treat. Once you've dug one plant from that row you'll know whether or not the rest of the plants in that row are ready too.

Later in the summer when the tops have died back I start harvesting the potatoes for storage. You can use a fork to loosen the soil and expose the potatoes, but I like to just use my hands. I use a shovel to loosen

Dry sand is an excellent way to store your potatoes.

the soil at the start of a row, and then I just go down the row pulling out the potatoes and placing them in a wheelbarrow. I "place" rather than throw because you don't want to bruise your potatoes. If your soil is not as sandy as mine you may need to use a shovel or fork, and you'll need to be careful not to spear the potatoes. Start outside of the area where you expect the potatoes to be and

Each plant should produce 6 to 10 potatoes.

then move gently towards them. I like harvesting them up close like this because it lets me eyeball each one to make sure it doesn't have any green exposed areas and also gives me an opportunity to knock some of the soil off them.

It doesn't matter how you do it, harvesting potatoes is a joyous, back-breaking, invigorating, exhausting thing to do, all at the same time.

Storage

Once you've placed all of your potatoes in your wheelbarrow you should let them sit for a few days before you start storing them. I leave them in the shade. Some people leave them on top of the soil in the sun to dry, but I would rather not give them a chance to develop any green spots. After a few days of drying I sort through them. I take out all the medium-sized potatoes, brush off any excess soil, and then put them in buckets. Once the bucket is half full I put in some peat moss and then add more potatoes. Once I've got the bucket filled with potatoes I top it up with more peat moss. I use buckets from the dollar store because they aren't too big. I've also had great luck storing potatoes in dry sand. The problem is that sand is heavy and the buckets become too cumbersome to

move into the root cellar. Many environmentalists are critical of peat moss because of the damage done to the peat bogs where it is harvested. I am also concerned about this, but my potatoes are grown sustainably and peat moss is an excellent material to store my potatoes in. I don't use much and as I use up each bucket of potatoes over the winter I save the peat moss and add it to my soil to help condition it. We have a local sawmill which has wood shavings and sawdust available, so I'm going to try that next year.

Ideally potatoes should be stored just above freezing with adequate ventilation. I can't really control the temperature of my root cellar, which is actually the old cistern under the kitchen of my century-old farmhouse. It never freezes and it's extremely dark. It doesn't have optimal air exchange, but my potatoes keep amazingly well. If you haven't built your root cellar yet, it's time to do so. I provide some guidance in chapter 63.

My favorite potato is the Red Norland variety. I love the crisp, white flesh, and I really like how the red skin seems much less likely to turn green if I'm ever negligent and they do get some exposure to the sun. I like them so much that I gradually got to the point where they were the only variety that I was growing, and all of my stock came from potatoes left over from the previous season. Then we had a really wet and cool summer a few years back and I had problems with scab and with black spots in the middle of many of them. This was a wake-up call to smarten up and diversify my seed stock.

The following year we added some Kennebec and Superior. Cultivars with a gold flesh like Yukon Gold are becoming very popular as well. I would suggest you peruse the pages of your seed catalog or the aisles of your local gardening center or co-op store and see what appeals to you. Plant several varieties and record which does best and the growing conditions that summer. Then you'll be able to narrow your list down to what you prefer in terms of eating and storage and what does best with your soil and growing conditions.

Growing Potatoes in Mulch

This year a friend introduced me to a concept developed by Ruth Stout that relies heavily on mulch. Ruth Stout has written a number of books about growing vegetables with mulch. Her premise is that mulch saves tilling the soil, retains moisture, and makes a fabulous supplement for the soil.

I tried this technique by growing some potatoes in mulch. It works well for beginner gardeners or gardeners with mobility issues because it's really very easy. You place the potatoes on the soil, or even on the lawn, and apply lots of mulch. The yield was lower for the potatoes I planted this way, but overall they did remarkably well. I really like Ruth's concept that mulch helps add organic material to the soil as it breaks down and decomposes.

My concern about this technique is twofold. I believe that a large mass of organic mulch is a great place for pests to hang out. This past summer was a cool and wet one in my growing area, the second cool and wet summer in a row. For a decade I had never seen a slug in my garden and now they are everywhere. The place where I found them to be most prolific was under the rotting hay anywhere that I had used it for mulch. This was fine when I was just using it to kill grass and make my gardens bigger, but around crops it was a problem. I know I had much more damage than usual from slugs on tomatoes and other crops. Mulch just makes it easier for them to stay cool during the day and hide.

My other challenge with planting potatoes or anything else in mulch is the fine line between having too thin a layer of mulch and too thick a layer. If it's too thick, which is what Ruth advocates, I would be concerned about the shoots being able to get through it. If it's not thick enough, the potato shoots won't have any problem getting through it, but then neither will the weeds.

That said I think this system worked quite well. If I'd added some compost on top of the mulch rain might have washed some of the organic material and nutrients down through the mulch and helped increase the yield.

No matter how you grow them, where you grow them, and what kind you grow, potatoes should be THE workhorse of your garden. Not only are they healthy and versatile, they store well, lend themselves to many methods of preparation, and are easy to grow. Potatoes are nature's perfect vegetable!

Grown in mulch, both my Red Norlands (left) and Kennebecs (right) produced well with very little maintenance.

40   Pumpkins

Pumpkins, like so many things today, have been taken to the max. Everything has to be extreme, so now we have extreme pumpkin-growing competitions in which people compete to grow pumpkins so big and heavy that a forklift is required to move them. A 1,500-pound pumpkin just doesn't sound practical to me. But a fall garden with a dozen brilliant orange pumpkins is a beautiful thing. Whether you want them to decorate the front porch or you think of them as the big squash that they are, pumpkins are great to grow if you have the space. There's something special about cutting into a nice, big pumpkin you have nurtured from a tiny seed.

Most of us are familiar with pumpkin pies made with filling from a can, but a pumpkin pie made from pumpkins that you planted and weeded and watered and nourished with compost simply tastes better. And it's not just about pies either. My current *Backhome Magazine* has a wonderful article on how versatile pumpkin is. Pumpkin fritters, pumpkin rolls, pumpkin bread, pumpkin bread stuffing, pumpkin soup…they all sound fantastic. Pumpkins are surprisingly good for you. They have 41% of the recommended daily requirement of vitamin A and almost 30% of your daily requirement of beta-carotene. That beautiful orange color is a hint of the health potential of pumpkins. Plus it has B vitamins and also vitamin C from basking in the sun all summer. It's got some iron, potassium, phosphorus, and folate. Not bad for something that most of us carve up for Halloween and would never consider eating.

Growing

Pumpkins are easy to grow and love the sun. Don't plant them as seeds in the garden until you're sure the chance of frost is over. They will not germinate in cool soil, so you should wait until you're sure of warmer weather. I usually plant pumpkins in hills with six or seven seeds per hill. Once they're well established I thin them to two or three plants per hill. When you see the size of pumpkins you have to make the assumption that they require a fair amount of feeding to get to that size. I make sure to add lots of compost and composted manure to the area where I make the hills. Once I've tilled or hoed the area, I pull in soil from a radius of three or four feet around to make the hills, which are at least a foot and a half across. I push the soil out from the middle so that the hill has walls, like a swimming pool (or a volcano crater). When I was a kid I liked to do this with my mashed potatoes and gravy. When I need to water the pumpkins I can fill up this little swimming pool area and know that the water is going to drain to where the roots can use it. It's helpful to have a system like this in the heat of the summer when I tend to

water only in the morning. If I've filled up some rain barrels that are raised off the ground, they will have natural head or water pressure to deliver water to where I want it. It won't be super fast, but it'll do the work for me. So I can put the hose in one of these hills, go and water elsewhere with watering cans, and then come back after six or seven minutes and move the hose into the next hill. With all of my squash-type vegetables growing in hills like this it's a very efficient use of my time to water with a system like this.

This year I had a pile of partially composted horse manure and I decided to try planting my pumpkins right in it. Manure can sometimes have too much nitrogen, which will burn your plants, but this manure had plenty of wood shavings in it as well, and the rain had washed much of the nitrogen down into the pile during the six months or so that it had been sitting there. We had a great crop of pumpkins this year, growing right in the manure pile. The real challenge was keeping them watered, because the manure pile was outside the main garden, so it was easy to forget.

My pumpkin patch grew out of a composted manure pile.

Novelty Pumpkins

Here's a gardening novelty trick I tried this year. I took a ballpoint pen and wrote "Cam" and "Michelle" into the green skin of two of the largest pumpkins. As they matured and ripened, the lines made by the pen formed scar tissue and ended up looking very natural, as if they were part of the pumpkin. I was hoping to be able to burst into the house one day with the miracle pumpkins to show Michelle. I was going to say "Hallelujah! Eureka! It's a message. Let's buy lottery tickets."

But, as Michelle has a tendency to do, she stole my thunder. One day she said to me "How come you wrote *your* name on the *bigger* pumpkin." Even so, I enjoyed having "his and her" pumpkins on the front porch this past Halloween.

Most people don't have the luxury of a spare, composting horse manure pile to grow their pumpkins in, so just make sure you put lots of compost into the area where you plan on planting your pumpkins. You may even want to top-dress them during the season, putting more compost around the base of the pumpkin plants once they really start growing.

Care

Pumpkins are very low-maintenance plants. Once they start growing you just need to keep them watered and keep your eye on them for pests. The biggest challenge with my pumpkin vines has been with squash bugs. While they tend to be attracted to butternut and acorn squash plants, they will also go after pumpkins. Look for them around the base of the plants. They are grey and have an armored look to them. Track them down and squish them. Not only will they lay eggs and produce babies that attack the plants, they will tend to spread viruses and wilts that cause the leaves to wilt and the plant to lose energy.

Pumpkins are monoecious which means that there are both male and female flowers on the same plant. When the flowers bloom the female have a small ovary or bump, like a mini-pumpkin, at the base of the petals. This is what will turn into a pumpkin if it is pollinated. If you have lots of bees

Female pumpkin flowers have a small pumpkin already starting at the base of the flower.

in the area, you should notice them fly from one flower to the next doing the pollination for you. If you don't see bees or other insects around, or if you see a lot of female flowers dropping without being pollinated, you can do it yourself. Remove a male flower, cut off the petals, find the anther, which will be covered in pollen, and rub it against the stigma of the female flower. With colony collapse disorder having a dramatic effect on the bee population in North America, it's probably worth having this skill anyway. If you are in an urban area where you don't see many bees, put on your Mother Nature hat and get out there and pollinate some pumpkins!

Pumpkin Seeds

Don't be tossing those pumpkin seeds in the compost bin yet! "Thar's gold in them thar seeds!" After removing them from the pumpkin, wash them and roast them. They taste great and are an excellent source of protein, zinc, and vitamins. They have lots of minerals in them and, like all seeds, are really good for you.

41 Radicchio

You may have trouble finding radicchio in your seed catalog because everyone seems to put it in a different place, and routinely not in the "R" section. Some catalogs have it with chicory, as it really is a type of chicory. Since radicchio is the trendy or more common name right now, I decided to classify chicory under radicchio. Radicchio is a leaf chicory and some people call it Italian chicory. It is becoming popular as a salad ingredient because of its unique bitter and spicy taste. The taste mellows when it is grilled or roasted, so you may see a warm radicchio salad on menus in trendy restaurants. It certainly adds colour and zest to salads with its white-veined burgundy leaves.

The unique spicy taste of radicchio is gaining popularity in North America, but it's been a staple on Mediterranean menus for many years.

In Italy radicchio is often grilled in olive oil or mixed with risotto. I can remember when I was growing up there was a television commercial that advertised a certain brand of coffee as being mellow because it had chicory added to it. If you wanted to you could grow chicory, roast its root, and grind it in place of coffee. With its deep, dark, rich color you can tell it is nutrient-rich, and like all vegetables it has powerful anti-oxidant properties.

Growing

You grow radicchio as you would any head lettuce. You can sprinkle the seeds in loose soil and rake it to make sure the seeds contact the soil. Then water, and the seeds should start germinating in 7 to 10 days. You may have to thin them if they've been seeded too densely. Radicchio is a cool-season vegetable, so I actually start mine later in the spring or in early summer. The cool nights of later summer and fall will enhance the taste, so don't rush planting it. You can plant it in the spring and see what you think of the heads you harvest in the summer.

I have had very few problems with radicchio. No insect seems very interested in it, but it is susceptible to a fungus called Botrytis, which can damage the leaves. Most of the cultivars in catalogs today have some resistance to this. Radicchio is very drought-resistant as well, so it's one of those vegetables you don't have to be too fanatical about watering. It will send down a big taproot which helps it handle low water conditions.

I have found that radicchio plants aren't very consistent in terms of the dark burgundy color that's so enticing about them. Some of the plants don't achieve the color and some don't form heads as uniformly as I'd like. It doesn't seem to matter whether I plant radicchio early or late, it's inconsistent. I'll keep trying new cultivars and perhaps I'll find one that does well in my soil and climate.

Harvesting

I cut the radicchio heads with a sharp knife just below the soil. If you start harvesting early, the root will continue to send up new growth. If you don't have a lot of plants because of space limitations, you can also just harvest some leaves for a salad, starting at the outside and working in.

If you are able to leave the root in the ground over the winter it will send up a five-foot-tall spiky plant with light blue flowers. These are edible and look nice on a plate. While I do have the room to leave things in my garden I usually like a clean start each spring and so I usually choose to clean everything up in the fall. The only time I've enjoyed the lovely blue flower of a radicchio plant was the year I left some plants in the garden by accident.

42   Radishes

Radishes are THE easiest vegetable you can grow, so they're a really good confidence-builder if you're just getting started. Put a row in the garden in the spring and in a couple of weeks you'll have a vegetable to toss in a salad. How cool is that!

If you're from Oaxaca, Mexico radishes have a unique place in your culture when you're celebrating Noche de Rábanos or Night of the Radishes on December 23rd. People carve the most amazing things you could ever imagine out of radishes, including nativity scenes! What a versatile little vegetable! There are some good health benefits in that spicy, crunchy radish, too. There is lots of vitamin C and vitamins K and B6, as well as riboflavin. Radishes have lots of trace minerals along with antibacterial and antifungal properties. I sense this when I bite into a particularly hot radish.

Growing

You can plant radish seeds as soon as the ground can be worked. With a day or two of sun they'll germinate, and with luck you'll have some ready to eat in three to four weeks. Since they mature so quickly, plant half or a third of a row to start, and then replant every couple of weeks. You can do this all summer, but it might be better to miss the extreme heat and start replanting again in August for a fall harvest.

Radishes aren't heavy feeders, so you

Radishes germinate quickly and grow well in cool weather, so they can be one of the first crops you harvest in the spring.

don't have to take any extra care to make sure they're in a good part of the garden. If you plant them in the spring you probably won't even have to worry about watering them, since you'll still have the spring rains.

Radishes are the sort of vegetable that you have to watch really carefully, because they mature quickly and need to be harvested over a short period of time. If you leave radishes in the ground too long they will react poorly. They may go to seed, their tops may crack, or they'll end up being tough and tasteless. So harvest them often and in small amounts, and harvest them regularly. While they'll store in the fridge for a week or two, they don't store well over a long period of time.

Some people actually use radishes to mark the rows of slower-to-germinate vegetables. In other words, you could plant a row of carrots and radishes at the same time once the soil warms up. The radishes will be up in a couple of days, but the carrots will take a week or two to germinate. The carrots will also start growing very slowly, so in three or four weeks, when you start harvesting radishes, the carrots will just be reaching the size where you can see the row and can keep track of them. You just have to make sure you harvest the radishes carefully so as not to disturb the small carrots too much. I like to make sure the soil is well watered, and then I get down on my hands and knees and watch as I pull each radish out. If I do disturb any of the surrounding carrots I take a second to put some soil in the empty hole and straighten the carrots and pat the area down. It's just like "replacing your divots" on the golf course, but in this case you end up with healthy, beta-carotene-rich carrots after you've pulled out the radishes.

I'm sure radishes are susceptible to some pests but I've never seen any of them. The radishes in my garden are never in the ground long enough for anything to get to them. You might have a problem with maggots on your radishes, but a floating row cover will deal with that problem. While you can grow radishes in the heat of summer, they seem to do best maturing in cooler weather. The challenge during the summer heat is making sure they get adequately watered. If they don't, you'll end up with tough and dry flesh in the root. Take the easy "root," which in this case means planting them early in succession and then waiting until you harvest your garlic to start more succession planting for the fall. Sometimes it's better to just accept limitations and put your efforts into other crops during the heat. It's hard enough to work in brutal heat, so this will mean one less thing to worry about.

This raised bed helps the soil warm up faster so you get that first crop of radishes even sooner.

Here you can see some small radishes with carrot seedlings that have just germinated, even though they were planted at the same time. Once you harvest the radishes the carrots will have room to expand.

Speeding up the Season TIP

I'm always looking at ways to speed up the season, especially for heat loving plants like tomatoes and peppers.

The water in this waterwall warms up during the day to radiate back at night and with less water in each compartment than the photo on the right, it will actually lean in to form a pyramid to protect plants in cooler weather.

43   Rhubarb

You've got to love a plant that you can use in fabulous tart desserts but might kill you if you use the wrong part of it! Now that's living dangerously! To be honest I've never actually heard of anyone dying after eating rhubarb, but while the stalks are perfectly safe to eat, the leaves do produce oxalic acid, which can be toxic. So you need to be careful to just eat the stalk and not the leaves.

I like rhubarb because it's a perennial, so once you plant it, it comes back every year without fail. It's also one of those beautiful plants that you should actually put in your flower garden because it looks great and produces food. Plus it's a great source of vitamin C and dietary fiber and it has significant levels of calcium, vitamin K, and potassium. Try getting that out of your geraniums!

Rhubarb does best in cooler areas where winter temperatures are cold enough to freeze the top two inches of soil and put the plant into dormancy.

Planting

I've been lucky in that all of the homes I've lived in have already had rhubarb plants growing somewhere in their yards, so I've never had to plant it. If you aren't lucky enough to have a rhubarb plant in your yard, you'll be able to acquire some roots from a seed company or a plant from a garden center. Rhubarb does best in a well-drained area, so a sandy soil is best. If you have a clay soil or clay subsoil fairly close to the surface, you really need to dig a large, deep hole before you plant rhubarb. You can backfill the hole with sand and compost so that the roots won't rot. Since it's going to be there for years, you'll want to add as much compost and rich soil as possible.

Rhubarb is a heavy feeder, and when you see the size of the leaves and stalks it produces you'll understand why. There is a rhubarb plant in an unused part of my garden that I have neglected for several years, and it's withering away and is now just a tiny little plant. So it's not enough to put the compost to it just when you plant it; this has to be an ongoing thing. You need to keep applying compost around the plant several times a year, and once it's all died back in the fall I put a good supply of composted horse manure around the whole area to ensure that its roots have good, fertile soil to grow out into.

If you really like rhubarb and want to put in a few plants, make sure they are a good three feet apart. They will ultimately get big and you don't want them crowding each other out. If you purchase plants from the greenhouse, plant them a little lower than the soil level in the pot. This will allow you to build up the soil around the crown over time and won't leave it overly exposed to dry out. You shouldn't harvest any rhubarb for the first two years after planting. If your plant is very healthy in its second year and the stalks are at least half an inch thick, you might get away with using just a few of the stalks. Waiting like this is always hard to do with a plant, especially when you've had to dig a deep hole and the prepara-

Rhubarb is a consistent perennial performer with big striking leaves that is beautiful in the vegetable or flower garden. Photo courtesy of Johnny's Selected Seeds www.johnnyseeds.com

tion has been fairly extensive. I understand. It's hard to be patient. I can't tell you the number of times I've planted raspberries and strawberries and they always say remove the fruit early, as soon as it's formed. You want all the energy in the early years to go into building a strong root system. I'll admit, too, that I have eaten the forbidden fruit when I should have pruned it off weeks before. No one was watching, though, so it was all right. I compensated by adding more compost later to make up for my guilt.

With such a deep root system rhubarb is less susceptible to droughts than some plants, but if you do have a prolonged dry period make sure you give it a good deep watering periodically. Add a thick layer of compost or manure in the fall and you should be on your way to a healthy rhubarb harvest.

Harvesting

As with asparagus, you can only harvest some of the rhubarb stalks. You have to leave some so that the plant can continue to store solar energy in its root system for next year. Once the stalks are large enough you can harvest for one to two months, taking every other large stalk. Of course you should remember to cut off the leaves and not use them.

Eventually the rhubarb will attempt to send up a large seed stalk. You should remove it as soon as you recognize that it's not just another leaf. As with garlic scapes, you want your rhubarb plant to put its energy into the plant itself and not into forming a flower. There's been the odd year when I've forgotten to remove the seed stalk and it has formed an amazing-looking seed pod. The abandoned rhubarb plant that I've ignored used to send up a seed stalk, which is another reason I think it's getting smaller and less vigorous each year.

Rhubarb does actually spread, and each year it will send up new growth beside the original main crown. I just leave these, so now I have a really full, bushy plant, but as with many perennials you can actually remove one of the side shoots and start it as a plant on its own. This is a good way to expand the rhubarb patch. If your plant is starting to look overcrowded, you might want to start removing some of these. You can plant them yourself or put them in a pot and sell them as a fundraiser at the local plant sale. Or of course you can take part in the ancient tradition of sharing a plant with a neighbor to show off your exceptional green thumb. Hey, if you've got it baby, flaunt it!

44   Rutabaga

Rutabagas are a cross between a turnip and a cabbage. They're also called "swede" or "winter turnip." They're a unique-looking vegetable because the upper part of the rutabaga is burgundy in color and the lower part is cream colored. They look like a 1950s style saddle shoe. You can eat the lower part of the rutabaga as well as the leaves, so it's a pretty versatile vegetable. It's the kind of vegetable that reminds me of my Grandma Grace Micklethwaite. Family get-togethers at her house usually included a dish of rutabaga, which was

Rutabagas are a healthy, nutritionally rich fall root crop that store well in your root cellar.

something that was never cooked at my house. At that age, I didn't mind the lack of rutabaga on our family dinner table because my definition of good food included items such as Cap'n Crunch cereal. Now that I've seen the light I realize the health benefits of root vegetables like this as well the importance of being able to grow plants that will store well into the winter in the root cellar.

As with all brassicas, rutabagas are a super-food, providing anti-oxidants to fight so many of the diseases common to North Americans, from arthritis to high blood pressure and heart disease, diabetes, and some cancers.

Planting

I start rutabagas in the garden because I'm not in a rush to harvest them. They are a cool-season crop, so there's no need to rush their planting. I often wait a good month after the last frost before I plant them. There's always a lot to do in the meantime.

I direct-seed them and thin them so they're about six inches apart. They grow really well in my soil, and if I leave them too close they crowd into each other. The other solution is to thin them as they get bigger to allow more room, but if you forget they'll end up losing some of their round shape. With the current trend of growing vegetables in boxes

Rutabaga tops get very dense, which is excellent for keeping weeds down and retaining moisture.

and making crazy shapes out of them, this may not be a problem for you.

I keep rutabagas well watered and weeded during the summer.

Pests

If you have a problem with cabbage root maggot or flea beetles you can use floating row covers in the season to keep these pests off. By planting them later in June or early July for the fall harvest, you'll be less likely to have problems with these pests. You might find that your rutabagas have a soft, brown interior. You can correct this with either lots of compost or the addition of borax, since this condition indicates a soil boron deficiency. There are also "black leg" and "black rot," which sound like names of characters from "Pirates of the Caribbean." To avoid these, try and rotate your brassicas so they're not planted in the same space each year. If you do have a problem with this be sure to dispose of the whole plant rather than composting it, because diseases like this will stay in the soil and your compost pile may not get hot enough to eliminate them.

Harvesting

I like to leave the rutabagas until we have experienced several frosts before I harvest them. The cold enhances their flavor. I dig them up and cut off their tops and then wash them well. After they've dried I store them in the root cellar. I leave them sitting on a shelf and they generally last four or five months. As spring approaches they'll start to send up new green growth and begin getting soft, so you should eat them before this.

Commercial rutabagas that you buy in the store have actually been dipped in paraffin wax to protect them during shipping and keep them from going bad in store displays. Obviously you should remove the skin of these commercially grown rutabagas, but this isn't necessary when you've grown them in your own garden.

45   Spinach

*"I'm strong to the finich
Cause I eats me spinach.
I'm Popeye the Sailor Man."*

Growing up there was always a huge disconnect for me between, on the one hand, the can of spinach that Popeye was able to open without a can opener and the positive effect eating it had on his physique and, on the other hand, the taste of this hideous vegetable that my mother would encourage me to eat. Popeye made it look so appealing, but somehow my mother managed to cook it in such a way that it triggered my gag reflex.

I'm happy to say, though, that I've matured and love spinach. I prefer it raw and Michelle makes a fantastic spinach salad with mandarin oranges and roasted sunflower seeds topped with an orange-juice-and-mustard-based dressing. It's unbelievably tasty. Michelle tells me that the vitamin C from the oranges helps make the iron in the spinach more readily available to your body. It's wonderful to be able to eat something that tastes great and also provides a huge health benefit. I've convinced Michelle to provide her recipe for this salad at the end of this section—it's that good and that good for you!

One cup of boiled spinach provides you with over 500% of your daily vitamin K requirements, close to 400% of your vitamin A, 85% of your manganese, and 65% of your folate needs. Plus it has the iron Popeye craved, B vitamins, and a whole array of trace elements and minerals. Without question it is a vegetable super-food, and I wish I had a graphic of spinach dressed up like Superman at the top of this page.

Researchers have identified at least 13 different compounds in spinach that act as antioxidants and anticancer agents. The vitamin E in spinach helps with brain function. Its iron is great for women and men, and spinach offers an excellent source of iron without the saturated fat and other negatives of red meat. Spinach even has omega-3 fatty acids, so you don't have to eat fish to get them.

So I'm hoping I've convinced you to grow spinach based on its health merits. But get this: it's also really, really easy to grow. In fact, it almost grows itself, so this should be Number One on your list of "Sure Things to Plant This Spring."

Planting

Spinach is a cool-season crop, so it can be one of the first greens you eat from the garden. You can direct-seed spinach in the garden as soon as the soil

Spinach—an easy-to-grow nutritional powerhouse!

Spinach seedlings emerge.

can be worked. When I said "it almost grows itself" I wasn't kidding. Spinach has a tendency to bolt, or go to seed, and often it does this when I'm not paying attention, so I end up with spinach in various parts of the garden dropping lots of seeds during the growing season. The following spring, before the snow has even finished melting in some of the garden, spinach will be popping up everywhere. So it can really handle the cool weather.

If you're really organized you might even want to rototill or prepare an area in the fall where you plan to plant spinach the following spring. That way, as soon as the snow is gone you can get spinach seeds into the ground. Spinach, like any green vegetable, likes lots of nitrogen in the soil, so compost is key to a good growing environment.

Spinach is something you should spend a little time on as you peruse your seed catalog. You'll find two main cultivars called Savoy and Smooth Leaf, and they'll be categorized as cool-weather and warm-weather spinaches. Savoy-leaf will be the more traditional, crinkly leafed spinach, while Smooth Leaf will be more like a leaf lettuce. While spinach traditionally has been a cool-season vegetable, there are now cultivars such as New Zealand that do well in hot, dry

weather. So if you're determined to have as long a season as possible, you'll want to get some of the cool-weather and hot-weather varieties. We like both Savoy and Smooth Leaf. The downside to Savoy is that I have a really sandy soil, and since spinach grows so close to the ground, rainwater tends to splash sand up onto the leaves and the ridges in the Savoy hold onto the sand. This just means I have to wash it well, but it's something for you to consider.

You may want to plan on getting some spinach in early and holding some back until summer to plant for a fall harvest. And you may want to try one of the warm-weather types as well. As I mentioned, spinach loves to bolt or send up its seed stalk. It does this because of either lack of moisture, which is easy to remedy with regular watering, or hot weather. This is hard to control, so it makes sense to have a few varieties on the go. When I see spinach "volunteers," the plants that seed themselves each year, I don't mind eating them when they're quite small since I don't want them to go to seed. The plant that produced them has already indicated that it's prone to bolting, which isn't a good characteristic for spinach, so I certainly don't want to do anything to extend this trait by using seed from prematurely bolting spinach parents.

Spinach is one of the vegetables I plant when I harvest my garlic during the third week of July, and I also plant some in the cold frame in late August to harvest until the snow flies. Spinach is a really wonderful, hardy plant.

Pests

I have very few problems with spinach other than damage from flea beetles, which eat small holes in the leaves. You can eliminate these with floating row covers, but you have to be careful because they create a small greenhouse effect and make it too warm for the spinach. I find that the spinach I plant later has fewer problems because I've missed the bugs, so this tends to be the crop we store. You should keep your eye on your spinach to see if it does bolt, and at the first sign of a seed stalk pinch it off so that the plant continues to send energy to the leaves. Chances are once the plant gets to the stage where it's sending up a seed pod you're best to just harvest the whole plant, and then you'll get a nice mix of large and small leaves.

Harvest and Storage

You can start harvesting leaves as soon as they appear, starting with the larger outside leaves and leaving the smaller inner leaves to grab sunlight for energy and get larger. Once we get enough on the go and we've had a few meals of it, we start freezing spinach. Spinach is one of the many reasons we're grateful for our freezer. It allows us to save some of that incredible, health-promoting spinach to eat in the winter months. You can take it out and add it to so many dishes.

To freeze spinach, wash it to remove any dirt and then remove any large stalks as well as any yellow or brown leaves. Blanch it by placing it in boiling water for about 1 minute. Take it out of the boiling water and either place it in ice-cold water or rinse it with cold water for about a min-

ute to cool it down. Once you've drained it well you can place it in freezer bags or containers, removing as much of the air as possible. Remember to label it with the year so you can be sure to use it this winter or next spring before more starts arriving.

Spinach tends to bolt in hot weather or if it doesn't receive enough water. These seed stalks will be a source of seed for next year's crop if you leave them.

Fresh Spinach Salad

Salad Ingredients

Spinach, wash and spun dry and torn into bite-sized pieces
1 can of mandarin oranges, or use a fresh orange that you've peeled, separated into segments, and cut into bite-sized pieces
White mushrooms
Red onion
Raw unsalted sunflower seeds

Dressing Ingredients

¼ cup olive oil
¼ cup orange juice
1 tbsp. honey
1 tsp. mustard
Salt & pepper

Clean and slice mushrooms. Slice red onion thinly and separate into rings. Toast sunflower seeds in a dry fry pan until aromatic and beginning to brown. Combine dressing ingredients and shake well.

Place spinach, orange pieces, mushroom slices, and onion rings in salad bowl. Splash dressing over salad and sprinkle with toasted sunflower seeds. Enjoy!

46   Squash – Summer – Zucchini

I decided that rather than putting this vegetable under "Z" for zucchini, which is what I call it, I'd put it with squash and call it "summer squash," as many people do. One of my greatest accomplishments after moving to the country was winning $15 at the Parham Fair one year for entering the "Biggest Zucchini." It was a proud day indeed. As time went on, though, and I realized that small zucchinis are more appropriate for eating, I was concerned that the prize was just a way to mock "cidiots" (city-idiots) like myself who should know better than to let their zucchinis get too big. But the prize category still exists, so I think it's just an example of the good sense of humor country people have, because anyone who grows summer squash inevitably ends up with some that are ludicrously big since they go from being just the right size to monstrous, seemingly overnight.

Zucchini is not necessarily a nutritional heavy hitter, but it is low in calories and has useful amounts of folate, potassium, vitamin A, and manganese. It shouldn't be eaten in its usual "roadhouse-type restaurant" appetizer form, breaded and deep-fried. This defeats the purpose of eating healthy vegetables! It's a wonderful addition to a summer pasta primavera, grilled on the barbeque,

A zucchini can produce an amazing number of blossoms and fruit.

A tiny, perfect zucchini almost ready to harvest.

cooked in a ratatouille, stir-fried with some olive oil, grated and baked in wonderful bread, and, if absolutely necessary, breaded and pan-fried in a bit of oil. If you want to be really fancy schmancy you can stuff and pan-fry the zucchini blossoms, because they're edible. Your dinner guests will be quite impressed by your dish of zucchini blossoms. I have to be honest though…I just can't bring myself to eat them. I know, I know, they're perfectly edible. I just have trouble getting past the idea of eating flowers.

Planting

I plant summer squash seeds in hills after the danger of frost has passed. The seeds need warm soil to germinate. I plant five or six seeds in a hill and then thin to one or two plants once they get going, because they'll get big. They need a good-sized area with lots of compost to produce that vigorous growth, and once they start producing fruit they're going to keep it up for a long time, so you need to make sure you've given the plant the nutrition it needs to keep growing and producing.

If your soil is lacking you may want to mulch around the hills with well-composted manure or compost once they get underway to give them a little extra kick. You should keep them well watered and watch for crawly pests like squash bugs and cucumber bugs, which you'll find in the flowers. Keep your eye on the underside of the leaves for egg clusters from the squash bugs, and scrape these off when you find them.

Harvesting

You probably think I was exaggerating when I said that the zucchinis that are a perfect size one day become monstrous overnight, and perhaps I have overstated it a bit. But zucchinis are best harvested when they're young and tender. I've learned that it's better to cut them off when they're too

Yellow zucchini—a nice addition to the more traditional green.

small rather than wait, because they'll become too large in the course of several days and you'll have enough other stuff going on in the garden that you could miss this window of opportunity. When you cut them leave about an inch of the stem to help preserve them, but they won't last more than a couple of days, so plan your summer meals to enjoy lots of zucchini!

Zucchini plants can get big, so leave lots of room around them.

Female and Male Squash Flowers

This photograph shows male and female flowers.

The female flower shows the beginning of the squash, while the male flower has does its job of pollinating the female and has now fallen off its stem.

So when you see blossoms falling of squash plants, don't panic, they are probably male and will have done their job.

47 Squash – Winter

The difference between summer and winter squash is that winter squash will store well while summer squash will not. So your winter squash are the ones you'll grow to eat as fall and winter vegetables. Your squash harvest will provide your root cellar with vegetables full of vitamins C, A, and K, some B vitamins, and a whole variety of other beneficial nutrients from omega-3 fatty acids to zinc, iron, and calcium. Full of fiber and cancer-fighting and healthy-heart-inducing goodness, they can be a great way to enjoy a local vegetable with major health benefits in the cold months. Plus you can store them without refrigeration in the root cellar, so they help reduce your carbon footprint even more.

There are lots of different squash varieties: acorn, buttercup, butternut, spaghetti, hubbard…the colors, shapes, and sizes seem endless. Some of them look more suited to a role in a *Star Wars* movie, but they're great in soups or baked with some maple syrup to sweeten them up a bit. With so much variety and versatility, they're a great addition to your garden. They have a tendency to take up a fair amount of space, so you should give some thought to how to grow them

Acorn squash trying without much success to climb the trellis provided.

if you have limited space. This year I tried growing some on a trellis and it worked fairly well. So if you're growing in a confined space give some thought to trying this. My only caution would be to keep your eye on them and make sure you help them along while they get trained on the trellis. They don't grow vertically by nature, so they need your help to steer them in the right direction. It's a little bit like parenting in that respect!

Planting

I try to get my summer squash or zucchini started as soon as the soil is warm enough, but I'm not in quite as big a rush with the winter squash. They have a much longer season to mature, and since I'm not going to be harvesting until the fall it's not quite as urgent to get them started. I plant six or seven seeds in a hill and space the hills a good four feet apart, so you can see that if you have limited space taking the time to build a trellis is worth the effort. You can plant squash seeds about one inch deep in the soil and they will still germinate. Once I have a number of seedlings sprouted I put toilet-paper-roll collars around them because of the challenges I have with cutworms. Then once they're big enough that a cutworm can't lop them off, I thin them to one or two plants per hill. These are going to be large plants with numerous fruit on each one, so too many plants in each hill will cause too much competition.

Once the plant gets going it requires little attention. You just have to make sure it stays watered. If I find the time, I like to top-dress the area around the hill once the plants are established to give the roots another boost of energy for the growing season.

Pests

The real challenge with squash is the bugs. Squash bugs, cucumber beetles, and vine borers may be a problem for your squash plants. This may be one plant where you use a floating row cover to try and keep insects from landing. You should try and keep the cover up and off the plants, and even though this lets sunlight in it maintains some warmth in the early going to help the plants get established. I still prefer to keep my eye on the plants and remove these bugs by hand. The squash bugs tend to hide at the base of the plants and they're easy to spot once you know what you're looking for. They lay their eggs on the underside of the leaves, so be sure to check these on a regular basis. One squash bug isn't a problem; it's the mass of babies that result if you let the eggs hatch. So I like to keep a lookout for the adults to make sure the eggs don't get laid in the first place. Cucumber beetles, which look like cute yellow ladybugs, are not beneficial. Some cultivars will tolerate cucumber beetles or you may want to treat them with a pyrethrum spray. Not only will they chew on leaves but they'll spread viral disease and bacterial wilt.

An immature butternut squash.

If your squash vines suddenly wilt, take a look around the base and see if you can see any sawdust-like piles. Squash vine borers will have left these. You may be able to see the hole and use a sharp knife to slice open the vine and remove the borer. To do this you'll need the dexterity of a surgeon, although the stakes are a little lower.

Squash take up a fair amount of room in your garden.

Lots of male flowers available to pollinate female flowers.

Just one squash plant can produce an amazing amount of vegetable protein and carbohydrates for your winter diet.

This past year was a weird summer for me because I had no bugs on my squash plants, and I mean none. I'm so used to them that I kept checking all summer and there was nothing. Perhaps it was because it was so cool and wet. Instead, my squash vines suffered from a downy mildew that caused the leaves to wilt and die early. Luckily, they seemed to suffer from it late enough that the fruit were fully formed and close enough to harvest that it didn't affect them.

Harvesting

I wait as long as possible before harvesting my squash. The first light frosts will cause the leaves to die back and turn brown, but the fruit will be fine. I use pruners to cut the squash off of the vine, making sure to keep an inch or two of the stem with them. You'll want to retain this stem, because if it falls off the squash will tend to rot at the point where the stem was. When I harvest the squash I turn them so that what was on the ground is facing the sun, and I leave them in the sun for several days. Then as time permits I put them in the barn or garage for a week or two. As the weather starts to get colder I start putting the best squash into the root cellar. I sit them on a shelf where they don't touch each other and I make sure to leave

accessible any squash that have marks or blemishes or have lost their stems so that we can eat those first. You should always store the best of the harvest and eat all the worst-looking stuff first.

A spaghetti squash.

Acorn squash store extremely well in the root cellar.

Part of our squash harvest this year.

48   Sweet Potatoes

I own several gardening books which are entirely devoted to just one vegetable. My copy of *Growing Great Garlic* by Ron L. Engeland has been a great help over the years, and we now grow 3,000 heads of garlic and sell some of it for pocket money. After 15 years of growing garlic I'm pretty comfortable with my skills and knowledge. My latest one-topic book is about sweet potatoes, and frankly, I'm still pretty intimidated by them. We grew some this year and we were happy with the results, but for some reason they still seem shrouded in mystery to me. I think that's one of the things I love about gardening. There are always little hurdles to get over, bumps in the road that seem scary as you approach them. I like to throw caution to the wind and give new things a try. Sometimes the results are awesome. Sometimes the results are abysmal. I'm still acquiring knowledge about growing sweet potatoes, but I'm happy to share what I've learned so far. I hope to become much more knowledgeable. I hope to be completely comfortable with growing sweet potatoes, but I don't think I'll ever get to the stage where I'll want to write a whole book about them. I like to be a generalist in most areas of my life, and gardening is the same.

One of the reasons I'm committed to improving my sweet potato growing skills is that they

The morning-glory-like flowers of the sweet potato plant are a joy to behold.

are incredibly healthy for you. They're not just healthy, they're insanely healthy. They are the superfood of superfoods. So if you like to eat them that's awesome! If you can grow them, even better.

According to the Center for Science in the Public Interest, when you look at fiber content, complex carbohydrates, protein, vitamins A and C, iron, and calcium, the sweet potato ranks highest in nutritional value of any vegetable. They really are the ultimate superfood, rich in fiber, complex carbohydrates, and protein. They have more than 300% of your daily requirement of vitamin A, 65% of your vitamin C, and almost 30% of your vitamin B6. The orange color is beta-carotene, which has many health benefits including better vision and protection against macular degeneration and cataracts. Sweet potatoes also have iron, calcium, and lots of trace minerals and nutrients. Sweet potatoes are great for diabetics because they have a low glycemic rating, which means that you digest them slowly which results in a gradual rise in blood sugar so that you feel satisfied longer. It doesn't matter how you slice them, sweet potatoes are the grand slam of healthy vegetables.

Regular potatoes grow well in cooler growing zones, which is where I garden. Sweet potatoes, on the other hand, are a tropical plant and like warmer climates. There are lots of different techniques that northern gardeners can use to improve their chance of success with sweet potatoes, but you still have to work at it. Regular potatoes are much easier for most people. I hope that eventually my sweet potato knowledge will make me casual about growing sweet potatoes as well, but I'm not there yet. I know I have to get cracking because Oprah is huge fan of sweet potatoes, and when Oprah endorses something, it becomes huge.

Sweet potatoes are native to South America and are technically distinct from yams, which are native to Africa and Asia. The plant is a beautiful perennial vine that produces wonderful flowers that look like morning glories. The vines are one of the nicest things I've ever grown in the garden. Ideally sweet potatoes need at least a hundred frost-free days to mature. This can be tough in the north, but you can help things along.

Most of my newfound knowledge about sweet potatoes was gleaned from an excellent book by Ken Allan called *Sweet Potatoes for the Home Garden, with Special Techniques for Northern Gardeners*. Ken Allan lives close to me and has turned his passion for sweet potatoes into a mission to spread the word on how to grow them. His book is an excellent resource if you want more detailed information. Ken has shared his knowledge with Brian Burt and Ruth Hayward, who run the greenhouse where we buy our transplants each spring. Brian and Ruth have been sharing their knowledge and enthusiasm about sweet potatoes with me as well.

Planting

Sweet potatoes prefer a loose and well-drained soil, so make sure you mix a lot of compost in prior to planting. The tubers form on modified roots called storage roots which swell up, so the lighter, airy soil makes it easier for them to grow and expand. The soil should be kept moist but not wet until the vines start to spread. After that the dense leaves keep a lot of the moisture in the soil, and you should only have to water them if you notice the leaves wilting.

As with all vegetables, make sure you move sweet potatoes around your garden from year to year to discourage problems with pests. The first way in which sweet potatoes are different from regular potatoes is in their planting. You don't plant a piece of the potato as you do with regular potatoes. You can start them in several ways. One is by using "slips," shoots that grow out of sweet potatoes you've stored from last year. These may come from sweet potatoes that you purchased at the grocery store. I say "may" because there's a good chance that sweet potatoes from a traditional food distribution network will not sprout. They're usually transported on chilled trucks and kept cool in the produce section of the store. This will basically kill the sweet potato, so try another source of sweet potatoes that have been properly cured and kept warm during the winter, or get plants or cuttings from a garden center. Another way to start sweet potatoes is to keep a few plants inside over the winter and then take cuttings from these plants.

If you aren't able to find a source for slips, you can start them yourself. In the late winter, two months before the final frost date, purchase some sweet potatoes from your seed supplier. Take them home, cut them in half lengthwise, and place them

I used clear plastic held down with wooden stakes in my raised bed to try and increase soil temperature since sweet potatoes are a heat-loving, tropical plant.

face down in an aluminum tray containing several inches of potting mix. Water the soil, put the tray into a plastic bag, and place it on a sunny windowsill. In two to three weeks you'll start to get small, green shoots growing out of the tubers. Like traditional potatoes, initially these will take their nutrition from the tuber root itself, but the difference with sweet potatoes is that they will quickly send out roots from these new shoots where they are below the soil, and these roots will start to seek out nutrition from the soil rather than relying on the tuber. After these have been growing for six or eight weeks and the last danger of frost has passed, you'll be able to separate these slips from the sweet potato tuber and plant them.

While you could plant the whole sweet potato as you would a regular potato, it's not recommended. Northern gardeners will lose a few weeks waiting for the shoots, and you need to get these growing vigorously as soon as the soil is warm or your season won't be long enough. You'll also get numerous shoots, which will mean too many growing too close together, and that can affect the harvest. There's also the possibility that the existing tuber will start to grow again and you'll end up with one big sweet potato the size of a car battery, which will not be convenient to store or bake unless you have an industrial-sized oven in your kitchen.

If you've stored tubers from last year they'll probably start to sprout as spring approaches, so you'll be able to use these as well. This year when we harvested our sweet potatoes we cut dozens of six-inch cuttings from the vines and rooted them in water. They shoot out roots very quickly, and we put these in the house in pots of potting soil. Right now on our windowsills we have lovely lush plants that look like many of the vine houseplants you can purchase. I sense these will start to lose their lower leaves as the spring approaches, but we'll still be able to use them for plants. What we'll do is cut slips off these plants that will now be twelve inches or longer and put them in glass jars with water. Each will send out roots, and when these are long enough we'll place them in

small pots in potting soil. We'll place each of these slips or cuttings in the garden and they'll become a sweet potato plant. You can actually skip the rooting in water stage and put the cutting with next to no roots right in soil. You should bury a number of leaf nodes to maximize root production. This sounds a little complicated, but we enjoy having houseplants anyway and these are just edible plants, or at least end up producing an insanely healthy sweet potato plant.

Sweet potatoes grow best in an average temperature of 75°F (24°C) with lots of sun and warm nights. Northern gardeners will be challenged to guarantee that kind of environment for their sweet potato plants. What they can do is try and optimize the growing conditions. To start, I

BEFORE and AFTER: Above, the four cuttings I planted, prior to covering with clear plastic. Below, the sweet potatoes that swallowed my garden! They are a lovely, vigorous addition to a garden.

would recommend using raised beds, since they get more exposure to the sun and warm up more quickly. You can see from my photos that I use a raised bed in our old barn foundation. I have 8 to 10 inches of topsoil that is actually on top of concrete, which really helps to radiate heat back on cool nights early in the season. Your raised beds can be permanent like this with a natural material like cedar or rock surrounding the soil. You can also make raised beds by hilling up the soil yourself. Just drag soil from the surrounding garden and make hills 5" or 6" high and 18" to 24" across.

Take a root slip, which will now be a beautiful small plant, remove it from the pot, and place it in a small hole you've dug every 12" to 18" apart. Plant the slip to a depth of half its length, which should be about 6" or 15cm. While southern gardeners don't have to worry about using plastic mulch, it is recommended for northern gardeners as a way of keeping the heat in the soil around the plants. Traditionally most gardeners who mulch use black plastic, the theory being that dark colors absorb heat. While black plastic helps prevent some heat from radiating back out of the soil at night, it might also restrict how much can get through to the soil during the day. So I actually

Prior to harvesting the whole crop I reached in and grabbed a few tubers to check their progress.

used clear plastic mulch on my sweet potatoes this year, and I was very impressed with the results. You should apply the plastic mulch several weeks before you plan on planting to prewarm the soil.

While you can purchase special clear plastic for this purpose, some of which is UV treated so that it will last many years, I just went with some clear plastic garbage bags which I cut open and held down with sticks. Since it was my first attempt at sweet potatoes I didn't want to go hog-wild, and the plastic did a good job of keeping the weeds down and the soil moist.

For the first six weeks or so I made sure to put lots of water in the twelve-inch open area in the plastic where the slip was growing. The soil wicked the water throughout the area. Eventually the vines were growing so vigorously that they covered the whole area with a thick mat of leaves, which helped shade the soil and prevent any weeds that might have germinated from growing. They also prevented moisture from evaporating.

Once the sweet potato vines start growing like this it's just a foot race to see how long the season will be to maximize your yield. I wanted to see how things were going, so periodically I would reach down into the loose soil and hunt around until I found a tuber and pulled it up. The plants around it kept growing fine. Ideally you should harvest your crop before the first frost. The further south you are the longer the growing season and the bigger the harvest.

Pests

We didn't have any problems with pests this year although some of the leaves were eaten, which I assumed was grasshoppers but which Brian Burt says were probably tortoise beetles. Sweet potatoes do not seem to have many natural insect predators, which makes them an excellent crop to grow organically.

Purchasing disease-free plants from a grower who specializes in sweet potatoes can prevent the most common causes of disease. You also avoid some problems by making sure the soil has lots of compost and organic material from a variety of sources to ensure that trace minerals are available to the plants. Nematodes may be a problem in the soil, which is an excellent reason to remember to plant in a different spot each year. You might consider applying beneficial nematodes if you have poorly colored or deformed potatoes. Wireworms and grubs are a problem with any root crop, and I always look for these when tilling and preparing soil. I find that if I plant in an area where I've only recently removed the grass I'm more likely to have problems, but over time they become less and less common.

Harvesting

I must say that harvesting my sweet potatoes was one of the hardest things I've ever done in the garden, simply because the vines are so pretty and the flowers are amazing. But it was tough love and up they came. We put in four slips of a variety supplied by Ken Allan to Burt's Greenhouse called Georgia Jet, and we harvested 25 pounds of sweet potatoes. This was pretty great for a first attempt. Unlike regular potatoes that form at the end of roots on the main stock of the plant, sweet potato tubers are the root or form as an outgrowth of the root.

Some of the sweet potatoes we harvested were beautifully shaped tubers, just like the kind you see in the grocery store. Others were shaped less conventionally, and one was about 3 pounds and almost as square as a box. It tasted fine when we cooked it, but it wasn't pretty.

Storage

I think the biggest challenge with sweet potatoes is their storage. Regular potatoes are very rugged. It doesn't matter if I dig them up in the heat or the cold, in wet weather or dry weather. As long as I let them dry out for a day and store only the best ones in dry peat moss they keep all winter, "no problemo."

Sweet potatoes, on the other hand, have to be "cured." This means that you have to hold them at a constant temperature and humidity for an extended period of time to help heal cuts and scrapes and to keep moisture in. As soon as they're

harvested sweet potatoes start to lose moisture, so curing is designed to stop the flow. The best way to cure sweet potatoes is to hold them at a temperature of 85°F to 90°F (30°C to 32°C) and 80% to 90% humidity for five to seven days. In tropical countries growers don't have to worry about curing, but North American gardeners need them to form a layer that will keep moisture in and keep them from drying out.

If you've got a second bathroom or a sauna

Before I dug the plants I took a lot of 12" cuttings that I rooted in water before planting in pots.

One of our beautiful indoor sweet potato vine plants that I'll take cuttings from this winter and root in water before putting it into a small pot with potting mix, ready to plant out next spring for next year's crop.

with its own heat control this can be a perfect place to cure sweet potatoes. If you have the boss and wife over to impress them, though, you may want to take the sweet potatoes out of the sauna before you all sit down for a good sweat. "So, John, why do you have sweet potatoes in the sauna?" A humidifier will help, and if you have small quantities of sweet potatoes, placing them in paper bags will help retain the moisture while allowing some of the off gases to leave.

The other requirement with sweet potatoes is

If you plant sweet potatoes leave lots of room for them.

that they should be kept above 55°F (13°C). If you keep them below temperature for very long they will eventually rot. Grocery stores don't want them to sprout as a result of being too warm but end up damaging them with the cold. This really is one of the wonderful things about growing your own. You have complete control over harvesting, curing, and storage, which will enhance their flavor over store-bought sweet potatoes. The flavor and sweetness actually improves during the fall and into early winter.

I'm hoping my description of growing sweet potatoes hasn't seemed too complicated. I think once you get into the groove you'll find them quite easy to grow. I know you'll love the plants when they're growing because they're a joy to look at. When you start baking sweet potato pies and integrating them into your diet your body will love them. They are the nutritional equivalent to hitting the jackpot on a slot machine, the difference being that there is no luck involved. You know that growing and eating sweet potatoes is really, really good for you, so the outcome is a given.

49   Swiss Chard

Swiss chard is a very hardy plant and nutritious vegetable, but perhaps another green leafy vegetable might sound a little boring at this point. Boring until you see some of the new varieties like Neon Lights Mix from Burpee Seeds or Bright Lights from Johnny's Seeds. The rhubarb-like stocks are pink and red and orange and yellow. They look fantastic in the garden. They take a plain old workhorse of a green leafy vegetable and give it a *Saturday Night Fever* flash.

Swiss chard is a member of the beet family, which means that it packs a really healthy punch. It's a great source of vitamins K, A, C, and E, as well as magnesium, potassium, and iron. It's also a good source of some B vitamins, calcium, and

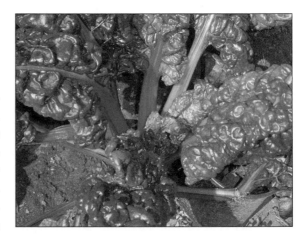

copper. So it's really worth growing some in your vegetable garden. Whether you're tossing it with some olive oil in a penne pasta, using it in omelets and frittatas or in vegetarian lasagna as a substitute for spinach, or using the young tender leaves in salads, it's a versatile addition to the garden.

Growing

Swiss chard is extremely easy to grow, just like beets, and prefers cool and mild weather, but I've found it to be fairly heat resistant. It's not a heavy feeder, so it doesn't have to be in a heavily composted area of the garden. I direct-seed it about half an inch deep with the seeds about one inch apart. Since the plants are fairly compact you can have rows closer together, in the range of 18 inches or so. I use succession plantings until early in the summer so that I have a fairly consistent supply all season. Once the seeds germinate and the plants start growing I thin them to about 4 inches apart, and I use the plants that I thin in salads. I like the red Swiss chard with red stocks and green leaves and red veins in the green leaf; it's a really striking addition to a plain old green salad.

When you look at Swiss chard seeds you'll notice that they're like members of the beet family and actually contain many seeds. So once they sprout you'll actually have several plants sprouting from the one seed. If you don't thin these for salads you'll have denser plantings, with more leaves to harvest later when they're bigger.

Like all plants chard needs a steady supply of water, but I find that Swiss chard can handle the dry weather. In fact it can handle heat as well. So many leafy vegetables have a tendency to wilt and can't handle the extreme heat of summer heat waves, but Swiss chard stands proud and wilt-resistant during the worst of it. I've had very few problems with Swiss chard. Sometimes the leaves will get small chew marks in them, which could be from leaf miners or a variety of leaf chewers that inhabit my garden, from grasshoppers right on down the line. Luckily I tend to have enough of any crop that I can discard really bad leaves and cut around the bad spots on others. Yes, if would be great to live in a bubble free of insect pests, but I do what I can and then try and relax when sometimes the smallest inhabitants of the garden get a small feed as well.

Harvesting

Once the plants get big enough you can start removing the outside leaves to eat. Leave the smaller inside leaves to get bigger for harvest later on. Swiss chard will go right into the fall frosts, so I do succession plantings during the late spring and early summer so that I have some later as well. In warmer climates chard may make it through the winter, and in colder growing zones you can actually mulch Swiss chard and it will begin growing again in the spring. During the second year of its growth it will be focused on sending up a seed head. You can let this go and harvest your own seeds or you can cut it back so that the plant puts its energy into the green growth and you get to eat the early shoots as a nice green vegetable early in the season.

With lush green leaves and brilliant red stalks, Swiss chard makes a dramatic statement in the garden or on your dinner plate.

Three Swiss chard seedlings grown inside and transferred to the garden.

50   Tomatoes

I'm a huge fan of lycopene! While not many people would admit this, once I discovered it I was hooked! Lycopene is a carotene that research has shown to be an excellent antioxidant and therefore effective in preventing some types of cancers. Your body produces free radicals which damage cells and have been linked to degenerative diseases like cancer, cataracts, and cardiovascular disease. While the FDA has been slow to recognize the data, there are many who feel that lycopene has powerful abilities to help protect your body against disease, and tomatoes are the best source of lycopene you'll find. The fact that they are fabulous-tasting and have all the usual benefits of vegetables, such as fiber, makes tomatoes all the more appealing.

When you cook most vegetables you diminish the nutritional benefits of the vitamins, but when you cook tomatoes you actually increase the concentration of lycopene available to your body. The lycopene in tomato sauce is four times more readily available than that in raw tomatoes. Cooking and serving tomatoes in oil-rich dishes like pasta and pizza sauces greatly increases the absorption of lycopene into your bloodstream.

Tomatoes are rich in vitamin C and a good source of vitamins A and E and the B vitamins. So whether you cook them to enhance their lycopene or eat them raw for the benefit of all of those C and B vitamins, tomatoes are an excellent addition to your diet.

Tomatoes are also pretty easy to grow, even in containers, so if you're living in an apartment or townhouse, as long as you get some good sun you should be growing tomatoes.

There are two main types of tomatoes: determinant and indeterminant. Determinant cultivars tend to be bushy plants that grow to a certain height and then stop so they can put all their energy into their fruit. These don't have to be staked and are really best for commercial growers who don't have the ability to stake every plant and who basically want all the fruit to mature at the same time to make harvesting easy. Indeterminant cultivars just keep growing until the frost stops them, so they should be staked or grown in tomato cages.

The tomato pages of a seed catalog are a joy to read. There are so many varieties and there's so much red on the page! It makes you crave pasta with tomato sauce for dinner. With so many cultivars it's easy for everyone to find a variety they like. I generally go with the varieties our local greenhouse owner has picked out. He's chosen them to suit our growing season and to have resistance to diseases that are common to my garden. I usually plant three or four varieties, some early, some later, some large, like beefsteak tomatoes, some smaller, and some Roma for our

I try and give my tomatoes all the help I can with marigolds to discourage nematodes and onions to discourage insect pests.

pasta sauces. With variety like this we maximize the possibility of a good harvest.

Planting

While it's a good idea to plant tomatoes in an area with fertile soil, don't overdo the compost or composted manure. Too much nitrogen and you'll end up with too much foliage and not enough fruit. When I built raised beds in the barn foundation I used soil that was wonderfully dark and rich and had been building up nitrogen for many years. The tomato plants that grew in those raised beds were huge and had lots of leaves but not much fruit.

Tomatoes are a great plant to start indoors in the winter six to eight weeks before your last spring frost date. We start some ourselves and rely on our local greenhouse for some transplants as well. Burt's does an exceptional job and their tomato seedlings are inevitably healthier and bigger than our own. Tomatoes are heat-loving plants, and they really need that heat in order to thrive when they're getting started. They also need it when you plant those transplants in the garden, so don't rush it.

For many years I've tried to rush the season, growing tomatoes in various "cloches" and using other techniques to speed them up. The one conclusion I've come to is that tomatoes love the heat but I don't have a greenhouse, so I can't control this. When it comes right down to it, the plants that I started early and tried to protect from the cold matured at just about the same rate as the plants that I set out later, several weeks after the last frost date. I've even found that setting tomatoes out on the date that traditionally is the last frost date isn't the best idea. We'll still have cool evenings and the plants just don't like this. I take the plants I purchase from the greenhouse and leave them out in the sun during the day and bring them into the house at night for a week or two before I finally set them out. If you want to speed up the season by all means go for it. Your seed catalog will have lots of products to help you do this.

When I plant my transplants in the ground I make sure to dig the hole extra deep and plant them so that the small bottom leaves are close to the earth. The lower part of the stem, which is darker in color, will have small hairs on it. This area will actually send out roots, so I make sure it's in the soil to encourage more roots to grow and help make the plants even healthier. I also stake them when I plant them to avoid damaging roots that I will inevitably hit if I wait until the plants have become established.

I prefer to stake, tie, and prune my tomatoes to keep them more compact than they'll be in a tomato cage.

If you've started some tomato plants yourself and they seem too tall and lanky without enough greenery toward the bottom, you can deal with this quite easily. Dig a small trench two or three inches deep, perhaps four to six inches long, and lay the tomato seedling down in it. Carefully bend the upper

leafy section out of the soil and then backfill soil on the lanky part of the stalk that's now in the ground. The buried stalk will send out new roots and you'll actually be giving this plant you probably weren't too enthused about a new lease on life. With that much extra root area, once the sun hits those exposed leaves the tomato plant will thrive.

I put collars on my tomatoes to keep the cutworms off and I also make a small circle with dirt walls around the base for watering to prevent the water from running away from the little plants. This way I can stand with the watering can and fill up the reservoir and the water will eventually trickle down to where the roots need it rather than running off to where it may do no good.

Care

Tomatoes do well in raised beds because they like the heat. They also like a consistent level of moisture, so regular watering is important if you aren't getting rain. Black plastic mulch is great to help retain heat and conserve moisture. Using a plastic

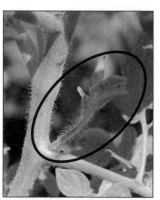

mulch with a drip irrigation system under it is optimal. You can use natural mulches like straw or leaves, and an advantage of these is that they'll keep the lower fruit from sitting on the soil and may also prevent disease-causing organisms from getting splashed onto the plant by the rain. When you water, make sure you just water the soil and keep the water off the foliage to help lessen the risk of disease.

I like to prune my tomatoes to help increase their yield of large, healthy fruit. When you look at the tomato plant you'll see small suckers growing between the stem and the main leaf branches. I pinch these off as soon as I spot them. By removing them you prevent the suckers from growing and making the plant too bushy, which results in too much of the plant's energy going into green growth rather than fruit. I also remove the suckers to encourage the plant to have one main stem, which is the one I've staked and the one where the fruit will grow. Removing suckers reduces shading of the fruit and allows the sun to penetrate evenly into the inner parts of the plants, assisting ripening and eliminating disease.

I try and keep this pruning up during the season and then six weeks before the first frost date I start pruning all the growing tips on the plant. I also remove any new blossoms that form because I know that late in the summer they're not going to have a chance to ripen anyway. By pruning this growth that isn't going to amount to any additional fruit I'm getting the plant to focus all its energy on ripening the fruit it already has. What you want is a reasonable number of big, healthy, ripe tomatoes rather than bushels of small green tomatoes.

I've compared the yield from my pruned, staked tomato plants and the tomato plants that I grow in tomato cages and don't prune. I get more tomatoes from the pruned and staked plants. The unpruned ones get overgrown, and the weight of the heavy green growth usually causes the entire tomato cage to topple over. The plants end up with a lot of top growth without a corresponding increase in fruit production.

Pests

The only insect problem I've ever had with my tomatoes was "a" tomato hornworm, a huge, green, terrifying caterpillar that I noticed on a plant where lots of the leaves were gone. I only spotted it because I was looking carefully at that area. Keep your eyes peeled for these and pluck them

Removing suckers like this encourages one main stalk and keeps the tomato plant more compact and manageable.

off and drown them.

Blossom end rot is a frustrating problem you may have with tomatoes, and it can be caused by a number of different things. You'll sometimes notice that the flowers that should turn into fruit after being pollinated will just drop off and no fruit will form. If this is a common problem in your garden from year to year, give some thought to doing a soil test. This will tell you if it's a deficiency in nitrogen, phosphorus, or potassium. Good compost from a variety of sources should prevent this. I believe, though, that the main reason for blossom end rot is cooler temperatures, especially at night. This summer was very cool and it took my tomatoes much longer than usual to start setting fruit. Often we're still having cool nights when they're setting fruit, and this stress can cause the flowers to drop off.

On the other hand, even though tomatoes love heat there's a limit to that love. If you have an extended heat wave where it doesn't cool off enough at night you may find that you lose blossoms then, too. Too much moisture in the soil can cause this as well, as this year proved, since our July was so wet and damp that I never had to water my tomato plants.

The good news about blossom end rot is that eventually the correct conditions will likely return and the tomato plants will return to being able to set fruit properly. This is why I like to plant four or five different varieties of tomatoes in different

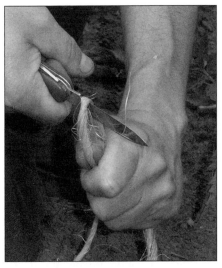

I like to use binder twine to tie tomatoes to stakes because it will break down over time.

Tomato Diseases

The main challenge you'll have with tomatoes is a variety of diseases that are invisible but can still have a negative effect on your plants. Rule number one with tomatoes is to keep relocating them each year and discard any plants that you have problems with. Don't compost them; throw them out so they don't bring the disease into your compost soil.

Here are the common problems you'll have with tomatoes:

V	verticilium wilt
N	nematodes
LS	leaf spot
ST	stemphylium
F	fusarium wilt
TMW	tobacco mosaic virus
ASC	alternaria stem canker
C	cladosporium (leaf mold)

This list might scare you off and make you wonder if you should bother growing something so disease-prone. Well, the good news is that many of the tomato cultivars available today have some natural resistance to these problems. When you're reading your seed catalog you'll see that a resistant cultivar has the corresponding letter next to its name.

Towards the end of the season I prune back the top growth so that the plant's energy is devoted to the fruit that are already set.

spots in my garden. My attitude is that I'm increasing the odds that, regardless of the problems I may encounter, from moisture to soil conditions to insect pests to soil-borne diseases, I'm more likely to get a good harvest from at least one of the varieties. When you see the number of potential diseases that tomatoes are susceptible to, anything you can do to increase the odds of success is a good idea.

Ripe Roma tomatoes are excellent for sauces and contain loads of lycopene when cooked.

Hybrids versus Heirloom

I know I'm going to take some abuse from die-hard organic, anticorporate, seed-saving heirloom fans, but I'm afraid I'm not a real fan of heirloom tomato plants. I haven't really enjoyed the flavor of any that I've tried so far. I'm sure some would say that's because I grew up on pale, golfball-like tomatoes that were shipped green from California and don't know what a real tomato tastes like. Point taken. As I've already admitted, I was a huge fan of Cap'n Crunch cereal as I was growing up, so I cannot claim to have refined, gourmet taste buds.

But none of the heirloom cultivar tomatoes I've ever grown has thrived, and none has provided a fruit that I would say is superior to that of hybrids. When I say hybrid I'm not saying a genetically modified Frankenfood produced in a lab with mammal genes and alien DNA. A hybrid is a plant produced by a hand-pollinated cross between two distinct parent lines. Hybrids tend to produce more uniform plants and fruit of better quality and with higher yields than open-pollinated cultivars. In recent years I've come to enjoy eating my tomatoes raw, whether in salads or sandwiches or drizzled with olive oil and basil and balsamic vinegar in a delicious caprese salad. While I understand the attraction of heirlooms, I've just had better luck with hybrids.

I would strongly encourage you to decide for yourself. There is a plethora of heirloom and heritage tomatoes available from mainstream seed catalogs, from growers who specialize in the heirloom seeds, and probably from local seed savers in your community. It's one of the joys of gardening—so much variety, limited only by your own ambition to try them. If at some time in the future you plan on saving your tomato seeds to grow your own, you'll want to stay away from hybrids. Since they have been bred from different cultivars, the plants you grow from their seed will not be "true," and you won't be able to get consistent plants in the future. I discuss this further in the seed saving chapter 64.

Harvesting

If you've chosen your varieties carefully you'll have early tomatoes, and seed catalogs today have some cultivars that should produce fruit in very little time. Once they start ripening, start harvesting. Be careful when you pick a tomato from a stem that has more than one tomato on it. Pull just the tomato and stem you want without disturbing the others. As the season gets going you'll probably find you soon have more tomatoes than you can deal with. This is when it's good to score points with friends and neighbors who don't garden themselves.

You can also start to think about storing tomatoes for the winter. I discuss canning in chapter 62, but we have taken to freezing a lot of our tomatoes. Michelle removes the skins by putting the tomatoes in boiling water for sixty seconds and then plunging them into ice-cold water. After they've cooled, the skins are easily removed and

A staked and pruned tomato plant makes it easy to get to the tomatoes and allows the sun to reach the fruit.

she puts the tomatoes in plastic freezer bags and into the freezer they go. They're great for using in sauces and soups. One of our favorite winter treats is to put some frozen tomatoes in a pot on the wood stove early in the day with some garlic and frozen basil. Over the course of the day much of the liquid boils off and a wonderful summer aroma of tomatoes, garlic, and basil fills the house. By dinnertime the soup is thick and delicious. It has next to no fat and is so tasty you don't need salt. With some fresh whole-wheat bread you have a meal low in fat and high in antioxidants and lycopene with wonderful flavor. A meal like this fits right into what Dan Buettner recommends in his book The Blue Zones, in which he describes the areas in the world where people live the longest. This meal is all vegetables. It's low in fat and it's a light meal late in the day, which is the best way to increase longevity. Makes me crave cold winter days!

When buying transplants at the garden center watch for sores like this which will make the plant more susceptible to damage.

Harvest time! There are going to be some happy neighbors once we've frozen enough for the winter.

51　Turnips

Turnips come from the cabbage family and are a pretty rugged, versatile vegetable. Not only do they do well in cool-season areas, you can eat both the roots and the green tops. Nothing goes to waste! They're a "green" vegetable even though the root usually isn't green. They also can mature fairly quickly, which makes them a great early root vegetable for the garden.

As with other members of the brassica family, the greens are high in vitamin A, folate or vitamin B9, vitamin C, and calcium. They have more than three times the daily recommended requirement for vitamin K, which is important for good health for a variety of reasons. The turnips themselves are very high in vitamin C, which is a good reason to grow some and store them for the winter. They're like a glass of orange juice that hasn't had to travel to you from Florida or Brazil.

Planting

Since they tolerate cool temperatures turnips are a good vegetable to plant very early. You can direct-seed them early because they really don't like the hot weather. I plant them fairly densely and then start thinning as the plants emerge. You can eat the little plants that you thin in your salad. As the turnip roots start to form I thin them again to leave about six inches between each plant, and those early small turnips are a very tasty, tender treat.

You shouldn't let turnips go too long or they'll lose some of their flavor and become woody and tough. So I plant an early crop and then plant again in summer for a late crop. They like the cool weather, so the ones that mature early in the fall taste great and are perfect for storing.

As turnips grow, the part that begins to form above the soil turns purple or red with most cultivars, but the flesh will be white throughout.

Pests

Root maggots may eat some of the early turnips, but since I'm still thinning at this time I usually have enough so that I can find lots to eat that haven't been chewed. The ones you plant in July or August for fall harvest will tend not to have root maggots because you'll have missed the fly's egg-laying stage.

Harvest

You've been harvesting the greens and young turnips all season to make room for the final storage crop. If you remove the tops the turnips should store well in your root cellar for a few months. Keep your eye on them to make sure they're not going soft.

Thick turnip tops like these keep the weeds down and help the soil retain moisture.

52   Watermelon

Growing your first watermelon is like a rite of passage for a vegetable gardener. It shows you've graduated to the big leagues; you're an adult now and can play with the big boys. Just the size of a watermelon leaves you feeling accomplished. And growing something that is so sweet is very rewarding. You start wondering, "how did such a sweet, tasty, wonderfully moist thing come from this soil I have here in my garden." Sweet things are supposed to come in plastic wrappers at the convenience store. Growing your own watermelons can be a transcendental moment.

Watermelons can also help define what generation you're from. So often I associate watermelons with a comedian called Gallagher whose trademark was smashing a big watermelon with a giant mallet and showering his audience with watermelon guts. Now that's funny stuff, although it seems a little wasteful in a world where almost seven billion people are competing for dinner.

Watermelons aren't exactly classified as a superfood for their nutritional benefits, but in terms of a sweet, thirst-quenching addition to your diet, they can't be beat. I must admit I don't usually eat them at the dinner table. I like to sit on the front lawn where I let the juices drip onto the grass and spit out the seeds.

Watermelons are 6% sugar and 92% water by weight, so you can think of them as the ultimate upscale flavored water that comes in an organic and easily compostable package. Watermelons are a great source of vitamin C with close to a quarter of your daily recommended allowance. They also contain vitamins A, B6, and B1 as well as potassium and magnesium.

As a spreading vine, watermelons need a fair amount of room, but you can actually train them to grow up a trellis. This year I raised some Tiger Baby watermelons on a trellis and they matured without any help. Ideally I should have used some form of netting to hold them up once they started getting big, but they just managed to hang on until they were ripe. So even if your garden space is limited there's no reason not to grow watermelons.

Planting

I'm not really going to talk much more about watermelons because I've already described how to grow them in Chapter 20, the cantaloupe–muskmelon chapter. You can grow watermelons using the same methods and they will be susceptible to the same pests as cantaloupes. They need rich soil with lots of compost to start, and they

want heat and consistent moisture. When you see the size of a watermelon and realize it's more than 90% water, it stands to reason you need to keep the water coming.

There's often a small, curly section of the vine near the stem of a watermelon that starts to go brown when it's ripe. You can also tap on the watermelon and if it makes a dull thud sound then it's probably ready.

While I've grown full-size watermelons in the past, I now tend to grow just the smaller, rounder varieties like Tiger Baby. They seem to ripen quickly and produce a wonderfully tasty melon and they'll produce a number of watermelons on each vine, which helps to extend the season. This year I even harvested some after the first light frost and they still tasted great.

Some Tiger Babies growing more traditionally on the ground.

A mature watermelon is over 90% water, so these two go hand in hand.

Some Sugar Baby transplants getting ready to climb the trellis made from a shelf salvaged from the local dump.

An unsupported melon on the trellis.

The black pot absorbs sunlight to help this heat-loving fruit mature faster and keep it off the ground on cooler nights.

PART III

Fruits and Berries

53   Strawberries

Eating sweet, juicy berries that you've grown yourself is one of the ultimate gardening rewards. And standing in the berry patch eating berries without having to wash them is pretty great too. Commercial growers are under a lot of pressure to grow cosmetically attractive fruit, but that can often involve a lot of the "cides" most of us would rather avoid...pesticides, insecticides, fungicides, herbicides…you name it. With the rising cost of these petroleum-based products and consumers demanding "cleaner" fruit, many farmers are moving towards an integrated pest management (IPM) program, which minimizes the application of these products and tries to maximize their effectiveness. Still, many fruits and berries have been identified as the most concentrated sources of these products.

Strawberries in particular can be a tough crop to get to market looking just right and tend to be one of the most highly sprayed fruits. In California growers use methyl bromide to boost their yields; not only is this bad for your body's nervous system, it's also bad for the planet's nervous system because it eats away at the ozone layer. And that's just to grow the berries. If you live in the north and eat those berries when you can't get locally produced berries, which is probably ten months of the year, the carbon footprint of those little red berries is monstrous.

So growing your own is better all around. The caveat that I think I need to add, since the subtitle of this book has the word "easy" in it, is that berries require a little bit more commitment on your part. Berries are perennial, which means that when you plant them they're going to be around for a few years. My attitude with my vegetable garden is that I know I can wipe the slate clean every fall and start fresh every spring. If I have one of those late summers and autumns where I lose interest in weeding, or get distracted with work and just don't weed properly, I know I can pump some gas into my rototiller and go at the garden and completely clean it up in time for spring planting. Yes, I know that if I've let the weeds go to seed and I rototil them into the soil some of them are going to germinate and I'm going to have more work weeding. But right now because each year the vegetable garden is a clean slate I can play a little fast and loose with the weeding rules.

Berries are not going to be so forgiving, and if you don't keep up with the weeding of the berry patch you won't be able to just start over again without disturbing your strawberry plants. So if you're going to plant berries make sure you're committed to keeping them well maintained; otherwise you're just setting yourself up for disappointment. When we first moved here I immediately planted strawberries, something that I'd always dreamed of doing as a gardener but had never had the room for. The dream quickly turned to a nightmare as enlarging gardens and doing one-thousand-and-one other things on our 150 acres and in our hundred-year-old farmhouse distracted me. The strawberries were ignored and when I did finally find a few minutes to devote to them it was overwhelming and depressing. Eventually I just gave up on them. Then last year after a long hiatus I got serious and planted berries again. I had a different attitude this time and am committed to having them thrive. So they are getting weeded and nurtured.

Planting

Strawberries like a slightly acidic soil, so you don't have to worry about liming or using wood ash. To prepare the area you should make sure the soil has lots of good compost worked in. Avoid planting strawberries in a low area because frost will tend to be worse there and strawberries are sensitive to frost. Try not to plant strawberries where you have grown tomatoes, peppers, eggplants, potatoes, raspberries, or corn because the soil may contain verticillium wilt.

You are most likely to purchase strawberry plants with roots on them ready to put into the garden. These bare-root plants will probably come in bunches of 25. Plant them so that the crowns are level with the soil. During the first year you want the plant to get established, so you should remove the blossoms and allow the plant's energy to go into its roots and runners and not into the fruit. The plant will send out a number of runners, which are basically little baby plants still attached to the mother plant by an umbilical cord. At the end of a runner a new plant will form and if it comes into contact with soil it will send down its own root system and get established. Another runner will sometimes grow out of the first plant,

so you'll have a runner from a runner. Sounds like something from *Invasion of the Body Snatchers*.

How you plant your strawberries will depend on what you want to do with the runners. If you have a lot of space you may want to plant them in a "matted row." This is more like a berry patch than a row, because the main plants are going to send out runners all around, like the spokes on a wheel, so the row is going to be very wide and haphazard since you can't always control where the runners will go. With this system you want to set the plants one and a half to two feet apart in rows that are three to four feet apart. You need big, wide rows because the rows are going to become patches that will be quite wide themselves.

Strawberry plants will come in bunches of 25. Plant so that the crown is level with the soil.

If your garden space is more limited you should put your plants about a foot apart and make the space between the rows less than three feet. You'll need to take the time to train the runners to go where you want them to and to get them to root in the space between each mother plant, not too far from the center of the row. Anytime you check the row and move a runner that has sent out some roots, just put some soil over those roots to hold them in place. The

Put lots of soil around the plant, pat it down, and water your new transplant well.

goal will be to try and keep the row reasonably compact and the plants fairly uniformly spaced. Don't let the mother plants and runner babies, sometimes called daughter plants, get too close together. If they do they'll end up competing for nutrients and water.

Strawberries send down a fairly shallow root considering that they're perennial, so they have to be well watered when you first plant them and you have to be careful to keep them watered for the whole season, especially if there's a drought. If you have strawberries that produce early it's easy to ignore them once the berries are harvested, but you have to continue to make sure the plants get the water they need to be healthy for the following year's crop.

A newly planted row of strawberries. I got the plants in first and started removing the neighboring weeds later.

Strawberries can benefit from good mulch, and as their name suggests, straw is a good mulch to use. You might be tempted to use hay if it's easier to buy, but hay has too many weed seeds. Avoid using leaves and grass as mulch as they are too thick and tend to weigh down the plants and smother them. Straw is the stalk of a grain plant, so it should contain very few seeds. Straw mulch helps to keep the moisture in and the weeds down. Once the plants start producing it also helps to keep the fruit off the ground, which is really important in order to avoid problems with the berries themselves. Mulch may prevent runners from rooting, so as you inspect your rows and notice a runner, pull the mulch back and root the runner by placing some soil over it.

Pests

Many of the main problems with strawberries can be avoided by buying from a supplier who provides good-quality, certified virus- and disease-free plants. Two of the most common problems are verticillium wilt and red steele. Some plants are also resistant to powdery mildew, which is a disease that will turn your wonderful red berries into big, fluffy, grey spore balls in no time. During some brutally cool and wet seasons a bit of mildew is inevitable, but make sure to keep your plants well spaced. If they're too close together it's easier for mildew to spread.

Sometimes you'll find a frothy mass of bubbles on your plants caused by a spittlebug sucking sap from the plant. These are gross but won't do too much damage. You can blast them off with the hose. If you find rolled up leaves, unroll them to look for a strawberry leaf roller inside. If you find any, remove the leaf and squish the larva inside. If your leaves turn brown and you can find a fine web underneath, it may be spider mites. A strong spray with soapy water should eliminate these.

If your fruit start looking kind of a gnarly, deformed, and unstrawberry-like, it may be because of tarnish plant bugs. These bugs actually inject a toxin into the buds while they're feeding on them. Pick these bugs off or use a pyrethrin spray if they're bad. I have also lost a few strawberry plants to cutworms early in the season. If you see leaves falling and stems toppling over, dig around in the soil and squish the cutworms.

Harvesting

After removing blossoms the first year you'll be able to start harvesting berries the second year. Be careful to leave the stem and other berries intact when you pick the ripe ones. I think of strawberries as one of the first great tastes of summer. Most of the cultivars you purchase are designed to be ready early in the season. There are now some cultivars called "day-neutral" or "everbearing" which are designed to provide berries right up until frost. I haven't had any experience with these and I guess I'm a bit of purist. I eat baskets of local strawberries for about four weeks while they're in season and I stop eating them when our local season is over. Often by this time, after eating so many I'm sick of them. We freeze some and make jam with some, so we're able to enjoy them year round in other forms. I can't speak to how well everbearing plants will do. It may be something I'll experiment with in the future.

After that first season when you get the plants going, your strawberries should continue to produce a crop for you for three to five years depending on a number of variables. To prolong their productive years make sure you continue to keep your plants well watered and composted. Sprinkling them with compost early in the spring and again in the fall should help keep them healthy. After a few years some of your original plants may start to look tired and won't perform well. Remove these and let the runner plants fill in and make up the difference.

Eventually, though, the patch will reach the end of its natural life and will need to be tilled under. You may want to put a cover crop like clover here the following year to try and rehabilitate the soil. Then you should pick a new location and start with new plants. If you have unlimited space you could start a new row every year and have the rows at different stages of production so that you're

Those first-year transplants are starting to look like a berry patch.

starting a new row and removing an old row each year. This would be a lot of work, though, and require a lot of space, but if you love strawberries it just might be worth it.

This runner has started to form roots which I'm helping along by planting in a hole I dug to increase the number of plants producing strawberries.

54   Raspberries

Raspberries are unbelievably tasty and unbelievably good for you, so they're a perfect investment of garden space and time. Raspberries are packed with vitamin C and antioxidants. They're like sweet and juicy little health drops hanging in the garden, sucking up all that solar energy to produce a powerful blast of disease-fighting and energy-giving goodness. Sorry if it sounds as though I'm writing a commercial, but why not? Companies that make sugary drinks and junk food spend billions of dollars advertising products with questionable health benefits. I've never seen an advertisement for raspberries, but there should be one because they're what keep you out of the doctor's office.

Along with vitamin C they have a variety of antioxidants. If you're ever in a health food store and see a supplement called ellagic acid, it's usually made from raspberries. It's a phytonutrient that helps prevent cell damage from free radicals. There are also elements in raspberries that are antimicrobial and may have cancer-protective properties. This is on top of the great fiber they add to your diet, along with 60% of your recommended daily allowance of manganese and 50% of your vitamin C in just a one-cup serving. Raspberries also contain vitamins B1, B2, B3, folic acid, magnesium, copper, and iron. If you're getting tired of trying to swallow a multivitamin the size of a horse tranquilizer, maybe it's time you started growing some raspberries and putting them on your granola in the morning. Your colon will thank you.

A raspberry is made up of about a hundred drupelets, each of which has juicy pulp and a seed. That seed is why your colon will be happy, because your system won't be able to fully digest it so it's going to work its way through your digestive system dragging with it all that nasty stuff that shouldn't be sitting around down there. So put away the powdered fiber that you mix with water and start eating lots of raspberries.

Planting

Raspberry plants are perennials that can live for decades, so you want to pick a good location for them. They'll need a fair amount of room. If you're still in an urban or suburban environment and you have limited space for your vegetable garden, it might be time to turn a flower garden into a raspberry patch.

Raspberries like a rich soil, so hopefully you've been building up those flower beds over the years. If you do plant them in or near the vegetable garden make sure that you keep them away from where the nightshade or solanum plants such as tomatoes, potatoes, and eggplants have been growing, and don't put them where strawberries have been grown recently. There could be root diseases left in the soil that you will want to avoid. It will also be a challenge to plant raspberries where there has recently been grass growing, because it can be pretty hard to eliminate. This is where long-term

While it may be a little thorny there's nothing more appetizing than a raspberry patch covered with sweet, juicy, red raspberries.

Raspberry canes come bundled from your supplier. Get them in water right away and into the ground soon after.

planning of your gardens pays off. This year work to get your vegetables growing and think about where you might put raspberries in the future. If the area you've chosen is grass-covered, put some rotten hay or a thick layer of leaves or mulch on the area to kill the grass this summer. Then turn it over with your shovel or rototiller in the fall so it's ready to plant in the spring.

I strongly recommend that you have a large open area without grass nearby, because grass will encroach upon your row of raspberries again and will be a major pain to get rid of. It's been my biggest downfall with any of my berries.

If you're lucky, you might find a friend or neighbor who is thinning a raspberry patch and is willing to provide you with a few plants. Otherwise you can order them through a seed catalog or pick them up at the local garden center. Make sure you prepare a really deep hole for the plants. Dig it much deeper than you need and then backfill with good healthy topsoil and lots of rich compost. You want to make sure the roots don't sit in water, and this is one of the best ways to ensure good drainage. Many of the potential problems with berries can be root related, and unlike strawberries that have shallow roots, raspberries can send down very deep roots. So the easier it is for them to make their way through the soil and the easier it is for moisture to percolate down through the soil and not sit around near the roots, the better it is for your plants.

Plants you've ordered from a seed catalog will be shipped bareroot, meaning that you'll receive about a 12-inch cane and root ball in peat moss. You should make sure you get some water on these as soon as they arrive. If you order them like this you should also have your row or holes prepared so that you're ready to plant the day you receive them. Put the roots in a bucket of water while you work. Plant the cane an inch or two lower than it was previously planted, which you'll probably be able to determine from the base of the cane. Spread the roots out carefully and then backfill around them and give the area a really deep watering.

Plant the canes a good 24 inches (60 cm) apart and if you have more than one row keep them from 4 to 6 feet apart. Raspberries are going to get very bushy

Make sure the white shoots sprouting from the root mass are planted several inches below the soil surface.

Forming a pool with the soil around the cane helps to ensure that water gets to the roots and doesn't run off.

and you need lots of space between rows. This is why putting them down the side of your backyard isn't a bad idea. Hopefully the neighbors on the other side of the fence like raspberries too in case your plants start sending roots onto their side.

Fresh shoots emerging from a newly planted cane.

During the first year of their growth you should remove any flowers before they set fruit. I know, it's hard, but it has to be done. You want all the energy to be stored for some serious growth next year. Once they get going you might also want to mulch them with a natural material. This will keep moisture in and keep the weeds down, and as the mulch decomposes it will add organic material to the soil. During the second spring you'll want to pull back any mulch while the plant starts sending up suckers. These are small green shoots that grow into canes. If the mulch is too heavy it can be difficult for the shoot to get through.

You want to maintain a good growing environment for raspberry plants, so add a liberal dose

Well camouflaged, the small, green raspberries will be ripening soon.

of composted manure or compost in the fall and again in the spring. When you see how big the canes can get and you see those stems laden with raspberries you'll realize that you have to keep providing energy to build all that biomass.

Pruning

There are all sorts of different cultivars of "brambles," as some people call raspberries: the common early-season red raspberry, the fall-bearing red raspberry, the purple raspberry, the black raspberry, and the blackberry. I'm just going to talk about what I plant, and that's the red raspberry. I plan to try others in the future but haven't prepared a spot for them yet. The common red raspberry produces its fruit midseason, usually after the strawberries, but there are now fall-bearing and even everbearing raspberries which can produce for most of the season. As with strawberries, I believe in the "eating when in season" philosophy, so I like the more traditional early-bearing raspberry.

Raspberry plants are perennial, which means they keep producing for many years. The canes they send up are actually biennial, working on a two-year basis. The first year the plant sends up a shoot that grows over the summer, starting out green and then getting firmer and almost woody. During this first year just the cane grows and it's unlikely it will produce any fruit. If you leave that cane it will produce fruit during the second year, after which you should remove it because it will just take energy that would otherwise go into newer growth. If you're organized you may even want to remove it as soon as you've finished harvesting all the berries. Sometimes this is an advantage because by the fall, once all the fruit is gone, it can be difficult to tell the canes that produced this year from those that will produce next year. Eventually you'll get a feeling for it if you wait until the fall. The cane will die on its own after its fruit season, so ultimately you have a Plan B if you don't get around to pruning back your canes in the fall. When you do remove old canes you should get rid of them by burning them if you can. Old canes can harbor disease, so you want to physically remove them from the area and make sure they don't end up in the compost.

With everbearing plants you can follow this strategy and remove the cane that produced fruit as soon as the second crop of raspberries has been produced later in the season. Or you can have just one set of fruit if you cut the whole patch down in the fall after the leaves have dropped. This means you'll get one late crop but the actual yield may be much better. You also eliminate injury to the canes during the winter as well as reducing the number of overwintering pests that may spend the winter burrowed in the canes.

Pests

Raspberry plants may produce for many years, but the older they get the more prone to disease they are. Gee, doesn't that sound familiar. You may want to consider starting a new bed every decade or so to cut down on some of these problems.

Raspberry plants are susceptible to the same pests and diseases as other berries. If it's a wet summer some of the fruit may have light gray fuzz. You can't do much to prevent this other than picking the fruit often and getting rid of any fruit that is too far gone to eat. You may also have fruit with a white powder, which is called powdery mildew. You have to make sure you keep pruning out old canes, and you should try and find cultivars that are resistant to it. If you have new canes that begin growing and then yellow and die this is probably from verticillium wilt. There is no cure for this disease, which stays in the soil, but you can reduce the chances of your raspberry plants getting it by not planting in an area where the nightshade family has been grown.

If you find thin white grubs a quarter of an inch long in the fruit, these are raspberry fruit worms. You can spray your plants with pyrethrin as soon as the buds appear if this is a problem. The most common insect pest will be the red-necked cane borer. If your cane tips wilt and then die this may be the cause. You'll probably be able to find swellings on the canes called "galls" where the larvae have been laid. The larvae will overwinter in the canes, which is why if you have diseased canes you should cut them out, burn them, and then make sure you keep any old and dead canes pruned out of the patch. You can also spray with pyrethrin just before the plants come into bloom if you have a really bad infestation of them.

Keep your eyes peeled for aphids and spider mites on your plants as well.

Look for the fine webs that mites leave and examine the leaves closely to see aphids. Blast away at these with the hose or use an insecticidal soap to get rid of them.

If you plant a cultivar that produces early and one that produces later you'll be able to prolong your raspberry season, or you could try some everbearing plants. If you have an exceptional harvest and can't find ways to eat all the fruit as it matures, raspberries freeze really well. We put them on cookie sheets to IQF (individually quick freeze) them, then pop them into freezer bags. Anytime you want some for muffins, or to put in a dessert, or to make a nice low-fat vinaigrette salad dressing with, you'll have some low-impact, 100-foot-diet, organic, amazingly healthy, absolutely fabulous raspberries ready to go.

55   Blueberries

You know how reformed smokers are always the worst antismokers? Well, I used to be a wild blueberry purist. "Oh yes, wild are way better than commercial/domestic blueberries, smaller, tastier, healthier…." Well, I'm now a reformed "wild blueberry snob." This year I picked some domestic "highbush" blueberries and they are fantastic! If you've ever picked wild blueberries you know that it's really, really hard work. They're very low to the ground, so it's hard on your back. Around here they grow near big granite outcrops, so the footing is always terrible. And of course they're ripe at the height of deer fly/black fly/mosquito season, so if the heat and terrain don't do you in, the bugs or black bears will generally send you screaming from the woods to the shelter of the screen porch.

My blueberry conversion/epiphany took place at Denice Wilkins and John Wilson's U-Pick organic highbush blueberry patch near the village of Tweed. The bushes are tall and each bush was bursting with berries, so you could stand in one place and pick half a pint from one position. It was heaven. Michelle and I picked 12 quarts in an hour. It would have taken two miserable days in

Tasty and incredibly healthy blueberries have it all.

the bush to pick that many wild blueberries. And they tasted great. So complete was my conversion that I've got a spot prepared to put in some highbush blueberry plants next spring.

As a child my only encounter with blueberries was in the original *Willy Wonka and the Chocolate Factory* movie in which Violet Beauregarde gets turned into a giant blueberry and rolled out of the factory. It was horrifying! I was scarred for life. Luckily I got over that early fear and came to appreciate blueberries because, like raspberries, they're unbelievably good for you. Researchers at Tufts University analyzed 60 fruits and vegetables and blueberries were the most powerful antioxidant, able to destroy free radicals that lead to premature aging and disease. Whether it's fighting cardiovascular disease, preventing cancer, or defending against other aspects of the aging process like cognitive functioning, it's time to put down the cheeses and start snacking on blueberries. With vitamin C, vitamin K, manganese, and trace B vitamins and minerals, blueberries pack a huge nutritional punch. If you were redoing the superman comic today that big red "S" on his chest would have to change to a rich blue "B."

Varieties

Blueberries come in two main varieties, highbush and lowbush, and there's also a variety that's popular in the south called "rabbiteye." Lowbush are close to their wild cousins and spread out low on the ground. Because I have "easy" in the subtitle of this book I'm just going to talk about highbush. This is because I believe these will be easier to plant and maintain, and as I enter my sixth decade on the planet, the less time I spend on my knees or bent over picking lowbush blueberries the better.

Planting

I've started to prepare the area where I'm going to plant my blueberry bushes next spring. I started off by putting rotting hay on it in the late summer to kill the grass. This works wonders because it not only allows me to save the topsoil from that area and work it back into the lower soil with my shovel or rototiller but also provides more organic material as the hay rots. I have a very sandy soil, so I've also added some compost and composted manure, although blueberries are not heavy feeders.

The key to success with blueberries is that they're acid-loving plants, which is the opposite of most of the things you'll grow. They in fact like a really acidic soil. On the pH scale on page 27 you can see that neutral (not too acid, not too alkaline) is 7. Blueberries like a pH of 4 to 5.5, so chances are you're going to have to work at creating the right conditions in the soil. I'm going to start with using natural and easy-to-obtain products to lower the soil's pH. I've added pine needles to the soil. I'm also going to use peat moss, which will make soil more acidic. Peat moss comes from peat bogs and these are the sorts of places blueberries love to grow, so it just makes sense that there's a good fit between the two. I've also discov-

ered a great soil conditioner designed for growing acid-loving plants that I'm going to add to the soil as well (see photo). If you have a farm supply store nearby see if they sell seed meal or soybean meal. Sometimes these are used as animal feed, but they can be a great soil amendment and these are naturally acidic fertilizers. Also, add your coffee grounds or ask your favorite coffee shop to save some for you. Coffee grounds are essentially coffee seed meal. After the holidays I'll cut up our

A ten-year-old row of highbush blueberries with a drip irrigation line installed to ensure adequate watering all season long.

Christmas tree and let the needles drop into this area as well. We have lots of oak trees on the property so I'll be mixing in their leaves too.

If you use a soil test kit and find that your soil is still not acid enough, give some thought to using sulfur. You can purchase this from your local garden center or co-op. There are ornamental plants like rhododendrons and azaleas that like an acid soil, so look for products with photos of these flowers and read the instructions to see if there are recommendations for blueberries. Most of these products are "ammonium sulphate," a nonorganic soil acidifier, so try to get powdered or pelleted sulfur. Once I get the blueberries planted I'm going to continue to heavily mulch them with acidic materials like oak leaves, pine needles, some peat moss, and hardwood shavings or chips.

Highbush blueberries can get quite tall and wide, so you should dig your planting holes four to five feet apart. This may seem crazy when you first plant them, but you have to look down the road, and these bushes will grow and produce for thirty years or more. Dig the hole one to two feet wide and deep and then backfill with lots of acid-enhancing amendments: peat moss, pine needles, pine bark, and oak leaves. If you get the plants shipped bareroot get them in the ground quickly and water them well. By digging the hole much deeper than necessary you've ensured that even if you have a clay soil there will be good drainage to keep the roots from rotting. Remember to keep the plants watered all summer even if you're not getting berries from them. This can be a challenge during a drought. You'll tend to be focused on beans and tomatoes and the vegetables that are almost ready to harvest. But in the long run if you want to make sure you have a good crop of berries, you have to pay attention to them as well.

Blueberries have shallow roots—usually growing in the top six to eight inches of soil—so water often but not for too long. They like to be cool and moist but definitely don't like wet feet. Three or four inches of mulch on top helps. If the leaves droop it's too late, and some or all of the plant will die, so make sure they don't get that dry.

With a basket tied to my waist I was a picking machine at John & Denice's U-Pick highbush organic blueberry patch.

The first year you're going to have to remove all the flowers from the new plants to ensure that their energy goes into developing roots and shoots for next year. Keep them watered and mulched to get them well established. You may even want to hold off harvesting berries the second year and wait until the third. This will depend on how old the plants are that you purchase. Some may be three years old, but some may be just two years old. If you're like me and can't wait and do pick blueberries the second year, make sure you've been diligent in keeping the area around the bushes well supplied with mulch.

Blueberries are like many other fruits that need another cultivar nearby to cross-pollinate properly, so make sure that you plant more than one variety. The companies that publish seed catalogs want happy customers, so they sell a "Plant Collection" which includes two or three different cultivars to ensure that you have proper pollination and a good crop each year.

Most highbush varieties are for growing zone 4 and up, but you can find some for zone 3. If in the spring you notice that last year's new green shoots or branches have turned brown, wrinkled, and died it's probably winterkill, which will stunt your plant and greatly reduce your production of berries. If you have only a few plants you can wrap them in burlap for the winter, which should help, plant them on a sheltered south-facing slope, or plant only hardier varieties.

Pests

Blueberries are similar to other berries in that you should pick and remove any fruit that isn't suitable for eating and get it away from the plants. "Mummy berry," which sounds like a sugared cereal I used to see advertised on Saturday morning cartoons when I was a kid, will cause mature berries to shrivel and turn grey and hard. Pick off and destroy these berries, and don't let them drop onto the soil. The diseased berries can overwinter and cause problems the following year. This is the advantage of adding fresh mulch on a regular basis, because you'll cover up any of these that you miss, minimizing the chance that they'll cause problems in the future. One of the biggest problems with blueberries is birds, because when they discover your bushes they'll be more than happy to help with the harvest. In fact if given a chance they'll eat all of your berries, with maybe a few going to the local chipmunks. If they become a pest and you don't have all day to spend in the backyard chasing them away, purchase some bird netting to drape over the plants when the fruit is ready to harvest. Birds don't like to land in netting and they get panicky about being able to get out, so it should do the job.

Harvest

It sounds like a no-brainer to say that you should pick the blueberries when they're ripe, but be careful not to rush it. Fully ripe berries provide the most health benefits, and if you pick them early you'll miss some of these. When you pick a ripe blueberry it should come off the stem easily. The sweetest and most nutritious fruit has stayed on the bushes for several days after the berries have turned blue. Try to not pick berries after a rain and wait until the plants are dry, because you're more likely to spread disease under wet conditions. Of course if you have a wet summer like the one we just experienced, you may not have any choice.

Pruning

You won't need to prune the bushes for the first two or three years. When you start to prune you'll want to encourage the straight and heavy main stalks. The best time to prune is early spring when it's easy to see which branches have lots of fruit buds. Fruit buds are fat, round buds that swell before the leaf buds, which are slender and pointed and emerge later. You need a balance of both. You should also remove any old and dead material.

Good acidic mulch, adequate and consistent water, and annual pruning will give you many years of healthy, productive plants and insanely healthy blueberries. There is no better "ounce of prevention" than the time you'll spend maintaining these little mini-fountains of youth.

You may not be the type who takes pictures of everything, but some garden images are too good to resist. Whether you're showing them off on your Facebook page or putting them on the fridge to remind you of summer in the dead of winter, have a camera handy!

56   Fruit Trees

I'm very torn about this chapter. I think I've kept the rest of the book very positive because I love growing food. I also think that with a reasonable commitment of time you can get excellent results and a great return on your gardening investment. Fruit trees, on the other hand, are a bit different. Since the subtitle of the book includes "easy" and "organic" I'm not comfortable including fruit trees here. Growing berries can be a challenge, but as long as you keep on top of weeding them they aren't too bad once you get them established. Growing fruit trees organically takes it up a notch in terms of commitment.

I think the best thing for me to do is to share my experiences with fruit trees as some background. Think of it as my "fruit tree blog." When we lived in the city we had an apple tree and a peach tree growing in our front yard that did very well. We also ran an organic produce co-op out of our garage and, each week sixty local families would pick up vegetables and fruit that were grown and delivered by local organic farmers. In the fall we had an apple grower deliver organic apples and apple cider. I was pretty excited about organic apples. So when we moved to our rural property 12 years ago I was determined to have lots of fruit trees.

There was a gap of six months between the time we bought the house and the time we moved in because the house was off the electricity grid. Not only did we have a learning curve with solar power, we also had to get a rural phone system installed, which was quite challenging. One fall weekend during this transition period I drove several hours to a fruit tree nursery that specialized in heritage fruit trees that should do well in our growing zone. I purchased a number of apple trees and several cherry and plum trees as well. I had already planted a peach tree. I then drove about five hours back to our new house (yes, I know, it was not a red letter day for my carbon footprint). I had spent the previous several weekends digging massive holes for the trees, removing all the sand, and filling them up with dark, rich topsoil from beside the old barn. I also tossed in some composted manure for good measure so that these trees would have everything possible going for them.

The trees I planted were bareroot, which means that the nursery had dug them in the fall after they had lost their leaves and were dormant, or basically asleep for the winter. Next spring they broke bud and grew lots of wonderful green growth. Soon after, they produced flowers that blossomed and should have ultimately turned into fruit. If my life were a Hollywood movie it would show me a few months later running and jumping through a field of daisies, in slow motion, and marveling at the branches laden with fruit as the wind gently blew my flowing blond hair. Okay, I don't have blond hair. And it's never been long enough to "flow". And my fruit tree experience did end like a Hollywood movie but this one was more like *Nightmare on Elm Street*.

During that first year green caterpillars ate every blossom and much of the foliage, ravaging the trees. I tried to keep removing them as best I could, but reality set in. My reality was that this dream home in the woods had been built in 1888 and required lots of upgrading and upkeep. The solar electric system needed work, the vegetable gardens needed to be planted and maintained, firewood needed to be cut and hauled and stacked, and I also needed to continue to support my family with our electronic publishing business, which kept me at the computer for 10 or 12 hours a day. Something had to give, and unfortunately it was the fruit trees. Each year I started off with the best of intentions. I'd spray them with lime sulfur in the late winter as you're supposed to. I'd make sure the bases were weeded and had lots of compost and composted manure. But as soon as the good weather hit and I had to get busy in the vegetable garden the fruit pests got even busier, and their tactical advantage was that they could work 24 hours a day. The best I could do was check the fruit trees a couple of times a week and realize that I was getting my ass kicked by the little green caterpillars. And each year as the caterpillars mounted their relentless agent-orange-like defoliation campaign the trees had fewer and fewer leaves to photosynthesize that solar energy and to store and prepare themselves for the following season, and each year the trees got weaker and weaker. Finally I just gave up and eventually the trees died.

I share this with you not to discourage you but just to let you know that fruit trees are a lot of work if you want them to produce well and you want to do it organically. When Joni Mitchell sang "Give me spots on my apples, but leave me the birds and the bees" in the song "Big Yellow Taxi" ("They paved paradise and put up a parking lot") I don't think she'd spent much time growing fruit. It's just not that easy. If you stop spraying and have some spots on the apples, you might end up with no apples at all.

I also share this with you to give you an appreciation for the food that you eat. I think I've shared my wonder for vegetables, but you should marvel in particular at the fruit you see in the fresh produce section of your grocery store. It represents a massive amount of skill and effort on the part of the farmer who grew it. She invested endless hours growing what you see and endless years developing the skills to do it. Yes, many fruit farmers spray pesticides on their trees, but they are well aware that consumers don't like it and try to minimize it. In the early days of chemical agriculture farmers sprayed the trees at regular intervals whether they needed it or not.

With the increasing cost of fossil-fuel-based pesticides and growing environmental concerns, most fruit farmers now use Integrated Pest Management (IPM). They carefully watch their trees and monitor weather conditions and insect populations to decide if spraying is actually necessary. If it is they apply the minimum amount for success and then continue to monitor the results. The natural conclusion of the IPM business model would be for the farmer to eventually switch over to organic methods, constantly monitoring the crop and using every technique possible to avoid the application of pesticides.

I know what you're thinking. People were eating fruit long before we had chemical pesticides. This is true. The advent of modern chemical agriculture occurred after World War II when the chemical industry needed to find a new outlet for its products. Prior to that agriculture was organic and it produced much less food and that didn't look nearly as nice. People's expectations were much lower. The world was populated by small farms and most people lived on a farm and knew how much work raising food was and were happy to just have a crop of small, ugly apples to make into

As much as you'll want to eat that apple, there'll be bugs lined up ahead of you to feed first.

a pie rather than expecting them to be big and consistent and cosmetically perfect.

One of the books I recommend to help you deal with pests in the garden is *The Organic Gardener's Handbook of Natural Insect and Disease* Control written by Barbara Ellis and published by Rodale Books. Rodale has been publishing fabulous information on this topic since the 1950s, and this is an indispensable resource to have. The book provides very detailed information about possible problems you can have with fruit and vegetables, and some of the largest sections of the book are devoted to fruit. It ultimately supported my decision to give up on my first attempt at growing fruit trees. I didn't have this resource on hand at the time, and even if I had I didn't have the time to properly address the problems as they occurred. Whenever I see a chapter on "problems" that's as large as the one on fruit problems in this book I know I need to look before I leap.

My new, prized Liberty in the barn foundation.

I'd like to caution you that if you want to grow fruit you'll need to be committed to it. It's going to require you to check the trees daily and be very conscious of what's happening with them. You'll have to do some research when something doesn't seem to be correct. There are ways to keep your trees healthy without using chemicals, but you'll need to invest the time to research them and put them into practice. You can do it, and you'll probably be marvelously successful. But as long as I've got "easy" in the subtitle of my book I'm not going to mislead you. My experience was that it was nothing of the sort.

My reality is this. While I fantasize about being a full-time gardener, I still need to earn a living. I've been a market gardener and grown produce for several local businesses, and we continue to grow and sell a large crop of garlic, but this is still my hobby. My day job is publishing books about renewable energy and sustainability. In the spring, summer, and fall most of my spare time is devoted to my vegetable garden, but I'm still at my computer eight hours a day. As you'll see in chapter 58 I've developed strategies that let me maximize the amount of water I can get on my vegetables in a minimal amount of time, and I have a very large garden. I also live off the electricity grid, and all the water I use has to be either harvested from the rain or pumped from the ground, using electricity, to the garden. So I'm pretty much at my max in terms of the amount of time I can devote to my garden.

I'm assuming that many of you are in the same boat and have a limited amount of time to invest in your garden. If you aren't yet retired or haven't won the lottery and can only invest a certain amount of time, it's best that you spend it where it will give you the best return on the time you've invested. As I've mentioned, I view potatoes as the best return on your investment of time. Potatoes are easy to grow, easy to harvest, and easy to store right through the winter. Most of us will continue to purchase some of the food we eat, and at this stage I'm letting other local farmers grow most of my apples and peaches. I've planted two apple trees this year and I'm going to describe my strategy with them to perhaps provide some background and give some guidance on whether or not you want to give it a try.

Cam's Fabulous Apple Orchard

After my miserable failure at my first attempt at growing fruit I've taken a radically scaled back approach this time. From my first fruit endeavor I learned that you should be able to check your fruit trees almost daily to ensure that they're doing well. So rather than putting in 12, as I did before, I just planted 2. I put them in a large raised bed in the barn foundation because I'm growing in a Zone 4 with an average annual minimum temperature of -20°F to -30°F. In other words, my winters can be very cold. I'm hoping this inspires you because very few people reading this book live in areas that experience weather this cold.

I'm hoping that the massive concrete walls of the barn foundation will provide some protection for my fruit trees. I also planted two different varieties, a Macintosh and a Liberty. Most fruit trees are what are called "self-incompatible." Sometimes when I'm alone with my thoughts in the garden I start thinking I'm self-incompatible, but for the fruit tree it means that it's unable to self-pollinate and therefore produce fruit all by itself. It needs another compatible cultivar to cross-pollinate with. The second tree needs to be within about 50 feet (15 m) to ensure that the bees or pollinators are able to spread the pollen from one plant to the other.

Peach trees are self-pollinating, which explains why the one peach tree that I planted in our front yard in the city many years ago produced prodigiously.

So the first thing to do when buying fruit trees is to determine whether or not they're self-pollinating; if they're not, you'll need to plant at least two different cultivars. Grafting is a technique in which branches from one cultivar can be grafted onto the root of another completely different tree. When I was shopping for my apple trees I saw "5-in-1" apple trees where the nursery had actually grafted 4 compatible cultivars onto a fifth tree so that you could in fact plant one tree and be assured of pollination. You have to be aware of when the trees blossom as well, because all the blossoms have to be out at the same time when the bees are buzzing about with pollen from the other variety.

After you've picked your varieties make sure you prepare the soil really well. You might have what appears to be good topsoil, but be sure to dig your hole at least two feet deep. You may find that you have six inches of topsoil on top of clay. If you discover clay you'll need to dig a huge hole and dig it deep. Three feet is a good minimum depth to go if you have clay. After placing the tree in the hole backfill it with a bit of sand as well

as peat moss and organic material such as leaves, grass, rotting hay, and anything else that will help to break up the clay. Mix some of the clay back in but try and stick with materials that will allow water to drain through. The city where I grew up

Joni Mitchell would be proud of me: "spots on my apples" and birds and bees galore.

had very little topsoil and very deep clay. My parents planted a birch tree in the front yard and it died shortly afterwards. I can remember digging it up and how badly it smelled because the roots had rotted. It had been well watered, but the hole wasn't deep enough and since it was such impermeable clay the water just sat in the hole and eventually rotted the root mass. Your fruit tree isn't going to be inexpensive, and if you treat it properly it will produce for decades, so it's worth investing the time to make sure the roots are going to have an optimal environment to grow in. For the first few years you'll want the roots to be able to easily move beyond the small ball they come in and have an easy time working through the soil to find nutrients and help anchor the tree. If you have a clay soil they'll eventually hit the tougher clay, but give them as much help as you can early on.

For my second experience planting fruit trees I didn't plant bareroot trees as I had the first time. I went to a local nursery and purchased trees in pots with soil. I wasn't organized enough early in the spring to order bareroot so I had to pay more ($60 each) to get trees that came in pots. We own a Honda Civic and I don't think my daughter

Katie will ever forget driving home on a four-lane highway peering through apple blossoms to check her rear-view mirror. The car has never smelled better though.

With this summer's cool wet weather many of my leaves got powdery mildew.

When we got the trees home we carefully removed the root mass with the soil from the pot and placed the tree in the hole I'd prepared. You can usually see where the tree has been grafted onto the root, so make sure you keep this area above the soil line; otherwise the upper tree will start to put down it's own root. I bought what are called "semi-dwarf" trees, which means that they'll stay relatively small. If you have a city-sized lot, dwarf or semi-dwarf is the way to go with fruit trees. A semi-dwarf tree is created when wood from a regular full-sized tree has been grafted onto a root from a dwarf tree. The wood graft will eventually heal and the tree will produce the same fruit as a full-sized tree, but its dwarf root will restrict the tree's growth. Rather than ending up with a fruit tree that takes up your entire backyard and requires a massive ladder come harvest time, you'll have a tree that you'll be able to harvest while still standing on the ground and you'll even have room in the backyard for a birdbath. Dwarf fruit trees are a wonderful addition to the landscaping of any yard, especially when they blossom.

After planting the tree you need to pack down the soil around the plant and water it well. I would also suggest that you stake the tree when you plant it. I place the stakes outside the root ball zone so that I don't damage it, and I put a piece of old garden hose on the wire to ensure that the bark isn't damaged.

Plan on planting your tree early in the spring, ideally long before it has broken bud, or at least before it's blossomed. The spars or small branches where the blossoms form are easily knocked off, and I did a real number on the two trees as I carefully crammed them into my Honda Civic. Luckily the blossoms that survived did very well and we ended up with some reasonably sized apples this year. I consider this cheating, though, because the nursery had done all the work getting it to this stage. The acid test will come next year when I'm on my own.

It was very inspiring regardless, so I'm even more determined to see them do well next year. I didn't overdo it this time and planted two trees. I may put in another two next year. I made sure to put lots of compost on them this fall and pulled back the mulch near the base because I don't want mice and rodents to overwinter in the mulch and use the bark as a food source during the long, cold months of winter.

My Plan of Action

The first thing I'll do next spring is spray my apple trees with lime-sulfur dormant oil. While "spraying" with anything sounds as though it shouldn't qualify as "organic," this spray is fine. Lime and sulphur are naturally occurring elements and the oil is a horticultural mineral oil designed to smother any overwintering insects and their eggs that are hiding in the bark or anywhere on the tree. Lime sulfur is a natural fungicide that kills fungus spores that are dormant on the tree. Both insects and spores can lead to problems later on, so you're trying to get a leg up on the problems before they even emerge. The timing for applying the spray is really critical, so read the instructions on the box very carefully. You have to spray in the late winter but you'll need to choose a day when the temperature is above freezing for at least 24 hours. If the forecast is wrong and it freezes, you'll have to spray again. You can also spray your raspberries while you're at it. Lime-sulfur spray really stinks! It smells like rotten eggs, so be sure to wear old clothes!

Lime sulfur will be my first line of defense. The second will be to ensure that the trees are kept well fertilized and watered all season long. Fruit trees have the best shot at fighting off pests when they're healthy, just like us. I'm going to inspect the trees once a day for their entire growing season. I'm going to be vigilant about looking for pests and disease. My nemesis in the past has been leaf rollers. Unrelated to any illegal-substance-smoking party animals, leaf rollers are the larvae of a brown, mottled moth that hatch in the spring, eat leaves for a month, spin webs at the tips of branches, and pupate by rolling leaves around themselves to cocoon until they can emerge as moths in July. Once they become moths their job is to lay eggs that will overwinter hidden in the bark. If I'm lucky the dormant spray will kill the eggs, but if not I'll have to inspect the leaves daily and squash the caterpillars.

The second thing I'm going to watch for really carefully is coddling moths. The apples that I picked from my two trees this year showed signs of this infestation. The larvae tunnel through the apples and leave a little pile that looks like sawdust outside the hole. Next year I'll try pheromone traps if I can locate some. These are little sticky traps you hang in the tree; the moths are attracted to the pheromone and get stuck to the trap.

I think I might have had apple maggots as well. The flies that lay the eggs that turn into apple maggots are attracted to fruit by sight, so I'm going to buy some dark red balls and suspend in them in the trees in mid-June and coat them with Tanglefoot®. I use it to trap insects in the vegetable garden, so I always have a container of it around. I'll keep my eye on the pheromone traps and Tanglefoot® balls and clean off the dead pests.

I'll be checking my fruit or leaves for a brown,

scabby surface called apple scab. I could reapply lime-sulphur spray, but I should be able to avoid apple scab by destroying any of the leaves that fell off the trees the previous year. Fire blight is another bacterial problem that can be controlled by pruning affected sections off of the tree and destroying them.

The Liberty cultivar that I planted is resistant to some of these diseases, so I'll be watching to see if there is a significant difference between the trees. There are lots of other problems I've read about and I'll try and come up with a solution when I encounter them. The key this year is that I'll be discovering problems early and dealing with them immediately. During my previous attempt at growing fruit trees I would check the trees when I thought of it, once a week or so, and by then the leaf rollers or other problems were so bad that I would just throw up my hands. This year I'll be vigilant and proactive. I also hope to blog about it to keep my readers informed about what I'm encountering. Our blog is at www.aztext.com.

A simple solution to airborne pests is a red cup coated with Tanglefoot® to trap insects before they get to your fruit.

I may not have all the answers, but I'll do my best to figure out how to address the challenges as they come along without resorting to heavy-duty, non-organic chemicals. I probably get enough traces of those chemicals on the food that I buy, so I'm going to try and do whatever it takes to keep my homegrown food as pure as possible.

Tree Guard Tape is double-sided and prevents crawling insects like caterpillars from climbing your fruit trees.

After I've tried hand-picking any bugs I'll try some of the sprays that are acceptable for organic gardeners, which I'll discuss in more detail in Chapter 60. These are insecticidal soap, Bt, and lime sulphur, and if things get really out of hand possibly something with pyrethrin, neem oil, or copper compounds.

Pruning

Proper pruning of fruit trees is essential for their ongoing health. The goal should be to encourage good air circulation around the tree and allow sunlight to get into the center. Don't allow the tree to become too dense. I'll look for any branches that cross other branches or rub against another branch in the wind and I'll prune these out. I'll also look for any diseased or spindly branches and remove those as well as any "water sprouts," which are branches that grow vertically straight

up from a main branch. I'll also remove any root suckers that emerge from the soil and any crown suckers, shoots that grow out from the bottom of the tree.

One of the keys to healthy fruit is to ensure that any diseased wood is disposed of and not left on the ground near the tree. I'll also rake up any dead leaves underneath the tree and remove them from the area, and I'll make sure that any fruit that's dropped to the ground is removed.

Other Fruit Trees

Other fruit trees are going to require a similar commitment of time. Digging the hole and preparing the soil will be the same. Watering will be the same as well. Pears and cherries do well in cooler areas, but peaches and apricots cannot withstand really cold weather. The further south you are the more luck you'll have with peaches. All of these fruits are worth growing, especially if you have enough space. While I think you should remain focused on potatoes and other vegetables that can get you through the winter, there's nothing like fruit to make a meal special. Learning to can and preserve fruit is also a good idea, especially if your fruit trees start producing good harvests. Life can be like a bowl of cherries, and it'll be even better if you can grow the bowl of cherries yourself.

I did it! A perfect, blemish- and insect-free organic apple!

Section IV
Maintenance and Harvest

57   Weeding and Thinning

While the subject of this chapter may seem pretty obvious, I thought I'd try and make it stand out because it's important. I also thought I'd share some of the tricks I've learned over the years to make this a bit easier. Weeding is one of the most crucial elements of a successful garden, both from a harvest or plant yield point of view and also from a psychological point of view. A weedy, overgrown garden can be discouraging and depressing to look at. And it becomes a vicious cycle because it will begin to look so bad that you won't want to spend any time in your garden, which means less weeding will get done and it will keep getting worse.

A well-weeded garden is a sight to behold, and after a weeding session I like to stand and admire my garden for hours. It's okay to stare and not be accomplishing anything if you've already weeded it. I believe weeding is one of the most spiritual components of gardening. Admire what you've created and recognize that the plants you have nurtured are now going to nurture your body. Gardening is a powerful antidepressant. It will bring joy to your soul. It's even more joyful if you're looking at a well-weeded garden where you've got the upper hand over the plants that

don't belong in your garden but insist on growing there nonetheless.

The Key to Weeding Success

The most important suggestion for getting rid of your weeds next year is this: get rid of them this year. The biggest mistake you can make is letting down your guard in the fall and allowing weeds that might have seemed pretty inconsequential in August to grow and go to seed. I say this from experience. Several years ago we produced a DVD called *Grow Your Own Vegetables.* Since I knew I'd be filming throughout the summer I worked hard to keep the garden pretty meticulous. The following summer I had a much easier job weeding since there weren't nearly as many weed seeds in the soil ready to germinate. Last fall I was writing my book *Thriving During Challenging Times* and I didn't have as much time to spend in the garden as I usually do. The weeds got ahead of me and many went to seed. This summer there were far more weed seeds to germinate because I had slacked off so much last fall.

So rule number one for weeding is to stay on top of them. DO NOT LET WEEDS GO TO SEED.

Rototilling

With a garden as large as mine, periodic rototilling has become part of my weeding regime. From a CO^2 emissions point of view I know it's not the right thing to do. My rationalization is that if, instead of growing my own food, I were to buy it at my local grocery store, much of it would have traveled 1,500 miles to get there so I'm much further ahead using my rototiller. I use it sparingly, but there are times when the weeds start getting ahead of me and rototilling allows me to clean up a large area quickly. I use it to go down between the rows, so this is one of the advantages of leaving lots of space between rows.

Even after rototilling I still have to use a hoe

My rototiller can cover a huge area in a short period. The wonder of gasoline!

and go down each side of the row to remove weeds closer to the plants. A rototiller will dig down fairly deep, so I don't want to get too close to my actual plants. For the area closer to the plants I use the manual cultivator or hoe. At a certain point in the summer I often can't use the rototiller anymore because I've run out of room; the crops have gotten large and are now crowding out the spaces between rows.

I have two rototillers. I use the larger one with air-filled or pneumatic tires early in the season when the soil is pretty rough and I want to cover a large area. I also use it in the fall to clean up the garden before winter. It's helpful because if you leave a lot of organic material on the soil from the previous harvest you leave lots of places for insect pests to hide and overwinter. The smaller rototiller has solid rubber tires and is better for close-up work, so I tend to use it for weeding during the growing season. It is also more maneuverable and has a smaller turning radius so that when I reach the end of a row and turn around and head back in the other direction it's much easier to get around the corner.

If you're serious about having a large garden a rototiller might be worth the investment. As I get older I'm not capable of accomplishing as much in the garden in a day, and yet somehow the garden gets bigger every year. I purchased both of my rototillers used; be sure to keep your eyes open for a fellow gardener willing to part with one.

Mulching

I have recommended using mulch a number of times in this book because it can be an excellent aid in the garden. It can help warm the soil and extend the season. It can retain moisture to help with watering, especially if you run a drip irrigation line underneath it to ensure that you keep the plants supplied with water. It is also an excellent aid in keeping down weeds.

Plastic

Black plastic mulch is the more traditional application of this technique. You prepare your row for planting, lay the mulch on top of the soil, and fasten it down at the edges by burying it in soil. These pieces of black plastic are generally about four feet wide, part of which gets buried to hold it down. This image shows me putting down some black plastic mulch. This doesn't look quite as neat and tidy as the photos you see in seed catalogs. I'm not as fussy about cosmetic touches, so I didn't take the time to get it perfect. The mulch I use is a corn-starch-based natural mulch rather than a petroleum-based plastic, so it has less strength. The great thing is that it worked well all summer, but by the fall it was breaking down and basically disappeared. Petroleum-based plastic mulch comes with a guarantee and can be reused, but from my experience it'll be pretty beaten up after a season or two in the garden and you won't be able to use it again. You'll also have to clean it and store it in the fall, and each year you'll have to put in vegetable plants that require the same distance between them since you've cut holes in it.

Here you can see me using my pocket knife to slice a hole in the mulch and insert a peanut plant in a peat pot. This biodegradable mulch is very lightweight and I found that it flopped around quite a bit in the wind, so I placed some wooden stakes on top to keep it in place. It did a great job

of keeping the weeds down and the peanut plants thrived in the heat that the mulch helped to retain. Mulch like this requires more time up front to set in place, but you'll save yourself some time and effort later on in weeding and watering.

You can also purchase reversible mulch which is black on one side and white on the other. For crops that prefer things cool, the white side reflects the heat away from the soil. This is the same concept as using a white roof to reflect solar heat rather than a dark color that absorbs it.

Organic Mulches

As I've discussed throughout the book, using mulches of leaves or grass clippings or hay or straw can have the desired effect of keeping the weeds down and retaining heat and moisture. Their advantage is that they're not made from a nonrenewable resource like oil and also that as they break down over time they're enhancing the quality of your soil by adding organic material. The downside to using these types of mulches is that they offer a great place for bugs to hide. As long as you keep your eye on them and inspect the area periodically to make sure you don't have any unwanted pests using your mulch as a little oasis from the summer heat, you should be fine.

I use rotting hay as mulch for many crops. Straw would be superior since it doesn't have seeds in it. Hay often has seed heads in it, but I find that if I lay it down thick enough the weeds are less likely to germinate. I also tend to purchase hay that has rotted to the point that it isn't suitable to feed to livestock, and since it is already quite

advanced in the decomposition process it enhances the soil. If you use leaves or grass be careful, because they can become very thick and impenetrable for anything like raspberry shoots.

Old-Fashioned Elbow Grease

The final technique for dealing with weeds is the time-tested method of hoeing. When you perform this simple act you feel a bond with our ancestors who did this for thousands of years. I absolutely love hoeing the garden. It's physically demanding and I spend much of the time feeling morally superior thinking about the money I've saved not having to belong to a fitness club or purchase expensive exercise equipment. All I need is a $15 hoe and some soil. Not only do I save the $500 that a health club membership would cost and the $1,000 I could spend on a StairMaster but I end up with $500 worth of food, so the way I see it my little "hoedown" puts me $2,000 ahead of the game. You too will be amazed at the level of oxygen going to your brain and the endorphins produced by your body when you engage in physical activity like this.

There are lots of different designs and variations on the hoe. Here are some I've worked with:

Traditional Hoe

This is the standard, tried-and-true hoe that's been used for thousands of years. It's strong and you can use it to chop at really dense weeds you may encounter. It's excellent for moving soil when you're forming hills for your cucumbers or hilling up your potatoes. While there will always be people working to build a better mouse-trap it's hard to improve on this traditional design.

V-Shaped Hoe or Cultivator

I really like this hoe when I've left things too long and I've got a really thick patch of weeds to break up. It's sharp and easy to plunge down into the soil to remove weeds. It's also not as wide as the traditional hoe, which means there's less drag on it and you're moving less soil each time you pull it through the soil. This can help reduce your fatigue as you work with it.

Cultivator

This is my very favorite tool in the garden. I know this because I have about three that I've broken from overuse that I'll have to repair this winter. This cultivator has four sharp tines and is excellent for weeding. The thing I like most about it is that as it moves through the soil it scrapes and drags weeds out by their roots but leaves a lot of the soil behind. This means way less resistance on

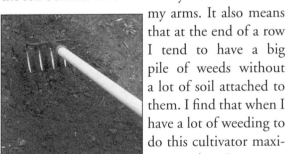

my arms. It also means that at the end of a row I tend to have a big pile of weeds without a lot of soil attached to them. I find that when I have a lot of weeding to do this cultivator maximizes what I can accomplish by minimizing the number of calories of energy I have to expend to make my way down each row. If I have the time and feel like a good workout

I use this to do all the weeding, even the large areas between rows that I could use the rototiller on. There's nothing quite as rewarding as standing back, sweating and exhausted, and admiring a freshly weeded garden. It really emphasizes how green the vegetables are when you look at them against the clean, newly exposed, weed-free soil.

Stirrup or Dutch Hoe

This is a new design I tried this year after doing some weeding at a local organic berry farm. The farmer, John Wise, suggested that many of these types of designs, including "wire weeders" or "collinear hoes," reduce fatigue during hoeing. John weeds the large area of space between his rows with a tractor, but the areas immediately around the strawberry plants need to be done by hand. Strawberry plants have fairly shallow root systems, so if you get in there with a big hoe and start dragging it around to remove weeds you'll also disturb the roots. Hoes like this allow you to work the area around your plants just below the surface of the soil. The goal is to sever the roots of the weeds while leaving good roots intact.

While I believe in the concept of these hoes I was never able to get into a groove with them this summer. I guess it's because I'm more like a bull in a china shop when it comes to weeding that I couldn't get into the slow, precise system. I prefer to weed most of the area with the cultivator and then get down on my hands and knees and use a smaller hand cultivator to get closer to the plants. I can be more patient and delicate with a handheld tool when I'm really close to the plant rather than when I'm standing up at the end of a longhandled hoe.

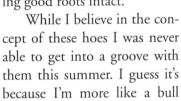

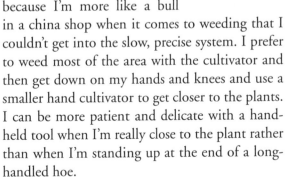

Thinning

While not necessarily the most physically demanding of garden tasks, I find thinning one of the hardest. Now that I save seeds I can be very

These freshly emerged carrot seedlings need to be weeded and thinned.

generous when sowing and plant way more than I need. This is fine if you are sowing a crop with a low germination rate, but when the germination rate is higher than you need you've got to thin the little plants as they begin to grow. I find this goes against every instinct I have. It's just not in my DNA to pull up and kill perfectly good plants. I know that if I leave them they'll be too crowded and I'll end up with a reduced harvest overall, but that doesn't stop me from having a mental block about it anyway.

The first way to minimize this challenge is to

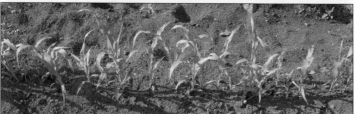

Corn before and after weeding and thinning.

not overplant. If you've purchased fresh seed from a reliable supplier and follow the instructions and don't plant the seeds too deep or too early, then you won't have to thin too much. But you'll often still find that you have more than what is recommended on the package. If it says plant seeds two inches apart and thin to six inches apart, it means that you've got to sacrifice two perfectly good little plants if they all germinate.

I do wait to make sure that cutworms don't decimate my tiny plants, which is the main reason I tend to overplant anyway. If I plant a thick row of beans it's easy to spot where a cutworm has been lopping off plants and I can dig around the chopped-off plants to find it. But if things are growing well you can't wait too long to thin. Sooner or later the roots will start to get too close together and removing one plant may disturb the roots of another.

As you can see from these photos I have obviously had great success with saving corn seed and therefore planted way too many. So I have to vigorously thin the row, because corn plants are big and if they're too close together the overall yield will be reduced. Sometimes I cheat a little bit and leave them slightly closer than recommended. I top them with some composted manure during the summer to give them a little boost.

Smaller plants like carrots can be a real challenge to thin. Since I've had problems getting carrots to germinate well over the years I tend to overseed. Then when I have a high germination rate suddenly I've got way too many seedlings and they need to be thinned. Carrots present a double whammy because they're very slow to germinate, which means that the weeds will be neck and neck with them as they emerge if not ahead of them in terms of development.

The first thing I do is to make sure the area is well watered before I begin thinning. I do less damage to delicate seedlings like carrots if the soil is wet. This serves to lubricate the carrot and root as you pull it out. I also find moist soil tends to be more malleable whereas dry soil will often become caked and stick together so that as you pull out a seedling it may take a chunk of soil with it that other carrots could be attached to. I remove the weeds first because if you're working on a large area there's a good chance you'll take the odd carrot with you in your haste. This way if you take some carrots by accident you're basically doing your primary thinning. Then I try and thin from areas where the carrots are too dense. Ideally you should have about one plant per square inch, but nature is never this helpful. I just try and leave a reasonable amount of space. If there's an area where I'm not sure whether to thin or not I tend to default to leaving them too dense and I thin later on. If I wait until they actually start developing that large taproot, sometimes I can come back and thin the area and end up with baby carrots as I thin the larger plants. If they're quite large as I thin I try and pour some loose soil back in the hole so I'm not leaving the neighboring carrots exposed.

I've learned over the years that you'll have very limited success replanting the plants you thin. Carrots in particular are just a large taproot, and when you pull it out you disturb all the smaller roots that were supporting and supplying it. You can try replanting it, but don't be surprised if it dies. If it does survive being transplanted its growth will be quite stunted.

I've tried replanting with other plants such as corn. As I've thinned I've attempted to replant the thinned corn plants into spots where there are holes from insect damage or poor germination. These transplanted corn plants will not thrive. They may survive but they'll be stunted and really just take up space without producing an ear of corn. It would be better to plant some new seed in those weak areas. Since you'll probably have eliminated the pest that caused the problem the chances are good that the new seeds will germinate and grow. If they're a bit behind the others in the row that's a good thing and should mean that you'll have some less mature plants to harvest later which will help extend the season.

As I mentioned, pulling out perfectly healthy plants will go completely against your instincts as a gardener, but it's "tough love." They've got to go. If they hang around they'll be too crowded and will compete with each other, and you'll end up disappointed with a smaller yield than you'd have enjoyed if you'd been proactive and thinned down to a reasonable number.

The Steaming Compost Heap

This steamy horse manure shows that natural decomposition is happening, breaking down organic matter and killing pathogens. If you turn over your compost heap on a cool morning you should see steam like this if it's working properly.

58   Watering

Water is essential for life, and it's crucial to your garden. The effects of climate change will cause water to become an issue for many gardeners. For some, depending on where you garden, it may mean more rain, but for most of us climate change will result in less rain, or less consistent rain. Droughts will become increasingly common and areas of the country that are already water challenged could get worse. So you should have a plan to harvest rainwater and store it and to use water as efficiently as possible in your garden. Many of us are already accustomed to having water restrictions in the summer that prevent us from watering our lawns everyday.

Like most things in life the type of soil you have will have some advantages but it will also have some disadvantages. A clay soil may not drain well and you have to be careful about plant roots being damaged by sitting in water. The upside is that when it rains or when you water, the soil should retain water well. If you have a sandy soil that water runs through you don't have to worry about things being overwatered and waterlogged but the soil will lose moisture much more quickly, so you've got to be even more proactive about watering.

Every one of your downspouts needs a rain barrel on it.

I deal with a triple whammy in my garden. To start with, I have a sandy soil that dries out very quickly. Secondly, I live in a little microclimate that is very drought-prone. I often watch the radar maps of storms headed my way only to discover that they've lost all of their moisture before they get to me. My final challenge is living off the electricity grid. Pumping and moving water around is one of my single biggest uses of electricity so not only do I have physical limitations on how much water I can pump, I have a finite amount of electricity to pump it with. Don't get me wrong, I love living off grid. I'm here by choice. It is very in keeping with my world view of the finite nature of our planet's resources. When you live on the electricity grid, power and water are infinite; they just keep coming out of that socket and tap as long as you keep them turned on. At my house electricity is very finite so I have to use it wisely.

Municipal Water

If you live in a city or urban environment your water is probably provided to you by a utility. Many of these utilities are challenged by the age of their equipment infrastructure and the new urban growth over the last decade. Historically we have paid extremely low rates for water. It's one of those amazing luxuries that we take for granted that have provided such a great standard of living for us. But city utilities are faced with many challenges, and just as many utilities have had to increase the cost of the electricity they provide, it's likely that you'll also see the cost of water delivered to your home increase. It will still be relatively inexpensive, but we're going to have to pay to replace the entire infrastructure somehow. So using water wisely is very important.

I suggest that you should put rain barrels on all of your downspouts to harvest rainwater, and you might even want to give some thought to having a rain barrel set up to put municipal water in.

The water coming out of the tap is quite cold and many plants prefer warmer water rather than being shocked by extreme cold. With an extra rain barrel or two you can keep them filled and allow the water to warm up to air temperature. If your water is heavily chlorinated some of the chlorine may have a chance to evaporate if you let the water sit. This will also help if you should get into a situation where you're being asked to water only on alternative days. You can fill the barrel on your day and let it sit until you need to water. Having a reservoir of water ready to go for the garden is a good idea.

Rainwater Harvesting

The most important theme of this chapter is the harvesting of rainwater. There are lots of ways to harvest rainwater and the easiest way is to take it off your roof. Your rain gutters or eavestroughs direct rainwater to a downspout and this is where you'll need to position your rain barrels. I use "barrels" plural because you should have more than one. I have about eight located under the downspouts on my house and barn. You'll need to get some good tinsnips so you can cut the aluminum downspout and move the elbow higher so that it will drain into your rain barrel. If you have plastic piping you'll need a hacksaw or another tool that will cut the plastic.

If you have a small garden and plan to water it by hand it will be fine for the rain barrel to sit on the ground. If you plan on having a bigger garden where you you'll need to save more water and use a faucet and hose, then you may want to have the rain barrel up off the ground. Find some rocks to build a small platform for your rain barrel. If the rain

Livestock water troughs can be used for rainwater storage.

barrel has a faucet or tap, raising it up a bit will make it easier to attach a hose to it.

You can see from photos that I'm a big fan of raising my rain barrels. I do this for the help it provides in moving the water over a longer distance. For every 2.3 feet you raise the barrel you get 1 psi (pounds per square inch) of water pressure. Municipal water may come out of your taps at 40 or 60 psi, so even if you could raise your rain barrel over two feet you'd still have far less pressure than you get from the city. But if you only need enough pressure to water your garden this isn't necessarily an insurmountable problem. Even if you were using a hose to get the water to a garden at the back of your yard you would get it there; it would just be a bit slow. In this photo you can see some rain barrels sitting on top of a crib that I built beside our barn foundation. The barrels are about ten feet above the gardens in the barn foundation and you can see from the picture that I get excellent pressure for watering the gardens.

You may not have a barn foundation but you may have some structure on your property that would allow you to raise your rain barrel higher. Perhaps you have a downspout that drains below your deck, but if you rerouted the downspout and sat the rain barrel on your deck, you'd have a one-story fall for the water to build pressure to help with garden watering.

You don't need to limit yourself to just one barrel at each downspout; you can have several. Some commercial rain barrels come with overflow valves that ac-

Raising your rain barrels provides natural "head" or water pressure.

cept a short piece of hose which allows water to drain from one barrel to the next. After the first barrel fills the second one starts filling up. As long as that second barrel has a faucet you can use its natural pressure for watering or you can just immerse watering cans into it. There are lots of other types of rainwater catchment systems that you can purchase. With water becoming such a huge issue in areas of the south there are a number of companies that specialize in providing huge storage tanks. You can purchase livestock tanks from a local feed and farm supply outlet. Or you can use a company like CorGal that provides much larger storage solutions.

Integrating rainwater storage systems will become commonplace in water-challenged parts of the country. Photo courtesy of CorGal Water Tanks, Inc. www.corgaltanks.com

If you live in a rain- and water-challenged location then it may be time to start evaluating these systems. There are even some that harvest rainwater for use inside your home. These systems have screens to remove most of the debris that may come off your roof. The system diverts the initial rainwater for use in your garden. This water may have pollen or airborne materials which aren't optimal in water you use in your home but won't bother your lawn or garden. Once that initial water has been directed for garden use the system will then direct the rest of the rainwater into a large tank for use in the house. This water will be

fine for bathing and other uses and it could even be filtered further for potable or drinking water.

While these may be more advanced than you need for garden water I have discussed them in order to get you thinking about water. If you have sporadic rain and your municipality is water challenged or you pump your own water from a well, you need to have a strategy to store a large amount of rainwater until the next time it falls. If you live in a rural area and pump your water from a well, this requires electricity and your well will have a replenishing rate. This is the rate at which groundwater will flow back into the well casing after the pump has drawn it down. Often in the summer groundwater levels can drop and well replenish rates decrease. So if you start increasing your water use by watering a garden you'll have to be aware of just how quickly you're using water and how quickly your well can replenish itself.

When we first moved to this off-grid house I used a regular sprinkler on the garden once. I checked my batteries after about an hour and noticed that they were very low even though it was sunny and the sunshine should have been charging them up. Then I noticed there was a large load on my inverter. It turns out that after 20 minutes of the sprinkler running the pump had come on to fill up and pressurize my water tanks. Twenty minutes later the tanks were drained and the pump came on again. This time, though, the pump drew the water from much lower in the well, so by the time the pump came on the third time the water level was below the pump, so it ran continuously. This can be very hard on a pump but it was even harder on my batteries, which were having to provide for this very large load for much longer than the usual four minutes it took to recharge the pressure tanks.

This taught me a good lesson. First, that water is precious and you have to be very careful how you use it. It also taught me that a traditional above-ground sprinkler, like the kind we ran through as kids, is a very inefficient way to provide water to your garden. Now we have to look at how to avoid this.

Watering

After the experience of pumping my well dry I got serious about using water wisely. I purchased rain barrels for all of my downspouts and after a big rain I had close to 500 gallons of water in my rain barrels. I also began to use the "dug well" beside my garden. My house has a "drilled well" which was drilled by a large truck with a drill on the back. As the hole was drilled into the ground a metal casement was inserted to keep debris from falling back into the well. This casement has holes in it that allow the ground water to trickle back in and fill the well up. My dug well was created just as it sounds; it was dug by hand. In my case it was dug 70 years ago when this area of my property had a barn and was used for cattle. After the well hole was dug about 15 feet deep a concrete wall was built to surround the well. When we moved here there was a little wooden shed that surrounded the well but the roof had fallen in and the walls were falling down. The floor was also missing. The pump, which was actually a wooden pump with a steel handle and faucet, had fallen into the well. So I removed the building and built a new cover.

When my vegetable garden was smaller than it is now I would lower a bucket attached to a rope down into this well and pull the bucket up full of water. Then I'd carry the water to where I needed it and put it in watering cans. As the garden grew bigger and my water needs became greater I just couldn't keep up. So my friend Bill Kemp, author of *The Renewable Energy Handbook*, designed a solar pump for me. It uses an inexpensive DC pump wired to a solar panel. When sun hits the solar panel, DC electricity is produced which activates the pump. The pump draws water from the well and hoses move it to wherever I need it in the garden. It's an absolutely amazing system and it's given me a huge appreciation for solar power. I live in a solar-powered home, but the electricity generated by the panels near the house is for appliances like fridges and freezers and TVs and washing machines that have always been a part of my life. I've never had to wash clothes by hand. I

moved a lot of water out of my dug well manually and it's back-breaking, exhausting work. The solar pump moves far more water in a day than I ever could, regardless of how much granola I eat for breakfast.

If you have a standing source for water, like a pond or stream near your garden, and no source of electricity nearby, there's a solar solution you can use.

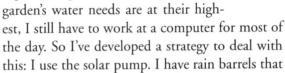

A drilled well casement head.

As I mentioned earlier, gardening still isn't my full-time job. At the height of the summer when we're often experiencing a bit of a drought and the garden's water needs are at their highest, I still have to work at a computer for most of the day. So I've developed a strategy to deal with this: I use the solar pump. I have rain barrels that I've placed throughout the garden. I run a hose from the solar pump to a rain barrel and the pump takes about 30 minutes to fill it. During the workday I head out to the garden four or five times to move the

A dug well with a hole for the pump line.

hose from one rain barrel to another until all of them have been filled up. My garden visits give my back and wrists a break and I end up with full rain barrels. Once they're all full I switch the pump water over to my drip irrigation system.

I use the water in these rain barrels early in the morning when I like to do some watering by hand. With a big garden it's always a challenge to decide what needs to

Our solar-powered DC pump for moving water from the dug well out to the garden.

be watered first, but you get into a groove where you know what needs the most water and where the driest areas of the garden are. So I pick my spots and I water really well.

Initially my instinct was to try and water everything everyday. But I've learned that once my sandy soil gets dried out it takes a while for it to be receptive to water again. The first water you apply will tend to puddle or run off the area where you want it to go. With each watering can, though, a little more water is absorbed. After three or four trips some of the water will start to make its way down to the roots, and if I keep going the plant will get a proper watering. By just applying a little bit of water to a larger area I wasn't really accomplishing much. The water was I guess what you'd

Watering barrels are everywhere in my garden.

call "topical," just sitting on top and not reaching the roots. Now that I select a smaller section of the garden and really water it well, the water penetrates to where I want it to go, down to the roots. A light shallow watering is easily evaporated in the summer heat while a deep watering gets down to the roots where it can be absorbed and moved into the plant.

So I get into a pattern of using two or three rain barrels of water and giving certain rows a really good watering. When Michelle helps me we can water a fairly large section of the garden in an hour or so. Some sections don't get watered each day but that's okay. When they do get watered they get a good drink. Letting the soil near the surface of the plant dry out a bit reduces some problems with insect pests like slugs. They like it moist, so by letting the soil dry out you're creating a hostile environment for them. Many fungal

diseases thrive in wet soils and during a summer that's particularly wet you're more likely to see some of the molds and mildews that you wouldn't see in a dry season.

Different plants will be at different stages of development and you'll start to get a feel for what needs the most water. When you pull up a mature tomato or broccoli plant in the fall and see how far down the roots have grown you'll realize that some of your larger plants have developed a fairly advanced root system to go out and down to find water. So even though your instinct may be to ignore the smaller plants and focus on the larger ones, often that's not the right way to go. The key is to keep your eye on the plant to see if there's any sign of wilting or stress that a lack of water is causing.

I raise some of the rain barrels in the garden on rock platforms or cribs to give me some natural "head" or water pressure. I grow my cucurbit family of vines, which includes my squash and melons, in small hills that I hollow out like a shallow swimming pool. I run a hose from a nearby rain barrel to each "hill" and let the hose fill up the hollow where the plants are growing. After five or six minutes I move the hose to the next hill of vines and let it run while I'm busy using a rain barrel and watering can to water an-

This limestone crib provides natural water pressure from the horse barn roof to nearby gardens.

other area. I also have several barrels placed very high over the raised beds in the barn foundation. These beds actually sit on concrete, which isn't an optimal setup, but you work with what you're given. During a hot, dry spell I have to be really careful about these drying out since the concrete around the garden will really absorb the heat and can therefore increase the rate of evaporation. So I drain the two rain barrels I have over the garden each day or every other day to ensure that these beds are well watered.

By the time the sun is getting high and the day is getting hot, most of our watering is done. By then the sun will be hitting the solar pump and I can start refilling the rain barrels to water again the following morning. Like municipal water the water coming out of the dug well is wonderfully cool, which would be great for a drink on a hot afternoon but isn't always optimal for vegetables. If you pump the well water into rain barrels and let them sit in the sun, the water has a day to warm up before it's applied to the vegetables. Generally at this time of year the nights are warm, so the water is a much more comfortable temperature coming from a rain barrel than directly from the well. So for the next few hours I just keep moving the dug well water hose from rain barrel to rain barrel until they're full. After that I begin using my drip irrigation system.

When I water with a watering can, I try to avoid getting water on the foliage or green, leafy part of the plant. I know this sounds difficult, and with some plants it's almost impossible, but if you can manage it it's recommended. If water sits on the foliage it can create an environment for disease and pests. There a number of very cool watering can designs that have much longer necks so that you can direct the water onto the soil under the plant rather than just pouring a rainfall of water down over the entire plant. You should also try to minimize how much water splashes back up on the plants while you're watering. There are bacteria and fungi and diseases that are soilborne and may be sitting in the soil near your plants. When you sprinkle water from above you are more likely

to splash some of those unwelcome intruders onto the foliage of your plants.

One of the best ways to minimize these risks is to water in the morning. This gives the sun the maximum amount of time to warm up and dry off that plant. You can certainly water in the afternoon, but by then it's often so hot that much of your water will just be lost to evaporation, so it's a bit of a waste of time. If you work outside your home you will probably tend to work in your garden after dinner to unwind and destress after your workday. While I completely understand the sentiment, it's not the optimal time to water. Watering early in the morning before you leave for work would be a better time. During a heat wave you should water whenever you can, but heat waves can sometimes be accompanied by high humidity, which can inspire spores to germinate, so by watering at night you're just creating a more attractive environment for some of these problems. You may never have a problem watering at night and your garden may thrive. I'm merely passing along tips to try and minimize potential problems that might be difficult to diagnose later on.

Sprinklers

From everything I've just described you can guess my feelings towards sprinklers. They are not a prime method for watering your garden. If you have a small garden and a healthy well that replenishes quickly, then by all means put your sprinkler on the garden in the morning. But remember that you're much more likely to splash problems onto the foliage of your plants than if you used other methods of watering. Sprinklers tend to create puddles in the soil by putting a large of amount of water on it in a short period of time. This increases the potential for soilborne disease being splashed onto plant foliage.

Sprinklers are also extremely wasteful as a means of applying water. First they spread water over the entire garden, even to the areas between rows where you don't need it. Not only is this wasteful, but it's also a bad strategy in terms of weeds. I have this love/hate relationship each summer. When it's hot and dry I'm consumed with watering. When it's cool and wet I'm consumed with weeding. The beauty of the hot summer is that most of your plants will love it and it will dry out the areas between your rows. Weed seeds need

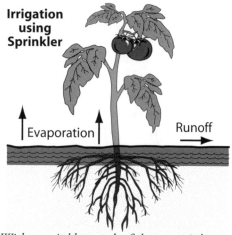

Irrigation using Sprinkler

Evaporation   Runoff

With a sprinkler much of the water is lost to runoff and evaporation and doesn't make it to the roots.

water to germinate, so in the midst of a drought you'll have far fewer weeds. Sure, you'll have to water more, but you get to weed less. Last summer was really wet here, which was a blessing because we didn't have to get up before sunrise to water. The downside was that the weeds grew like

crazy. The time I would normally spend watering was spent on weeding.

So by using a sprinkler you're ensuring that any of those weed seeds that would otherwise have remained dormant in your soil are assured of a good environment to germinate. Using a watering can or hose and directing it just under the vegetables ensures fewer weeds in between plants and rows.

Sprinklers also lose an incredible amount of water to evaporation. If you look at your sprinkler while the sun is behind it you'll see how many small water droplets get blasted out of the nozzles and become airborne. They're not going to make it to your garden, and these are just the droplets you can see. That wonderful mist reflected against the sunlight may be a great way for Las Vegas resorts to cool guests when they're outside in the desert heat, but they're not the best way for you to get a precious resource to where your plants need it. In a water-constrained world a sprinkler is not the ideal method of delivering water.

Sprinklers can actually pool water or create puddles on the surface of the soil. With so much water being applied in such a short period, if you have a soil with poor drainage the pooled water is likely to evaporate. The rapid application of lots of water can also mean that sometimes it flows to low points, which can be between rows, and is therefore wasted.

I understand what you're probably thinking. But we've always watered this way. And I see huge farms using sprinklers so why shouldn't I? Well, we're now aware of the limitations of sprinklers, so whenever possible we should use alternatives. There aren't economical alternatives for many farmers. Most of us still rely on farmers to provide the bulk of our food, so I would rather they waste some water to evaporation if it means they can produce a good volume of marketable food at the end of the day. As water is becoming more of an issue in areas where large volumes of food are grown, such as California, there are increasing economic incentives for farmers to invest in more efficient methods of watering crops.

This is a home gardening handbook, so I'm suggesting that you try and make optimal use of your water. Your well or municipality will thank you. And the most efficient way to water your vegetables is with a drip irrigation system.

Overwatering

Overwatering has never been an issue for me because my sandy soil has good drainage and can handle large volumes of water. As our snow melts in the spring the topography of my garden deals with it well. The garden slopes gently and the water all drains to a low area I don't currently grow on. This is where the dug well was placed some 80 years ago. Apparently when the farmer dug the well back then he knew that the natural slope of the land down to its low location would ensure the maximum amount of water to replenish the well when it was pumped.

If you have a clay soil you'll probably have the opposite problem. The water will not effectively drain and it's more likely that roots will be damaged by waterlogged conditions. Fungi also love this type of environment. Your first line of defense should be to add a lot of organic material. When you're starting the garden add lots of compost and peat moss and leaves and dig them deep into the soil. If you have thick clay you should use a shovel and dig your rows a foot or even two feet deep as you're planting. Then as you backfill, break up the clay with all the organic material you can. You may even want to add some sand to help break up that clay. You probably don't want to use mulch with soil like this because you don't want to hold moisture near the plant any more than you have to. If you have access to mulching material like leaves or rotting hay add it to the soil as you're working it to help break up the clay rather than leaving it on top of the soil.

You might also want to try raised beds if you have a clay soil. As you dig deeper into the ground you'll find that soil is stratified with different layers of material. If you have clay topsoil you'll probably find even more clay and firmer clay below. This will create a challenge for water to drain down through. Yes, you want water near your roots but you don't want it sitting there, and with some clay it's like having your plants sit in a bowl of water. Prior to planting you should dig down and add sand and organic material to these deeper areas. Then make use of the healthier soil above and rake and pull it into raised beds. These don't necessarily have to be bordered by wood or rock. As you're planting your carrots just pull the topsoil from around your row into a pile 12 to 24 inches wide. This allows the upper soil to drain better and gives your roots another 4 to 6 inches to grow down into before they hit the tougher clay where water may tend to accumulate. I prefer raised beds of this type that aren't permanent because in the fall after harvest you can rototill or hoe them all down and keep spreading the organic material around the garden.

If you're finding that water is sitting on your garden and it's severe then you may want to look at installing a drainage system of perforated pipes to drain excess water away from your garden. You'll have to decide the best place to drain the water to and then dig trenches to install the drainage pipe. Water runs downhill and it's suggested that for every 100 feet of run you should have a three-inch fall. You should also try and avoid having any dips in the pipe where the water might accumulate. This may appear to be a fairly major undertaking, but if you have a heavy clay soil and you're noticing that water is pooling and puddling and that during the growing season your plants aren't performing well, it may be worth investigating.

> ## WATERING TIPS
> - Water in the morning.
> - Try and let your water sit for a day to warm up to air temperature.
> - Try and avoid getting water on the foliage if you can by directing it under the plants rather than on the leaves

If you have a smaller garden you could try digging a ditch to drain the water. Take a look at where the water seems to be pooling and find an area you can move that water to. This might be the excuse you were looking for to put in that little pond in the backyard. Try and position the pond so that you can dig a trench from the garden to drain water that may otherwise impede healthy plant growth. The advantage of the drainage system is that the piping is out of site.

Obviously if you have this type of soil you also have to be aware of overwatering, so as the summer progresses try and monitor how moist your soil is. It may be worth purchasing a moisture meter to test the soil around your plants to determine how much water is present in the roots and if it's actually necessary to even add water.

Soaker Hoses
You can purchase commercial soaker hoses, but I've never had much luck with them. I find that they tend to shoot water in all directions and it's not easy to control where it goes. It also tends to shoot out in a really fine spray that just evaporates.

The fact that soaker hoses shoot the water into the air first is a bad sign in terms of how much water actually ends up in the soil and how much is watering your plants.

Before purchasing my drip irrigation system I did make some of my own soaker hoses. I took an older hose I wasn't too concerned about, added a screw cap to the end, and drilled holes along the length of the hose. Since I use this with my solar-powered pump, the water is under fairly low pressure, unlike what you get if you're using your household water pressure. I drilled holes at about two-inch intervals. Since I knew the tendency would be for water to drain out the first holes it encountered, I used much smaller drill bits for the initial holes and then as I worked my way towards the end of the hose I used progressively larger bits. This allowed the water to flow out fairly consistently throughout the length of the soaker hose.

A homemade soaker hose.

This system is much more effective in getting water right to your plants where you need it. There is less lost to evaporation than with a sprinkler and it tends to go right to the base of the plants rather than wetting the area between rows as well. If you have a mulch on the vegetables in the row it will tend to hold the water and ensure that it gets directed into the soil rather than spilling out away from the plants. A soaker hose like this would work on an elevated rain barrel with some natural head or water pressure. If you use it with your municipal water system make sure the water pressure isn't too high and isn't eroding the areas in your soil where the water runs out. If it is, turn down the pressure.

Drip Irrigation

As my garden has become larger and my microclimate has become more drought prone, I've been on a collision course with water. I've had to find a better way to get water where I want it and not waste it in the process. Drip irrigation has been the solution, and I've become a huge fan. Drip irrigation is simply a system of moving water directly to the base of the plant and applying it slowly. It minimizes losses to evaporation and maximizes the amount of water that actually gets to the roots where it's needed. Drip irrigation is considered 95% efficient compared to about 65% for overhead sprinklers.

Here are some graphics to show you how water moves through soil. The graphic on page 209 shows a sprinkler using a large amount of water and delivering it to a large area of garden, covering it fairly uniformly. Often only the upper area of the soil actually gets water, as much of it evaporates before it reaches down to the roots. With a drip irrigation system the water is delivered close to the base of the plant. When water gets into the soil it travels through what is called "capillary" action. A good way to illustrate this is to take a big, fluffy towel, dip the corner in water for a second, and then take it out. This first dip in the water wets the area immediately around the corner where you dipped it in. Now do it a second time with the same corner. This time the water spreads a little further into the dry part of the towel. Each time you do this the towel absorbs more water, like a sponge. At a certain point it's hard to lift the towel because the capillary action of the water causes the whole towel to be wet even though it's only the corner you dipped in each time.

Water acts the same way in soil. If you keep applying water to the same place in the soil, over time it won't just be that area that's wet; the water will have been wicked to cover a much larger area than that initial entry point. If you have sandy soil the water will tend to move down through soil particles easily, forming a vertical wet pattern. In clay soil that doesn't drain well the water will tend to move horizontally and spread out below the

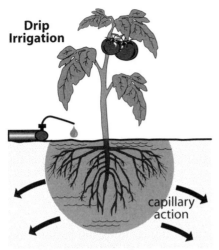

Drip Irrigation

capillary action

Wetting pattern in most loam and garden soils

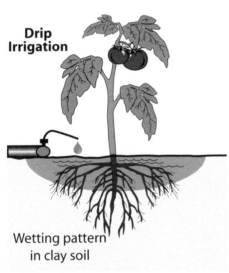

Drip Irrigation

Wetting pattern in clay soil

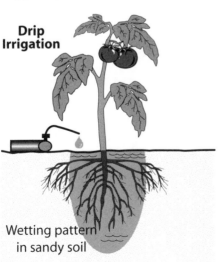

Drip Irrigation

Wetting pattern in sandy soil

surface of the soil and not penetrate too deeply. This is why you worked so hard to add organic material—so that the water wouldn't be prevented from moving through the soil and down to deep roots.

Hopefully your soil follows the pattern where the capillary action of the soil pulls the water both horizontally and vertically so that it has a fairly uniform distribution around the roots of your vegetables. Even if your soil isn't perfect the over-riding theme of this book is the importance of building up your soil with organic materials. All that compost and compostable material you've been adding each year is going to create a soil which allows water to drain well through the soil and not rot the roots but at the same time retains that moisture for when the plant needs it. That clump of leaves from last fall is going to do a great job of grabbing some of that rainwater or irriga-tion water as it slowly makes its way through the soil. It will hold onto that moisture until a nearby root encounters it and decides it needs it. This is one of the many benefits of adding compost and organic material on a large scale.

System Components

There are number of suppliers of drip irrigation equipment, and I provide a list of some of them at the end of this chapter. Some seed catalogs now sell it as well. You'll need adapters to connect to your water source and pipe to get the water to the garden and pipe in the garden with drippers to get the water to the soil. The faucet assembly consists of an anti-siphon adapter, a pressure regulator, a T-filter, and a swivel adapter.

The anti-siphon adapter attaches to your gar-den hose or outside wall faucet and is required by many municipalities. While there is little likeli-hood that irrigation water will flow back into your domestic water supply, I have had problems with siphoning in my own garden. Sometimes after my solar pump has filled one of my garden rain barrels I remove one length of hose to move it to my drip irrigation system. Meanwhile I've left one length of garden hose in the rain barrel and the other end

Faucet Assembly

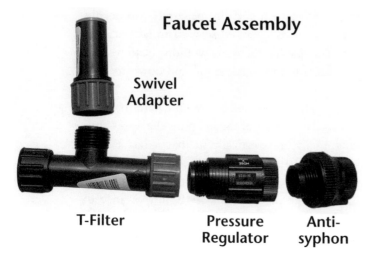

Swivel Adapter

T-Filter   **Pressure Regulator**   **Anti-syphon**

is lying on the ground. On more occasions than I care to admit I've come back later expecting to have a full rain barrel only to discover next to no water in it and a big wet spot and a small stream bed cut through the garden at the lower end of the hose. When I removed the one hose it created a siphon effect that drew the water out of the barrel. This would be a danger in your home if water from your irrigation system got drawn back into your house.

The next fitting is a pressure regulator. One of the beauties of a drip irrigation system is that it works under low pressure, making it perfect for applications that use a slower solar-powered DC pump or even an elevated rain barrel. Most drip irrigation systems run at 15 to 30 psi (pounds per square inch), but the water pressure in your home is probably between 40 to 60 psi. This low flow rate is nice in that your drip irrigation system won't be competing with other water pressure uses in the house. Your shower may not have much pressure while a sprinkler is running, and heaven forbid someone should flush the toilet, but with a low-flow drip irrigation system you don't have to worry about this. You do have to worry about having too much pressure in the lines, however, so the pressure regulator drops the higher household water pressure down to one more manageable for the drip system.

The pressure regulator fits into the T-filter. It's best to place the filter in a vertical position, just

as if it were hanging down from an outside faucet. The filter removes any sediment and particles from the water before it's fed into the drip lines. The holes for the water to drip out of the system are small and easily plugged up, so this filter is designed to prevent that. I use a dug well, and many people use other sources of water that may contain sediment and other materials that can plug up the system. After a few weeks of use I clean the filter out and I'm amazed by how much stuff it has collected. My well water looks clear but obviously has sediment and particles in it. I also have what's called a foot valve in the well that has a screen on it. The foot valve prevents water from draining out of the system, and the large mesh screen is designed to prevent any large debris and particles from entering the system.

The final fitting is a swivel adapter that threads onto the T-filter. You insert the pipe into the swivel adapter that will take the water to where you want to start dripping it onto plants. When it reaches the garden there's a "T" adapter that sends the water to each row, where there's another "T" or "L" adapter. A drip line extends from

This shows a strainer screen clogged with material from our dug well. The pressure was low in the system and when I investigated I discovered that this was the culprit.

this adapter to each row to water the vegetables or fruit. These fittings are barbed and you just push the pipe onto them. It helps to have a bucket of hot water with you to put the pipe in before pushing it onto the fitting. This helps it expand and makes it more malleable so that it fits on more easily. My system works under such low pressure that just hand installation works fine—no clamps required.

The Drip Line

The drip line is the same black plastic material as the pipe that feeds the water. The difference is that every 12 inches there's a drip hole. This is a reinforced section of the pipe with a very small hole that allows water to drip out. Once the system is pressurized water will begin dripping from these holes onto the soil. These holes are sometimes referred to as button drippers. Here you can see a close-up of the drip line turned upside down with the water starting to accumulate underneath it. The drip line doesn't have to be pointed down to work properly. It drips based on the water pressure in the line rather than the direction it's facing.

How long you leave the drip line irrigation system on will depend on a number of factors, including the pressure in the line and the rating on the drip emitters, which will typically be 1 to 4 gph (gallons per hour). This differs greatly from a lawn sprinkler that may be rated at 1 to 5 gpm (gallons per minute) or from 60 to 300 gph. It may sound as if you're not getting enough water on the plants, but you're not losing any from evaporation or running off and puddling or just being blown away by the wind. All the water is going where you want it, right to the roots of the plants. If you're irrigating your carrots you may want to make sure to give them a good, deep watering to get down to end of that long taproot. Strawberries, which have roots much closer to the surface, won't require as much watering.

Nozzles/Drippers

Drip lines that come with evenly spaced holes or button drippers deliver water to the plant based on the flow rate in the system, so the higher the

Drip holes deliver water to soil.

water pressure the more water the dripper will deliver. If you keep your eye on the system and have a good idea of how much water is being delivered button drippers are fine for most home gardeners provided that your rows aren't too long and you don't have huge elevation differences.

Some people like to have more control to deliver the water and for that they use drip emitters or drippers. These are a separate part and you actually punch a hole in the line and insert them into it. These drippers can control how much water they deliver, generally between .5 and 4 gph. Regardless of how much water pressure is in the system, they will deliver the same amount of water. They often have a self-flushing mode so that as pressure builds on start-up or reduces on shutdown they flush themselves to clear out debris. They work well on a very long line where it is difficult to maintain consistent pressure and water flow down the entire length of the line. With drip emitters you can increase the pressure through the system and be assured that each dripper will still deliver the required amount of water. Finally, they work well on a system that isn't on a level surface and may have different elevations in the drip line. With the button drippers you may find that more water is delivered at the bottom of the hill than at the top, whereas with these more advanced

A drip emitter to better control the water flow rate.

This shows a typical garden configuration. Water comes from the source in the lower pipe, then goes out to various driplines in the rows of vegetables. "L" ribbed connectors are for the end of the line and "T" connectors are used when the water continues to additional rows.

drip emitters you'll be able to deliver a consistent amount of water throughout the drip line regardless of the elevation. They will increase the cost of the system marginally and will take a little more time to install but may be worth it depending on your application.

Kits

Many of drip irrigation companies and seed companies sell kits that include everything you need to get started. For my first experience with drip irrigation I bought a complete kit. It came with instructions and I spent that summer getting comfortable with the system. After that I understood how it worked and knew what I needed more of and what I didn't really use, so on my subsequent order I just purchased the specific pipe and adapters I needed. I highly recommend one of the kits to get started.

Photo: www.northerngardensupply.ca

Cleaning

At the end of each of my drip lines is an adapter with two plastic "Os" that fit completely over the pipe so that it looks like a number "8." After you insert this adapter at the end of the line you fold back and pinch the pipe and move the other open end of the adapter down onto the very end of the pipe. This seals it and prevents any water from leaking out. In my garden I have two issues in terms of getting materials in the drip lines. First of all I have an outside source of water (my dug well) which contains materials that may clog things up. Secondly, I move the drip lines around the garden as the summer progresses. Some areas may be drier than others or some plants may be thirstier than others. Anytime I move the system pipe adapters fall onto the soil and get dirty. I try to keep a bucket of water handy to dip each item into before I hook the system up again, but dirt eventually gets into the system.

This type of adapter allows for really easy cleaning of the system. You just have to have pressure in the system and then remove the open end of the figure 8 stop and water gushes out, removing all the soil and debris with it. It's hard to tell from the photograph but the first burst of water out of the system is fairly brown and has lots of materials in it that you don't want in your system. I'm sure I could be more careful as I move the drip lines around the garden to avoid so much build-up, but you know how it is. You get busy and you rush things and lo and behold—compromises occur. That's what I like about this type of system: it's very forgiving. In a garden environment with non-municipality-treated water it's going to be very tough to keep the system pristine. Having a means to conveniently flush the lines is a really logical way to deal with this.

Flexibility

I've become a really big fan of drip irrigation. It's incredibly flexible. You can use different nozzles based on the layout of your garden. You can use different input sources: household water supply, low-pressure outside pump, or elevated natural pressure from a rain barrel. You can also expand the system as your garden grows by ordering more pipe and adapters. And, finally, I like it because you can move it around. In the photo on page 123 you can see that I plant my onions in two rows very close together. I can put a drip line down the middle, give it a good deep watering, and then move the system without having to worry about watering again for three or four days. While moving the system around takes a little time and effort, it's flexible. It would be best to be able to leave it in place, especially if you had it under black plastic mulch. But with the size of my garden and the changing needs of plants at different stages of their lives, I love my drip irrigation system. The fact that it's extremely efficient with water is just the icing on the cake.

My Watering Routine

My watering routine starts early in the morning, before the sun's up and before it's too hot outside. I use watering cans and rain barrels that I position throughout the garden. I give any row and section that I water a really good, deep watering. If it's a short row I put anywhere from five to ten watering cans of water on it. I generally water two or three different rows with each can to avoid overwatering and having the water run off and be wasted. I find it's better to water in lots of small applications allowing the water to soak in between each trip.

While I'm using the watering cans dipped into some of my rain barrels in the garden, I'm draining some of my raised rain barrels either into hilled plants like squash or into soaker hoses which work well under really low pressure. As the sun starts to rise and hits my solar panel, the solar pump starts and I begin filling up empty rain barrels.

After an hour or more of this it's time for breakfast. For the next two to three hours I come back out to the garden every 30 minutes or so and move the solar pump, which is filling up rain barrels from the dug well near the garden. Once all these are filled I attach the hose to the drip irrigation system and it irrigates a large area of the garden for the rest of the day. Depending on the vegetable and how dry it is, I may leave the drip irrigation system there the next day or move it to

A "Figure 8" line terminator.

Opening and flushing the dirt out of the system. The first water is dark and has soil and debris in it.

Once the water is clear you can close it back up again.

the next location for the following day's watering.

This probably sounds overwhelming, and it helps that I work out of my home. Your garden will probably be much smaller than the half acre I work on. And if you don't want to take the time to hand water you can get timers for drip irrigation systems that allow you put the lines down once and water properly each day and have the system shut off automatically. There's lots of flexibility, and I'm sure with the suggestions I've made you'll find one system or a combination that's right for your garden, time, soil, and climate.

I think you'll find that you want to spend some time hand watering. There's something about taking rainwater and giving it to your plants. It's very ancient. I believe it's in our DNA to do this. Humans have been doing it for generations. The more of us who do it, and do it on an increasingly large scale, the greater the chance that future generations will also get to enjoy this simple pleasure.

Drip Irrigation Sources

Many seed catalogs now sell drip irrigation components. Here are some on-line companies that specialize in them.

www.dripirrigation.com
www.dripdepot.com
www.rainbird.com
www.irrigationdirect.com
www.digcorp.com
www.dripworksusa.com

Canada
www.northerngardensupply.ca

Rows getting a good watering with drip irrigation during a drought.

Lettuce is one vegetable that doesn't mind water on its leaves.

If you're gardening on a smaller scale you might want to try a homemade drip irrigation system. Grab some pop bottles from the neighbors recycling bin, drill several holes in the cap, one in the bottom, fill with water and put in the soil near the base of that tomato plant. You might want to tie it to a stake to help it stay upright. More holes will let the water out faster. This can be helpful if you find yourself forgetting to water, especially containers on your porch that can dry out quickly in the hot summer sun.

59   A Little Midseason Boost

Ever have one of those afternoons when things are really dragging? You didn't have a very good lunch, or the office is really hot, or work in the warehouse is more physical than usual and you're kind of tapped out? If you were at home you'd probably have a nap. But you're at work and that's frowned upon. Well, it's frowned upon in many places, but some companies are starting to recognize the value of a nap in the afternoon. Heaven knows cultures in warm climates have found siestas to be effective. I know that when I hit that wall a 15-minute nap can really help to make me feel re-energized. Okay, I know what you're thinking … what does this have to do with gardening?

Partway through the summer some of your plants may be feeling the same way. You've done everything right. You worked really hard and you made great compost and you applied it liberally to the soil to help the plant through its entire growing season. Maybe you found a great source of composted manure that you mixed into the soil in the spring. Or you found some great bagged manure on sale locally that really helped enrich your soil. You've done everything right, but sometimes your plants hit that little midafternoon, or midsummer, naptime when they could use a bit of a boost. So here are some ideas that you may want to try. I don't really believe these are necessary, but sometimes they can make the difference between a good harvest and a great harvest.

Top Dressing

At some point during the growing season I like to top-dress some of my plants with composted manure. I usually pick the heavy feeders like corn. I figure if I have the compost or composted manure available I might as well be making use of it. I compost on a large scale, and at any given time I have various piles at different stages of decomposition and even if it's not perfectly composted it's not a problem. I use it anyway. If you've grabbed a hundred bags of leaves the previous fall they'll have started to break down by midsummer and will be mixed up with the rest of your compost. Feel free to use this. It's going to be a great boost. Plus it's going to help the semi-composted material break down faster because it will be exposed to more moisture and light. The worms are going to help you as well. They love this sort of stuff added to the garden. They'll work their way towards the upper reaches of the soil to deposit their castings and if they hit a nice pile of rotting leaves they'll be thinking, "Woo hoo, party time." Worms will pull some of the material down into the soil, so they'll help make this little midsummer top-up much more readily available to the plants.

If you had some materials you were thinking of using as a mulch, like those straw bales you grabbed from the neighbor's Halloween display last fall, now's a good time to apply them. Any mulch is going to help retain moisture but a natural mulching material like this will also start to break down fairly quickly, so some of this organic matter will end up washing down to the roots during watering and rain.

Top-dressing corn with composted manure.

Compost Tea

This sounds horrible I know, but it's worth some consideration. The concept of a compost tea is to make nutrients readily available to the plant by spraying them in liquid form onto the plant's foliage. This is also called a "foliar spray." The nutrients can enter the plants through openings or pores in the leaves rather than traveling up from the roots. While it technically isn't the best way of doing it, since the plant has evolved to bring the nutrients up from the soil, when the plant is in a vigorous growing phase a little boost like this isn't such a bad idea. It's like a Mars bar at about 3:30 in the afternoon on a hot day in the office.

Younger corn getting a topdressing boost

Manure tea can help with problems caused by some diseases like fungus. Things like powdery mildew, which appears as a grayish powdery substance on plants, is attacked by organisms in the compost, and several applications can sometimes slow down or stop problems like this.

Mixing up some compost tea.

You can use a variety of materials to make compost tea, including your own compost or commercial compost that you find at the garden center. You may also find bags of worm castings or similar natural products that are very rich in organic material and healthy organisms. Regardless of what compost you use, try mixing about a quart of the compost in a five-gallon bucket of water. Mix it up really well and stir it occasionally over the next day or so whenever you walk by. After a day or two you should strain it before putting it into a watering can. You can use a sprayer if you have one, but be extra careful about straining out all of the solids that might plug up the spray nozzle.

Then it's just a matter of spraying the foliage of the plants to provide a readily usable source of nutrients right where the plant needs it. While I don't usually do this myself, if your soil seems to be lacking in nutrition and you weren't able to add enough compost and organic material during the previous fall and in the spring, this is a way to give your plants a real boost. You can put any excess on the base of the plants along with the materials you strained out.

Manure Tea

Manure tea is the same concept but you use manure instead of compost. You have to be much more careful with manure because it can deliver pathogens like E. coli that can be very harmful to humans. Some E. coli outbreaks have been caused by manure getting into water that people drink or that is used as irrigation water for crops. Be sure not to use manure tea on any plant that's close to maturity or that has fruit that's nearly ready to pick. Manure tea is more of a boost to use when plants are setting fruit, which is when those flowers are about to turn into small fruit. You don't want to risk delivering pathogens to something that may be eaten soon. Manure tea isn't appropriate for use on strawberries, for example, after fruit has set.

The second thing to make sure of is that you use composted manure. This is manure that has been sitting in a pile exposed to the sun and the rain. Microorganisms will have begun the decomposition process, which creates heat that helps kill the pathogens. To make manure tea you need to suspend the manure in water in a perforated bag so that the nutrients can leech out. After a day or two of "steeping" you can use it as a foliar spray after straining. Some organic gardeners make manure tea and dip the roots of their transplants in it to give them a shot of nutrition before they're planted.

While manure tea is growing in popularity I'm always cautious with manure. I have access to horse manure that I compost before I apply it to the garden, but I'd be very careful with cow manure, which is often the source of E. coli contamination. Chicken manure is very high in nutrient value but is more difficult to find. My philosophy with manure is to compost it and then either work it into the soil or use it as a top dressing underneath the plants, being careful that the fruit never touches it. I never top-dress tomatoes because the lower fruit often hangs down and ends up on the soil. Corn, on the other hand, grows a foot or two up the plant and never gets close to the soil, so since it's a heavy feeder I often top-dress corn.

Stinging Nettle Tea

It's good to have a green thumb and be successful in your gardening efforts. It seems to be a given, though, that you'll be most successful at growing things you don't want to grow. Dandelions are one example of this. Now dandelions are an amazing plant. They are an extremely healthy addition to a salad and they are even used to make wine. Their long taproot, which is hard to kill, is a superhighway to transport nutrients from deep in the soil up to the leaves. When you're finally successful at eliminating the dandelions, the path that the taproot has punched through the soil helps to prevent your garden plants from sit-

The invasive and nitrogen packed stinging nettle.

ting in water and makes it easier for them to get down deep into the lower soil areas.

While I long ago accepted dandelions as a healthy and beautiful part of my lawn, there's a plant called stinging nettle that grows uncontrollably around my property. I've noticed that you can actually purchase stinging nettle seeds, but you might want to grow it under controlled circumstances. Stinging nettle is a perennial that spreads by sending out rhizomes and roots underground, and it spreads very quickly. It's extremely healthy in terms of its food and medicinal uses, being exceptionally high in vitamins A, C, and D and also containing iron and some trace nutrients. If you prepare it properly you can eat it or make tea out of it and it contains 40% protein, which is very high for a green, leafy plant.

There's a downside though, and that's the "stinging" part. When you touch it with your bare skin, it hurts. Its tiny hairs or needles give off several chemicals that really sting. If you're weeding and you grab one in your bare hands by accident you will yell words that you won't want your children to hear. The stinging can last for a few minutes or it can last all day. Occasionally the area of skin that made contact with the stinging nettle plant will be sore for half an hour but will be itchy and irritated for the rest of the day. I continue to fight it in the garden but around the property it grows like crazy. It spreads and takes over and in a good location the stalks can be seven feet high. That's great when someone like me forgets about it and wanders into it while contemplating the meaning of life. Ouch!

I have finally learned to embrace my stinging nettle and I'm starting to make use of it. Along with all those wonderful vitamins stinging nettle is an outstanding source of nitrogen, which as you know is key to a healthy garden. So I now "harvest" my stinging nettle. When it gets big enough I cut the stalks and add them to the compost. I

Stinging nettle tea steeping.

always have lots of carbon-based inputs like leaves and hay, so stinging nettle makes a superb nitrogen supplement. Adding it to the mix really makes the compost hot and working it in helps to get the decomposition process under way.

Stinging nettle is also a great raw material to use for making a foliar spray. In the photo I've added some to a garbage can full of water and stirred it up. After a day or two it's ready to spray on plants and is a huge energy booster without the potential risk that using manure can add to the process. Nettles also supply magnesium, sulphur, and iron to the leaves, so I'm pretty excited to have finally realized it was kind of stupid to be trying to eradicate such a powerhouse of potential nutrition for the garden. The reason it was so hard to eradicate was also the reason to embrace it.

Be sure to use it with caution, though. Always wear gloves and long-sleeved shirts around it and be careful to keep it away from your face as you're harvesting and cutting and moving it and immersing it in water. Not that I've ever done such a stupid thing, but having one of these slap you in the face really lets you know you're alive! If you choose to introduce stinging nettle to your garden be aware that it can be very invasive. It's like mint in that you'll grow it with the best of intentions and the next thing you know it will grow well beyond where you envisioned it. If you have the space, grow it in an isolated area and use some rocks or something to delineate where you

want it to stay. Even if you surround it with rocks it WILL spread beyond them by sending roots underneath them. The rocks, though, can serve as your "line in the sand," and you should lop off any new growth that springs up outside the line. Also be aware that if you make a foliar spray out of stinging nettles you'll want to use it up within 48 hours or so. There have been times when I've forgotten about the batch that I was brewing, and after more than a few days in the hot sun it turns into quite a bubbly, stinky mess. Those batches just ended up being dumped right into the compost heap and it was like one of those science experiments gone horribly wrong. It really did teach me, though, about all the wonderful nutrients that started working in a big way once the nettle was immersed in water.

A Midsummer Boost from the Ocean

While it may sound appealing for your vegetables to have a little midsummer holiday by the ocean to charge up their growth batteries, this is not in fact a realistic option. What is an option, though, is to bring the ocean to your plants in the form of seaweed emulsion and fish emulsion. Fish emulsion is created from the waste of the fish processing industry; it has an N-P-K rating of about 5-2-2 and also supplies some micronutrients.

There was a movie made in 1990 with Richard Harris called *The Field* about a Scottish farmer who had worked his whole life to build up the field he farmed, but the field was owned by a widow. When she decides to sell the land things go horribly wrong. I was struck by the image of him hauling seaweed from the ocean to work into his soil. People who have farmed near the ocean have been doing this forever, and now you can use some of it in your garden too. Seaweed fertilizer is sold as a solid in bag form which you can spread on your garden or as a liquid emulsion that you can use as a foliar spray. From a convenience standpoint this is probably the easiest of the foliar spray options because you can just mix it with water and spray it without having to strain it.

I would be careful about using these items,

though, because you can't control where the fish or seaweed has originated. As you move up the food chain toxins are more concentrated, and fish are pretty high on the chain. Small fish acquire toxins from their diet and big fish eat the small fish, and the toxins become more concentrated in these larger fish. So fish emulsion should be used in moderation. You should also be careful with seaweed in terms of its potential salt content. If you do have access to seaweed near your home, though, it would be worth harvesting some that washes up on the beach and adding it your compost or using it as mulch.

Commercial Boosters

We've all seen the commercials for fertilizers you can apply to your plants for miracle results. Bigger tomatoes, greener lawns, more azaleas—whatever. I don't think there's any question that these products will produce the results they advertise. You just have to question whether they're a product you want to add to your garden. While they may not be harmful in any way, they're often not a product that will add to the long-term viability of your soil. They're a quick fix, and like all quick fixes there can be consequences down the road. In other words, if you start using it on your tomatoes each year and have a huge harvest, then you may

feel it's not necessary to continue putting the effort into your compost application. I really do believe that for the health of your soil it's a "no pain, no gain" proposition and that these quick fixes often result in your soil being depleted and hooked on the short-term fix. It's like eating that chocolate bar in the middle of the afternoon. Yes, you'll feel great for an hour, but you also know you'll probably have a sugar crash after the spike that the chocolate bar gives you. You'd be much better to have some carrots that will provide a slower lift and will also add fiber and beta-carotene and other healthy things to the mix. The energy will also tend to last longer and you won't have a fast sugar crash.

All these techniques are provided as suggestions for you to consider. I believe that if you've really done the groundwork by building up a rich, healthy soil with compost they may not be necessary. If you feel your soil may be really lacking in organic materials and nutrients and if it seems as though your plants are not making the progress you'd like, then by all means give them a little push with a foliar spray. If you're keeping a journal of your garden these are the things you should note each year so you can decide whether or not they're beneficial and if you want to continue with them from year to year.

Don't forget the ultimate goal of all this work. Here's a "wagon o' brassicas" filled with brocoli and cauliflower. You're going to need a big family, good neighbors or a freezer to use all these healthy, tasty veggies!

# 60	Insects and Pests

Insects are essential to the success of your garden. They pollinate many of the flowers that turn into wonderful and delicious fruit. Thank goodness for the pollinators! The problem is that other insects are a potential problem in your garden and if left unchecked they will be able to completely wipe out some of your vegetables. You need to have a strategy to deal with the unwanted pests without destroying the beneficial ones. Ladybugs are a beautiful addition to any garden with their lovely orange color against the green of the plants. They're in your garden because there is food for them and they eat insects like the aphids that want to suck the juice out of your vegetables. If you use a traditional chemical approach to dealing with the aphids you may also kill the bees and ladybugs that your garden really needs.

The dreaded Colorado potato beetle.

Most of us have come to the realization that we probably are exposed to too many chemicals already, so growing food organically is a great way to reduce some of the exposure. There is nothing more direct in terms of chemical exposure than ingesting it into our bodies though our food. Growing food without these chemicals gives your immune system a huge boost by reducing your exposure to them.

Growing organically isn't some magic utopia that you'd see in a fairy tale. Nature is all about birth and death and there are lots of little creatures out there that will survive and thrive by taking nourishment from your garden. Your job is to watch for these invaders as the season progresses and try to create an environment that is as unwelcoming to them as possible.

I've been discussing many techniques for pest control throughout the book, but this chapter integrates all of this information for easy reference just in case you're having one of those summers where the bugs have you at your wits' end. I have been dealing with pests for 30 years and have used a variety of sources to come up with strategies and techniques for success. One of the best books I've come across for more detailed information is *The Organic Gardener's Handbook of Natural Insect and Disease Control*, written by Barbara Ellis and published by Rodale Books. Rodale has been publishing great information on organic gardening for decades, and this book is an outstanding compendium of detailed solutions to garden problems. While it's probably got far more detail than most home gardeners need, if you want to take pest control to the next level, this 500+ page book is for you.

It summarizes the four main control methods for dealing with pests:

Cultural controls are methods like rotating your crops and cleaning up your garden in the fall to remove places where pests are likely to overwinter.

Physical controls include methods that I've discussed in other chapters, such as putting collars on plants susceptible to cutworms or knocking potato bugs into a bucket of water with a badminton racket.

Biological controls involve methods such as releasing ladybugs to eat aphids or spraying with a microorganism like Bt, which is discussed in previous chapters on various vegetables.

Organic sprays and dusts are a last resort since they are also toxic to beneficial insects.

Cultural Controls

The main cultural control that I use is crop rotation. The purpose of crop rotation is to keep pests from getting spoiled and expecting to find the same crop planted in the same spot each year. By moving things around each year I've been able to minimize the pests and disease that would occur if I left the same crops in the same place season after season. There are lots of different strategies for rotation, but I have been successful with a "seat of my pants" system. Each spring there is usually something left from the previous fall or some biennial going into its seed stage that I don't want to disturb, so I don't technically have the luxury of starting with a blank slate. Ideally you would have a square garden divided into four equal quarters. Each year you would move the main crop types from one square to the next. If possible, it would also be beneficial to use one of the quarters for a green manure planting that would allow the soil in one quarter of the garden to be replenished naturally. If you plant one of your quarters in legumes like peas and beans this allows you to a get a crop and still have the soil enriched by these nitrogen fixers.

I purchase plants from a supplier who believes in disease prevention as much as I do. I do not want to bring seeds or plants that already have problems into the garden. While it is next to impossible for anyone to guarantee immunity from disease, it's good to know that the seed catalogs that I use and the greenhouse where I purchase transplants are committed to providing the highest-quality, disease-free seeds and plants possible. This is especially important with items like berries and potatoes. Make sure your suppliers provide details on their system of disease prevention and their commitment to providing disease-free plants for your garden.

I also purchase seeds that have resistance to disease before I even plant them. This is one of the most basic ways of minimizing problems during the growing season. It's worth the investment to take extra time in the winter to look for seeds that have been bred to be less susceptible to the common problems encountered by home gardeners. For most gardeners it's next to impossible to know exactly what may be causing problems in the garden, so your seed choice will come down to a gut feeling of what sounds tasty and what has the most resistance.

Another great way to keep your garden as healthy as possible is to take the advice you give your kids and "keep it clean." In the fall it's a good idea to remove all the debris from the summer and turn the soil over or rototill. The debris can make a perfect home for pests to winter over, so by removing it you create a more hostile environment for them. By going that next step and tilling up or cultivating the top few inches of soil you'll disturb any pests that haven't burrowed deep enough yet and hopefully disrupt their plans for hibernation. I've often wrestled with tilling in the fall because I hate to see soil exposed to winter winds. Luckily the soil is usually fairly damp, which helps prevent erosion, and here we often get a snow early enough to cover up the soil and prevent it from blowing away.

Tilling your garden can also make it tough for some pests to venture into and around your garden. This past summer was so wet that slugs suddenly became a problem. As I observed how slowly they were able to move across a level pathway, I realized just how much a soil that is well worked with peaks and fissures would prevent their movement. I would hope that tilled soil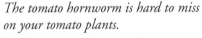

The tomato hornworm is hard to miss on your tomato plants.

is a big "Keep Out" sign to pests hiding in the areas around your garden. I always pay attention when I'm tilling because white grubs are easy to spot against a dark brown soil background, so tilling provides an excellent opportunity to get rid of really nasty pests. Grubs feed on roots and so many times an unexplained problem with a plant is caused by a grub underground munching on its roots. Looking at a row of healthy plants with just one wilted and dying can often indicate grubs. Digging around in the soil should expose a grub that had eaten all the roots off the plant. Sometimes you have to sacrifice a plant to see what's going on under the soil and diagnose the problem. If you have one plant that's growing but is struggling among healthy plants there's a good chance that a grub or wireworm caused the problem.

Most of us wash our kitchen utensils, but it's

easy to be lazy about tools in the garden. It's just a shovel, right? It's in the dirt. How bad can it be? Well, it can actually be a source of diseases that are being spread from one place in the garden to the next, so it's a good idea to keep your tools clean. I like having a lot of rain barrels around because it lets me wash tools close to where I use them. Some people will even use alcohol, especially on tools like pruners that can easily spread some fairly nasty problems. It's common sense but worth mentioning that anything that moves around your garden, from your rototiller to your workboots, can spread disease. If you're having a particularly wet summer, be careful about moving things around on a wet day when pathogens find it even easier to hitch a ride on your pant leg. Try and do most of your work on dryer, sunnier days.

Physical Controls

Physical controls are the ones I use the most, probably because I tend to spot the problems once they're underway and it's easy to address them when they're out in the open. I got pretty comfortable with squishing bugs in my fingers a long time ago, probably because I usually discover them after they've started to chew on my plants. I have to admit I've been known to take a bit of joy in seeking retribution for a slight against my garden.

As I discussed in the potato chapter, I watch for adult potato beetles early in the season by planting just one row to attract them. The bugs are easy to spot and the eggs are even easier. By eliminating the bulk of the bugs early in the season I have much less to worry about later on. If they do get out of hand, a few minutes spent squishing them by hand or using a

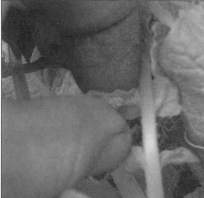

Eliminate potato bug eggs by rubbing the bright orange egg cluster on the underside of leaves.

badminton racquet to knock them into a bucket of water helps me stay on top of them.

Tomato hornworms like the one on the previous page are so large they're hard to miss. If you're spending time in your garden regularly you should spot their damage fairly easily, so just spend some time hunting them down. These are big enough that you may want to drown them in a bucket of water.

This past summer was the second wet summer in a row, which caused the slug population to skyrocket. While slugs are slow, they work tirelessly and cause lots of damage to plants. I used two techniques to deal with them. One was to place wooden boards throughout the garden that I would turn over in the morning. I found many slugs that took refuge under them. I also used aluminum tart tins that I

filled with beer. Slugs and earwigs were attracted to the beer and drowned themselves. For the beer lovers among us this will not seem to be such a terrible fate. This past fall I found a particularly high number of snails, presumably seeking refuge for the winter, wherever I had used rotting hay for mulch. I eliminated these under my boot.

Ponds and forests surround me and every summer we have a large population of deer flies. They don't affect the vegetables, just the vegetable gardener. So I take a piece of boxboard from a cracker box, duct tape it to the back of my hat and then smear it with Tanglefoot®. This is a natural product made from tree resins that is very sticky and traps insects when they land. Deer flies seem to be programmed to

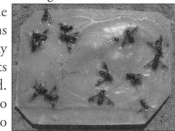

attack people's heads from behind, and after a few hours I have dozens of them stuck to the boxboard, where they can't bite me.

I've begun using the same principle in the garden, placing flat sticks around plants that flying insects are attracted to. You can paint the wood different colors like blue or yellow, but I've had good success leaving the wood unpainted. I then smear the wood with Tanglefoot®. Many of the pests on your vegetables will have will have landed there from the air in the form of moths and butterflies that use the plant as the host for their larvae.

Floating Row Covers

The logical best defense against these types of attacks is to prevent the airborne pests from landing on your plants, and floating covers are the way to do that. This photo shows plants growing in mulch covered by a floating row cover which is made from a spun material that allows sunlight, air, and water to pass through but prevents butterflies, moths, and other flying insects from landing on your plants. The first limitation to floating row covers is that you won't want to use these if and when your plant has flowers that need pollinating because the bees won't be able to get through either. The other challenge is that you'll have to keep the row cover well secured and avoid letting it lie on your plants, especially if they're immature. As plants get larger and stronger you'll be able to just lay the row cover on top of them, but early on you'll have to be careful about causing damage to young seedlings. That's where hooped row covers are an advantage. These pieces of curved steel help

to keep the cloth off the plants.

You can see from this photo what an amazing environment you can create. You've basically

These heat-loving peppers are helped by plastic mulch and a hooped floating row cover which helps keep heat in and flying insect pests out. (Courtesy of Johnny's Selected Seeds: www.johnnyseeds.com)

made a little mini-greenhouse that will help extend your season and keep your plants safe from late frosts and cool nights. You've also got a row cover to keep flying pests off. The downside to all this is the time required to set it up. Unfortunately, the time when I would need to be setting this all up is also the busiest time for me, so I haven't made significant use of floating row covers. This is probably the wrong way to look at it in terms of the "pay now or pay later" theory. I end up paying later, having to deal with the results of the eggs that the flying insects lay. Row covers will also protect against some pests that may not be as common but still do lots of damage. Cabbage maggots are laid by flies that would be prevented by a row cover. Carrots also have problems with maggots and other pests that originate from airborne insects.

The Brassica Ballet

The brassicas, including cauliflower, broccoli, and cabbage, are all favored places for the lovely white cabbage worm butterfly to lay its eggs. The butterflies have two or three black swatches on each wing, and as they flit and flutter around the garden they add to the lovely pastoral scene. This jaunty dance masks a sinister intent, and if you don't deal with them they lay eggs that hatch into little green worms that love to eat brassicas. One of the ways that I deal with them is to pick up my badminton racquet and go after them. In the gardening DVD I produced several years ago called *Grow Your Own Vegetables* there is footage of me performing this butterfly-killing dance. It has proven to be the most popular part of the gardening DVD. It looks like a combination of an epileptic seizure and a sasquatch's first experience on ice skates. It isn't pretty. The butterflies are completely erratic in their movement and my attempts to eliminate them are not graceful. This is not something I would recommend if you're on a first date and you've invited your date over to see your garden before you head out for dinner. While you were chasing the butterflies with your badminton racquet in hand you might not notice your date slowly backing away before turning and sprinting for the car to make a fast exit. As I mentioned, it isn't pretty, but it works.

This innocuous cabbage butterfly lays eggs, and the larvae that hatch will do major damage to your brassicas.

Cutworm Collars

Cutworms are my nemesis. Too often all of my spring enthusiasm for gardening is diminished by these dull-colored caterpillars that emerge from the soil to lop off plants just as they begin to grow. Then they pull the piece of the plant back down into the soil to munch on it. They can do a lot of damage to your early garden, but I've discovered a number of ways to deal with them. The first method is to use sacrificial plants. These are plants that I put into the garden as early as possible to attract the cutworms. If I have a volunteer plant that's growing where it's not supposed to, I transplant it close to one of my rows of crops. I also start flats of plants such as lettuce or sunflowers and I save a lot of these seeds from year to year, so I have plenty of seeds for growing sacrificial plants. When I plant a row of beans or peas

My nemesis, the dreaded Dr. Evil, a.k.a. cutworm.

I also plant my "sacrificial sunflowers" throughout the row. As I plant onions or leeks I plant a few lettuce plants throughout the row too. My hope is that by the time the beans or planted crop is emerging I'll have been able to find any cutworms that have been attracted to the nice, green sunflower or lettuce plants and I'll be able to dig them up and eradicate them.

This photo shows a row of basil transplants that I started in flats and have just set out. I want the basil. The lettuce plants are sacrificial plants that I'm using to attract cutworms. With all the leaves on the plant it's easy to spot damage from a cutworm. Once I've located an area with a cutworm at work it's just a matter of

rooting around with my finger and removing soil in the area until I expose it. It's a time-consuming process, but it's either that or losing the plants that I want to thrive.

Another method I use against cutworms is the collar. I make collars by cutting a toilet-paper roll in half and then cutting down the side so that it opens. This way I can wrap it around a plant and mound some soil around it to keep it closed. This past year I experimented with using three-quarters of a toilet-paper roll so I could place it more deeply into the soil to prevent the cutworms from tunneling under it so readily. You can use other materials for collars, such as rolled up and molded newspapers or tin cans with the tops and bottoms removed. These need to be removed when the threat has passed or you'll have to collect the cans in the fall when you're doing cleanup. I have enough to do, so I don't want to add another job. The beauty of the toilet-paper rolls is that they last for a couple of weeks when I need them the most. Then they start breaking down and in six or eight weeks there's no sign of them. This seems pretty natural to me.

Apple Barriers

Some of the problems with fruit trees can come from caterpillars that crawl up from the soil. The photo on page 196 shows a barrier that is basically double-sided tape that you wrap around the base of the tree. Any pest that tries to crawl over it will get stuck. Simple but effective.

Eggshells

Another barrier you can use is eggshells. I save and dry eggshells and then pound them with a mallet to break them into small shards. When I have a problem with crawling pests making their way across the soil and onto plants, I sprinkle a thick layer of crushed eggshells around  the plant. Many garden pests have soft underbellies that are torn as they travel across this field of broken eggshells.

Biological Controls

I have not made significant use of biological controls in my garden, or at least not consciously. These controls use the natural enemies of insects to control them, and while I'm hoping I have fostered an environment where there are lots of predators, I haven't gone out of my way either to attract them or to purchase them commercially. There are a number of companies that now specialize in controlling pests with predators, such as Natural Insect Control (NIC) at www.naturalinsectcontrol.com and www.planetnatural.com.

These companies sell predators that are happy to make a meal out of the insects that are making a meal out of the vegetables that you hope to make a meal out of. You may even find that your garden center is now selling some of these sorts of controls. Ladybugs are one that you may have encountered before. They really love aphids, which can be quite troublesome in your garden.  You'll often find aphids because you'll see lots of ants on your plants, which is better than having ants in your pants. Aphids are quite small and they cluster together, so they can be quite well camouflaged. As they suck juice from your precious vegetable they secrete a sticky sap that the ants like. If you've got ladybugs in your garden, catch some and carry them over to where the aphids are and let them go there. Or you can buy a bag of ladybugs to release. I know what you're thinking: How can I control them? What if they all fly over to my neighbor's yard? That might be a good sign, because it means that your neighbor has pests that you don't have.

Praying mantises can eat a huge volume of pests and because they're so big that they can eat big pests. I haven't purchased them because I know that I have a lot of them in my garden already, and I'd be concerned that a non-native variety might dominate

The voracious pest-eating machine—the praying mantis. (Photo by Jeff Moore)

my natural mantises. If you don't have any now and are finding a large number of insect pests, it might be worth purchasing some.

There are a number of interesting beneficial insects you can purchase, such as wasps that lay eggs in a number of pests in the garden. The eggs hatch and kill the host, just like in an *Aliens* movie. There are also soldier bugs that eat various harmful beetles and cabbage loopers.

The one beneficial creature I've purchased is so small you can't see it with the naked eye: "beneficial nematodes." Nematodes are a microscopic parasitic worm that infests the insect larvae of grubs, fly maggots, and whole variety of soil-dwelling bad guys. I originally bought some for areas of my lawn that grubs were chewing up and destroying. In recent years I've tried them in the vegetable garden where cutworms have been particularly damaging. They're sold by the millions on a sponge that you put in water and then apply to your soil with a watering can. Your soil temperature has to be above 60°F (15°C) for these to thrive and be effective, which is a challenge for me because the cutworms are most active in the spring when the soil is still fairly cool. I waited until the soil was warm enough and applied them anyway, with the thought that it was worth being preemptive to try and lessen next year's damage.

Bacillus Thuringiensis

Bt or Bacillus thuringiensis is one of the most common organic beneficials used today. This bacterium is ingested by a variety of insect pests which shortly afterwards stop eating and die. It works on a variety of caterpillars such as cabbage worms, tomato hornworms, and cabbage loopers. This is the

If you do spray with Bt make sure to get under the leaves of your brassicas as well as on top.

one item that I don't hesitate to spray in my garden, and although it feels weird to be out there with a sprayer you have to remind yourself that these microscopic organisms are harmless to humans. Bt is much easier to find these days and I can purchase it at a local garden center. It is sold by a number of companies under names such as DiPel, BTK, and Caterpillar Killer. The BTK that I use comes as a liquid that I mix with water and spray on all

my brassicas, being careful to direct the spray over the entire plant, especially the underside of leaves where the cabbage loopers and cabbage worms feed. I make sure I apply it when there's no chance of rain washing it away.

My application of Bt is basically an admission that I should have used floating row covers. If I had used row covers, my brassicas wouldn't have as many cabbage bugs chomping away at them. This is still a choice I'm comfortable with. Floating row covers last only a year or two and then have to be replaced. In a good season when I'm on top of the garden I keep my eyes open for eggs that are small and white and easy to spot on the underside of broccoli and cauliflower leaves. And as I mentioned, I do my best to eliminate the butterflies that lay the eggs with my handy and deadly high school badminton racket.

Ducks and Chickens

Whenever I'm picking strawberries at John Wise's farm it's always fun to watch his ducks helping him control pests. The geese love to move up and down the rows, pecking around for insects in the soil. Chickens are also known to be beneficial in the vegetable garden. They love bugs and are happy to root around in the soil in search of them. These are not organic pest control methods to be entered into without thought. They involve expense and require care, they have to be penned, and they could be the target of predators such as foxes and raccoons. You have to feed them year round since they can only feed themselves when the garden has a ready supply of bugs for dinner. But they are another potential ally in the war against insect pests and in some settings can certainly add to the surroundings. Although some cities are now allowing chickens, you'll have to decide if they're worth the potential wrath of neighbors who don't share your enthusiasm for our clucking friends.

Organic Sprays and Dusts

The final line of defense in our war against diseases and pests is sprays and dusts. For years many organic gardeners made their own, but now these are becoming much easier to find at gardening centers. As some municipalities have declared a moratorium on the cosmetic application of pesticides, companies are filling the void with more natural varieties. You still need to research them and be aware of what the product is that you're using. You can make many of the easy sprays yourself, and their advantage is that you know exactly what's in them.

Oil Sprays

I have already mentioned some of these, such as lime-sulfur spray, which is applied to fruit trees before they break bud. These sprays consist of horticultural dormant oil which kills insect pests that overwinter on trees. Previous versions of dormant oil tended to be heavier and you needed to avoid getting it on foliage, which made late-winter spraying most effective. Newer oils are lighter and you can use them year round. They work by smothering both the pest and its eggs.

Sulfur is a very old pesticide and works as a fungicide as well, which makes it particularly effective with fruit trees. It can protect against apple scab and powdery mildew. Applying lime-sulfur dormant oil in late winter provides some protection against various mites, scale, scabs, mildew, rust, and fungus. You need to spray it in the morning so that it will dry, and it should not be sprayed in temperatures below 39°F (4°C) or above 80°F (27°C).

You can use a lime-sulphur spray on its own during the growing season when leaves have appeared, but if you have fruit trees it's best to use it in conjunction with the dormant oil before the leaves emerge.

Diatomaceous Earth

I have used diatomaceous earth when I've had some major pest problems. It's the crushed dust from ancient fossils and contains microscopic jagged, pointy bits, like glass shards, that puncture the bodies of insects. They have an exoskeleton on the outside of their bodies that covers their soft, juicy insides, and if you can pierce that protective coating they gradually lose vital body moisture and die. Sounds like a violent video game to me, rated "VG" for Vegetable Gardeners. You dust diatomaceous earth directly onto your plants or onto the soil around the base of plants to kill any insects that attempt to crawl across the soil and up onto them.

Diatomaceous earth can be effective for a variety of other insect pests as well. Insects with soft bodies like caterpillars, thrips, leaf hoppers, aphids, and the larvae of many pests like Colorado potato beetles, corn earworms, cabbage loopers, and root maggots are particularly vulnerable to having their skeletons punctured. Remember that diatomaceous earth is nonselective and will kill beneficial insects as well as pests, so you should use it only if you have to. While it's considered safe for humans it can irritate your lungs, so wear a mask when you apply it and try and stay

I use an old baby powder container to apply diatomaceous earth and am careful to not breathe it in.

upwind since some will end up airborne. Rain will wash it off, so you'll have to reapply it if the pest persists.

Sprinkling it around the base of plants helps control soil-dwelling pests like slugs, cutworms, and root maggots. If you dust the leaves or foliage with it, chewing insects like cabbage loopers and potato beetle larvae will be affected. Diatomaceous earth is a great test of your resolve to garden organically. It may be working well, but it will look as though it's having the opposite effect. The affected insects will become dehydrated and they'll begin looking for moisture. You might suddenly notice a huge increase in insects after you've used this treatment, as they all come out of hiding looking for moisture. You have to be patient. It might take a couple of weeks before it's worked its magic on the insect pests. We're conditioned to want immediate results, but sometimes when you're trying to use natural products you have to be patient and let Mother Nature work her magic. You can purchase diatomaceous earth on its own, and there's also a commercial product called DIATECT® which includes pyrethrin.

Bugs by Mail

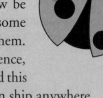

While many natural and organic pest control products can now be found in local stores, here are some companies that specialize in them. I provide the location for reference, but since they are internet based this may not be relevant as they can ship anywhere.

Montana	www.planetnatural.com
Arizona	www.arbico-organics.com
California	www.organiccontrol.com
California	www.groworganic.com
Vermont	www.dirtworks.net/Organic-Pest-Control.html
Massachusetts	www.extremelygreen.com
Canada	www.naturalinsectcontrol.com

Pyrethrin

Chrysanthemums have a relative called the pyrethrum daisy that can be used to make a broad-spectrum neurotoxin spray. It can kill insects on contact. While you can grow your own daisies and make your own spray, there are a number of commercial products with pyrethin in them. They can be effective for sucking and chewing pests like cabbage loopers, tomato pinworms, leafhoppers, Mexican bean beetles, and potato bugs. When you apply a pyrethrin spray wear protective clothing and be careful with it. While it is derived from daisies you still want to target the insect pests and try not to come into contact with it yourself.

Rotenone

Rotenone was one of the earliest pest control methods that organic farmers employed. It is derived from tropical plants, which gave the impression that it was safer than commercial pesticides, but it can be mildly toxic to humans and can be very toxic to fish and birds. As with any control this powerful, it will also kill beneficial insects which you're trying to encourage in the garden, so it should only be used as a last resort. With so many excellent and less toxic alternatives available today, I wouldn't suggest that you use rotenone.

Neem

Neem oil has been used in India in toothpaste and soap, but it works very well as a broad-spectrum insecticide. Plants absorb it and it moves around the plant and through its root system. Insects don't like the taste of plants that have been sprayed with neem. It has been shown to successfully deal with mealy bugs, root maggots, mites, squash bugs, leafhoppers, caterpillars, and the Japanese beetle. It also controls black spot, powdery mildew, anthracnose, and a fungus called rust. There are now some commercial sprays which use neem as their base.

Insecticidal Soap

"Soap" doesn't sound like the heavy-duty spray we want to take out into the garden and blast away with at all those pests chewing on our vegetables, but it can be surprisingly effective in the fight against pests. Insecticidal soaps work by using fatty acids that cause the contents of insect cells to be damaged and leak out, causing the insect to die. Soaps are most effective against insects that have soft bodies, such as thrips, spider mites and aphids. Some of the larger soft-bodied insects like caterpillars and leafhoppers may be killed by it, but luckily most beneficial insects like bees seem not to be bothered by it.

Insecticidal soaps may do some damage to plants, causing spots on leaves or burned tips. Try spraying a small area first before covering a plant completely. Cucumbers and beans don't seem to like soap sprays, so you'll have to find an alternative if you have a pest problem with these. There are lots of commercial insecticidal soaps, but you may want to try making your own. Try mixing about three teaspoons of liquid soap into a gallon of water.

Homemade Sprays

One of the first sprays I made myself made use of some vegetables that I talk about in chapter 61 on companion planting. Members of the allium family, like onions and garlic, have a natural ability to keep many insect pests away. If someone's just enjoyed a big meal with lots of either of these, it will have the same effect on people. Luckily insects can't offer these vegetables breath mints, so they just stay away from them. I mixed some minced onion, garlic, about a teaspoon of cayenne pepper, and a tablespoon of liquid dish soap in about a quart (1 liter) of water and put it into a spray bottle. It proved to be quite effective. The only thing that didn't work effectively was the spray bottle, since I hadn't strained the mixture. Straining it through a cloth solved that problem. These are all products you eat or come into contact with every day, so I believe they're well worth trying. You're combining the insecticidal properties of the fatty acids in the soap with the natural ability of alliums to discourage pests and throwing in a whoop-ass dose of stomach-ache-inducing cay-

enne pepper for any insect that makes it through the other lines of defense.

Staying in Touch

Insects and vegetable plants are all part of a much larger ecosystem that has infinite combinations of weather and moisture and nutrient inputs that can produce infinite outcomes. You can't always control what happens in your garden. Mother Nature is the ultimate final authority on what sort of garden you're going to have each year. What you can do is to try to provide an environment that stacks the odds in favor of your plants as much as possible. You do this by building up the soil with compost and making sure your plants get enough water. A healthy, vibrant plant is the best defense against an insect invader. You can't always control

outside variables such as the weather that may foster a climate that helps insect pests thrive. So spend time in your garden and pay attention to your plants. Try and spot pests early and deal with them directly by hand-picking them. If the problem gets overwhelming you can resort to some of these other techniques, but make them your second option. And only use them in response to a problem. There's no need to spray your garden if the pests aren't having an adverse effect. Stay in touch with your garden and spot "challenges" early before they turn into problems.

This squash bug will hang around the base of your cucurbits (squash and pumpkins) and lay its eggs in clusters, often on the underside of the leaves. I eliminate both by squashing them before they damage my squash.

61   Help in the Garden

Beneficial Insects

Many years ago I was in my corn patch checking things out. I noticed a small, black, ugly-looking, soft-shelled insect crawling on a leaf. It looked nasty, so I squished it. I hadn't had many problems with my corn and I wanted to keep it that way. Occasionally some of the corn that I harvested late would have a worm at the top of the ear or that had tunneled in from the side, but it didn't happen very often. I noticed a few more of these bugs so I squished them too. Anything that ugly had to be bad. The bug was all spiky and jagged, like something you'd see in a movie that was intended to gross you out. Over the next few weeks I kept squashing these and felt pretty good about my gardening prowess. Hey. Mr. Ugly Bug. You want a piece of my garden? I don't think so. Take that! Splat!

Over the next few years I began trying to identify insects so that I could determine which were helpful and which were in fact pests. We purchased a great color insect guide that listed a huge number of insects. That's when I discovered that I was squishing ladybug larvae. Ladybugs are

Larvae of my friend the ladybug. (Photo by Jeff Moore)

the model beneficial insect in your garden. It's as if the Governor of California in his previous life as the Terminator were prowling around your garden and saying "hasta la vista, baby" to aphids and a whole bunch of juice-sucking, planting-destroying pests. And what was I doing? Squashing ladybug babies. It wasn't a red-letter day for me when I discovered what I had been doing, but a valuable learning experience nonetheless.

"Know your enemy" has become my mantra. When I encounter a new insect, unless I actually see it chomping on a vegetable plant in my gar-

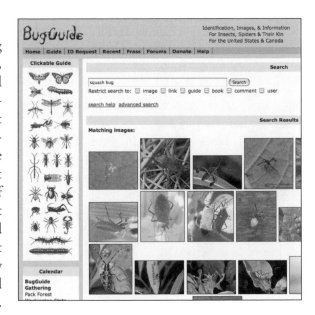

den, I get out my book and figure out what I'm looking at. If you can't conveniently find a book try www.bugguide.net, a website maintained by people who are really into bugs. I know what you're asking: "Did you say people who are into bugs?" Yes! And there are lots of them. I actually know many people who are into insects and I must say it's starting to become a bit of a passion of mine. I think one of the main reasons I've been so attracted to learning more about bugs is that they have so much power over the success of my garden. When they cooperate, things go well. When they get out of control, things can go very badly.

You can use BugGuide.net to identify insects. On the upper left-hand side of the website is a black and white "Clickable Guide." You click on the insect shape that most closely approximates what you're looking for. Some insects are hard to categorize, especially beetles. But this gives you a place to start once you get to the "beetle" sub page you may see a photograph that will more closely approximate what you're looking for. If not try another shape from the "Clickable Guide". As I was writing this book during the summer I spent a fair bit of time on this website and got to know some of the contributors. I was trying to obtain some photos to potentially use in this book. Normally I would have just taken my own photos of the bugs in my garden, but because of our second cool and wet summer in a row I didn't have many of the pests I usually have. Any other year this would have been a blessing, but this year I had a new digital SLR camera all ready to photograph them. And they never came. Apparently this is a sure fire method of insect control…buy a really good camera to take pictures of them. So are bugs camera shy?

Another resource, which I mentioned in the preceding chapter, is *The Organic Gardener's Handbook of Natural Insect and Disease Control*, written by Barbara Ellis and published by Rodale Books. This book identifies problems and their causes and includes some good graphics of specific plants and illustrates the symptoms and the pest responsible.

Resources such as these can be a great tool for successful vegetable gardening. They can prevent you from eliminating beneficial insects and help you target the real pests. Some pests will be obvious. When you see a big, fat, orange blob of an insect chomping away at your potato leaves there's little doubt that it is in fact the larva of the Colorado potato bug and needs to be eliminated.

Sometimes insects may look similar, but it's fairly easy to distinguish between the beneficial and the pest. Brown stink bugs are shaped like a shield with sharp points on their shoulders. They love to suck the sap from all sorts of vegetables. When you disturb them they emit a rancid-smelling odor that contains cyanide. "Holy stink bug Batman, we've got to get rid of this dastardly demon bug."

A spined soldier bug looks almost the same. The difference is that the spined soldier beetle has a sheathed proboscis on its head, which is like what a mosquito uses to suck your blood. In this case the big, long, pointy sticker is designed to be jabbed into grubs and caterpillars to suck their juice out, like a permanent straw in the beetle's

Brown Stink Bug
Photo: Phil Huntley-Franck

Spined Soldier Bug
Photo: www.planetnatural.com

mouth. Yes, I know, it sounds gross, but nature can be that way. When someone is channel surfing in our house and we hit a nature program that shows insects really close up, it's always a contest to see how long we can stand the high yuckiness factor.

Some bugs are much tougher to identify. Raspberry cane borers are a real problem if you grow raspberries, and I've discovered an insect that looks remarkably like one. It's a slender beetle with a long, black abdomen (back end), orange thorax (middle), and black head. It has long, black antenna. It lays eggs on the raspberry canes and the eggs hatch into grubs that spend the winter in the canes and then start munching away when it warms up the following spring.

Soldier beetles look almost identical to raspberry cane borers but they are incredibly beneficial, feeding on cucumber beetles, corn rootworms, aphids, grasshopper eggs, and other soft-bodied pests. The main difference between the two seems to be that the cane borer has red legs and two black spots on its thorax.

So you need to start paying attention to the insects in your garden and learning which are friends and which are enemies. You already know lots of beneficial insects you want in the garden, like bees, ladybugs, and praying mantids (mantises). Next you'll start to recognize other really helpful beneficials like assassin bugs. Maybe you've heard of the movie *Ninja Assassin*. These bugs are like little versions of ninja assassins, wreaking havoc on caterpillars with roundhouse kicks. Well, actually they look like many other beetles except they have a long, curved beak and their job, which they choose to perform daily, is to hit the garden running and suck juices.

In keeping with the movie theme is the "minute pirate bug," modeled after Captain Jack Sparrow of *Pirates of the Caribbean* fame. This small, black-and-white-winged cross between a fly and a beetle swashbuckles its way through a crowd of thrips, spider mites, and other small caterpillars with impunity.

Lacewings have a lovely, refined name and are fine, green or brown, delicate, transparent winged insects that emerge from larvae that look a bit like sow bugs. They eat a whole smorgasbord of small, juice-sucking pests.

Most of the wasps you see in the garden are also your friends. Well, let me qualify. Some are your friends. Some will sting you if you piss them off. Many, however, are parasitic and will actually lay their eggs in hosts like caterpillars. When the eggs hatch they feed on the host until they're ready to emerge, killing the host. Remember the scene in the first *Aliens* movie with the person who comes back into the spaceship and has the really bad reaction to that one meal? I notice a lot of wasps in my garden and many aren't the traditional kind. They're much smaller and more delicate, but they look like a smaller version of the big paper wasps. They have a large stinger on their abdomen designed to sting and paralyze prey while they inject them with eggs. I love seeing these insects in my garden.

Beneficial Plants

So while many insects are pests, many are very beneficial and you should attract them and keep them in your garden. Encouraging them requires a healthy environment for them, so the less you spray of any of the concoctions from the previous chapter the better. You should try and create an environment that attracts the beneficial insects. Since many of the beneficials you want feed on nectar and pollen, the more of this that's available the better. Sometimes my gardening oversights turn into positives. I always plant radishes but I don't always get to harvest and eat them before they go to seed. And when a radish goes to seed it goes big time. It sends up an enormous flower stalk that is covered with hundreds of small white and pink flowers. It's a like a big "Welcome" sign to many of the insects you want. My early broccoli often flowers as well, and walking by a broccoli stalk in flower can be deafening because of the bees and winged insects buzzing in and out of the flowers.

A number of herbs, like fennel and mint, also produce small flowers. Some people like to have borders around vegetable gardens that are actually flowerbeds that attract the good guys to the vegetables. Michelle often helps out in this department by planting a few rows of flowers in the garden to use as cut flowers. Her zinnias and asters and other cut flowers not only provide wonderful color and smells but also create a big bull's eye target for all those nectar feeders as they fly about the area. Insects often need water, so having a backyard pond near the garden is a great attraction. I always have

I discovered this great tool for companion planting. You can take it with you into the gardening to help you with deciding what to plant with what. For each of the main vegetables it tells you which other vegetables are "Good Companions", which are "Neutral" and which to "Avoid".
I know after years of gardening I've learned some of these, but having it right with you in the garden as you're planting could be really handy. You can order them Calendula Publishing, http://calendulapublishing.net (902) 273-2467

some large, shallow clay pots filled with water in the garden to attract birds, but insects like them as well. If you're planning to plant a wildflower garden, put it near the vegetables. Anything that keeps beneficial insects attracted to your yard is a great idea. Many organic gardeners like to have borders with catnip, fennel, lemon balm, parsley, rosemary, savory, and yarrow to attract beneficial insects.

Plants that Repel Insects

Some plants help discourage insects from getting comfortable in your garden. Garlic and onions are a good example. Garlic when combined with mineral oil and soap is a great spray for dealing with aphids and other insect pests, and it's been shown to kill mosquito larvae when sprayed on ponds. Planting garlic in your garden is an excellent way to discourage many pests. You can plant some bulbs anywhere in the garden to achieve this effect, and spraying it in areas where you have problems with rodents and rabbits can discourage them from feeding in that area. Chives also help discourage insect pests and are helpful to have near carrots. Planted in orchards they help prevent apple scab that lives in the soil.

Nasturtiums, which have a wonderful, colorful, edible flower, keep squash bugs away from squash plants and repel white flies and aphids near broccoli. Pyrethrum daisies discourage any pest from coming near, so if you have a vegetable that's particularly heavily infested with pests, next year grow some pyrethrum daisies nearby. Sage grown near brassicas helps discourage cabbage butterflies, and since they lay the eggs for the larvae that will eat these plants this is a great combination. Stinging nettle, which surrounds my garden (not by choice), is an excellent plant for discouraging pests large and small from venturing inside. I can just imagine a rabbit getting a face full of it as it approaches the garden. Ouch!

Basil, which is excellent when served with tomatoes, is also a great herb to plant near them because it discourages flies and mosquitoes. A perennial called tansy has been used for centuries

as an insect repellent and is toxic to anthropods like earwigs and sow bugs or woodlice. If you have a problem with maggots in your carrots and radishes, try sprinkling tea leaves around them to keep flies from landing to lay eggs. Horseradish helps repel potato bugs.

If you're planting a border to discourage pests consider anise, calendula, coriander, savory, sage, mint, and wormwood.

Amazing Marigolds

I really love marigolds. I don't know whether it's because of all the Bollywood movies where they're so prevalent in weddings, but they're an amazing flower. They grow vigorously and produce beautiful orange and yellow flowers all season. Marigolds are the anti-nematode. Nema-

Tomatoes are always planted with marigolds in my garden.

todes are a microscopic worm that lives in the soil and feeds on roots, which stunts the growth of many vegetables. Nightshade plants like tomatoes, eggplants, and peppers are particularly susceptible to nematodes. Marigolds help to control nematodes and I always plant marigolds near tomatoes. Nematodes seem to be attracted to marigold roots, but once they get there they can't lay eggs. I realized this year that I have grown tomatoes in the same raised bed in the barn foundation for several years in a row. So last fall I grabbed seeds from marigolds, and I have lots of them. I'm going to plant them very densely in that garden this year and then next fall I'm going to turn it under. I'm hoping this will really knock out any nematodes that were getting established there and give the bed some resistance to them for a few years.

I discussed "beneficial nematodes" in the previous chapter. They're a great natural control because they actually feed on grubs and other harmful insects in the soil rather than on roots.

Some companion planting isn't necessarily about insect repelling. Some plants just grow well together. Planting lettuce under corn later in the summer helps shade it from the brutal sun and heat it doesn't like. In the photo of the raised bed on page 149 I've planted radishes with the carrots. Radishes germinate very quickly and carrots are very slow. By the time the carrots are a half-decent size, the radishes are ready to be harvested, so as you harvest the radishes you're making room for the carrots. Many years ago I read a book by an organic gardener who claims that everything grows better with basil in the vicinity. We like basil so much and we start so many seedlings that I plant it everywhere, and I certainly can't dispute the theory. Since basil can go to seed in the summer heat I like to plant it near tomatoes; as the tomatoes get large enough it's usually time to harvest some of the basil, which leaves room for the tomatoes to expand into.

A toad house.

A leopard frog.

A toad.

Amphibians in the Garden

I am always thrilled by how many frogs and toads I have living in the garden. These wonderful creatures live on bugs and I figure that if they thrive in my garden they're doing their job of keeping the population of some harmful insects down. In the spring I'm careful and watch for them as I rototill since they're much slower in the cold weather. By the summer they hightail it anytime you're nearby weeding or working. I also try and make sure there are places for them to hang out. Here I've used a broken clay pot with an opening for them. The bottom is broken on this one so I put a piece of wood over it. Make sure the floor of the house is just soil because sometimes they like to burrow. I also find leopard frogs in the garden as well as toads. There's a wet area near the garden which must be where they spend the winter.

Snakes

Snakes eat insects and I have lots of insects in the garden. I've seen photos of snakes with insects in their mouths, and any time I have big piles of rotting hay I always find lots of garter snakes.

Last year I set up a "Garter Snake Hotel" in the garden made out of hay, but it didn't seem to matter how many snakes I placed near it, they didn't choose to hang around. I'm not sure if they're free spirits and resented being told where to live or if they prefer grassy areas to give them more cover when they hunt for food. I shall continue to try and get inside the local snakes' heads to figure out how I can train them to live exclusively on slugs, cutworms, and some of the pests I have problems with.

As you spend more time in your garden and observe what does well and what doesn't you'll start getting a feel for things that grow together well and plants that shouldn't be close to each other. The more diverse the plants in your garden and the more places there are for beneficials to seek refuge, the less likely you will be to have major infestations of harmful pests.

62 Harvesting and Storage

Harvesting is the easy part of the gardening game. You'll know when things are ready. Just pick some peas and shell them and if they're big and sweet enough, they're ready. When the broccoli resembles what you would buy at the grocery store, it's time. If you leave it too long, though, the flowerettes will get too big and actually start to flower. When the tops of the potato plants start turning brown and dying back late in the summer, start digging them up. If your garden is big enough you'll need a good-sized basket or wheelbarrow! This is a good thing because there really is nothing like filling an entire wheelbarrow full of vegetables you've grown. It's magic!

As I've discussed each vegetable in this book I've given you some ideas about the best way to store them. You'll eat many of them as you pick them. Hopefully you'll have extra of the ones you really like so that you can store them to eat later. Lettuce won't store well, but if you build yourself a cold frame you'll have lettuce and spinach right into the fall months.

The key to your success in "putting things up," as some people call storing food, is to preserve it soon after picking it and always preserve the best of the harvest. This seems counterintuitive if you're about to cut it up and can it. Who cares what it looks like? Microorganisms live on everything, including all those wonderful vegetables and fruits from your garden, but they particularly like damaged and bruised parts of fresh food. If something has insect damage, even if the insect is gone it's likely that pathogens will be on it. One of the main reasons you want to keep insects off your plants is that many of them harbor diseases that cause damage as the plant is growing. It's not enough that these pests like to chew away on your plants; often they spread various other problems like viruses and bacteria. These may not necessarily be harmful to you and are more of a problem for plants, but why take any chances?

Canning

Choose the prime specimens from your garden for preserving and eat the less-than-perfect produce right away. Vegetables and fruit spoil for a number of reasons, including moisture loss, reaction with oxygen, the activity of food enzymes, and the growth of yeasts, molds, and undesirable microorganisms and bacteria. Proper canning removes oxygen, destroys enzymes, and prevents the growth of undesirable bacteria, yeasts, and molds. The canning process creates a high-pressure vacuum in the jars which forms a tight seal that keeps the liquid in and the microorganisms and air out.

Some vegetables can lose nearly half their vitamins in a few days if they are not preserved or kept cool in the refrigerator. The process of canning will destroy 30% to 50% of vitamins A and C, but after canning very little loss occurs. If you can shortly after harvest, your canned vegetables will have the same or more nutrition than fresh produce that is purchased at the grocery store, especially if the store produce was picked weeks before and trucked a long distance.

The real danger with canning is "botulism," or Clostridium botulinum, which is a food poisoning that can kill you. The bacteria exist as spores in the soil and they multiply in environments such as a moist, low-acid food at a temperature between 40°F and 120°F (4°C and 48°C) with less than 2% oxygen. Botulinum spores are present on most fresh food surfaces but are harmless because they only grow in the absence of air.

Washing fresh food reduces the number of bacteria, yeasts, and molds that are on food surfaces, but only slightly. Peeling tomatoes and root vegetables helps, but you still need to properly process foods to avoid spoilage and potential hazards.

Acidity

Foods like tomatoes and most fruit are acidic enough to block the growth of botulinum bacteria and can be canned using boiling water. Foods like peas and corn are not acidic enough and require the use of a pressure canner to ensure that the temperature is high enough to kill botulinum spores. You can increase the acidity levels in foods by adding lemon juice, citric acid, or vinegar. Examples of foods with added acidity are pickles, jams, marmalades, fruits, and sauerkraut.

The temperature of boiling water, 212°F (100°C), may not destroy botulinum spores, so low-acid foods should be sterilized at temperatures of 240°F (116°C), which can be reached only in a pressure canner. Depending on the food and the size of the jars you may need to leave them for 20 to 100 minutes in a pressure canner but 7 to 10 hours in a boiling-water canner. For the sake of energy efficiency and the realization that the world is running out of easy and cheap energy, the less time you need to process your food during the canning process the better. A pressure canner is going to be well worth the investment over its life.

The focus of this book is the process of growing your food and so I will leave the specific details on canning for you to find elsewhere. There are a number of good websites that have excellent information. Ball® fresh preserving products have been around since 1884 and there is lots of good information on the website at www.freshpreserving.com. The *USDA Complete Guide to Home Canning, 2009 revision* is available at www.uga.edu/nchfp/publications/publications_usda.html.

Ball® Brand has published an outstanding book on home canning called the *Ball Blue Book of Preserving*. The USDA guide is also published in book form and is available at the Purdue University website at www.extension.purdue.edu/store. Both of these books are very reasonably priced and will be an excellent addition to your library. You need to be careful when canning and you need a detailed step-by-step guide to follow so that you're sure whatever you preserve looks and tastes as good as possible and is safe.

As food and energy become more expensive, many people are looking to develop some of the skills our parents and grandparents had, and there are an increasing number of courses on offer that deal with canning. Check out your local library or community center or grocery store flyer board to see if any are being conducted in your area. You may even want to ask someone you know (such as a grandparent) who preserves his or her own food for some one-on-one instruction. If you are able to find someone to "show you the ropes" be sure to also consult the above websites and be aware of the current guidelines for the optimal and safe way to can. I'm not questioning your grandmother's ability, and heaven knows she's eaten her canned goods long enough to prove that they're safe. It's possible, though, that this has been partially based on some degree of luck, so at least be aware of what the current standard of safety is as you observe her technique so that you can decide if you want to err on the side of caution in your own kitchen.

I have not been able to find a good comparison of the cost of canning your own vegetables versus buying commercially canned goods. Obviously there are an infinite number of variables that make this difficult, including what fuel you are using, the cost of the fuel where you live, and the technique you use for canning. The one thing you're assured of with home canning is control of the raw material, and I hope I've provided the motivation and tools you need to grow your garden organically. Purchasing organic vegetables, even canned ones, usually carries a premium over conventionally grown produce.

Freezing

A freezer is an excellent alternative or supplement to your canning. Recently we invested in a 10-cubic-foot freezer. While this may not sound like a big step, for someone living off the electricity grid it is. We had to evaluate how much additional load the 282 kilowatt-hours per year represented and determine if we could afford the electricity from the finite amount we produce with our solar panels and wind turbine. With our recent upgrade to more solar panels we felt we could. We also decided to put the freezer in our basement. Our house, which was built in 1888, has a concrete basement that is not heated, so it's more like a crawl space and stays very cool in the winter. Our feeling was that since the air temperature is close to zero the freezer wouldn't have to work that hard. And so far it appears to be the case. We haven't been able to notice any significant difference in our electricity loads.

If you were on the grid and paying 12¢/kWh, the electricity to run the freezer would be $42 (282 kWh x 12¢ = $33.84) a year. We filled up our freezer with vegetables last summer. We froze beans, peas, basil, cauliflower, broccoli, and lots of tomatoes. Now on a cold winter day we take out a bag of tomatoes, put them on the wood stove in the morning, throw in some garlic and basil, and let it simmer all day, filling the house with a wonderful aroma. A bowl of this soup is like having a bowl full of summer. The tomatoes didn't go through a lengthy heating process by being canned; they were just put in bags and frozen, so I think we preserved some of the healthful benefits of freshly picked tomatoes. Freezing won't improve the texture or flavor of food, but when done properly it can preserve most of the quality.

Some vegetables need to be "blanched" before freezing. To blanch vegetables you immerse them in boiling water for a brief period of time and then remove them and plunge them into ice-cold water to halt the cooking process. Blanching stops the enzyme action that can cause a loss of flavor and nutrients as well as affecting color and texture. Beans and broccoli are examples of vegetables that require blanching. You can use a similar process to remove the skins of tomatoes prior to freezing. Place a few tomatoes in a pot of boiling water for 60 seconds or so. Remove them and plunge them into ice-cold water. Drain them and let them cool. Peel off the skins and place the tomatoes in heavy freezer bags or plastic containers. Always leave some room at the top of the container for expansion.

Purée basil in a food processor with enough olive oil to make a smooth paste. Place a dollop in a sandwich-sized, zippered freezer bag and spread it into a thin layer. Freeze it, and whenever you'd like a bit of basil for a recipe, break a chunk off.

We also freeze some vegetables without blanching them. We put shelled peas directly into freezer bags and freeze them. We put high-bush blueberries into plastic containers and freeze them. This works really well because you can grab the container of blueberries and thaw just enough for your morning granola. During corn season we make a point of cooking more ears than we can eat so that we can freeze the corn that doesn't get eaten. We cut the corn off the leftover cobs and put it in freezer bags. It's comparable to the bagged frozen corn that you can buy, but it's your own!

Frozen fruits and vegetables should be eaten within the year. Freezing is a great alternative or supplement to canning. I really like the idea of getting things from the garden to the freezer quickly in order to preserve vitamins. If you have an efficient freezer they can be frozen and maintained at a fairly low cost. The real challenge comes if you live in a place prone to power interruptions. If you do have a power outage, make sure you don't open the freezer because you want to keep all that cold air in there. Throw a big, thick blanket or comforter over the freezer, being careful not to cover up the back where the compressor is.

Dehydration

Another process you might want to look at for preserving your harvest is dehydration.

There are a number of commercial food dehydrators available for purchase. They are designed to use heat and air flow to reduce the water content of food. Fruits and vegetables are 80% to 95% water (this explains the importance of watering them as they're growing), and removing moisture discourages bacteria from growing and spoiling the food. A dehydrator heats up to between 130°F and 140°F (54°C and 60°C) as a fan circulates air around the food, which sits on a mesh tray to aid circulation. Countertop designs are available. Be aware that the trays receive different heat penetrations and juices can drip down onto the heating element. If you're trying to dehydrate different vegetables at the same time, this might mix their flavors. A dehydrator has limited

An Excalibur food dehydrator.
www.excaliburdehydrator.com

capacity, and twelve square feet of drying space translates into about half a bushel of vegetables, but dehydrating can play a role in your garden preservation strategy.

Fruit Leathers

You can make your own fruit leather by pouring puréed fruit onto a flat surface and rolling it when it has dried. This is a good use of some of your fruit and your homemade leathers have far less sugar than those that are commercially prepared. Add two teaspoons of lemon juice or ascorbic acid for every two cups of fruit and purée until smooth. Pour this mixture onto a cookie sheet lined with plastic wrap. Some dehydrators come with special plastic sheets for this. At a temperature of 140°F (60°C), fruit leather takes 6 to 8 hours to dry in a dehydrator, up to 18 hours in an oven, and 1 to 2 days in the sun. It will last about a month at room temperature or a year if frozen.

Sun Drying

Dehydrating food can be as simple as slicing it and putting it in the sun on a warm day. What you're attempting to do is remove the water through evaporation. The warmer and drier the air the better. Fruits are high in sugar and acid, which makes them better candidates for this than vegetables. To speed the process you may want to look at building a solar dryer. We have a solar oven, and during the hot sunny days of August we often don't need it since we have more than enough electricity for all our cooking. We experimented with putting tomatoes in it and it was amazing how quickly they went from the garden to "sun dried," usually in one hot day. The challenge is air movement, since you want to remove moist air and keep hot, dry air entering the oven. Most models have a central drying shelf with a glass cover that creates a greenhouse effect, with a vent system at the top and bottom to bring hot dry air in at the base and vent the moist air out the top.

A simpler design is to use a large, clean, stainless steel or fiberglass screen across some saw horses. To keep birds and bugs off you'll want to place a second screen on top.

If you're planning on using a dehydrator you'll need to consider the cost of electricity in your area. If it's relatively high, using an electric foot dehydrator may be an expensive way to preserve food. As energy and food get more expensive it's going to make more and more sense to take the time to build a solar food dryer and dehydrate fruits and vegetables from your garden. You'll need to determine when the time is right for you. Building a solar food dryer may only require $50 in materials, but it may take a couple of days or even a week if, like me, you're not a natural-born carpenter. Most people with gardens know that when the harvest comes in you inevitably find that you've planted more food than you can consume, so it just makes sense to have a low-energy way to save it.

Pickling

Preserving food by anaerobically fermenting it in brine (salty water) and storing it in vinegar is called pickling. Unlike canning, the fermentation process does not require that foods be completely sterile before they're sealed because the acidity or salinity of the solution kills any bacteria present. Regular dill pickles and sauerkraut are fermented for about three weeks. The acidity of a pickle is as important to its safety as it is to the texture and taste, so make sure you follow recipes carefully. Don't alter the vinegar, water, and food mix which must be uniform to keep botulinum from growing.

Jams and Jellies

Preserves, jams, and jellies are fruits that are jellied or thickened by the addition of sugar. Jams are thick and are made by cooking crushed fruit with sugar. Jellies are clear and firm and are made by cooking fruit juice with sugar. Preserves are whole fruit or pieces of fruit in clear, slightly gelled syrup. During fruit season there are lots of sources of information in the fruit- or canning-supply sections of grocery and hardware stores. There are now recipes for uncooked jams, so experiment and find one your family likes.

Storing

Once you've canned or pickled your harvest you should store it in a cool, dark place. Your root cellar may be ideal as long as it doesn't go below zero. It's best not to expose your glass jars to direct sunlight to avoid discoloration of what's inside, and keeping them cool preserves your hard work. Jars should not be stored above 95°F (35°C), so make sure to keep them out of furnace rooms or uninsulated attics that may overheat.

Roma "sun-dried" tomatoes after eight hours in our solar oven.

When you open your jars of canned fruits and vegetables, check to make sure that the lid is concave and still well sealed. Next, make sure there are no streaks of dried food that come from the top of the jar where a seal may have leaked. Also check for any rising bubbles and unnatural color. When you open the jar make sure the contents smell good and look for any mold on the top of the food or on the inside of the lid. If there is anything to indicate that there is spoilage, discard the whole jar, contents and all. Afterwards, wash your hands really well and clean any surfaces that might have come into contact with the contents. With botulism it's better to be safe than sorry.

Summary

After putting so much work into your garden it only makes sense to save as much of the harvest as you can. Canning, freezing, drying, and dehydrating are ways to enjoy your harvest of fruits and vegetables all year long. Each requires energy of some sort for the storage process, and in a future with rapidly increasing energy costs you'll want to use the technique which requires the least amount of outside energy. A root cellar fits this bill and I'll discuss root cellars in the next chapter.

63   Root Cellars

Root cellars are the original refrigerators of our pioneer ancestors and our not-too-distant grandparents. If you go to www.rootcellars.com you'll find yourself at the website of Elliston, Newfoundland on Canada's East Coast, which calls itself "The Root Cellar Capital of the World." Elliston is a small community with 135 documented root cellars, some of which have survived for nearly two centuries. I'm confident that no refrigerator will last that long. Many of the root cellars shown on this website use the old design of digging into a hill or just digging a hole, lining the insides with rock, and then mounding soil back over the whole structure. These root cellars are beautiful and have become part of the landscape.

A root cellar is designed to keep food at low temperatures and steady humidity so that it doesn't freeze in the winter and stays

Elliston, Newfoundland—the "The Root Cellar Capital of the World." Photo by Neal K. Tucker.

cool in the summer to prevent spoilage. There are an infinite number of designs, but many of the original structures were separate from the main house and were built right into the ground. If you have a hill on your property you can tunnel into the slope and contour the root cellar into the natural lay of the land. It's not necessary to have a hill, though; you just need to ensure that an outside root cellar is covered with a thick layer of soil that acts as an insulator. You'll want to dig the hole for your root cellar about six feet deep. As you would with any building, you'll have issues with moisture and drainage, so you'll need to have a plan for dealing with it. One of the most common techniques is to build the root cellar using concrete blocks. You'll need concrete or rock stairs down to the root cellar and a well-insulated door.

Having your root cellar below grade like this ensures a steady, cool temperature without any outside source of energy. Having a strong roof that you cover with a thick layer of soil helps to ensure a steady temperature inside. Some designs incorporate a vent that allows warm air to leave the root cellar, and it's important to screen the vent to keep small visitors out. If you've ever lived in an older home you know how damp a poorly insulated basement can be, but in the case of a root cellar this is actually a good thing. Having 80% to 90% moisture in the air helps vegetables last. Since they're mostly water they're likely to lose too much moisture in a dry environment. You can put a concrete floor in your root cellar, but I prefer a dirt floor. For one thing, you don't have to be concerned about the dirt that falls off your vegetables. Root cellars can be fairly messy places. For another, a dirt floor acts as a great moisture buffer, keeping the air nice and moist. If your root cellar has a dirt or gravel floor and the air is too dry you can just dump some water on the floor. In order to have the best of both worlds, some root cellars have two rooms, one with a dirt floor for vegetables that like moisture and one with a concrete floor for things that don't.

If you're planning on building an outdoor root cellar there are two sources you may want to refer to. There's an excellent book by Mike and Nancy

Bubel called *Root Cellaring*, published by Storey Publishing. There's also The *Renewable Energy Handbook* by William Kemp. This book is primarily about solar and wind power, but it has an excellent section on correct building and insulation techniques. Depending on how cold your winters get, how much rain you receive, what kind of soil you have, and the drainage in the area of your root cellar, it will be worth doing some research to develop a strategy for an outside root cellar.

As glamorous and romantic as an outside root cellar sounds, it's still outside. That means that if you get up on a cold, snowy Sunday morning and decide you feel like some hash browns, you'll have to pull on your snow boots and parka and hike out to the root cellar in your PJs. A nicer option is to have the root cellar in your home. Some people build root cellars into their home design, extending the basement out to add a room that's below grade but separate from the rest of the house so that it's easy to isolate it from the home heating system. Some homes have rooms under the front porch that are appropriate for use as a root cellar. There are lots of different configurations for incorporating a root cellar into your home.

If you want to add a root cellar to your basement there are some basic guidelines. You'll want to locate it on the north side of the basement if at all possible. This will minimize the amount of solar heat that may be absorbed if part of the room is above grade. It's common for a basement to be mostly below grade but have enough room above grade for a window at the top. This is a good set-up because you'll be able to use the window to help with ventilation. You should fill the window in with plywood or an insulated panel if you're in a colder climate. If there isn't a window, you can provide ventilation by cutting holes in the walls and running pipe through them. Use four-inch vent pipes like the type used for your clothes dryer. The top pipe should be in a straight line from the root cellar to the outside. Since it's positioned high in the root cellar the warmer air near the top of the room can exit. The second pipe uses an elbow joint to direct the pipe right down to the

This newly built outside root cellar is both beautiful and functional, the ultimate low-energy cold storage method.

floor. This allows heavier, cool air to drop to the floor of the root cellar. These two vents create a siphon which brings cool air in and allows warm air to leave; it also allows for some air circulation, which can help prevent spoilage.

If possible, use a northern corner of the house for the root cellar, which means that two walls are outside walls that will help to keep the root cellar cold. This reduces the number of insulated walls you have to build when you box the root cellar in. We should almost call this a "cold room," because that's what you're trying to create. If there's a furnace vent or source of heat for this area you should remove it. Be sure to insulate the walls, preferably with rigid insulation, which resists mold in the humid environment of a root cellar. You'll want to make sure that the ceiling is insulated as well in order to keep any warm air from entering from above.

You need to isolate your cold room from the rest of the basement and the heating system by using insulated walls, maximizing the exposure to cold outside walls, and developing a ventilation system to bring cool air into the room at floor level and allow warm air in the room to leave. Having some air circulation like this is a good idea from an air-exchange standpoint. Vegetables will release some elements into the air as they go through their slow decomposition process in the root cellar, and some of these gases can adversely affect your other

Viola Davis' root cellar is well stocked with a summer's worth of canning and preserving.

Now you see it, now you don't. Like so many heritage farmhouses a trap door covers Viola's root cellar. Michelle emerges with samples of Viola's canned goods.

stored crops. Apples, for instance, release ethylene gas that causes fruit to ripen faster. It will cause potatoes to sprout, which is exactly what you don't want. Since it's difficult to isolate all the different processes that the food in the root cellar is going through it's best to make sure that the air is exchanging periodically to remove anything that might be detrimental to neighboring produce.

"Root" cellars are called this for a reason, which is that they're optimal for storing root crops. They're great for storing a variety of vegetables, but root crops will last the longest and that's one of the reasons I emphasized crops like potatoes and carrots in my book *Thriving During Challenging Times*. They grow well and can be stored with no energy inputs, which will be important in a future with rapidly increasing energy costs. I store a variety of vegetables in the root cellar, but I know that root crops will store the best and keep the longest.

Most people build shelves in their root cellar, and there are various containers you can use. Wooden trays are a great find at garage sales and auctions, or you can build your own. Many of us have romantic images of apples and crops stored in wooden crates in a root cellar. These are a really handy storage container to have. Bushel baskets, which are becoming increasingly harder to find, are good too, especially for things like apples and pears. One has to be realistic, though, and realize that plastic has taken over our lives and sometimes it's convenient to use plastic storage tubs and trays. I like plastic buckets because they have handles and are easy to move. They're also small enough that you'll be limited by how much stuff you can get into one. I find that if I make the mistake of using a plastic storage tub that's too large I tend to overfill it and it ends up being too heavy to move around. So experiment and find out what works for you and your set-up.

What to Store

Potatoes are my number-one crop to grow and store. They make up a big part of my diet because along with their convenience and versatility they're extremely healthy. I started storing my potatoes in buckets of dry sand. This works exceptionally well. My root cellar is actually the cistern under the kitchen of our 1888 farmhouse, so anything that goes into it must be lowered through a trap door in the pantry floor. When I stored the potatoes in sand I not only had to lower heavy buckets into the root cellar but also had to haul the sand-filled buckets back out again at the end of the season. So I switched to peat moss. It's lighter and works very well if you're comfortable with its environmental impact. You can also use wood shavings or sawdust. Sometimes I put potatoes in the root cellar that I intend to eat soon, so I don't put them in anything. These potatoes store just as well as the potatoes stored in sand or peat moss. While I feel better about storing them in a medium that removes any extra moisture or at least keeps them at a fairly constant level of moisture, it's not necessary.

Choose very carefully when you select the potatoes that you're going to store. Remove any with cuts or nicks or rough or blemished skin. Gently squeeze them as you put them into the bucket to ensure that they're firm. I learned this lesson the hard way one year when we had experienced a wet fall and I wasn't careful as I packed potatoes into buckets and accidentally included a soft one. You would not believe how bad a rotten potato can smell! It was no small chore trying to track it down when there were 20 buckets of potatoes in peat moss and all the ones on the top looked fine.

If you store the best ones and eat the others early in fall and winter you'll have an excellent chance of successfully storing potatoes for six to eight months. In the early spring, even though the root cellar is inky black and the temperature doesn't vary much at all, the potatoes begin to form eyes or sprouts. By April some of these spouts start growing and because there's no light in the root cellar/cistern they'll start stretching to reach it. Some of the potatoes that I take out to plant in June have dense, white shoots and look like a bucket of spaghetti overflowing at the top.

Carrots like a little moisture while they're in storage, so I actually dampen the peat moss slightly with the garden hose before I add the carrots. When stored without damp peat moss, carrots dry up and begin to lose moisture. Alternatives to moist peat moss include moist sand or sawdust. I store other root crops like turnips, rutabagas, beets, and parsnips in a moist environment as well. They dry out much faster if left to the open air.

I store some crops on open wire shelves in the root cellar. If I choose the best squash for storage they will often keep right into February. If left much longer than that they start to get soft. If they're left forgotten in a corner of the root cellar, by spring they'll have turned into a scary ball of moldy fuzz that you won't recognize as ever having been food. Cabbage keeps well for about two months if you choose a really good head for storage. Too often even my best cabbages have a bit of pest damage that leads to premature decomposition or mold. This is why it's always good to start some cabbage early to eat during the summer and some much later that you'll store. Bugs inevitably go after the first crop, which bears the brunt of insect damage. The later crop is much more likely to avoid pests, and you'll harvest them in the cool weather, which often really enhances their taste.

Celeriac, the root crop that tastes like celery, and kohlrabi store well in a moist environment like wet sawdust. As you get more confident in your gardening you'll want to become more adventuresome in your root cellaring too. Leeks do very well in the fall garden through a few frosts, but unless you put really thick mulch on them you'll lose them eventually. To store them in your root cellar you should dig them out with their roots intact and put them in a bucket or pot with soil or sand. They'll store for about four to eight weeks in the root cellar.

Onions are one of our other key root cellar storage crops, and I grow and store a lot of them. I also eat a lot of them. It's really important to dry onions well before you store them. I cut the tops and dry them on a rack in the barn for a good month. As I package them for storage I make sure each onion is firm. It's easy to have a soft one slip by and turn into a mushy mess. I used to store onions in plastic buckets until I found some wire mesh baskets at the local dollar store. These are fabulous for onions. I can load them up and then hang them from the rafters, which ensures that there's good air circulation around them. I've found these wire mesh baskets indispensable for harvesting and drying. I store garlic in them while we're going through the various cleaning stages. The plastic mesh bags that you purchase oranges or onions in are also excellent for storing and hanging onions in your root cellar.

My apple trees aren't large enough to produce a large crop yet so storage isn't an issue. We do get apples from a nearby General Store that brings in large wooden bins from a local farmer and offers a wonderful selection. We usually load up with a bushel or two for the root cellar. Initially we're just eating them raw, but as the winter progresses they start to get softer so we use them in pies and apple crisp.

Our root cellar, with the summer harvest stored and ready to feed us this winter.

Additional Storage Methods

Sweet potatoes are one crop that you don't need to store in the root cellar. The key with sweet potatoes is to cure them properly. After harvest they need to be cured at 85°F to 90°F (30°C to 32°C) and 80% to 90% humidity for five to seven days. This is a fairly tough task and you have to be a fairly committed sweet potato fan to undertake it. Once you've properly cured them, long-term storage is much easier because they can be stored for up to six months if they're kept between 55°F to 65°F (13°C to 18°C). A root cellar will be much cooler than this, so sweet potatoes are better stored in a spare bedroom with the door closed or a cool pantry without a heating vent.

Garlic too doesn't need to be kept in the root cellar. If it has been dried and cleaned well to make sure there's no soil left to trap moisture, you can store it in a cool environment for the winter. We actually store our garlic in our bedroom closet, which is on a north-facing wall, is not heated, and is very dark. The garlic will not smell unless as spring approaches it starts to get a bit soft, which means it should be eaten up.

For eons humans ate in rhythm with nature. They ate a huge variety of vegetables and fruit in the summers when it was abundant and grew root crops to store in their root cellars to get them through the winter. Eating food that we grow and store is part of our human heritage and was probably starting to become part of our DNA until this latest generation was able to experience summer 12 months of the year with every fruit and vegetable available all year long. It's a tremendous privilege to live in a time of such abundance. It is premised on plentiful and cheap fossil-fuel energy, and there are many geologists who tell us that these days are drawing to a close. I believe that the best steps you can take to prepare for this are to learn how to grow your own food and to build a good root cellar or cold room in your basement. A root cellar is a definitive low-energy way to deal with challenging times and benefit from your summer garden all year long.

64 Seed Saving

We all have some things that we do well and some things that we need to work on. I think I garden well and I want to become an excellent seed saver, but right now I'm just an OK seed saver. Saving seed makes an incredible amount of sense in terms of saving money and being in control of your garden. Some seeds are easy to save and others are difficult, and I'm still learning. I've had great success saving many seeds like peas and beans and pumpkins and lettuce. These are all pretty easy to save. If you leave fruit on the plant long enough it matures and you'll find seeds inside. While it sounds straightforward it can be fraught with hazards. Not as hazardous as falling off a cliff, but after going to the effort of saving seeds and planting some of those seeds the following season you run the risk of being disappointed with the results.

To understand why seed saving isn't as straightforward as we might think, we need to discuss hybridization. Many of the seeds and plants that we buy have been hybridized. In hybridization a plant breeder uses two parent plants and breeds them so that the resulting plant has characteristics of both parents. This promotes better yields and better disease resistance, which is so important for successful gardening. The process is one of the reasons we can feed so many humans today, because we've been able to take the best characteristics of a variety of plants and combine them to improve the offspring. When you see the "F1" hybrid designation in the seed catalog it indicates that the plant combines the best of several different parent plants and will probably produce an excellent crop.

The downside to hybrid plants is that you can't rely on the seed from them if you save it because a hybrid cannot reliably produce true copies. This means that the new plant will not be "true-to-type." So if you save the seed you might get unexpected results, with some dominant char-acteristics of the plant taking over. You might end up with a fine result, but it's often not as good as if you planted the original hybrid each year. While this may sound like a plot by the seed companies, it's really just how hybrids work. It provides compensation for the person who went to the effort of producing a high quality seed that will be very productive for people who use it. As I learn more about seed saving and the production of hybrids I'm glad that someone is doing the work to provide such seeds.

Self-pollinated plants like wheat and lettuce are easy to save. The seed kernels of wheat are ground into flour to make bread.

I guess I should have warned you that we need to discuss sex in this book. A flower has a male part called an "anther," which produces pollen, and a female part called the "pistil," which is receptive to the pollen and conducts it down the "style" to the "ovary," which has "ovules" or egg cells that develop into the fruit or seedpod when fertilized. Phew! Thank goodness that's over! Luckily it was a lot easier for me to deal with that subject with my daughters. I just left it completely with Michelle, and I have no idea how she handled it.

Some plants are self-pollinated, using pollen from their own anther to fertilize themselves.

They can also use pollen from another flower from the same type of plant growing nearby. The blossoms of self-pollinated plants are called "perfect flowers" because of their ability to pollinate themselves. In the vegetable garden, beans, peas, tomatoes, lettuce, peppers, and eggplants are all self-pollinated. Many of the major cereal and grain crops that are so important to the world, like oats, wheat, barley, and rice are also self-pollinated.

If you don't harvest your broccoli heads in time they'll produce wonderful yellow flowers (right) which bees and pollinators love and which then turn into seed pods you can harvest for next year (left).

Open-pollinated plants cannot pollinate themselves and must rely on pollen from a different plant. Pollen can be spread by the wind or by insects such as honeybees. In your vegetable garden open-pollinated plants include broccoli, cauliflower, spinach, corn, radishes, and all your cucurbits like squash, melons, cucumbers, and pumpkins. Some open-pollinated plants like cucurbits are "monoecious," which means that they produce both male and female flowers on the same plant. On the photograph on page 157 you can identify the female zuccini flower because it has a large part at the bottom that forms the fruit. Before I figured this out, I'd notice the flowers on my squash and other cucurbits falling off and I'd blame it on some bug. Turns out it was just the male flowers falling off after they had served their purpose.

There are also "dioecious" plants where some of the plants are "male" and others are "female." Spinach is an example of a dioecious plant. When you plant a row of spinach some of the plants produce pollen while others produce only seed. This explains why some of my plants, that looked as if they were flowering and should have produced seed, didn't. They were the male plants whose purpose was just to pollinate the females. Crazy stuff goes on in the garden when you're not watching!

In the seed catalogs you'll see heirloom and heritage seeds for plants that have been around for generations. If you want to be successful in your seed saving these are a good place to start. Growers of heirloom seeds have tried to isolate their plants and keep them "true to type." If a plant is the self-pollinating type this is pretty easy, but if it's open-pollinated it's more difficult. You have to physically isolate the flower you want to remain true to keep it from pollinating with a plant whose characteristics you don't want. Sometimes you need to grow the plants quite a distance away from other plants that might cross-pollinate. Some breeders grow their plants in frames with screens or netting around them to keep out pollinating insects like bees.

Corn is an example of just how amazing nature is. The tassel on the top of a corn plant is the male part, which produces pollen. The corn ear is the female part and consists of hundreds of individual silk styles that run into the plant, with each one producing one kernel (or seed) of corn. So every kernel of corn has a silk that runs out the top of the ear and is fertilized by pollen that lands on it. Anyone who has walked through a cornfield while the tassels are producing pollen has a sense of just how much pollen they produce. There seems to be clouds of it. Corn is wind pollinated, which is why you should plant your corn in a box shape consisting of multiple rows. This ensures that the wind will blow the pollen around and onto the ears and that each silk will be exposed to pollen and form a proper kernel. If you plant your corn in one or two long rows it's less likely to be successfully pollinated. When you shuck an ear of corn and discover misshapen or missed kernels it's because those silks never got pollinated.

This is where seed saving starts to get more complicated. It's not too bad with self-pollinating plants, but open-pollinated plants can give unexpected results depending on where the pollen comes from. Cucurbits are a good example. Many members of this family can pollinate each other, such as a squash pollinating a pumpkin. If their female flowers are open at the same time there's nothing to stop a bee from visiting a male squash plant and then heading on over to a female pumpkin.

I don't always clean my garden up as well as I should in the fall. Occasionally I've left a pumpkin rotting near the compost pile. The next growing season I'll notice a "volunteer" there and I'll let it grow since it looks just like a pumpkin plant. Usually I end up with crazy results. The fruit doesn't look exactly like a pumpkin and it isn't so much a squash as some kind of bizarre green gourd that never does turn orange. I guess you could call it a "pumpkuash" or a "squashkin." Either way it really isn't good for anything. So this is where things get tricky, and you'll need to be careful about saving seeds from open-pollinated crops.

If you're interested in learning more about saving the seeds of open-pollinated plants I'd suggest you read *Seed to Seed* by Suzanne Ashworth, published by the Seed Savers Exchange. This is a group of people dedicated to ensuring that we keep a diverse supply of seeds available for everyone to choose from. The documentary *Food, Inc.* explains that 90% of the soybeans grown in the U.S. are the same variety of Roundup Ready® seeds from Monsanto. Soybeans are in many of our food products and are a reasonably big part of our diet, especially if you consider how much of the soybean crop ends up being fed to livestock. Do we want to be so dependent on one variety of seed controlled by one corporation?

I think we need to keep the seed stock as diverse as possible, and this becomes even more important as we begin to experience the effects of climate change. We'll need a good variety of ge-netic material to choose from as the environment each of us gardens in begins to change. I'm going to continue to learn more and become a better seed saver. A group of people in my village has begun meeting to form a seed exchange so that we can trade seeds with others in our community. This is a smaller version of the Seed Savers Exchange (www.seedsavers.org), which is a "non-profit, member-supported organization that saves and shares the heirloom seeds of our garden heritage, forming a living legacy that can be passed down through generations."

If you leave a leek in the ground over the winter, next spring it will produce a brilliant purple flower. Each of these white seed pods (right) will have three leek seeds for next year.

I am motivated to become a better seed saver because my teenage mutant ninja pumpkuash wasn't my only seed saving failure. First I'll share a success. I've had some good luck saving carrot seeds, which are a little bit more of a challenge to save because carrots are a biennial plant. This means that they produce the seed during their second year of growth. If you live in a warm growing zone and can just leave your biennials in the ground all winter this isn't a problem. I live in a cold zone where the ground freezes completely and any biennial left in the garden freezes and dies. So these plants have to be brought into the root cellar. Cabbage and turnips are also biennial and require a period of cold temperatures called "vernalization" before they're able to form flowers for seed production.

To save your carrots for replanting the following year, store them in damp sawdust. Most years they'll make it through the winter. In the spring they'll begin growing yellow leaves at the top and you'll be able to plant them in the garden. The tops will green up and turn into big bushy plants that flower and eventually produce seeds. Cabbage, on the other hand, doesn't always store well through the winter. To save a cabbage for seed production the following year remove the cabbage from the garden with the roots still attached and put it in a bucket of slightly damp sand. Store it in your root cellar. In the spring it won't be pretty, but as long as it isn't too moldy and rotted you should be able to get it growing again. Plant it back in the soil and new growth will start from the bottom, growing tall and forming flowers.

I've also had good luck saving seed from onions and leeks, which are biennials. I find I often have some of both that don't get harvested, and they survive the winter and send up an amazing seed pod the following year that is a huge, beautiful, purple flower (see photo on previous page).

A bucket of carrots left in the root cellar are ready to plant in spring. By replanting them in the garden you'll end up with a beautiful flower that produces an abundant number of seeds.

If you were to look at the flower of a carrot plant and the wildflower called Queen Anne's lace (which some people call "wild carrot"), you'd have difficulty telling them apart. I love Queen Anne's lace, and we have a lot of it growing on our property. This is a good thing unless you want to save carrot seeds and you don't have all the information you need. I managed to save some carrots through the winter and I planted them the following year. This first attempt worked so well that the following year I decide to "go big." This time I left

two rows of carrots in the ground in the fall and I heavily mulched them. We had a good snowpack and the deer didn't dig through and eat them, so I ended up with two rows of second-year carrots and they successfully flowered and I collected the seeds. I ended up with two bucketfuls of them.

As it turned out these were ready just as I was beginning my fall schedule of *Thriving During Challenging Times* workshops at local colleges. Part of my message is the importance of starting a garden and developing your own ability to grow food. So that fall as a bonus I handed everyone a plastic sandwich bag full of my carrot seeds. I didn't identify them right away and we played the game "Name This Substance." A baggie full of a green seed-like material can be easily mistaken for a hallucinogenic substance that one shouldn't be handing out in public. After people finished with the jokes, we discussed carrots and the importance of growing lots of root crops.

These carrot seeds turned out to be a valuable lesson about "open-pollinated" plants. Carrots can be crossed with wild carrots (Queen Anne's lace). Not only can they be crossed, they are easily crossed, and I have lots of Queen Anne's lace growing near the garden. My wonderful little bees that were so busy pollinating my carrots with pollen from neighboring carrot plants were also making sure there was a liberal dose of wild carrot pollen thrown in for good measure. Thank you bees. Now if you've ever had a genetics lesson in school you might remember learning about dominant traits and how characteristics such as eye colour are determined. Turns out that the white colour is dominant in carrots, so if you cross carrots with Queen Anne's lace, which has a white root, the white root color will eventually win out.

I experienced success the first year I saved carrot seeds either because the orange color managed to win or because the bees didn't cross-pollinate the carrots with the wild carrots. The seeds from this first attempt resulted in wonderful orange carrots. My second much larger attempt was not so successful. Either the white trait skipped a generation or with the larger size of my second crop of carrot flowers the bees couldn't help but mix and mingle with the wild carrots. What's worse, not only did I make a huge mistake but I inadvertently shared my big mistake with the people I happily shared my carrot seeds with. I'm hoping that maybe they didn't ever get around to planting those seeds. If they did, I look like an idiot. I never claimed to be a seed expert but as you can tell from my tone in this chapter I am truly humbled and admit I have much to learn. I also learned to not share seeds until I've planted them myself to be sure that I have a good quality, true-to-type seed to share.

The orange color of carrots indicates the presence of vitamin A and beta-carotene. This year many of the carrots that I dug up were white and were a reminder that I have much more to learn. We subscribe to the "lifelong learning" approach to living, and with seed saving I'm just getting started on my education.

I've had many successes, though. Here are bean seeds I saved this year. Some will end up in soup this winter and I'll plant some next spring. I've saved soybean seeds and lots of peas. Every year I save my own spinach seeds and lettuce seeds. I've saved some broccoli seeds, but I think they may have been from a hybrid plant. This is where good record keeping comes in. The broccoli plants I grew from those seeds were pretty good as I recall, but technically, since they were the second generation of a hybrid, they might not have been as good as the original hybrid plant. Then

This cabbage made it through the winter in the root cellar and you can see small shoots on the bottom. Once planted this year-old cabbage sent up shoots that turned into flower- and seed-bearing stalks.

again the breeder who made the hybrid took two broccoli cultivars that had good traits, so if I grew a seed from that hybrid I might not get all the good traits but I'd probably still get a fine broccoli plant. The challenge will be growing broccoli seed on an ongoing basis from these seeds. Ultimately, if I want to produce a true-to-type plant I should be starting with an heirloom seed or non-hybrid seed to make sure I can produce a plant consistently. I also have to consider where to grow that broccoli plant for seed and what nearby plants the bees might cross-pollinate with.

While I will continue to try and improve my seed-saving skills, for now I shall be grateful to the many and talented seed growers who put untold hours into producing wonderful hybrids that thrive in my garden. I buy lots of other creative works like music and books, and purchasing hybrid seeds from seed catalogs just ensures that the creative people who produce amazingly tasty and disease-resistant plants get compensated for their work.

Stay tuned!

Beans are seeds you can save either for soups in the winter or for growing new bean plants next year.

65   Container Growing

If you are new to vegetable gardening or you have limited space, container gardening is a great idea. You have much more control in terms of sunlight, water, weeds, soil, disease, and other important variables. You won't be able to grow the same volume as you could in a garden, but the produce from your container gardens will provide a good supplement to your diet.

Suitable containers are made with a variety of materials such as plastic, clay, or wood. Plastic pots eventually break down over time as a result of the effects of the sun and other elements but will be lightweight and inexpensive. Clay pots are heavier and more breakable and they tend to dry out faster because the clay wicks moisture from the soil. Wooden containers are great as long as you use the right wood. Choose cedar and be sure to stay away from pressure-treated wood. You can get creative with your containers and use almost anything, such as the clay lining from the inside of a chimney or a wooden barrel.

The nice thing about using a container is that finding soil for it is a fairly easy undertaking. A good potting mix from the garden center is fine, or you can use some of the dark, rich soil from the bottom of your compost pile. The advantage of commercial potting mixes is that they're weed- and disease-free, and since you're growing the plants in isolation you're likely to have good results. The plants in your containers have less opportunity to search for food, so you have to make sure the soil they're growing in is extremely rich. Compost is the perfect solution, but remember that it tends to dry out quickly if it's above the soil line in a container and exposed to sun, so you have to be really careful about keeping containers watered. Be sure to ask someone to water your containers regularly before you head off to the cottage for a week.

Make sure that any container you're considering has drainage holes. Without them water will collect at the bottom of the container and damage the roots. Some water may run through the drainage holes so keep this mind if your containers are on a deck or something you're careful with. Place another dish under the container to retain this water.

You'll have to water your containers more often than you'd water vegetables in a garden. You should also consider adding some sort of booster to the soil in your containers as the summer progresses. Compost tea will help, as will any of the liquid fish emulsion or liquid seaweed plant boosters you can purchase.

Herbs are a favorite for container gardening since they do so well. It's nice to have them located on the back porch near the kitchen so that when you're preparing dinner you can pick some to add to the meal. Just about any herb will grow well in a container. Some, like chamomile, will become very large, so keep that in mind if you have limited space on your porch or patio or balcony. Every summer we start basil seeds in small pots to move into the kitchen in the fall. It's really nice to have fresh basil handy in the kitchen, and if you've started a variety of herbs in pots there's no reason not to move them inside in the fall if you have room. With the shorter days and less sunlight they might not thrive after you bring them in, but they'll give you another month or two of fresh herbs and might even last through the winter.

Tomatoes are the most common vegetable that people grow in containers, but all of the nightshades like peppers and eggplants also do well. They need large pots, so choose containers that are from 3 to 15 gallons in size. Those oak half-barrels work well. You can certainly use a smaller container, but if you're making the effort to grow food in containers you might as well make sure your plants have room to thrive. If you use fairly small containers you may want to purchase some of the commercial tomato grow food. Earlier I discouraged the use of these types of fertilizers and compared using them to getting your plants hooked on crack. I made that comment in the context of using them in the soil in your garden. Container gardens are separate and temporary and therefore I don't consider them such a long-term investment. If you don't have a garden plot to use your compost in, then of course you should use it in your container gardens.

Cherry tomatoes are particularly well-suited to containers, and Michelle has grown lots of them in pots over the past few years. If you're choosing cherry tomato seeds from a seed catalog be sure to choose the ones that are recommended for use in hanging baskets. These plants are better suited for growing in a confined area. I love the look of the flowers on eggplants, and I think having an eggplant or pepper plant on the porch would be beautiful. In cooler growing zones this would be advantageous early on, as you would be able to bring them inside on cool nights or if a frost was called for. If you have a spot on the south side of your house it will be nice and warm on sunny days, and these plants do well in heat. Just remember to keep them well watered.

You can grow beans in containers, as they should stay fairly compact. Onions and garlic also work well. Probably some of the easiest things to grow are lettuce and spinach. They'll do well in a spot that receives some shade, since they don't always thrive in heat. A planter box with a nice lettuce mix sitting by the back door is a major inspiration to eat more salad. A larger container for your tomatoes and peppers will allow you to grow some lettuce around them. You may want to harvest the lettuce fairly early, but this is one way of making the most use of the space you have.

One other plant to consider for a container is strawberries. Strawberry pots are available in a variety of materials and styles, but they all follow the same cascading design with small terraces on the side for additional plants. They're extremely attractive and look great on a deck. They also help to ensure that the berries stay off the ground. They're perfect for someone with back or knee problems because they make berry picking a dream. The yield isn't as high as it is from a large patch of berries, but there isn't as much weeding and maintenance either.

In order to enjoy success with container gardening you need to start out with a good potting soil mixture. Be sure to stay on top of watering because pots dry out faster than your garden plot, especially in hot sunny weather. The convenience of having vegetables and herbs close to the house is worth effort. Even if you live in an apartment that has a sunny exposure you'll be able to grow something in a container!

Mike Lieberman takes container grower to the extreme on his balcony in New York City. These photos show various vegetables getting started and further along in his home-made self-watering containers. www.urbanorganicgardener.com

66   Enjoying the Bounty

A garden is a joyous, wondrous place. Amazing things happen there.

A garden serves as a great metaphor for life.

Early in the spring the garden looks lifeless, but as the sun and rain start to warm it up life begins to emerge. You take this tiny, amazing seed and plant it in the soil. That tiny seed has the genetic encoding it needs to know to form roots, shoots, leaves, flowers, and fruit. It can produce chemicals to deter pests, and some plants like sunflowers even have little solar receptors so they can track the sun as it moves through the sky. That tiny seed can produce food for your body with unbelievable health-giving qualities.

Early in the spring the plant is growing quickly and starting to assume the form it will take when mature. As spring turns into summer those adolescent plants start to grow into big, healthy, vigorous adults. The potential in the flowers they sent out is now starting to show. The fruit is developing and taking shape. For many vegetables the fruit matures at different rates, with some ripening early and others ripening right through until frost.

For others, like cabbages, all the energy goes into one big main event. The philosophy of a cabbage might be, "It's better to burn out than to fade away."

Eventually, though, as you approach fall, everything in the garden starts to slow down and come to the end of its natural life. Winter brings on that final period of sleep. Depending on where you stand spiritually, you can decide if winter is indeed the end or just a period of downtime before the garden is born again in the spring.

Despite my springtime enthusiasm, by the fall I'm usually pretty burned out on gardening. By then I've put a lot of work into it and it has consumed much of my spare time for the last three seasons. I'm thrilled with the bounty in my root cellar and freezer, but I look forward to the winter when I can get caught up on reading and other projects. I bounce back pretty quickly, though, and by late in the winter as the sun starts to get stronger and the snow starts to melt I can feel my enthusiasm for gardening starting to build again. By the time the snow is gone and the soil is warm and dry enough to work, you can't keep me out of the garden. A coaster that Michelle bought for me sums it up perfectly: "I live in the garden. I just sleep in the house." The garden is a symbol of rebirth. I just can't describe the joy I get from getting my hands down into the soil every spring and helping to bring it back to life. Every day that I fall into bed exhausted after a day in the garden is a red-letter day at Sunflower Farm!

The garden radiates positive energy all season. Visitors love to walk through my garden, especially in July and August when it's going full throttle. It provides me with energy every time I'm in it and every time I eat something from it.

I hope you will feel the same energy from your garden. Many things are happening in our world which indicate that having the skills to grow your own food is going to take on great significance in the future. The fact that developing these skills is an infinitely fulfilling process is just a bonus. Someday as you sit weeding your carrots and your brain is at its full potential as your lungs draw in fresh air and oxygen and you're surrounded by all these amazing green plants, I'll bet you'll actually answer the big question:"What's the meaning of life?" "What's my place in the universe?" "What should I do next with my life?" And if you don't actually find the meaning of life in this weeding session, at least you're going to end up with some sweet, crunchy, beta-carotene-packed, health-giving carrots. Not a bad result for your efforts!

For three seasons of the year, if Michelle can't find me I'm in the garden. Solving the big questions. Recharging my soul. Growing dinner. In the great scheme of things, could you really ask for anything else?

"See you in the garden!"

Appendix 1

Remote Water Pumping Overview
Make sure pump intake is strained!

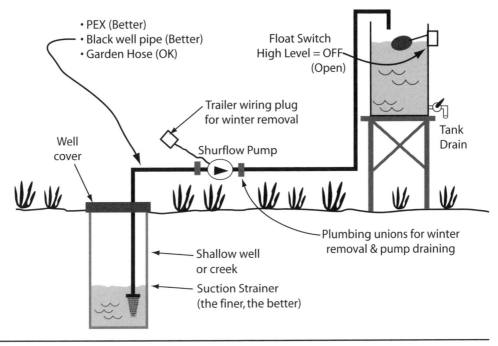

- PEX (Better)
- Black well pipe (Better)
- Garden Hose (OK)

Float Switch
High Level = OFF
(Open)

Trailer wiring plug
for winter removal

Shurflow Pump

Tank
Drain

Well
cover

Plumbing unions for winter
removal & pump draining

Shallow well
or creek

Suction Strainer
(the finer, the better)

Remote Water Pumping Wiring Schematic

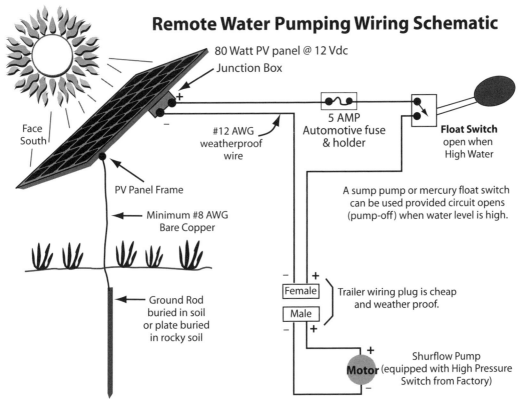

80 Watt PV panel @ 12 Vdc
Junction Box

5 AMP
Automotive fuse
& holder

Float Switch
open when
High Water

Face
South

#12 AWG
weatherproof
wire

A sump pump or mercury float switch
can be used provided circuit opens
(pump-off) when water level is high.

PV Panel Frame

Minimum #8 AWG
Bare Copper

Female

Male

Trailer wiring plug is cheap
and weather proof.

Ground Rod
buried in soil
or plate buried
in rocky soil

Shurflow Pump
Motor (equipped with High Pressure
Switch from Factory)

Appendix 2

U.S.D.A. North American Hardiness Zones

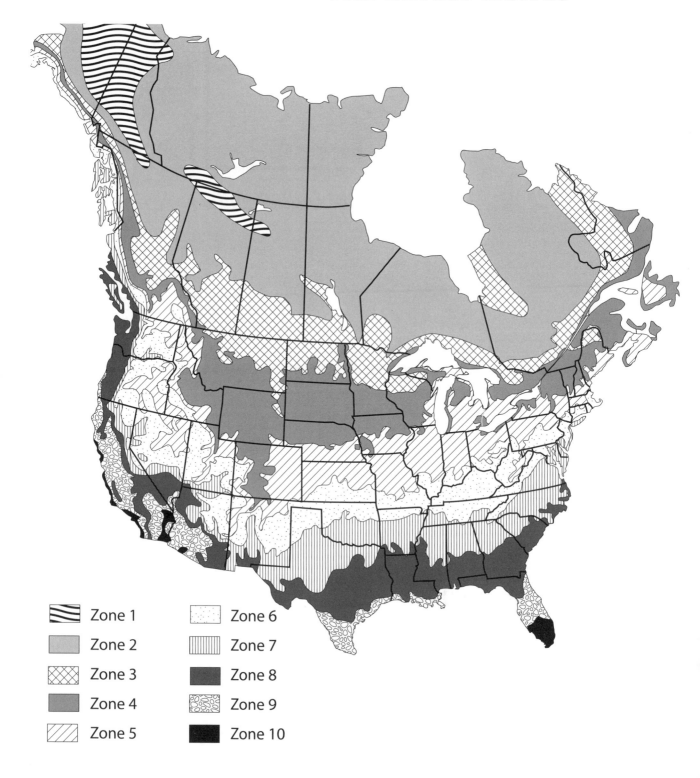

Zone 1		Zone 6	
Zone 2		Zone 7	
Zone 3		Zone 8	
Zone 4		Zone 9	
Zone 5		Zone 10	

Hardiness zones have been identified by the United States Department of Agriculture (USDA) as a way of indicating which areas certain plants can grow in. This includes the plant's ability to withstand the average annual minimum temperature for that zone. The main factors determining this are the latitude, altitude and proximity to the coast since large bodies of water have a regulating effect.

Seed catalogs will sometimes use these zones for woody plants like trees and perennials and for some annuals that require a long hot growing season. While it may be tempting if you are in a Zone 4 to attempt to grow a certain cultivar that is identified as being hardy to Zone 5, this will often end in disappointment as the plant simply won't handle the cooler temperatures of the lower zone. There are a number of other factors to think about as well. The zones do not take summer heat levels into account which can be quite different within a given zone as can precipitation levels. You should also consider the reliability of the snow cover in your area. Snow protects the roots of hibernating plants by acting as an insulator. Berry plants will be able to withstand much colder temperatures and suffer less winterkill if they are tucked under

a thick, cozy blanket of snow. Remember as well that urban centers act as huge heat sinks that absorb heat. If you are in a city you may find that your area is slightly warmer than the actual zone that you have been identified as.

There is one other wild card in all of this and that's climate change. Our increasing emissions of carbon dioxide into the atmosphere are altering the climate. This often takes the form of warmer temperatures but can also take the form of more erratic weather from temperature to precipitation extremes. The existing hardiness map was not considered fool proof because of anomalies like El Nino and El Ninja years when Pacific Ocean currents wreaked havoc on our weather. But climate change is a much larger potential problem and one that could have much greater consequences for gardeners. For someone growing in a colder zone this may seem like a good thing and certainly if it means a few more days for sweet potatoes and artichokes to mature it's not a bad thing in the context of growing vegetables. If on the other hand it brings much more violent storms that blow over taller plants or dump a deluge of rain on the garden that washes away topsoil, then it's not a good thing.

So use this chart as a rough guide and start to become more aware of the climate in your area. Use your gardening notebook to record the final frost date each spring and first frost date each fall so you have a record of what's unique about your particular growing zone. Detailed records of how well warm season crops matured will help you decide what you can and can't grow realistically. Records may also help you to analyze if you're making the correct choices in terms of cultivars of vegetable seeds you're ordering each year.

Average Annual Minimum Temperature

Zone 1	Below -50°F	(-45.6°C)
Zone 2	-50°F to -40°F	(-45.6°C to -40°C)
Zone 3	-40°F to -30°F	(-40°C to -34.4°C)
Zone 4	-30°F to -20°F	(-34.4°C to -28.9°C)
Zone 5	-20°F to -10°F	(-28.9°C to -23.3°C)
Zone 6	-10°F to 0°F	(-23.3°C to -17.8°C)
Zone 7	0°F to 10°F	(-17.8C to -12.2°C)
Zone 8	10°F to 20°F	(-12.2°C to -6.7°C)
Zone 9	20°F to 30°F	(-6.7°C to -1.1°C)
Zone 10	30°F to 40°F	(-1.1°C to +4.4°C)

Appendix 3

Seed Catalog Companies

Starting with good quality seeds is key to your vegetable gardening success. This listing is provided as just a small sampling of the many available. These are seed companies that offer a large variety of vegetables to choose from. There are many seed companies that specialize in just a few specific vegetables, but since I have included the word "easy" in the subtitle of this book, I think a one-stop seed supplier to get you started is a good idea.

Johnny's Selected Seeds
www.johnnyseeds.com
955 Benton Ave
Winslow, ME 04901
207-861-3900 or
877-564-6697

Pinetree Garden Seeds
www.superseeds.com
PO Box 300
New Gloucester, ME 04260
207-926-3400

Burpee
www.burpee.com
W. Atlee Burpee & Co.
300 Park Avenue
Warminster, PA 18974
1-800-333-5808

Territorial Seed
www.territorialseed.com
PO Box 158
Cottage Grove, OR 97424
800-626-0866

Park Seed Co.
www.parkseed.com
1 Parkton Ave.
Greenwood, SC 29647
800-213-0076

Burgess Seed & Plant Co.
www.eburgess.com
905 Four Seasons Road
Bloomington, IL 61701
(309) 662-7761

The Cook's Garden
www.cooksgarden.com
PO Box C5030
Warminster, PA 18974
1-800-457-9703

Seed Savers Exchange
www.seedsavers.org
3094 North Winn Rd
Decorah, Iowa 52101
(563) 382-5990

Thompson & Morgan
www.tmseeds.com
220 Faraday Avenue
Jackson, NJ 08527-5073
(800) 274-7333 or 1(732) 363-2225

Seeds of Change
www.seedsofchange.com
1 Sunset Way
Henderson NV 89014
888-762-7333

Abundant Life Seeds
www.abundantlifeseeds.com
PO Box 279
Cottage Grove, OR 97424-0010
541-767-9606

Evergreen Enterprises
(specializes in Asian vegetable seeds)
www.evergreenseeds.com
P.O. Box 17538
Anaheim, CA 92817
Fax : (714) 637-5769

Jordan's Seeds
www.jordanseeds.com
6400 Upper Afton Rd
Woodbury, MN 55125
651-738-3422, 651-739-9578

Ornamental Edibles
www.ornamentaledibles.com
5723 Trowbridge Way
San Jose, Ca 95138
408-528-SEED (7333)

Sieger's Seed Co. (specializes in
commercial growers)
www.siegers.com
13031 Reflections Drive
Holland, MI 49424
Phone: (616) 786-4999

Vermont Bean Seed Co.
www.vermontbean.com
334 West Stroud Street
Randolph WI 53956-1274
800-349-1071

Canadian Seed Companies which sell in both
Canada and the United States

Veseys Seeds
www.veseys.com
PO Box 9000
Charlottetown, PE
C1A 8K6
1-902-368-7333

Stokes
www.stokeseeds.com
PO Box 10
Thorold, ON
L2V 5E9
1-905-688-4300
1-800-396-9238

William Dam Seeds Ltd
www.damseeds.ca
279 Hwy 8 RR 1
Dundas, ON
L9H 5E1
905-628-6641

OSC Seeds
www.oscseeds.com
P.O. Box 7
Waterloo, ON
N2J 3Z6
519-886-0557

Index

Index

Index

Index

Index

Index

About the Author

Cam Mather and his wife Michelle live independently off the electricity grid using the sun and wind to power their home and their business, Aztext Press. Cam publishes books and DVDs about renewable energy and sustainability. He has produced best-selling DVDs on organic vegetable gardening and installing a home-scale wind turbine. He has been gardening organically for 30 years and operated a market garden. He continues to speak to large and varied groups about all aspects of sustainable living, from integrating renewable energy into your life to the importance personal food independence.

Also by Cam Mather

There's never been a better time to be in control of your fuel, food and finances.

Thriving During Challenging Times

The Energy, Food and Financial Independence Handbook

Cam Mather

316 pages 6" x 9"

ISBN 978-0-9733233-6-8

$19.95 Cdn/US

Most of us have never lived through times as tough as these. The economic crisis, peak oil, rising food costs, climate change and water shortages all converge to make it a very challenging time. This book provides a road map to allow you to return to the independence of previous generations. Independence in how you power your home, where you get your food from and how you control your financial destiny. The amazing thing is that the recommendations are not only good for you; they're good for the planet. Showering with water heated by the sun and eating a "100 foot diet" with food grown in your backyard will help you to reduce your carbon footprint. They also give you back control of your budget. By providing a step-by-step guide on how to get the fastest payback and invest the money you save, you'll discover the joy of being in control again.

From where you live, to how you heat and power your home, to producing your own food, controlling water and getting your financial house in order, this book proves that money doesn't buy happiness, but using what you have wisely helps.

The fact that most of the recommendations are good for your health, good for the health of the planet and good for protecting yourself financially, sets out a win/win/win scenario. Challenging times provide a tremendous opportunity for personal growth while giving your soul the joy a return to a saner pace in your life provides.

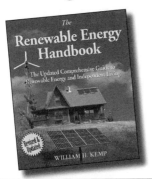

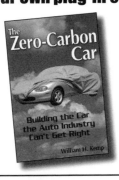

DVDs from the Renewable Energy Publisher

A video tour of author Cam Mather's enchanted vegetable garden.

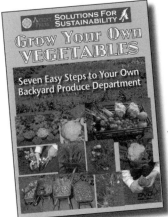

Grow Your Own Vegetables

With rising fuel and food costs, this 2 hour DVD provides everything you need to turn your backyard into your own personal produce department. Host Cam Mather covers soil preparation, starting seeds, planting, weeding and watering, dealing with pests, and harvesting and storage of your bounty. This DVD is entertaining and enlightening and you'll feel as if you've spent the summer in Cam's garden and learned from his 30 years of experience growing healthy, organic vegetables.

ISBN 978-0-9733233-9-9

Home-Scale Wind Turbine Installation

This video is a step-by-step guide to putting up a home sized wind turbine using a common tubular steel tilt-up tower hosted by author Cam Mather. From evaluating your location, installing anchors, wiring, assembling the tower and using the winch to properly raise the tower, this DVD will guide and inspire your move to green energy.

ISBN 978-0-9810132-0-6

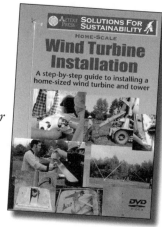

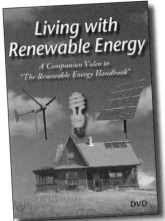

Living with Renewable Energy

This 2 hour companion DVD to "The Renewable Energy Handbook" is a guided tour of author William Kemp's off-grid home (as well as Cam Mather's). It shows how to enjoy a typical North American lifestyle, powered by the sun and wind. It also includes interviews with the author about renewable energy and sustainability.

ISBN 978-0-9733233-8-2

Biodiesel Basics

This companion DVD to our book "Biodiesel Basics and Beyond" is a one-hour tour of author William Kemp's small scale biodiesel production facility and shows how to produce ASTM quality biodiesel from waste vegetable oil.

ISBN 978-0-9733233-7-5

For more information visit www.aztext.com